The Tenth Muse

A HISTORICAL STUDY OF THE

OPERA LIBRETTO

THE
Tenth Muse
A Historical Study of the
Opera Libretto

BY PATRICK J. SMITH

NEW YORK

Alfred · A · Knopf

1970

Siccome questa musica segue
fedelmente la parola, bisogna
che la parola sia degna
d'essere seguita.
—ANTONIO FOGAZZARO

. . . what the librettist
needs is a command, not of
great poetry, but of operatic
dramaturgy.
—ERIC BENTLEY

PREFACE

THIS BOOK was generated by a growing exasperation at the persistent stream of uninformed and misleading comment on the opera libretto, fostered by ignorance and perpetuated by indifference. As the libretto is an integral component of the operatic entity, such comment necessarily distorts the view of opera, and more often than not results in codified misinterpretation, not of fact, but of emphasis, outlook, and tone.

It is not surprising that this has been the case with relation to the libretto, the foundations and influences of which lie not in music and music theory and development but rather in the history of the written and spoken word: in poetry and in drama. Those who have written on opera have had, by and large, neither exposure to nor training in these two fields, so that they have extrapolated from fragmentary data. Those who could have commented fruitfully on the history of the libretto and its relationship with the music usually have had neither exposure to nor training in music and operatic history, and have moreover not been attracted to the opera libretto, a smaller subject than drama. Thus the libretto has been forced to languish between two stools.[1]

This book seeks to provide a corrective to this inadequacy of vision.

Any attempt at a study of the opera libretto is a vast undertaking—for instance, well over twenty thousand Italian librettos survive from the seventeenth and eighteenth centuries alone. The task has heretofore been subject only to patchwork study. As with the whole field of opera, then, the amount of virgin ignorance far outweighs what information has been gathered. The following pages

---

(1) Evidence of this is the woeful lack of information on librettists in musical—or even operatic—encyclopedias, where they are clearly considered superfluous.

have been rendered somewhat easier, however, because the libretto is a sufficiently minor art form to permit a greater degree of generalization than, say, the novel. "If you've read one, you've read them all" may be an exaggeration, but, with the exception of the major librettists and some isolated librettos, it is not a gross exaggeration. What is more important for the purposes of this book is to proceed from this assumption and not end at it: if a pine forest is the endless repetition of one tree its interest has only in one specific been diminished.

Nevertheless, the very size of this undertaking has necessarily led to pruning in order to keep this book within reasonable limits. Since I had from the first determined to write a chronological study which would be "complete" only in the sense that it would uncover the entire field of the libretto (much as the surgeon at one stroke lays open the operating area), I have had to curtail severely or cut out entirely discussion of peripheral areas of librettology. All librettos that are not opera librettos have been omitted: librettos for masques,[2] oratorios, and the like. This omission should in no way suggest that I consider these works undramatic or even unoperatic: Winton Dean, Joseph Kerman, and others are entirely correct in emphasizing the "operatic" qualities of the oratorios of Handel and the cantatas of Bach. I have also chosen to follow the main line of operatic development, particularly in the case of seventeenth and eighteenth centuries, when opera centered in Italy and France, with the Italian influences spreading to the German-speaking countries. I have thus omitted peripheral manifestations of the libretto in Spain, to some extent in the German states, and in England.

My greatest regret, however, lies in the omission, except for passing references, of the Slavic nineteenth- and twentieth-century librettos, for if these have not had the influence on the art form that Slavic music has had on musical history, they nonetheless deserve attention as an important body of work. But my ignorance of Czech and Russian would cripple any systematic discussion, and I shall leave librettos in those languages to more competent commentators.

As will be seen, this book has attempted to isolate the libretto

---

(2) The purist will note some relaxation of this injunction in the conceptual broadening of "opera" since Wagner. The Thomson-Stein *Four Saints in Three Acts* may be more masque than opera, but Miss Stein's contributions to the history of the libretto are so important that such a hybrid could not be ignored.

and to examine it in and of itself, and only secondarily has sought to view the libretto in its relation with the music. The aim has been a "libretto-eyed" view of operatic history, which is a distortion, but which affords a much-needed corrective to the usual "composer-eyed" or "music-eyed" slant. The landmarks, are therefore seen from another side and in a differing light: at times the effect may be startling. I have also sought not to reiterate commonplaces about librettists already well known, but rather to discuss their contributions in a fresh way.

This book, then, is a selective rather than exhaustive study—I have avoided the word "history" in its title for that reason—but it is my hope that it will serve to open the field for further, more intensive research. Certainly the opportunity is ample, for this book and its companions trace but an indistinct camel trail through a desert. If the following pages can awaken new interest in the libretto and its problems, and if this book has succeeded in laying down some of the broad lines of influence and development that have been operative in the history of the libretto through the centuries of its existence, I shall feel amply rewarded.

N.B.: The number of variant readings of any given libretto, especially the Italian librettos of the seventeenth and eighteenth centuries, is staggering. I have in general tried to do my research in the first published edition, or from the collected editions over which the librettist presumably had some control. I have tried not to consult the librettos as published in the vocal scores. There are therefore bound to be some variations as to words and speeches. In case of drastic change, as for instance the interpolated final duet of the Monteverdi-Busenello *Incoronazione di Poppea*, which does not appear in the version in Busenello's collected works, I have of course noted the changes.

As to the quotations in the original language, I have respelled them in accordance with modern usage and, in the matter of Italian accents, brought them into conformity.

P.J.S.

Acknowledgments

I HAVE RECEIVED valuable assistance from many people during the course of the research and writing of this book, but those individuals who have been particularly helpful I should like to single out for special thanks. They are: Professor Alan Curtis, Professor Robert Freeman, George Martin, Fabrizio Melano, Maria Teresa Muraro, Virgil Thomson, William Weaver and my wife Elisabeth. The constant encouragement and advice of my editor, Herbert Weinstock, has been of prime importance in the genesis and fulfillment of this study, and to him I extend heartfelt thanks.

CONTENTS

xiii

Contents

ILLUSTRATIONS

INTRODUCTION

THE RELATION of word and music and the changes in their relative importance—in short, the entire subject of the interaction of the two major components of opera—has over the centuries become an exceedingly tangled Gordian knot of theory, opinion, and plain cant. Those who have tackled the subject—most notably Saint-Évremond, Dryden, Arteaga, Marcello, Algarotti, Diderot, and Wagner—have produced discussions of greater value as reflections of their ages and of the conditions of opera at the times in which they wrote than as objective evaluations of the relation of word and music. Books can and have been devoted to the problem in macrocosm and microcosm: to be misled into discussion of each would seriously damage the central purpose of this book, which is to unfold the chronology of the libretto in terms of the works themselves. Indeed, with few exceptions—for instance, in France, where in artistic matters theory has always had an important influence on practice—the debate can be phrased in terms of the works rather than of the theories. For, as with most branches of art, the success of a specific work will do more to influence the course of the practice than the reasonings of ten graybeards assembled.

It is not surprising to find that the comparative weight given to the word and to the music in opera is directly related to the development of the sonority and diversity of music over the years since 1600. Because "opera" grew out of the seed of the word, the early commentators on the fledgling art form naturally insisted on the primacy of the word over its musical accompaniment. In Italy, the quick transference of the operatic center of interest from the literature-oriented Florentine Camerata to the huge Barberini theater in Rome and thence to the public theaters of Venice served to accentuate the decline of the word in relation not only to music, but also to spectacle. Only in France, with its preponderant theatrical tradition, did the word retain its power, even in the face of endless spectacle—so that today "attention to the cadence of the French speech" remains an important criterion in judging much French opera.

Clearly, the development of opera away from poetic declamation necessitated a different evaluation of the qualities of the librettist, for he no longer was primarily a poet to be judged by the musicality of his lines and the aptness of his rhythms, rhymes, and similes. The librettist had become more: he had become a dramatist as well. *As well* and *primarily*. To consider the librettist merely a poet is to denigrate his function in the creation of an opera, for in the vast majority of cases the librettist supplied the original, motive force for the composition of the opera and created the dramatic node around which the final work was constructed. Our point of view, almost always through the composer's eyes, has distorted the truth of this statement, because the composer has arrogated the position of dramatist to himself—especially since the nineteenth century—by the increased impact of his music, in terms both of force and of characterization. If a librettist can pen three words as innocuous as "*per lui, pietà*" and have the composer transform them into a moment of unbearable poignance which illumines an entire character (Elvira's in *Don Giovanni:* the end of the "*Mi tradì*" aria), where does that leave the librettist? The fatal temptation is to assume that the omnipotent composer is therefore omniscient, the librettist but a utilitarian appendage employed to crank the composer's dramatic ideas into some sort of serviceable verse. We accept this as the lesson of the Verdi-Ghislanzoni *Aida:* we tend to infer beyond. As we shall see, even Verdi had distinct limitations as a dramatic librettist.

This belief in the omniscience of the composer, which may also be termed the Pathetic Fallacy of Opera, is perhaps the most consistent mistake of those who write about opera. It consists in ascribing to the music qualities that can be found only in the libretto or qualities that cannot be empirically traced to the composer. It is rife for two reasons: because it is easier to write "Verdi" than to check which one of his librettists the comment applies to, and because we have known very little about librettists and a good deal about composers. If this book can correct this one fault, it will have contributed importantly to a judicious evaluation of opera.[1]

The librettist therefore cannot be considered merely a wordsmith stringing out lines of mellifluous verse: he is at once a dramatist, a creator of word, verse, situation, scene, and character, and —this is of vital importance—an artist who, by dint of his professional training as a poet and/or dramatist, can often visualize the work *as a totality* more accurately than the composer. This totality includes not only the "story" but also the means by which that story will be most effectively presented on stage both organizationally and scenically. The abuses to which the scenic elements of opera have been lent throughout its history have tempted commentators into denigrating or dismissing those elements in part or in full as extraneous trappings added by self-inflated stage technicians working against the spirit of the opera. The cardinal fact is that these elements are tools in the librettist's workbag just as much as rhyme and simile, and that all the resources of the opera house—mechanical, fantastic, or improvisatory —form an integral part of the librettist's plan for his libretto and should be considered apart from it only when they clearly have been added later. Although Goldoni wanted to control the excesses to which comedy in his day had developed, his Harlequin was envisaged as a role for an artist trained in the stage tricks of the *commedia dell'arte*. Although Wagner never ceased to fulminate at the cheap theatrics of the French school of *Grand Opéra*, he never ceased to adapt them for his own use, and those who feel that the fogs and lightning flashes and pantomime of the end of Act II of *Die Walküre* are extraneous posturings will

---

(1) Citations of the Pathetic Fallacy would fill a volume; I will confine myself to one from a musicologist who should know better: ". . . indeed, [Shakespeare's] habit of relieving the mood of a tragedy by interspersing a few comic scenes was shared by many *Italian composers* of serious operas from Monteverdi and Landi to Scarlatti, and became almost universal in the early romantic period" (italics mine); Winton Dean: "Shakespeare and Opera," in *Shakespeare in Music*, ed. Phyllis Hartnoll, p. 93.

An ancillary consideration, outside the scope of this book but of importance in the study of opera, is the extent to which the music, because of its melodic sweep, assumes a quasi-dramatic function in holding the listener's attention while not being particularly "dramatic" in and of itself. The operas of Gounod, for instance, abound in such moments.

never come to terms with Wagner—or, for that matter, with opera. Indeed, as the importance of the verse and the rhyme began to be subsumed by the growing primacy of the music, the librettist was forced—to a great degree unconsciously—to rely on his other tools to convey the story to the audience. The awareness of all of the resources at the command of the librettist, and how he utilized these resources, will underlie the pages that follow.

Even among commentators on the libretto as distinct from opera, the scope of the librettist's choices has rarely been acknowledged. The single most notable criterion for judging librettos has always been the quality of the verse. This was understandable as long as the poetry was in fact paramount, but it became more and more anachronistic as the balance shifted toward music. Yet, until late in the nineteenth century, judgments being made on the libretto were still not qualitatively different from those made in 1650. Few would seriously question the first half of the following quote from Ulrich Weisstein, but many might question the second half: "Metastasio . . . must be regarded as the most influential of all librettists, with the possible exception of Eugène Scribe"[2]; but any student of the libretto would readily agree with Weisstein. Scribe was consistently damned—most often by Théophile Gautier—for his atrocious verse and cardboard characters, and Gautier was right. Yet Gautier's criticisms were *au fond* irrelevant, for the power of the music had vitiated Scribe's verse and the power to create character musically meant that a well-cut cardboard could be used as a starting point. Thus, *Les Huguenots*, *L'Elisir d'amore*, and *Un Ballo in maschera:* all originally by Scribe. What guarantees Scribe his position and influence is not his obvious faults but the multitude of innovations he codified in the development of the opera libretto and which Gautier and others chose to ignore.

The relative unimportance of verse in the making of a libretto probably goes back farther than we are willing to allow. The moment that a musical line is added to a line of verse, it necessarily imposes its own "poetry" upon the words, so that even such composers as those of the Florentine Camerata or the twentieth-century Leoš Janáček, who sought to keep the musical line "the humble servant" of the inflections of the speech, have

---

(2) Ulrich Weisstein, ed.: *The Essence of Opera*, p. 99.

been to some extent deluded. Certainly in the preponderance of cases music has taken over the very function of the poetry, and has thus drained the verse of the "musical" qualities that render it poetic. Verdi's emphasis on the *parole sceniche* (note: "scenic words," not verse) showed his instinctive awareness of this fact, though he clung to the outmoded verse forms. Michael Tippett, referring to Elizabethan lute music, writes: "The music of a song destroys the verbal music of the poem utterly."[3] If this can occur when a single instrument provides accompaniment, how much more thorough the process will be with greater sonority. Louis Gallet's wry definition of the *poème lyrique* as "a work in verse which one gives to a musician so that he can make it into prose" may have come as a disagreeable shock to him as a librettist at the end of the nineteenth century, but this only demonstrates the blinkered attitude most librettists, as well as writers on opera, continued to have about the libretto.[4] The libretto had become prose far earlier, and although we can admire beautiful poetry when it occurs, in Metastasio or in Hofmannsthal, we shall see that both these librettists brought a great deal more than verse to their works—which is why they loom so large in any history of the libretto.

Once the proper scope of the librettist's contribution to opera has been recognized and acknowledged, the hoary argument of *"Prima la musica e dopo [poi] le parole"* shrinks to its significance as symposium badinage: charming, relevant, but secondary. Concomitantly, the librettist himself gains in stature and can be judged as a co-equal of the composer: two complete artists in their respective fields intent upon the creation of a synergic unity neither could create alone.

Finally, the most important point must not be forgotten. The opera libretto itself, shorn of the magic of the stage, is in essence a negative or, at best, weakly positive, form. Strong music can

---

(3) Michael Tippett: *A History of Song*, p. 462, as quoted in Imogen Holst: *Tune*, p. 86.

(4) "The right defence of the Mozart librettos would start, I think, with the observation that great poetry set to music is not an ideal recipe for opera, in fact that there is no great dramatic poetry yet written that operatic music would not ruin"; Eric Bentley: *The Dramatic Event*, p. 235.

"Great poetry, which already has its intricate rhythms and overtones, is far harder to set to music than plain pedestrian verse"; Dean: "Shakespeare and Opera," p. 95.

dominate a libretto, can elevate it in our estimate of its qualities, can even survive as music without the words. Very few, if any, librettos have survived without the music (except those which were carried over practically intact from the stage); those which have survived have been staged as plays partly because of the novelty of the idea. Even fewer—if any—first-class librettos tied to inferior music have caused the opera to survive.

The constricted, esoteric nature of the art form—demanding not only ability to write for voice and the sung stage but also ability to collaborate with a composer—has caused the libretto to be shunned by many of the great dramatists and poets: those who have written librettos have, with very few exceptions, produced work far inferior to their non-libretto oeuvre. The fact that the vast majority of librettos are reworkings of materials in other forms only partially accounts for their weaknesses, for great playwrights—Shakespeare neither the first nor the last—have drawn on other sources for their materials. What matters is that these libretto reworkings, by and large, have little novelty and less interest. The sources would better have been left untouched.

Yet those librettists who will be discussed in this book have done more than rework and refashion: they have done more even than renew a story or a situation or an idea. They will be remembered as librettists because they managed to inject personality into the work they performed: not such an autobiographical exegesis as the Romantic Age held to be the chief aim of writing, but a point of view that is theirs and theirs alone. This point of view may extend to only a single character or to an outlook on life, but it will serve to give the libretto itself a personality that will set it off from its monochromatic companions. The libretto has literally been the plaything of kings and popes; at its best it has been far more. It has had stature, dignity, and honor in its own right and as a vital component of opera; and its practitioners, the great librettists, have shown not only a glimpse of themselves and their minds but also, in the apt words of Eric Bentley, a command of the dramaturgy of opera.

The Tenth Muse

A HISTORICAL STUDY OF THE

OPERA LIBRETTO

Chapter One

The Seventeenth-century Italian Libretto

T HAT OPERA as we historically determine it emerged from the word and not from the music is today a commonplace. What is lacking, however, is a proper consideration of the resources that the "word" had at its command at that point of time when the men of the Florentine Camerata took the pastoral play and stretched a complete framework of music over its form. The date 1600 has been somewhat arbitrarily adopted as an easy watershed at which the amorphous developments of the spectacle, the pastoral, and the intermezzo were transformed into what we call opera: the date was made easier by its simplicity and because at around that time the group of theorists, poets, musicians, and amateurs known as the Camerata publicized its efforts in staged and sung play both as a departure from the haphazard practices of the time and as a return to the ordered, classic practices of the Ancients (in this case, the ancient Greeks). We shall see this process of "ordering from without" become a constant feature of the criers of reform in opera throughout its history, and we shall also see that, in the development of the opera libretto, it will be less the orderers from without than the organic growth from within which will serve to change and direct the history of the art form.

The men of the Florentine Camerata—nobles such as Giovanni de' Bardi and Jacopo Corsi, composers such as Vincenzo Galilei and Jacopo Peri, poets such as Ottavio Rinuccini—had based their ideas of reform not so much on the Greek drama as on what they thought to be the way in which the Greeks had produced their plays: that is, on the fact that the Greeks sang rather than spoke their lines. Thus, the content of their works, though superficially Greek in setting and employment of the myths, had far less to do with Aeschylus, Sophocles, and Euripides than with the pastoral plays of sixteenth-century Italy.

The vogue for pastoral plays, which were often staged out of doors, sometimes on an island on the estate of a wealthy patron, had grown from the middle of the sixteenth century. Two of the most famous pastoral plays were Torquato Tasso's *Aminta* (1573) and Battista Guarini's *Il Pastor fido* (1581–90). Of the two, *Aminta* is clearly the superior in poetry and in form, but *Il Pastor fido* has been referred to more often as influential in the writings of Italian librettists. This paradoxical situation arose not so much because librettists have preferred works of a lower order of talent to masterpieces as, probably, because the Guarini work combines serviceable poetry with a more certain sense of the theatrical.

Aminta carries its own music with it (Tasso was one of the foremost Italian lyric poets), and its dulcet sounds influenced not only Guarini but also many of the Italian librettists—and some of the French—up to and including Felice Romani in the nineteenth century. From *Aminta* such lines as

> *Mira là quel colombo*
> *che con dolce susurro lusingando*
> *bacia la sua compagna;*
> *odi quel lusignuolo*
> *che va di ramo in ramo*
> *cantando: "Io amo, io amo" . . .*
> . . . .
> *Cangia, cangia consiglio,*
> *pazzarella che sei.*[1]
>
> (I, i)

with their reiterated liquid "o" sounds, wafted the perfumes of Arcady and the sweet-sad flutings of forlorn shepherds through the libretto. The suppleness and variety of the metrics—if not of the sounds, which generally avoided the harsh except for infre-

---

(1) "See that dove, who with a sweet murmuring flatteringly kisses his companion. Hear that nightingale who goes from branch to branch singing: 'I love you, I love you.' . . . Change, change your mind, foolish girl that you are."

quent humorous use in the mouths of villains—and the fact that the Italian language, which abounds in vowels and in end-word vowels, offers less of a chance for emphatic, end-stopped rhymes (except in short rhymed couplets) enabled the Italian libretto from the first to escape the fate of the French libretto, which was to be more or less chained to the twelve-syllable alexandrine couplet, with long declamatory speeches, and which worked so well for the classical theater but was more than a little uncomfortable when set to a musical line. The early Italian libretto had its share of long, declamatory speeches, but it also made frequent use not only of mixed metric lines (seven- and eleven-syllable lines were more popular than the rest) but also of fast, humorous give-and-take (probably originally from the Greek *stichomathia* by way of the dramas of Seneca and the improvisatory comic intermezzos) such as this scene between the heroine and a satyr in *Il Pastor fido*:

> CORISCA: *. . . se tu credi*
> *che Corisca non t'ami, il vero credi.*
> *Che vuoi tu ch'ami in te? quel tuo bel ceffo?*
> *Quella sucida barba? quelle orecchie*
> *caprigne, e quella putrida e bavasa*
> *isdentata caverna?*
> SATIRO: *O scelerata*
> *A me questo?*
> CORISCA: *A te questo.*
> SATIRO: *A me, ribalda?*
> CORISCA: *A te, caprone.*[2]
>
> (II, vi)

Naïve, direct, lyric, with emphasis on the poetry and opportunity for musical accompaniment, the pastorals appealed to the men of the Camerata, the more so because their leading poet (and the first librettist), Ottavio Rinuccini, was a disciple of Tasso.

Rinuccini's librettos for *Dafne* and *Euridice* (both published

---

(2) ". . . If you believe that Corisca doesn't love you, you believe the truth. What do you think I should love in you? That lovely mug of yours? That filthy beard? Those goatlike ears and that stinking and drooling toothless cavern?" "Do you dare say this to me, you villainess?" "I say it to you." "To me, you rogue?" "To you, you old goat."

in 1600, although the *Dafne* dates from 1596) owe almost everything to the pastoral play, but their brevity is probably a legacy
from the intermezzo.[3] The men of the Camerata, in their search
for purity, stressed simplicity and brevity as Greek ideals, and
the latter trait, present in the Italian libretto from the first, may
be the one salient characteristic of the Italian libretto throughout its history. When Rodolfo and Marcello toss Rodolfo's play
manuscript into the flames in Act I of *La Bohème*, Colline comments that the fire goes out quickly. *"La brevità, gran pregio"*
("Brevity, it's priceless"), Rodolfo replies: a sentiment that echoes
down from Rinuccini and is far more indigenous to the Rodolfo of
Illica, Giacosa, and Puccini than the Rodolphe of Murger's novel.

These two early operas presented a mixture of mortals
and gods, and relied heavily on a Greek type of chorus to comment on the action. Yet they are both little more than divertissements, and the intermezzo-like quality of their gentle, undramatic
poetry soon became isolated into the Prologue, which was a
standard feature of the early seventeenth-century opera and
which often served to comment on the action of the following
story by the use of gods or allegorical figures.

It is commonly acknowledged that opera as we recognize it
appeared at the moment when the ubiquitous messenger (another
Greek borrowing) appeared to Orfeo in Alessandro Striggio's
version of the Orpheus myth (1607) and said to him:

> *A te ne vengo, Orfeo,*
> *messaggera infelice*
> *di caso più infelice e più funesto.*
> *La tua bella Euridice—*
> ORFEO: *Ohimè, che odo?*
> MESSAGGERA: *La tua diletta sposa è morta.*
> ORFEO: *Ohimè.*[4]

(II)

Drama here made its entrance onto the operatic stage, but
in addition Striggio created in Orfeo a character who could rea-

---

(3) A short, comic interlude between the acts of a serious play or
opera. The story had nothing to do with that of the other work.
(4) "To you I come, Orfeo, an unhappy messenger of the unhappiest
and most tragic event. Your beautiful Euridice—" "Alas, what do I
hear?" "Your beloved wife is dead." "Alas."

son, feel, and express himself. His first thoughts, as he recovers from the news, are eminently in character and yet serve to further the action: "You, my life, are dead, yet I breathe. You have left me, never to return, and I remain. No . . ."—and he makes the decision to fetch Euridice from Hades. As he leads her out, doubts assail him: "But, as I sing, alas! who can assure me that she is following?" Eventually, he turns, as he must. "O sweetest light, I can see you, I can . . . but what eclipse, alas! obscures you?"[5] The eggshell of shepherds, chorus, and intermittent gods is still present, but the fledgling drama begins to squirm free.

Rinuccini's *Arianna* (1608) also shows a considerable advance over his earlier librettos. There is an awareness of the dramatic possibilities inherent in the story, particularly in the scene in which Arianna is pitted against the chorus to cry out: "Where, o where is that constancy which you so often swore to me?" And yet, withal, the suffering is not allowed to become acute: Arianna ends the opera with Bacco, sighing, "Blessed is the heart that has a god as its consolation." This little aphorism combines the reconciliation of Hofmannsthal's Ariadne (who forgets Theseus in Bacchus' arms) and the worldly cynicism of his Zerbinetta: "When a new god arrives we meekly surrender." Arianna's earlier lament, however, has completely obliterated the compromising ending, for it is the only music from Monteverdi's setting to survive. The lament, detached, played by itself, recomposed, became a classic of the early seventeenth century, and there is every reason to believe that its popularity influenced other librettists to include similar laments in their works. The lament-Arianna heads that list of distraught females whose *gran' scene* spotlight the corridors of opera.

We do not know how much of a share for the improvement of the dramatics of the libretto must be credited to the composer of *Orfeo* and *Arianna*, Claudio Monteverdi, but there is no doubt that his suggestions changed what Striggio and Rinuccini originally wrote. Monteverdi's influence on the libretto is directly comparable to Verdi's two centuries later in that it went beyond

---

(5) These passages reveal a constant trait of librettos and madrigals of the Renaissance and post-Renaissance period: the juxtaposition of opposites (light—dark; life—death). This artistic conceit is also found at the same time in Shakespeare (especially in the early plays, such as *Romeo and Juliet*), and continues to become one of the ordering principles of the exit aria of Metastasio in the eighteenth century.

tinkering with this or that specific to a thoroughgoing collaboration with the librettist on the plan of the entire work. It would seem probable, lacking further evidence, that the directness of the story line and the opportunities for dramatic highlighting (as in the antiphonal scene between Arianna and the chorus) were owing to the composer. Certainly the constant emphasis on the humanity of the characters, evident throughout the music that survives and carried over into the libretto, especially that of Striggio, must be traceable to Monteverdi. Yet his judgment was not infallible: it is thought that he insisted on the change of the end of *Orfeo*, in which Striggio planned either to have Orfeo killed by the bacchants or to leave him sorrowing while the bacchants had the final word. Monteverdi cranked down a *deus ex machina* who removes Orfeo to celestial bliss with Euridice.

Too much emphasis, however, has been devoted to the problem of the endings of operas in the seventeenth century. It is thought, by our age steeped in the necessity for the "logical" culmination of the drama—which to us means that nature takes its course—that the *lieto fine*, or happy ending, runs counter not only to the myth but also to the inevitability of the drama. There is a legitimate distinction, however, between the *lieto fine* of the later seventeenth- and early eighteenth-century operas, in which the tyrant-villain, who has displayed various nasty traits throughout the evening, suddenly forgets and forgives, and the metamorphosis endings of the early myth-operas, which are not so much happy as transfigured. When, as Hofmannsthal puts it in *Die Frau ohne Schatten*, higher powers come into play, purely mortal words have little or no meaning. It is possible to object to the mechanical nature of the *deus ex machina*, but a good deal of our objection rises from the fact that we reject the notion of the overseeing gods. Given the assumption (valid to the seventeenth century) that Man was still in some sense in thrall, the gods can interfere when they please. The results are neither illogical nor "unhappy."

It would be all too simple to deduce from the preceding pages that by 1610 the youthful form of opera had succeeded in emerging from the chrysalis of the pastoral play—which had left it a legacy of brevity, directness, and sweetness of sound—and, through the medium of Monteverdi, had found a dramatic voice that boded well for the years ahead. This is unfortunately the impression that can be derived from cursory histories of opera. The fact was that the

"pastoral" librettos of the Camerata—and Monteverdi's influence—
were but two of a number of sources which had contributed to the
birth of opera. It was soon to become evident that several of its other
sources would take over its development. Further, the emphasis
in the pastorals on simile and flowery language had sown the seeds
of the *stile gonfiato*, or inflated style, similar to the euphuistic style
of Lyly and the followers of the Spanish poet, Luis de Góngora,
which was to seize and dominate the libretto in its years of early
abandon. "The influence of humanism and of esthetic theories on
[the birth of opera] has been exaggerated," writes Professor Nino
Pirrotta.[6] The actions and publications of the Camerata had highlighted a developing situation, while the extraordinary popularity of the new art form—and the novel means by which it was
presented—had left estheticians turning gently in a backwash as
opera tumbled over itself downstream in its own ebullient growth.

One of the principal factors in the rise of opera was the use of
stage machinery for spectacular effect. Grand effects had been part
of the circumstance of great feasts, weddings, and other celebra-
tions of the sixteenth century, but with the development of the
proscenium arch,[7] which could effectively hide the workings of
the stage from the audience, such effects began to make their
way into the theater. Tasso's *Aminta*, when first performed in
Ferrara in 1573, was limited to simple arcadian scenery. When it
was presented in 1590 in Florence, the "engineer" Bontalenti (!)
created all sorts of magical illusions and stage witchery. Peri's
Euridice—that simple pastoral—was first presented clothed in
machines and effects—and, by the way, also was encumbered with
intermezzos between the acts, as was the custom. Neither the Camerata nor Monteverdi wished to do away with the machinery, and it
was not until late in the seventeenth century, when the stage effects
came regularly to dominate the story and such characterization as
there was, that any systematic outcry against their use was heard.
Scenic effects were for many years a novelty, and early opera was
more interested in parading and testing its toys than in adapting
them for restrained and subordinate use.

The Italy of the early seventeenth century was an exuberant

---

(6) Nino Pirrotta: "Commedia dell'arte and opera," *Musical Quarterly*
(July 1955), p. 315.
(7) Probably in Italy at the end of the sixteenth century or the beginning of the seventeenth.

and extrovert society, eager for learning and diversion. The pastoral play formed only a very small part of that diversion, for the Italian of the period, if he could read, would more likely be scanning the novellas of the time than the works of Tasso or Ariosto. Many of these novellas—and a great number of the plays presented—came from Spain, which was undergoing a theatrical boom of incredible proportions. By 1700, Spanish dramatists would have written the staggering total of thirty thousand plays,[8] notable in general for their theatricality, their zest for life, and their emotionality. The plots were complicated, bizarre, and disjunct; the intrigues rife; and the emotions poured forth in floods of tears and metrics. Yet Spain was not the only source. In 1611, Flaminio Scala edited a volume of fifty plays, mostly comedies, from countries as distant as Russia and Poland, which included pastorals but also comprised magic, fantastic happenings, and every sort of stage effect.[9] It is reasonable to assume that a number of these plays were staged and seen by the dramaphiles of the period. Horror plays were also popular: in *Isifile*, a play by Francesco Mondella dating from 1582, Isifile is presented with the heads of her slaughtered children and the hands of her flayed-alive husband along with a bowl of poison, in full view of the audience.[1]

In the realm of comedy, the *commedia dell'arte* had by the early seventeenth century established itself as a major art form, and was known throughout Italy. Its influence on the earlier intermezzos is evident: Pirrotta believes that it also created many of the conditions necessary for the acceptance of opera by the public.[2] Certainly its influence on the opera libretto cannot be exaggerated, not only in the seventeenth century but also in the eighteenth. The stock characters of the comic sections of seventeenth-century librettos derive directly from the improvisatory antics, codified into ritual and known as *lazzi*, of the *commedia* "scripts." The character of that prince of barbers, Figaro, springs originally from a *commedia* characterization made wildly popular in France in the beginning of the eighteenth century by the celebrated actor Mezzetin, who survives in a portrait by Watteau.

---

(8) John Gassner: *Masters of the Drama*, p. 186.
(9) Flaminio Scala: *Il Teatro delle favole rappresentative*; see Allardyce Nicoll: *The World of Harlequin*, for a fuller description.
(1) J. C. Walker: *Historical Memoir on Italian Tragedy*, pp. 105–6.
(2) Pirrotta: "Commedia dell'arte and opera," p. 315.

It is easy to see why this torrent of dramatic possibility would quickly overwhelm the pastoral play and naturalize the wide range of subject matter of the libretto: mythic, heroic, chivalric, fantastic, and historic. Because of this, and because a great number of librettos either have been lost or have not been discovered (the music of the early operas was rarely published, the libretto far more often), it becomes arbitrary to assign to a specific work claims of primacy in one area or another of the libretto. For many years the *Incoronazione di Poppea* (1642) of Giovanni Francesco Busenello[3] was considered the first historical opera. It may have been, depending on the definition of the term, but the *Sant' Alessio* (1632) of Giulio Cardinal Rospigliosi,[4] which may be considered not an opera but an oratorio or a pageant, has a quasi-historical background. *Sant' Alessio* has also been called the first *opera buffa* because it includes comic scenes, and the first opera that reflects its times in that the characters of the comic scenes are realistically drawn. It can be argued also that *Sant' Alessio* is neither: the comic scenes are definitely subordinate, and the opera is not about Rome in 1632. As to what is the first *opera buffa*, Romain Rolland and Angelo Solerti choose Parisani's *Diana schernita* (1629), but others prefer Rospigliosi's *Che soffre, speri* (1639), and Winton Dean chooses Rospigliosi's *Dal Male il bene* (1653).

It is safe to say that somewhere, in some libretto, almost any aspect of seventeenth-century dramatic thought and practice can be found. What is saddening is the fact that, with all these riches at its command, and using them all at one time or another, the libretto gradually settled into a series of tropes and conceits that were to be reproduced with minor variations from city to city and which characterize, almost at a glance, any libretto of the seventeenth century. The analogy with the growth of television in the United States is apt, as in both cases an infinity of wealth was quickly channeled into certain standard types, written by mediocrities, with reflections of this or that artistic novelty but largely faceless and gray.

Seventeenth-century opera grew to fullness in the public opera theaters of Venice after 1637, but Venice in turn was affected by

---

(3) 1598–1659. The first great librettist. See Chapter Two.
(4) Roman librettist; see next page.

the developments in opera instituted in Rome between 1620 and 1640. There in 1632, the Barberini family, passionate devotees of the new form of spectacle, caused a theater to be constructed which accommodated over three thousand people. It is true that the theater was populated entirely by an audience invited by the owners (as distinct from the Venetian paying audience), and that therefore the viewers of the spectacle were more or less confined to the upper classes, the clergy, and a few hangers-on. But what is far more significant is that the Barberini theater brought indoors and systematized the pageants, festival spectacles, and the like that had been taking place for almost a century. Whether these operas be considered pageants or quasi-oratorios is immaterial to the history of the art form: they served as the cold frame from which opera was transplanted to Venice and, through Antonio Barberini, papal legate to France, to Paris.

Many of the works were effective, also, as operas. Granted, they relied heavily on spectacle in terms of huge casts, immense choruses, and elaborate machinery. Granted also, some of the works were didactic, in that elevated language and sensibility were intended to teach the audience the virtues of Christianity. Sant' Alessio, the nobleman turned penitent, is mocked by the comic rabble, but perseveres, as much (Rospigliosi hints) because he is a member of the aristocracy as because he is a martyr. But the works of Giulio Rospigliosi, the future Pope Clement IX, expanded and enriched the libretto, for though he did not have a particularly sharp dramatic sense, nonetheless he had read widely and was totally committed to the idea of opera—so much so that, when he became Pope in 1667, he was accused of paying more attention to opera than to the affairs of the Holy See.[5] Rospigliosi deserves more attention as a librettist than he has received. (Romain Rolland first discussed his contributions.) His knowledge of the Spanish theater[6] as well as of the *commedia dell'arte* is evidenced in his comedies, and his grand crowd scenes brought the bustle of seventeenth-century Italy to the stage. Rolland details the spectacle elements of *Che soffre, speri*: rain, hail, tempest, battles, and, in the last act, a fair reproduced in detail, with merchants, strollers, nobility in carriages, a chariot pulled by oxen, and a sunset. Rospigliosi

---

(5) Romain Rolland: *Opéra avant Lulli*, p. 139, fn. 5.
(6) Fostered when he was papal nuncio in Spain.

was also able to write decent verse with some characterization, as this excerpt, a soliloquy of Sant' Alessio, demonstrates:

> *Alessio, che farai?*
> *Userai crudeltade*
> *a chi come ben sai,*
> *vuol il Ciel, vuol il mondo,*
> *che tu mostri pietade?*
> *Che fo? devo scoprirmi,*
> *O pur m'ascondo?*
> *Ah, silenzio crudele*
> *cagion d'aspre querele.*[7]
>
> (II, v)

Opera in Rome lasted a few years after the founding of the first paying theater in Venice in 1637, but it was a dwindling endeavor. The rivalry of the great Italian princely houses (most of whom were represented in the College of Cardinals) and interest in wars commanded the attention of those who had supported opera, and the "engineers" (as the machine makers were called) and the composers headed northward to Venice or Paris, taking with them the learning they had acquired in the Barberini theater. Rome continued to produce opera toward the end of the century, depending on the whims of the Popes, but its great days were gone, to be seen only in a dim way today at the Baths of the Caracalla, which preserves the spectacle if not the machinery, the moralisms, and the élan of the original.

In 1637 the Tron family opened the Teatro San Cassiano in Venice with *Andromeda* (music, Francesco Manelli; libretto, Benedetto Ferrari). By 1641 there were four Venetian theaters; by the end of the century sixteen, although some were in disuse.[8] The public opera theater had an impact upon Venice comparable to that of the Spanish Renaissance or the Elizabethan theaters on their audiences—or, more contemporaneously, to the impact of motion pictures or television. It generated great enthusiasm among the devotees, who flocked to the various theaters, which were gen-

---

(7) "Alessio, what will you do? You will be cruel, as you well know. Does Heaven, does the world expect that you show pity? What should I do? Should I disclose myself or hide? Ah, cruel silence, the cause of bitter quarrels."

(8) Leo Schrade: *Monteverdi*, p. 346; S. T. Worsthorne: *Venetian Opera in the Seventeenth Century*, p. 28.

erally open only in the fall and during the winter carnival (until Lent).[9] It was not uncommon to go to the opera every night during those months, and to see operas twice or three times over. As with television, however, there was a constant demand for "novelty," which meant not that every new opera would be a path-breaker but that every year the operas were newly composed. Popular librettos were retained or refurbished and embellished (especially with added scenic effects), but the music had to be new. This situation endured until well into the eighteenth century (there are many examples in the nineteenth), and it accounts for the fact that the great librettist Metastasio could write a single work and have it set by as many as a dozen composers over a thirty-year period. In turn, this reflected the continuing importance of the word vis-à-vis the music, for the word—or, better still, the basic story line—remained constant while the music, more ephemeral, disappeared after one or two productions.

All the opera houses of Venice were operated on more or less the same basis. Each was situated in a separate parish of the city and was owned by a noble family, who leased it to an entrepreneur.[1] The boxes were also leased, by the year, to noble families and to foreigners of rank, especially diplomats, while the parterre was open to the general public, which often had to stand: as in the Elizabethan Globe Theater, there were no seats in the pit. The boxes existed in a world almost apart from the rest of the theater and were treated as private drawing rooms of the renting family. Dinner could be served there, transactions and gossip discussed, and now and then the inhabitants would pause to marvel at the working of some miraculous occurrence on stage or listen to a particularly well-sung aria. The parterre in turn was open to refreshment sellers, who hawked their wares during the performance. The idea of dead silence in the theater so that the opera could be heard was totally unknown: travelers from France (where silence was more general but certainly not universal) invariably commented on the hubbub of the Italian theater (although Naples rather than Venice seemed

----

(9) The passion for opera was not confined to Venice, and it is thought by Paul Henry Lang and others that many "oratorios" of the seventeenth and eighteenth centuries are nothing but operas disguised so that they could be performed either during Lent or in areas where the ruling authority disliked opera.
(1) Schrade suggests that the number of theaters reflects less the popularity of the opera than the rivalry of the noble houses.

to be the noisiest opera city). Undoubtedly both the composer and the librettist despaired of this situation, for only a minimum of the music and/or words ever was listened to across the proscenium. But it is difficult to prove that this scared away any potentially great librettists. Noise in the theater was a general concomitant of seventeenth-century Italian drama, and the librettists simply relied even more heavily on visual means in order to get their stories across.[2]

At the beginning of the performance, the lanterns and candelabra in the auditorium proper were extinguished, so that solely the playing area remained brightly lit. There also was a curtain which was raised to begin the action.[3] The operas themselves often lasted until two in the morning, and, for the public, cost about $.42 per admission.[4]

Notwithstanding the posthumous fame of Monteverdi, it was the librettist and not the composer who dominated the collaboration in those first Venetian years. As Worsthorne writes,

> . . . the onus of the production depended on the poet. The formalities of publication were his responsibility; he chose the patron to whom the play was to be dedicated; he derived an income from the sale of the libretto. . . . The music, either in parts or score, was never printed, irrespective of the success of the work. . . . Clearly, then, the poet had a far larger public for the spread of his work than the composer, whose score was allowed to moulder in some lumber-room of the theatre.[5]

The librettist and, quite often, the engineer. Few of the early librettos directly name the composer (he is more likely to be found in the author's preface than on the title page), but a good many of them name the machine maker, and a few even include a preface

---

(2) The importance of noise in the theater *as far as the librettist is concerned* has been exaggerated. The paradox is that the autocrat who imposed the idea of dead silence on the audience, Richard Wagner, transferred his hubbub to the orchestra, so that even he had to rely on visual means and *parole sceniche* to make his points; for outside of Bayreuth, only a minimum of the words ever reaches the audience's ears.
(3) Worsthorne: *Venetian Opera in the Seventeenth Century*, p. 25. There is some question as to whether or not this curtain was a proscenium curtain, which was introduced in France at the end of the eighteenth century. It may have been some sort of mid-stage scrim, which served to hide the trompe l'oeil set and/or the machinery used in the Prologue.
(4) Ibid., p. 6.
(5) Ibid., p. 119.

written by him.⁶ The composer, clearly tertiary, fitted in as he could.

A study should be made of the librettists' prefaces to seventeenth-century Italian librettos, for their amusing, informative, and irreverent tone is often more enjoyable than the work that follows. The usual format for a "Venetian" libretto would be a title page giving the date of performance and the name of the dedicatee, followed by a grandiloquent preface, written by the "poet,"⁷ vowing his eternal respect for and gratitude to the noble patron who had allowed himself to be so humbly honored.⁸ This, in turn, was followed by the author's foreword to the readers, entitled *"a chi legge"* or *"ai lettori"* (the portion of the libretto referred to earlier). Next came the *"argomento,"* or chronology of events that had taken place before the action of the opera begins (it sometimes also included a gloss of the opera story). These *argomenti* grew in length and complexity as the century progressed (they often ran to four closely printed pages), and their inordinate wordiness, added to the impossibility of assimilating all the pre-events, became a target of those who wished to reform the libretto at the beginning of the eighteenth century. The *argomenti* find their echo in the nineteenth century in the Prologues to several of Verdi's operas, most notably *La Forza del destino* and *Il Trovatore,*⁹ but neither of these can compete in complexity with some of the seventeenth-century examples. The cast listing followed, almost invariably without any mention of the artists, and separated into the singing roles and the extras (or *"personaggi muti"*). Last would come the scene changes, the ballets between the acts, and, not infrequently, a listing of the machines and magical effects that would be seen during the course of the evening. It should be remembered, however, that the format of a seventeenth-century libretto was highly flexible, de-

---

(6) *L'Ulisse errante* (Venice, 1644), preface by Giacomo Torelli, one of the most famous stage engineers.
(7) In later years, the preface would more often be written by the entrepreneur who ran the theater; this was usually the case if the libretto was used in another city.
(8) Such Uriah Heepish dedications were obviously a matter of course for the seventeenth century and did not strike readers as degrading the author's dignity.
(9) I use the word "prologue" in both senses here: the antecedents of the opera as well as the primary scene, labeled as such in *Simon Boccanegra* or *La Forza del destino.* Seventeenth-century Prologues were, of course, an entirely different genre.

pending on the publisher and on the city in which it was published (and presumably on other variables such as amount of paper available, publication time, etc.), and that, apart from the dedication, which almost always appeared first, the other sections could be scrambled or omitted entirely.

The published librettos fall into two distinct species. The first, or *cereni* librettos (librettos meant to be read by candlelight), were intended for use during the performance and were usually on sale outside the theater. They were printed on cheap paper against the deadline of the performance, and abounded in typographical errors, misspellings, mislabelings (Act II as Act I), so that not a few of them included a table of corrections inserted at the last moment or for the second printing. Although the format of the librettos changed somewhat with the centuries, the poor quality of these *cereni* works lasted until well into the nineteenth century. The second category encompasses the collected editions of certain librettists, published usually at the author's expense and invariably a more professional job. One of the finest of these editions is that of the works of Giovann' Andrea Moniglia, published in Florence 1689–90.

As the century progressed, refinements appeared in the format of the librettos. The *argomento*, for instance, was often separated into two portions, that for which there was historical or documentary precedent, and that which was the author's embroidery or invention. The two are separated by the words *"che si finge,"* set in larger type.[1] In Rome, and in other cities under papal domination, the librettos had to have the approval of the Church (given in an imprimatur at the beginning or the end), and it was customary for the author to affirm his belief in the Catholic faith despite the pagan wordings of the libretto.[2] This affirmation (or *protesta*) became a commonplace in the eighteenth century, and the formula was reduced to a few words. The name of the stage engineer was

---

(1) This (that is, the separation of the "true" from the "invented," along with a list of the historical sources) has often been thought to be one of the reforms of the early eighteenth century, but, as with practically all the reforms, examples can be found as early as 1650. The "reformers" were codifiers rather than inventors.

(2) *"Le parole Fato, Idolo-Adorare, Dio, Nume, + altre son scritte da penna Poetica, ma chi le scrisse si vanta d'esser vero Cattolico."* ("The words *Fate, idol worship, God, Heavens*, and others are written in a poetic manner, but the person who wrote them is proud to be a true Catholic.") *L'Aiace*, Rome, 1697.

the first to appear in the libretto after those of the librettist and/or composer, but it was not until the eighteenth century that the artists and technicians received credit by name. Finally, with the growing importance of the aria in opera, variant editions of certain popular librettos began to appear.[3] In a supplement (often not by the original librettist), scenes or arias would be included which could be substituted for other scenes or arias (or, conversely, were cut in that particular production). The choice of aria would depend on the singer. Although it may at first appear that such a procedure would wreck a libretto, in fact it did nothing of the kind, for very few librettos (Busenello's are an exception in the later seventeenth century) had over-all structural unity that could be impaired. Most often these librettos were a series of loosely connected scenes, any one or two of which would be eliminated without detriment to the whole. The functions of the exit aria will be discussed in the chapters on Zeno and Metastasio: it is enough to say here that, as pictorializations of effects, they were often (even with Metastasio) interchangeable.

The Prologue, so important a part of the Camerata librettos, slowly became assimilated into the body of the work. At first it had only an allegorical connection (if any at all), its characters often being independent of the rest of the opera or reappearing only in the apotheosis finale. Gradually, however, the gods infested the opera; then the mortals (rather than allegorical figures such as Vendetta, Furore, or Ribellione) appeared in the Prologue, and finally it ceased to exist as a separate entity. The *licenza*, or final choral ode to the dedicatee (or the ruler), became a fixture of the Vienna reform operas, but was occasionally employed in the earlier seventeenth century. Its use declined, however, with the temporary disappearance of the chorus from opera.

What, then, were some of the features of seventeenth-century Italian opera? The chief ones were stage panoply, action taking the form of complex intrigue interwoven with love, little attempt at logical cohesion, and rampant emotionalism. In a theater where subtlety would count for naught, everything had to be exaggerated in order to make an effect. Huge, varied casts were employed (although by the end of the century they were growing smaller);

---

(3) Often librettos were subject to complete reworkings "to conform to current usage," as one preface puts it. *La Circe*, Venice, 1679.

comedy was often mixed with the "tragic"; and a tortured plot wound its mazy way through every kind of spectacle and magic.

As has been said earlier, several situations, scenes, and characters became stereotyped and reappeared in opera after opera. Most if not all of the comic characters were taken over from the *commedia dell'arte* (and can be found, along with many other evidences of the Italian drama, in Shakespeare). The wrinkled nurse laments her old age and gives frank and rational advice, sometimes conversing directly with the audience, as she undoubtedly did in the *commedia* plays. The comic servants stutter and stammer their way through interminable scenes in which they manage only to pronounce the first letter of the rhyme while the audience, to its glee, quickly guesses the word.[4] The younger cousin of the nurse, the *damigella*, or lady-in-waiting, became the classic *soubrette* of Italian opera: pretty, cheeky, and a flirt. Despina in *Così fan tutte* is one of her more famous incarnations, and she can be seen in this century, on a slightly different social level, but essentially the same *damigella*, in the Amelia of Menotti's *Amelia al ballo*. The worldly-wise and cynical page is probably drawn more from court life of the period than from the *commedia*, and can be seen in latter-day operas among the courtiers in *Rigoletto* or as Oscar in *Un Ballo in maschera*.

Most of the stories revolved around the tribulations of a knightly hero (or heroine, more Valkyrie than Fidelio) pitted against a tyrant, with elaborate love chains as subplots (A loves B, who loves C, etc.). After many vicissitudes (usually including being thrown into a dungeon), the hero overcomes the tyrant and gains his beloved,[5] in a triumphal final scene in which allegorical figures, such as Glory, often appear. For the ending of these operas was almost invariably the *lieto fine*. The librettist of *L'Ulisse errante* (1644), Giacomo Badoaro, says in his preface that the first librettists composed tragedies in order to show the tyrants their defects and to teach the populace to hate tyranny and to love liberty, but

---

(4) The stuttering servant survives in the yawning and sneezing servants of Beaumarchais' *Le Barbier de Séville*. We have forgotten their existence because Sterbini largely excised them from the libretto he gave Rossini, but they appear in full yawn and sneeze in Petrosellini's libretto for Paisiello.

(5) There is probably a connection between the hero-tyrant story line and the puppet plays of the period, still extant in Sicily, one of whose ancestors is the *Orlando furioso* of Ariosto.

that these tragedies lèd to sadness and death, while the *lieto fine* did all these things while making people happy. Thus the tyrant realizes at the final moment the evil of his ways and decides to reform, or realizes that his evil prime minister has misguided him, as Caligula does in *Caligula delirante* (1672; m., Giovanni Pagliardi; l., Domenico Gisberti). Wounded, he sees his blood spurting[6] and says, "Through the open wound my madness escapes; as my blood flows my mind is restored. . . ." Everyone, presumably including the tyrant, goes home happy.

The operas included several stock scenes, the most widespread of which was the slumber scene. Some say that its popularity was owed to its appearance in Busenello's *L'Incoronazione di Poppea*, but its use antedates that opera. The fact that Shakespeare had strolling players well versed in the slumber scene of the *Murder of Gonzago* suggests a common occurrence;[7] certainly the slumber scene was well known in Italy during the first part of the seventeenth century. These scenes became ubiquitous, and were divided into several categories. They usually take place in a garden or a bosky wood in which someone falls asleep (in *Giustino*, 1683; m., Giovanni Legrenzi; l., Nicolò Beregani—Giustino falls asleep on his plow). Sometimes he talks in his sleep, revealing his true feelings about the tyrant or his beloved. Sometimes (as in *Gonzago* or *L'Incoronazione*) a villain enters to kill him. Sometimes his beloved arrives, overhears his unconscious declarations of love to her, and is happily surprised. Sometimes he sleeps unnoticed, and wakes to overhear some plot. The slumber scenes developed into dream scenes in the later seventeenth and early eighteenth centuries (in the Handel-Marchi *Alcina*, for instance), which could then be used as excuses for elaborate ballets.[8] At times, as the sleeper slumbers, a shade or ghost appears to him to warn or guide him. These scenes— which need not be allied to the slumber scenes—were categorized

---

(6) The blood was often genuine (if ox blood), and added to the spectacle.

(7) Hamlet says, "His name's Gonzago: the story is extant, and writ in choice Italian . . ." (III, ii); it comes from a novella. Slumber scenes—and of course *ombra* scenes—are integral to Shakespeare. One of the most powerful is the scene in which Prince Hal sees the crown in the room of his dying, sleeping father (*Henry IV, Part II*; IV, iv).

(8) A practice, known as the "dream sequence," which is endemic to Broadway and Hollywood. The dances of the Weill-Anderson *Lady in the Dark* were all built around this idea (modernized into psychoanalytical dreams).

as *ombra* scenes, and can be found in many of the operas of the period (as well as in both parts of Berlioz's *Les Troyens*).

Another stock scene is one in which a letter is read out. Seventeenth-century librettists obviously took great delight in including these scenes, and invented excuses for having letters given to characters on stage so that they could be read out. I confess to being at a loss as to why so many of these particular scenes appear: the only explanation I have is that, most of the audience having been illiterate, the act of reading a letter was as magical as the stage tricks of the *maghi* (sorcerers) and *maghe* (witches). Admirers of *As You Like It* will recognize another "writing" trait: that of lovers scrawling their love over every rock and tree.[9]

Stage props were also very popular. These were smaller items than the great chariots and clouds of the stage machinery. Mirrors were often used, to be gazed into by ur-Marschallins and others: I suppose that this act also was quasi-magical. Basins abounded: usually they were brought in covered with a cloth which, when removed, would reveal either a crown and scepter or a set of chains, which meant *"Orride prigione!"* Chains—*catene*—clanked and rattled through all of seventeenth-century opera, and librettists seemingly vied in depicting the dank and smelly dungeons in which their heroes were immured.

Disguises were rife. It was rare that an Italian seventeenth-century opera ran its course without one or more changes of sex through costume. Although the practice had its origins with the *commedia,* it was not confined to the comic characters: early Fidelios became men so that they could save their lovers, and swains donned the garb of *damigelle* to come closer to their hearts' desires. The realism of the travesties was unimportant, as by this time many of the roles were being assumed by castrati and, in a world of exaggeration, a little more or less made not much difference.

And then the machines. It is fascinating to read the description of the machines for a given opera, and to look at the plans of their operation, for these machines were no amateur toys. In the operas of Agostino Steffani there are lists of the machines needed: a Theban wall, which moves forward; a monster, which becomes a

---

(9) In Aurelio Aureli's *Alessandro Magno in Sidone* (1679) the young king writes on a rock with the blood of a dead soldier.

squad of warriors; two infernal dragons; the collapse of innumerable buildings in an earthquake (all from *Niobe*); Merlin the magician rising from the depths of the earth on a ball of fire and returning; an earthquake that shakes the library and breaks seven statues, the fragments of which change into seven human figures (from *Marco Aurelio*). It is easy to see why such possibilities challenged the powers and the imaginations less of the composer and librettist than of the stage engineer, and it is equally easy to see why their workings, coupled with the more straightforward magic of puffs of smoke and potions of *maghi* and *maghe*, would always astound and delight.[1] The composer Cavalli is supposed to have felt that his librettos were but "themes offered to his fantasy": the same could be said of the librettist and the master stage engineer of the seventh century.[2]

The stage sets of the early Venetian operas were usually constructed along the lines of Sebastiano Serlio's famous engravings for the comic and tragic theater; that is, with a central perspective vanishing point and balanced wings. When the god descended in the machine, he was cranked down stage-center-upstage at the meeting point of the perspective lines; if other gods appeared on clouds, they balanced him along the sides of the stage. With the elaboration of the libretto and the machines, however, this ordered stage picture began to give way to greater and greater clutter. The work of the later members of the family of Galli da Bibiena in the eighteenth century imposed a new sense of order on the magnificence of the now fully "Baroque" sets by angling the vanishing point so that it cut through a many-tiered construction, giving the impression of vaulting heights and layers of depth. Librettists obviously considered the stage picture of prime import, and sets were very often minutely described in the libretto.

The seventeenth-century librettist and stage engineer also liked to work with height. Obviously, when a god came down out of the ceiling and sang an aria or an extended recitative above the stage, he was at once symbolically and physically above the mortals; when Orfeo is removed by Apollo in Striggio's libretto, he is literally lifted above the pains and pleasures that the bacchants

---

(1) As they do even today, judging from the wistful nostalgia on the part of many critics at the disappearance from the stage of that splendid relic of the seventeenth century, the fire-breathing dragon in *Siegfried*.
(2) Henry Prunières: *L'Opéra italien en France avant Lulli*, p. 289.

are experiencing in the temporal world. This visual symbolism was of striking use in an opera theater, where the words either could not be heard or were not worth being heard. When the use of the *deus ex machina* declined (except for triumphal appearances), the librettists continued to work with height by the use of towers. Towers are a standard fixture of the middle and late seventeenth century: tyrants bully heroes from their ramparts, heroes are immured in them—sometimes even two towers (or two elephants) are present on stage, with combatants on each shouting imprecations. Ships were also used for this purpose, as someone standing on the deck of a ship was above the stage (besides giving the stage engineer a chance to show off his wave motion). The use of the tower to symbolize either domination over those below or agonizing removal from them remained a standard operatic and theatrical device, as *Il Trovatore* and *Pelléas et Mélisande* demonstrate. That inspired magpie Richard Wagner, who had the surest instinct of any librettist when it came to the visual reinforcement of the action, uses height for both purposes. In *Lohengrin*, Elsa appears on a balcony to sing of her happiness, and is forced by Ortrud, below, to come down to her and give her her blessing (thus, the physical act of *coming down* becomes the first indication of the spell of mistrust that Ortrud will cast over Elsa). In *Parsifal*, Klingsor from his tower full of magic devices calls up Kundry, who appears from below in his thrall. Finally, Brangäne from her watchtower weaves a spell of song over the lovers below, but, not being an all-seeing god in a machine, does not spy King Mark until it is too late.[3]

Undoubtedly the stage engineers led many composers and librettists by the nose and forced on them unnecessary and redundant effects simply to show off their own prowess and skill, but it is a grave mistake to think that they worked against the wishes of the operatic collaborators. Spectacle was an integral part of seventeenth-century opera, and one test of the worth of a librettist is to determine whether he was able to handle its resources or whether its resources mishandled him.

It is certain that some of the seventeenth-century librettos, most particularly those written in the close-knit, comparatively lax,

---

(3) Wagner based Brangäne's song on the Minnesinger aubades (cf. Ernest Newman: *The Wagner Operas*, p. 257) sung from towers: the visual and symbolic connections with gods are obvious.

and incorrigibly gossipy Republic of Venice, were *livrets à clef*, in that they satirized and mocked specific conventions and individuals in thin disguise. Michael Robinson mentions a Viennese opera, *La Lanterna di Diogene* (1674),[4] as being one of these, and there are doubtless others. The problem is that, although we can often spot the mores being satirized, our ignorance of the models on whom the satires were based effectively prevents detection. Again, it is certain that some of the more outrageous librettos were parodies or quasi-parodies of the exaggerations of the times,[5] but so many librettos stand as self-parodies that it is difficult to distinguish between them without outside evidence. We shall see in the works of Busenello a mocking spirit that more than one librettist shared, though not with the same vigor or consistency.

The men who wrote the librettos of the seventeenth-century Italian opera began by being dilettantes and ended by being hacks. Very often they were noblemen or men with money and background (Moniglia was chief physician to the Grand Duke of Florence) who wrote, as one of them says in a preface, *"per capriccio."* Benedetto Ferrari became one of the first to compose the music and write the libretto. It is not strange that Busenello, the greatest seventeenth-century librettist, should have titled his collected works *Delle Ore ociose* (From Idle Hours; i.e., In My Spare Time): precisely that feeling of divertissement led many of his fellow-librettists to try their hand at the new genre. If they met with success, they continued to write: there was ample demand.

Yet it should not be thought, because many librettists arrived as amateurs of the art, that they were bumblers (although a few assuredly were). Men such as the father-and-son Cicogninis were librettists of great learning. Jacopo Cicognini wrote one of the earliest librettos, *Andromeda* (1611), corresponded with Lope de Vega, and is credited with introducing the riches of the Spanish theater to the Italian stage. His son Giacinto disseminated those riches in librettos in the pure seventeenth-century manner, was

---

(4) Michael F. Robinson: *Opera Before Mozart*, p. 77.
(5) The best approach to the problem of intentional parody or self-parody would be a study of operas presented in one city over a period of years, as the parody would most likely follow quickly on the success of the opera (as was the case in France). Andrea della Corte states that Moniglia was rudely satirized by one Menzini; *Drammi per musica*, vol. I, p. 38.

said to be the inventor of the *lieto fine*, and wrote one of the most celebrated librettos of the time, *Giasone* (1649). Count Niccolò Minato held the splendid title of Caesarean Poet at the Austrian Court from 1669 to 1698, which meant that he was required to furnish librettos for operas and oratorios on demand, and which in turn led to his writing well over a hundred of them.[6] He would be succeeded in that post by two of the most important librettists, Apostolo Zeno and Pietro Metastasio.

As was to be expected, the more verse came to be used on an operatic stage—and especially on an operatic stage dominated by extra-verse considerations—the more it adapted to the surroundings. At first it was not uncommon to have inordinately long speeches from the major characters (as late as *Il Ratto di Cefalo*, 1650 [m., Mattioli; l., Berni], Aurora appears, riding Pegasus, declaims sixty-two lines, then gets off and allows Pegasus to fly away before declaiming twenty-six more), but *brevità* intervened in the form of the fast exchange, the short sentence, and the shorter speech. The growing popularity of the aria also limited the words, as composers liked the shorter form, in which they had opportunity for repetition and extension. By Metastasio's time the exit arias were models of brevity and grace.

The suppleness of the verse was aided by the ever-greater use of *versi sciolti*, or blank verse, and its directness through the discovery of *saffici*, or broken verse. Broken verse—that is, with a complete cesura in the middle of the line—usually found in choral writing, became a staple of the Italian *melodramma* of the late eighteenth century and the nineteenth, but it is occasionally encountered in the seventeenth.[7] Although the librettos of the seventeenth century did not show the arsenal of short epithets which was to be developed in the later eighteenth century, they used a number of stock words which reappeared regularly: "*tiranno*"—"*furibondo*"—"*catena*"—"*superbo*"—"*germano*"—"*saetta*"—"*pupille*"—and many more.

The librettist Aurelio Aureli is typical of the many strains that went into the make-up of the seventeenth-century libretto.

---

(6) He is remembered today, if at all, through his famous apostrophe to a tree in Handel's *Serse*, so redolent of the verbiage of the century: "*Ombra mai fù/di vegetabile/cara, e amabile,/soave più*" ("No shade of a tree was ever more dear, lovable or mild").
(7) Walker: *Historical Memoir on Italian Tragedy*, pp. 195–6, asserts that *Aristodemo* (Padova, 1657) contains the first example of *saffici*.

He wrote librettos from 1652 to 1707 for many of the famous composers of the day, and demonstrated all the virtues and vices of the libretto at that time. His poetry was, at best, serviceable, as he himself admitted in *Medoro* (1658): "You already know that I compose for my own pleasure and not out of aspiration for the title of Poet." He sometimes included Prologues; his story lines were complex, with plots and subplots, with ample opportunity for spectacle, and with, always, the *lieto fine*. He adapted and cut to suit the tastes of the composer or the impresario,[8] and seemingly cared little about the fate of his works. Yet contained within the farrago of incident, aria, and wonder are some striking situations and characters, which demonstrate that Aureli knew how to write effectively for the theater in which he was working. For instance, *Alessandro Magno* (1679) opens with a cliché-filled seventeenth-century love lyric: "*Su' letto di rose,/pupille amorose,/mie faci, miei strali,/andianne a goder.//Vezzoso mio Nume/sì morbide piume/non porgan mai l'ali/al nostro piacer.*"[9] This scene is between lovers, but who are a married king and his mistress, and in the next scene the Queen enters. One of Aureli's best librettos, *Claudio Cesare* (1672), tells the story of the Emperor Claudius, married to Agrippina, who loves Giunia (who in turn loves the King of Spain). Giunia's nurse naturally counsels her to marry Claudius and become Empress instead of Queen, while Agrippina, a majestic termagant, tries to prevent the marriage. She is brought a portrait of Giunia (a common seventeenth-century device): "If I cannot kill that wicked woman . . . I shall at least revel in scratching her face." (She scratches one part of the portrait, then, unsheathing a knife, indignantly stabs it several times.) "Take that, O abhorred monster!" (II, xxiii). After much opportunity for intrigue and spectacle (a gladiatorial combat in the Colosseum becomes an excuse for a ballet), and after Agrippina is locked in a dungeon, Giunia renounces the throne and Agrippina magnanimously pardons her. To those who know Busenello, Aureli's story is a watered version of *L'Incoronazione di Poppea*. Nonetheless, it

---

(8) Andrea Della Corte, ed.: *Drammi per musica*, vol. I, pp. 39–40, severely condemns Aureli for giving in to the taste of the times so easily.
(9) Roughly: "On a bed of roses, O you with loving eyes, my torches, my arrows: let us go to our pleasure. O my charming god, such soft feathers can't forever be offered for the wings of our love."

contains the seeds of the operas of the reform and of the Italian operas thereafter: a coherent story line, a series of strong dramatic situations, and plenty of opportunity for the play of human emotions.

It is becoming more evident to scholars that the Italian opera of the later part of the century—at the moment of its greatest decadence in terms of swollen language, story line, and spectacle—was beginning to move toward the "reforms" that were to become popularized in Zeno and Metastasio. Attempts were being made at greater logicality and coherence, and audiences sated with the endless novelty of the machines were no longer demanding something more or something different. These developments, however, coincided with the growth in importance of the aria (and of the star singer) as replacement for the spectacle. At first the aria could be found throughout the opera, but gradually, as the century wore on, it gravitated toward the end of each scene, where it would be sung by a character who then left the stage. The florid aria constituted his flourish before leaving, and became conventionalized as the exit aria of *opera seria*. Aureli's *Claudio Cesare* supposedly contains sixty-six arias (many of them exit arias).

Harold Powers mentions two versions of Minato's *Scipione Affricano* to show the trend: in the 1664 edition, the hero discovers that his beloved is about to be burned alive in an abandoned ship at anchor. He shouts, "*Che tardo?*" ("Why delay?"), and swims off. In the 1678 edition (also by Minato) he gives the same shout, but pauses to sing an exit aria.[1] It would be up to Zeno—and more especially Metastasio—to fit the new vogue for the aria into the framework of a cogent drama.

---

(1) Harold S. Powers: *"Il Serse Trasformato," Musical Quarterly* (October 1961).

Chapter Two

Busenello

GIOVANNI FRANCESCO BUSENELLO (1598–1659) is the least known of the major librettists, and but for Monteverdi would hardly be known at all. He was born in Venice and lived all of his life there, a lawyer from a very rich and influential family of the "second nobility." We know very little of his actual life, but it appears that he rarely traveled any great distance, though it has been said that he once went to Spain. As a member of the upper classes of Venice, he became involved in the artistic and social affairs of the city; as a dilettante fretting at the bonds of the law, he wrote love lyrics and satires. He welcomed opera as a new outlet for his talents when the new art form made its debut in Venice in 1637, and there is evidence that he began writing librettos within a year after the first opera had been presented there. He published his collected operatic works in 1656, shortly before his death.

In an age when librettists wrote to order and the demand was great, Busenello's total output was minuscule: five librettos.[1] Yet two of these five are outstanding works and two more have within them a greater amount of originality and spark than any ten by any other seventeenth-century writer. For Busenello, unlike Striggio or Faustini or Aureli, injected himself into his works so that they formed an oeuvre reflective of Busenello the man. It is undoubtedly true that we can tell more about Busenello from his librettos than from what we know of his life. Such a statement can

---

(1) Professor Arthur Livingston, who pioneered work on Busenello at the end of the nineteenth century and has done practically all the research on him up to now, adds a sixth libretto to the canon: *La Discesa di Enea all'Inferno* (1640).

very rarely be made, for in most cases libretto writing hides rather than reveals the writer.

Carlo Goldoni wrote in the preface to his libretto *Statira* (1756): "When I write for music, the last person I think of is myself." To which Paul Henry Lang adds: "This is the attitude of the true librettist."[2] Not exactly. It is the attitude taken by one type of libretto writing in an age when the music clearly overrides. Such librettos cannot properly be called "negative" because they do not negate, but as reflections of their writers they could more properly be called "neutral." The neutral librettos are generally the ones that are most famous, for in them the adaptive rather than the creative powers of the librettist are paramount: much of Da Ponte's work, especially *Le Nozze di Figaro*, and Boito's three adaptations of Shakespeare and one of Goethe fall into this category, as do adaptations by composers of stage works, such as *Pelléas et Mélisande* and *Wozzeck*. Yet two factors should be noted in even these neutral librettos: that the librettist becomes a conduit for the personality and ideas of the original writer (strongly shown in *Pelléas;* watered down, but nonetheless in evidence, in *Le Nozze di Figaro*), and that even in adaptive librettos the personality of the librettist shines through. Da Ponte's *Don Giovanni* is an amplification of Bertati's libretto on the same subject, but it contains a great deal of the devil-may-care sexuality of its librettist which is missing in Bertati's rendition.[3] On the surface the vast output of Scribe would seem the perfect exemplar of the neutral libretto, but the bourgeois virtues and titillations that run through it accurately reflect the mind and thoughts of its creator.

But it is a much smaller group that can properly be called creative librettists, and of this group Busenello is the first example. What emerges in the four best librettos he wrote is not only organizational and dramatic ability above that of his fellow-dramatists, but also a point of view. The two salient features of a Busenello libretto are a stoically pessimistic outlook toward life and

---

(2) Paul Henry Lang: *George Frideric Handel*, p. 194. Lang neglects to mention that Goldoni's preface is to one of his *opera seria* librettos, which were few compared with his comedies, and quite inferior to them. Goldoni could not have made the same statement about his comedies, which teem with his ideas and personality.
(3) One reason why the notion that Casanova also had a hand in the writing of *Don Giovanni* is appealing is that the libretto accords with his personality.

a robust appreciation of love. Both of these traits are rare in librettos, for pessimism has never been a popular attitude for the operatic stage, and Busenello's concept of love is neither the milk-sop affection displayed by the majority of librettos nor the mystical union of *Tristan und Isolde,* but, rather, undisguised enjoyment of sexual pleasure. This last is found undiluted in Busenello's dialect poems.[4] It is interesting to note that a streak of pessimism has run through the Italian libretto from the first (although it lies largely unnoticed) from Busenello through Casti and Boito to Busoni, and in all cases has been coupled with a mordant sense of humor particularly apposite today.

Although Busenello's outlook appeals far more to the present century than do the works of his fellow-librettists, he was nevertheless entirely a man of his time. Indeed, his philosophic orientation and his ability to manipulate the enlarged framework of the Spanish-derived plots have prompted most commentators to compare him to his contemporary, Shakespeare.[5] Apt though the comparison is in certain areas, a comparison with Bertolt Brecht is even more apt, for Busenello shows that same feeling of dispassionate detachment and even anti-romanticism which Brecht calls "alienation." Busenello presents the world as it is, refusing to embellish or denigrate, with now and then a minor character who comments on the world's vanities. His most amazing achievement, *La Prosperità infelice di Giulio Cesare, Dittatore,* is far closer to the epic theater of Brecht than to that represented by Shakespeare's *Antony and Cleopatra.*

Busenello's first libretto was *Gli Amori d'Apollo e di Dafne* (1640), with music by Cavalli, who was to set all his librettos except *L'Incoronazione di Poppea.* The work is closely tied to the pastoral play, with imitative poetry and not much drama, a flower ballet, use of machines, and long, set declamatory speeches. It is easily the weakest of Busenello's librettos (leaving aside *La Discesa di Enea*). His second libretto, *Didone* (1641), represents a considerable improvement. Busenello in the preface refers to the "Spanish usage"

---

(4) "The sensuality contained in them gives vent above all to an intense and minute contemplation of feminine beauty"; Arthur Livingston: *La Vita veneziana nelle opere di Gian Francesco Busenello,* p. 233.
(5) It has been conjectured that Busenello wrote Shakespeare's plays, but I favor H. L. Mencken's hypothesis that the author was Beethoven.

in computing the Aristotelian rules,[6] and the libretto makes it certain that he had been studying Spanish plays. With *Didone* the Spanish concept of epic theater enters Busenello's world. The cast is large, and the scope is equally great. Didone herself does not appear until the second scene of the second act, for the first act is taken up with the death of Cassandra and the escape of Enea from the burning Troy. Didone's appearance, moreover, is not at the moment of Enea's landing, but when Iarba, King of the Getuli, comes to ask for her hand in marriage. The whole of the scene is a delightful example of stichomatheic banter, ending with Iarba's *"Lasciam' di disputar, Didon, t'adoro,"* to which Didone replies, *"Lasciam' di contrastar, Iarba, non t'amo."*[7]

As the libretto unfolds, it becomes evident that Enea and the plight of the Trojans are entirely secondary. Didone does not have a full-fledged love scene with Enea, and their only scene together occurs when he has decided to leave. Iarba, meanwhile, dominates the stage as a major comic character. He blusters and swaggers his love and chews the scenery with great gusto when he learns of the Didone-Enea liaison.[8] Busenello shows his growing grasp of character through the poetry of Iarba's comic declamations and of Didone's lament (III, xi), which is appropriately proud and regal and looks forward to the first of Metastasio's great librettos.

The ending of *Didone* is novel in that Didone does not die. She swoons away at the departure of Enea, tries to kill herself, and is prevented by Iarba. He then attempts suicide, and Didone comes to the reasonable decision (as Arianna had in 1607) that a man in hand is worth an ideal on the seas, and accepts the overjoyed Iarba. At this point the structure of the libretto works to its advantage, for had Didone and Enea been the focus, the ending would have been ludicrous.[9] But as Iarba has been kept in the center of the action, and as the epic nature of the story has served to

---

(6) The influence of the Aristotelian rules will be discussed in Chapter Five.

(7) "Let's not argue, Dido, I adore you." "Let's not fight, Iarba, I don't love you."

(8) II, xii, using as a refrain *"Son gemelle le donne e le bugie"* ("Women and liars are twins") and tearing his clothes.

(9) Unless the opera had been intended as a burlesque. There is no doubt that the speeches of Didone and Enea—and certainly those of Iarba—contain elements of satire at the overblown declamations of other librettists, but the work is not meant as a parody. We are always left unsure when Busenello is laughing and when he is dead serious.

diffuse the focus, the *lieto fine* is convincing. The separation of Busenello from the later, French-influenced, librettists of the reform is here most clearly evidenced. Busenello had little belief in Honor, Duty, and Sacrifice:[1] he realized that life goes on despite such good intentions, and that all such high-flown ideals end in the dust of vanity. As "Un Vecchio" says at the end of the second act, upon seeing the lovesick Iarba: "In the short span of a single day we pass from love to madnesses." The ending is thus technically a *lieto fine*, but its tone differs radically from the mechanical examples of the later seventeenth century, as well as from the glorified ones of the eighteenth. The cardinal point should again be emphasized that, although the *lieto fine* is judged on the basis of the specifics of the story, that can all too often be misleading. All of Busenello's operas end with a superficially *lieto fine*, but all of the endings differ in meaning, and only a fool would ignore the undercurrent of satire and pessimism always present.

Busenello's third libretto again took a giant stride forward, and must stand as one of the greatest of all librettos: *L'Incoronazione di Poppea*. Within its confines can be found not only most of the traits of seventeenth-century opera (the comic characters, the slumber scene, disguise, the appearance of gods, the *lieto fine*) but also, far more importantly, the traits that are particularly Busenellan: vigorous, masculine poetry, rapid and distinct delineation of character in verse, aphoristic compression, an unwavering point of view, a clear and logical unfolding of the story, and a total grasp of scenic and librettistic structure.

The story itself remains highly unusual even after three centuries: Nerone, in love with Poppea while married to Ottavia, insists on replacing Ottavia with Poppea as Empress, forces his tutor Seneca's suicide when he opposes the divorce, and gains his ends through exiling the reigning Empress and marrying Poppea. In keeping with the *à clef* nature of many librettos, it is thought that Busenello probably chose his historical subject because it paralleled an actual occurrence that had been the subject of gossip in

---

(1) Seneca in *L'Incoronazione* would seem to contradict this, but Busenello has presented a far more complex character than one simply motivated by Honor. There is a distinct distaste for the world in Seneca, and a yearning to be rid of it, so that death is welcomed as a release.

Italy for years. From 1617 to 1627, Vincenzo II Gonzaga had been unsuccessfully trying to divorce his wife, Isabella Gonzaga di Novellana, on the grounds that he had married her when she was forty (in 1616) and could no longer bear him children. The case became a *cause célèbre*, with both sides shamelessly trying to influence the decision of the Holy See, which finally decided in favor of Isabella when she was past fifty. Vincenzo died soon afterward, at thirty.[2]

In addition to a greater compression of word, Busenello had developed his ability to characterize in verse. The minor characters, such as Arnalta, Poppea's nurse, and Ottone, Poppea's unrequited lover, are excellent sketches. This ability was of prime import in dealing with the large number of characters of a seventeenth-century opera: each must be quickly and indelibly placed. Busenello outshone all his rivals in such portraiture.

The great confrontation scene between Nerone and Seneca is a fine example of his use of verse for dramatic purposes.[3] It begins with Nerone's opening throwing-down of the gauntlet, *"Son risoluto . . . di rimover Ottavia"* ("I am resolved . . . to remove Ottavia"), upon which Seneca politely demurs. With each demurrer Nerone's rage increases: the verse thins to one-line exchanges. Nerone's reason sways as, in his selfishness, he denies reason: *"La forza . . . bisogno non ha della ragione"* ("Force . . . has no need of reason"). In a final outburst, he says that he will have Poppea in spite of everyone. The hammering, constricted nature of his rant, with its repeated "e" both as a word and as vowel sound, is immediately contrasted to Seneca's relaxed and confident reply. The device of jarring contrast—highly dramatic—is a Busenello hallmark and will be discussed later in a larger, scenic connection.

---

(2) Some commentators have felt that the idea was derived from the annulment of Vincenzo I Gonzaga's marriage to Margherita Farnese in 1583, two years after his marriage, but this is unlikely, for the annulment took place without fanfare, as a matter of course, while Vincenzo II's tribulations were the scandal of Italy and were quite obviously widely discussed in the cafés of Venice at a time when Busenello was beginning to write.

(3) It cannot be too greatly emphasized that poetry *qua* poetry is of secondary importance in a libretto. Busenello's verse is solid, if rarely distinguished, but as drama his verse has few, if any, librettistic peers.

NERONE: *Tu mi sforzi allo sdegno; al tuo dispetto,*
e del popol in onta, e del Senato,
e d'Ottavia, e del Cielo, e dell'abisso,
siansi giuste od ingiuste le mie voglie,
hoggi, hoggi Poppea sarà mia moglie.

SENECA: *Siano innocenti i Regi,*
o s'aggravino sol di colpe illustri;
s'innocenza si perde,
perdasi sol per guadagnare i Regni,
chè il peccato commesso
per aggrandir l'Impero
si assolve da se stesso;
ma che una femminella habbia possanza
di condurti agli errori,
non è colpa di Rege, e Semideo.
E un misfatto plebeo.[4]

(I, ix)

Busenello shows his versatility most impressively in the love lyrics, for in them he manages to contrast three specific types. First, Nerone and Poppea: directly sensual, immediate, steeped in their desire for each other and their enjoyment of each other.[5] Second, the love scenes between Ottone and Drusilla: far more superficial, light, with a pastoral flavor (the superficiality reinforced dramatically because Ottone is on the "rebound" from Poppea's rejection and is in part using Drusilla's love as a salve). Third, the frankly airy and tinselly scene between the page and the *damigella*, full of diminutives and cute euphuisms that would become the bane of the libretto for the next hundred years, but here apposite, in contrast to Nerone-Poppea and to the scenes immediately preceding: those leading to the suicide of Seneca.

None of Busenello's characters is single-motivated, a fact that immeasurably enriches the work. Nerone insists on the marriage as

---

(4) "You make me angry; in spite of you, in spite of the people, the Senate, Ottavia, Heaven and Hell, no matter whether my desires are lawful or not, today, *today*, Poppea will be my wife." "Let Kings be innocent or commit only illustrious crimes, let them lose their innocence only to gain a kingdom. Because a crime committed to enlarge the Empire contains its own absolution; but if a mere woman has the power to lead you into error it is no longer the crime of a King, of a demigod—only a vulgar mistake."

(5) Although Busenello tries to disguise it, I am convinced that the scene following the Nerone-Seneca confrontation begins as a post-coital dialogue, appropriate in its conjunction with the rage before.

much—or more—because he wants to demonstrate his absolute power over gods and mortals as because he is lost in love, and Poppea well appreciates the advantages accruing to her new position as Empress. Busenello, however, is far too subtle a librettist to be dismissed as a cynic: none of the aspects of his characters eclipses any of the others, and in their interaction he produces not a caricature but a portrait of a human being. The facility with which he is able to perform this with even minor characters stamps him as a dramatist of the first order.

Rolland was only one of the writers who has commented on the "psychological correctness" with which Busenello draws his characters. The observation is correct, but Busenello's genius lies in using these psychological traits for dramatic purposes. In the great Nerone-Poppea scene after the Nerone-Seneca scene (I, x), Poppea is eager to have Nerone's tutor's influence curbed, if not vitiated entirely. Because she realizes that Nerone would naturally have a great attachment for (and fear of) Seneca as a father-figure, she uses the one argument that will penetrate Nerone's armor and arouse him at once: "*Seneca . . . che sempre tenta persuader altrui,/che il tuo scettro dipende sol da lui*" ("Seneca . . . who always seeks to persuade others that your scepter depends solely on him"). Instantly, Nerone orders Seneca's death. Similarly, when Ottone, in his rage at being rejected by Poppea, begins to champion Ottavia's cause, he finds that such revenge comes at a high price:

> OTTAVIA: *Voglio che la tua spada*
> *scriva gli oblighi miei*
> *alla tua cortesia*
> *col sangue di Poppea; vuo' che l'uccida.*
> OTTONE: *Che uccida chi?*
> OTTAVIA: *Poppea.*
> OTTONE: *Poppea?*
> OTTAVIA: *Poppea: perche dunque ricusi*
> *quel che gia prommetesti!*
> OTTONE: *Io cio promisi?*[6]

(II, ix)

---

(6) "I want your sword to write my debt to your service with the blood of Poppea. I want you to kill her." "To kill whom?" "Poppea." "Poppea?" "Poppea. Why then do you deny what you once promised?" "Did I promise that?"

The excerpt shows the highly dramatic nature of Busenello's

Evident throughout the libretto is this directness and drive combined with complexity, in contrast to so many other librettos that were hazy, filled with language that tiptoed around the desired point, embroidered on a flat and simplistic situation.

Finally, Busenello in *L'Incoronazione* arrives at control of the scenic form, which can so easily become unwieldy and shapeless. Each scene exists as a scene, but each contributes to the whole. Busenello is especially aware of the dramatic effectiveness of juxtaposing violently dissimilar scenes, an option that all but disappeared with the growth of the single-situation, logical-development libretto.[7] The contrast between scenes ix and x of Act I has already been mentioned—even more effective is the opening of the second act. The four scenes of the death of Seneca are beautifully realized in their stately progression (so akin to Seneca's Stoic nature): first, the appearance of Mercurio to inform Seneca of his impending death; second, the arrival of Nerone's messenger with the same message (the movement from the supernatural to the realistic parallels that from the Prologue to the first scene in so many seventeenth-century operas—as well as in *L'Incoronazione* itself). Seneca's resolution and his happiness at the coming release from the world strangely move the messenger. Third, he assembles

dialogues, and if the libretto is compared with a score (or, more easily, with the libretto included in the complete recording conducted by Alan Curtis for Cambridge Records [CRM B 901; CRS B 1901], where the word-repeats added by Monteverdi are given in italics), it can be seen that the composer heightened the effect of the drama by repetition and emphasis. Monteverdi was a great opera composer because his natural dramatic ability enabled him to see at once the key words and phrases to be emphasized—for instance, the repetition of the word "*tornerai*" ("Will you return?"), which Poppea dwells on at the end of the first Nerone-Poppea scene (I, iii), drawing out the anguish of parting—but it is willful negligence to ascribe even the major share of the dramatic pace of the opera to him, as many commentators steeped in the tradition of the Omniscient Composer have done. The orchestral accompaniment is simply so light that the weight still remains with the librettist. It is also probable that Monteverdi's disciples, such as Cavalli, and their followers, seized on this device of repetition and emphasis to break up lengthy speeches (as Monteverdi did).

(7) In truth, there are few examples—Wagner is one—of dramatic scene contrast on the level of Busenello until *Wozzeck*. Da Ponte's *Don Giovanni* could have used them effectively, but the feeling is that the librettist never appreciated their power. The most striking example in that score, the scene after the Don goes to Hell, is more convention than calculation, and its foreignness to our concept of a logical ending has persisted until today (*vide* Paul Henry Lang: *Music in Western Civilization*, p. 664).

his friends, who try to dissuade him (the contrast here is between the immediate and the eternal, for Seneca is gradually becoming one of the gods). Fourth, in a scene that Monteverdi did not set, Seneca is transfigured among a chorus of "Virtues." Immediately following this comes the light and inconsequential scene between the valet and his *damigella*, providing the greatest imaginable contrast, and following that is Nerone's orgy scene with his friend Lucan, in which he tries to forget his conscience through exaggerated—and more than a little hysterical—praise of woman (that is, Poppea) and song.

Although the opera centers upon the two lovers, Busenello has managed to use the scenic approach to enlarge the scope so that every level of society is seen, from the opening scene of the soldiers on guard bitching over the conditions of service to the final imperial triumph. Low-life scenes would become increasingly rare as the libretto moved upward in the social scale. The true mastery of the epic libretto, however, would be the task of Busenello's next work, *La Prosperità infelice di Giulio Cesare, Dittatore* (1646). Its scope is nothing less than the history of the Mediterranean world from 49 B.C. to 44 B.C.

In the course of its five acts (unusual for Busenello) Pompeo splits with the triumvirate ruling the Roman Empire, is defeated by Cesare, and escapes to Egypt, where he is killed by Tolomeo (Ptolemy); Cesare arrives and dallies with Cleopatra, then returns to Rome, to full power and assassination, and the opera ends with the vindication of Pompeo's death. Even to envision such a libretto is first of all an incredible tour de force, but when the stock seventeenth-century scenes and characters are added to the mixture, to bring it off would seem an impossibility. Yet Busenello does so, and does so brilliantly, in such a way that old ladies, hard-bitten soldiers, magicians, tutors—even the stock subplot lovers[8]—are caught up in the whole and transformed into positive forces: into a picture of the classes and the history of the known world. *Giulio Cesare* is an epic journey through history, told with the straightforwardness and dispassion of a chronicler who wishes to present things as they are, without pausing to rhapsodize over the "great" moments. Although the libretto does not have the psychological

---

(8) Already flourishing long before their codification in the Metastasian reform operas. Busenello justified them as appearing in *Il Pastor fido*. See also their use in Shakespeare's plays.

complexities or the focus[9] of *L'Incoronazione di Poppea*, it remains in many ways Busenello's greatest achievement, and certainly a vindication and triumph of the esthetic bases of the Spanish-derived, sprawling seventeenth-century libretto. Those who dismiss the seventeenth-century libretto as unsuitable to opera should study the master.

Busenello's task was made simpler by his strengths: command of a clear and consistent story line and ability to bring a character to life at once. Also, by maintaining such focus as there was on Pompeo's family (the subplot love story involves Sesto, Pompeo's son) and its desire for revenge, Busenello added a unity to the recounting of historical events. The first act presents Pompeo at the time when he became sole consul. In an *ombra* scene, his dead wife Giulia (Cesare's daughter) warns him not to fight her father, but he cannot shirk what he believes to be his duty. After a scene in which the inevitable "Old Lady" bewails the miseries of the famous, the scene shifts to Cesare, and again Busenello exploits the contrast between the high-minded Pompeo and the hard-bitten soldiery surrounding Cesare. Here is an excerpt:

FIRST CAPTAIN: *Nell' ultime rassegne*
dimmi, se il Ciel l'astutie tue non guasti
camerata mia fida
quante paghe rubbasti?
quanti, deh dimmi? quanti
e di nome mutati, e di mantello
hebbero doppia, e triplicata paga?
Diciamlo qui trà noi, che alcun non ode;
e se ci udisse ancora il Mondo tutto,
il rubbar cauto è diventato lode.[1]

(I, vii)

One of the most interesting scenes of the libretto follows, for the first ballet (between the first and second acts) depicts the de-

---

(9) The focus is not on Nerone-Poppea, or even on their love, but rather on "love" itself in all its forms: sexual, flowery, self-love, ambition (love of power), love of honor, love of law, etc.
(1) "In the last muster, tell me (if Heaven has not destroyed your cleverness), my trusty colleague, how much pay did you rob? Tell me, how many? How many names were changed or double and triple pay gained by switching cloaks? We can admit it here to each other: nobody is listening, and even if the whole world could hear, cautious robbery has become praiseworthy."

feat of Pompeo by Cesare at Pharsalus. There are numerous other examples in seventeenth-century opera of ballets using people involved in the libretto itself, but this is the only one I have come across in which the ballet forms an integral part of the story line and actually furthers its development.

The second act is the weakest, being largely involved with subplots (the character of Davo, Sesto's cynical tutor, recalls Seneca): Pompeo leaves his current wife Cornelia and flees to Egypt, although he is warned by Davo of Tolomeo's treachery. The third act opens on another of Busenello's great scenes, in which the eunuch prime minister argues the weak-willed Tolomeo into having Pompeo killed.[2] The deed itself takes place between scenes, and the locale shifts to Cesare's camp. Cesare reads in Pompeo's death a foreboding of his own:

> *Fortuna io non ti credo,*
> *troppo sei favorevole, e feconda,*
> *tue sovverchie lusinghe*
> *di tradimento son sospette: i Dei*
> *così avversi a Pompeo*
> *fanno, che mi sovvenga*
> *d'esser un huomo anch'io,*
> *e che non lunge forse*
> *m'attende al varco il precipitio mio.*[3]
>
> (III, ii)

He tells Cornelia that he did not order Pompeo's death, and she understands. The fourth act, which takes place in Egypt, includes a Cesare-Cleopatra love duet and an attempt by Tolomeo's servant to kill Cesare as he sleeps (again a stock scene). Cesare curses Egyptian perfidy and returns to Rome. The fifth act opens with this triumphal return, and Busenello once more refuses to be content with the usual happy chorus scene. He introduces Cicero (a dramatic stroke of genius), who, with the chorus singing praise in

(2) Busenello appreciated the dramatic power of scenes in which there was a clash of wills, with the stronger will prevailing. Later, Wagner was also to appreciate the power of such scenes (Wotan-Fricka, Gunther-Hagen, Kundry-Klingsor).
(3) "Fortune, I don't believe you, you are too favorable and fertile. Your excessive flattery has a suspicion of betrayal: the Gods, by being so adverse to Pompeo make me remember that I too am a man and that perhaps not far away the edge of my precipice is waiting for me."

the background, tells Cesare that as Pompeo's friend he cannot congratulate him. Cesare, magnanimous, understands, but the foreboding of the future runs in counterpoint to the superficial joy. The plot is hatched. Cesare sings a farewell ode and disappears (as usual, the death is off stage), the conspirators sing of their liberation from the tyrant, and Cornelia rests content that Pompeo has been avenged. A *lieto fine*? Strictly speaking yes, but as Busenello has never portrayed Cesare as anything less than a noble, strong-willed leader, the accusations of "tyrant" have a very hollow ring. In fact, as in all his librettos, there are no villains: simply human beings in the act of life.

Busenello's last libretto, *Statira* (1655),[4] is an anticlimax. As usual, there are well-drawn characters, some effective scenes, and an overriding pessimistic outlook, here taking the form of anger at the futility of war (the Indian servant's aria at the end of Act II is an example). Yet the conventions of seventeenth-century opera —disguises and complexities—have here upset the logic of Busenello's development of the story, and the description of the battle, which takes up almost all of the second act, is more tidy and polite than stinging. It is not clear whether Busenello had become bored with the form and was merely cranking out a libretto, or whether this work was possibly a collaboration or a reworking of something earlier (*Statira* was an immensely popular libretto subject, as it involved Darius and—sometimes—Artaxerxes, and Statira operas were composed well into the eighteenth century). The libretto, however, belongs with *Didone* on a lower level than Busenello's two finest efforts.

It has become commonplace for writers to note that Busenello was almost forgotten while he was still alive and not rediscovered until the twentieth century. The explanation usually given is that his satiric outlook became increasingly at variance with the temper of opera, which was developing toward euphuistic superficiality and heroic concepts unrelated with the way life was actually lived.

---

(4) The libretto as published bears no date, but in the preface Busenello says that *Poppea* was written thirteen years before. It is noteworthy that Alfred Loewenberg's *Annals of Opera* does not list performances for operas based upon either of Busenello's last two librettos, although the *Giulio Cesare* was apparently given at the Teatro Griman (according to the printed libretto). The Library of Congress Catalog of the Schatz Collection, however, gives the theater as the Teatro Novissimo.

There is some truth in this, but I suspect that the major reason why none of Busenello's librettos was especially successful when first given in Venice lay in the fact that his sharp pen had created many enemies. He apparently never ceased to write biting satires of his fellow-Venetians, and it would have been only natural for them to reply by sabotaging his works.[5]

If Lorenzo Da Ponte is the most overpraised librettist in the pantheon, Gian' Francesco Busenello is the most neglected. He is historically the first great librettist, and his fame transcends historical bounds. Certainly *L'Incoronazione di Poppea* is one of the handful of librettos that can be called supreme, and *Giulio Cesare* is not far inferior. Other men—Cicognini, Moniglia, Minato—better demonstrate the bizarreries and grandiloquent faults of the seventeenth-century libretto, but Busenello demonstrates its virtues. With him, the libretto achieved manhood.

---

(5) It was natural for writers like Charles Burney to consign Busenello merely to a listing of librettists, for Burney wrote in an age still steeped in the Metastasian ethic (and its Gluckian offshoot, which was just as far removed from Busenello). George Hogarth, in 1838, dismisses "Busenelli's" *Didone* as typical of the deficiencies of the libretto of its time. This neglect persists even today: Ernest H. Wilkins: *A History of Italian Literature*, p. 316, says that Rinuccini was "the most successful" librettist of the century, and does not mention Busenello. Ulderico Rolandi calls him *one* of the best. Only Arthur Livingston and Romain Rolland can be said truly to have appreciated his contributions.

Chapter Three

The Beginnings of the French Libretto

IN FRANCE the development of the libretto followed a very different route from that of its counterpart in Italy. The paramount distinction between the two lay in the greater centralization of all of the arts in France, a concomitant of the centralization of power in the hands of the Bourbon monarchy as initiated by Cardinal Richelieu and carried to a triumphant conclusion by Louis XIV. It is no exaggeration to state that what took place in the city of Paris and in the royal palaces of its environs determined the course of French opera,[1] whereas in Italy the center of operatic attention shifted from city to city and often encompassed separate, vigorous centers, such as Venice and Naples in the later seventeenth and eighteenth centuries. This centralization, codified in the establishment of a French National Opera which, until the Revolution, constituted a monopoly, resulted in a greatly heightened awareness of all national operatic developments. The opera produced by the national trust became the French opera of the year, and critical response to it was likely to take the form of parodies produced by acting companies of the Paris fairs, which only attracted more at-

---

(1) This generalization loses force in the nineteenth century, which saw Berlioz's major operatic work *(Les Troyens)* written (though never produced) for Weimar, and his last opera *(Béatrice et Bénédict)* produced first in Germany; which saw Saint-Saëns' *Samson et Dalila* first produced at Weimar, and many of Massenet's later works in Monte Carlo. The important distinction is that the French did not consider these works seriously until they had achieved the coronation of a Paris production.

tention to the work itself.[2] Because all of these productions, as well as operas imported into France by visiting companies or produced by the Opéra, could easily be seen by an inhabitant of Paris, the composer and his librettist were kept constantly at the center of attention. If there were necessarily fewer composers and librettists, each one was subjected to a scrutiny all the more thoroughgoing. In the context of a strongly nationalistic artistic tradition that gave great weight to the artistic product as end-result of intellectual ratiocination, this centralization fed the fires of debate and contributed to generalization. The free and easy qualities that distinguished the Italian libretto were not unknown in France, for *opéra comique* grew out of the haphazard, carefree japeries of the fairs, but it is not surprising to note that even here that growth was aided by the philosophical esthetics of the intelligentsia, in this case Diderot and the Encyclopedists. In French opera, there is always a reason behind every action, or so it seems, and there always seems to be a writer in the audience willing to discuss the opera of the night before at interminable length, thus subjecting the work to a great deal more attention than it doubtless needs or deserves.

The chauvinistic aspect of opera in France appeared almost immediately. Prior to the development of the Camerata opera in Florence, Paris had been captivated by the idea of ballet. Its vogue began around 1580 and continued into the seventeenth century, attracting great crowds from every level of society. Usually the aristocracy took part in the performances, and there was great use of machines. Along with the rage for ballet went the French love of the theater, both for native companies and for those groups of *commedia dell'arte* players from Italy who appeared regularly. As it developed, French opera absorbed all of these earlier dramatic modes, most particularly the ballet and the spectacle (known in France as "*le merveilleux*"), and also that attention to word which came to typify the performances of the Comédie-Française. Of course, all of these characteristics could be found in Italian seven-

---

(2) There was never more than one *tragédie lyrique* per year produced in Paris, in direct contradistinction to the plethora of new operas in Italy. The psychological import of a Paris production is evident throughout French operatic history: even though Berlioz despised the artistic standards of the Opéra, he went to every length to have his operas mounted there.

teenth-century opera, but they continued to be factors in French opera long after they had diminished or disappeared from Italian opera. After a time, they came to be considered French in origin.

A few words should be written about one of the most often mentioned characteristics of French opera: the attention paid to the word, and the subordination of music to the declamation of French verse. The idea achieved its force because of the constant proselytization of Jean-Baptiste Lully, who had his singers study the actors of the Comédie-Française in order to learn the inflections of their speech, and who himself composed according to its precepts. Lully had attained a monopolistic position in French opera, and his words therefore carried more weight than they otherwise would have; so much weight, indeed, that they became a touchstone for all future French opera. The generalization that the importance of the word is greater in French operas than in Italian opera has a certain validity —and in certain specific cases, such as *Pelléas et Mélisande* and the operas of Massenet, it is vital. Yet the truth in this constantly re-iterated platitude has been exaggerated, especially with regard to nineteenth-century French opera. A study of Auber's attention to the Scribe libretto of *Gustave III* compared with Verdi's to Somma's for *Un Ballo in maschera* will not reveal more intensity on the part of the Frenchman, and the music of Meyerbeer's operas often rides roughshod over the verse.[3] The French gave greater weight to the word because of their love of the spoken theater, but that weight is revealed less in the through-composed operas than in the *opéras comiques*, which grew out of the *pièces mêlées d'ariettes*, in which spoken words were intermingled with sung set pieces. The legitimate distinction is between the French spoken portions and the Italian *recitativo secco*.

The first operas seen in Paris were attempts by Cardinal Mazarin to import the grandiose Roman seventeenth-century opera into France. Mazarin adored opera, had taken part in the staging of *Sant' Alessio* in Rome, and was naturally eager to transplant the art form onto his adopted soil. The three imported "Roman"

---

(3) It has been said in extenuation that Meyerbeer was not a French-man. This has some peripheral value, for he and his fellow-German, Offenbach, paid less attention to the word than did some French composers. Yet Meyerbeer cannot both have and eat his cake: his operas form one of the glorious chapters of French operatic history, and his mature works cannot be considered other than French.

operas—Luigi Rossi's *Orfeo* (1647), Carlo Caproli's *Le Nozze di Peleo e di Theti* (1654), and Francesco Cavalli's *L'Ercole amante* (1662)—could all be classed as failures, in the sense that those who saw them rejected them as non-French. Yet the truth is, as usual, a great deal more complex. The attitude of the Italian artists imported for the *Orfeo* had been extremely arrogant, and after its expensive failure the French reacted by throwing the famous engineer Torelli into jail. Mazarin foxily dissociated himself as much as possible from the fiasco, and tried to sweeten the pill seven years later by cramming *Le Nozze di Peleo* with ballet (the young Louis XIV danced the *entrées* of the ballets with his courtiers) and by having a few French singers hired. The operas, however, faced problems over and above nationalistic ones. The three librettos were written by Abbé Buti, the private secretary to Antonio Cardinal Barberini, and all of them were typical examples of the magniloquently bizarre, incredibly complicated libretto that lay at the opposite pole from the growing classical spirit of the rigorously controlled *tragédies*.

Yet the Roman operas were to influence French opera profoundly, despite their failure. They accustomed French audiences to a mixture of story, spectacle, and ballet which gave greater range of delight than the severe plays of the classical stage, and they set all of this within a lavish framework that aspired to high art. The series of operas by Lully and Quinault were direct outgrowths of those Roman experiments.

The "Abbé" Pierre Perrin (c. 1619–75)—his title was assumed—was the first important French librettist. He spent his life writing verse for music and pondering its relationships, and wrote, with Cambert, a pastoral opera for the small royal theater at Issy. It was his idea that French opera should attempt to move away from the grandiose postures of the Italian opera, toward a smaller, simpler form not burdened with the baggage of the overblown stage picture, the attitudes and the language. Even the French verse would not be the alexandrines of the theater, but lyric verse of short, supple lines.

Perrin's ideas were at first successful, for the charm of the pastoral opera led Louis XIV to think in terms of creating a national opera along the lines of the already created national theater, the Comédie-Française. He therefore granted Perrin in 1669 letters patent to establish an Académie d'opéra. In 1671 the first French opera, *Pomone*, music by Cambert and libretto by Perrin, was presented in Paris, with admission charged and the public admitted.

Yet Perrin and his ideals of pastoral French opera were not destined to be successful. There was the inevitable financial difficulty, which he could not control, and soon he found himself in debtor's prison. He died in 1675 a complete pauper, but not until he had sold his letters patent to Jean-Baptiste Lully (born Giovanni Battista Lulli).

Lully, eager to establish himself as the leading French composer, used the letters patent and his friendship with the King to consolidate himself in power as an operatic monopoly. Adroitly sidestepping his many enemies at court, Lully chose the young dramatist Philippe Quinault as his librettist and, working with him from 1673 until his own death in 1687,[4] created a body of operatic work which became the cornerstone of all subsequent French opera.

The ideals that Perrin had espoused did not disappear forever. Traces of them remain even in the Quinault librettos (notably the suppleness of the verse and its adaptability to music), but they were destined to flower anew in the writings and the pastoral operas of Jean-Jacques Rousseau in the eighteenth century. Indeed, the whole of the "bourgeois" movement that led to the creation of *opéra comique*, in itself a reaction against the high-flown *tragédies lyriques* of Lully's time and after, can be said to look back to the "Abbé" Perrin: he who was reacting against the high-flown Italian opera.

---

(4) Except for a brief hiatus in 1678–9, when Quinault's enemies managed to have him dropped as librettist for two operas.

Chapter Four

Quinault

LULLY SHOWED GREAT JUDGMENT when he selected Philippe Quinault to be his collaborator and stayed with him despite the urgings of many of his friends, for Quinault had several outstanding requisites for a librettist. First was his ability to work with the strong-willed Lully and to accept the secondary position that Lully demanded of all who worked for him.[1] Next, and more important in the finished product, was Quinault's ability to write singable verse and to produce logical stories while still making use of all the elements that constituted the Louis XIV *"gloire"* aura —which Lully (and his patron) felt was indispensable for a national opera reflecting the age. Quinault's achievement over the span of the twelve operas that he wrote for Lully, beginning with the *Cadmus et Hermione* in 1673, could probably not have been duplicated by any of his contemporaries, with the possible exception of La Fontaine,[2] for although Quinault began his career as a dramatist, he was able to divorce his operatic work from the stately fustian of the alexandrine of the theater and to write varied and highly *musicabile* verse.

---

(1) There is a paradox inherent in the statement, for, although Lully was definitely in charge of the totality of the operatic endeavor, the seventeenth-century public and critics of the new art form considered the music the less important aspect, serving merely to enhance the declamation of the verse. Lully himself subscribed to this idea, and therefore his accompaniments often sound thin to our ears. The later complaint made against Gluck's operas, that they "stank of music," reflects the unwillingness of the old-fashioned critics to give up the primacy of the word.
(2) A not very probable contingency, for La Fontaine's volatile temperament could not long have submitted to Lully's dominance.

The influence of the drama upon French librettists is far more marked than upon their Italian counterparts. The importance of the play in France and its relative unimportance in Italy account for the distinction: most French librettists from Quinault to the twentieth century began life as playwrights or wrote plays concurrent with their operatic oeuvre, whereas most Italian librettists, with the obvious exception of Goldoni, considered themselves poets rather than dramatists, and wrote few if any works for the spoken stage until late in the nineteenth century. The Italians contented themselves with adapting French librettos and plays from France, England, Germany, and Spain, in the process preparing them for operatic treatment.[3] In general, the French never lost sight of the confines of the theater; they always thought in terms of a succession of scenic moments[4] rather than of an unfolding unity, using the elements of the production as well as the characters in order to tell the story; whereas the Italians by and large concentrated on the plot and focused on the characters themselves.[5] Nemorino in *L'Elisir d'amore* sings of his *"gioia inesprimibil"* at seeing a furtive tear steal from the eyes of his beloved, thus signifying that she indeed does love him,[6] while the French librettist Sedaine (1719–97), wishing to express the lonely isolation of the

---

(3) While it is true that what constitutes effective or great drama on the spoken stage does not necessarily constitute the same in opera, care should be taken about going to the other extreme and positing entirely separate dramatic criteria. There remains a large area of overlap between the two, and this overlap is seen more clearly in the French libretto. Alfred Oliver's statement, nevertheless, is true: "[Quinault] recognized that literary and operatic dramaturgy are not identical, a fact overlooked by later French librettists and not definitely pointed out until nearly a century later by Jean-Jacques Rousseau"; *The Encyclopedists as Critics of Music*, p. 9.

(4) Cuthbert Girdlestone's statement remains valid to an amazing extent throughout the history of the French libretto: "French opera is not a form in which the progress of the action is the sole source of interest. It consists in a succession of tensions and relaxations obtained by pathetic scenes alternating with festivity." *Rameau*, as quoted in Michael F. Robinson: *Opera Before Mozart*, p. 93. Note once again the extent to which the esthetic bases of seventeenth-century Italian opera transferred themselves to France.

(5) One evidence of the dichotomy is the general absence of stage directions in Italian librettos, and their presence in French ones.

(6) William Weaver rightly remarked to me that ninety-nine tenors out of a hundred do not pay attention to Romani's words, and thus sing the *romanza* with exaggerated sentimental sadness, which is entirely inappropriate.

captive Richard the Lion-Heart, has him appear on a terrace of a fortress surrounded by an iron grille in such a way that he cannot see his faithful minstrel, Blondel, who has been searching for him throughout Europe. In both cases an emotion is expressed, but in one it is expressed by word and music alone, whereas in the other it is expressed visually as well.

Quinault occupies an important position in libretto history because he was the first major librettist to be recognized as such by his contemporaries. The French, particularly in the generation after his death, overpraised his work and read his librettos as dramatic poetry apart from Lully's music, and he continued to be revered as a master until late in the eighteenth century, almost a hundred years after his death, by Jean-François Marmontel and others who refashioned his works for the then-current usage. With Hugo von Hofmannsthal, Émile Zola, and Wagner he is the only major librettist whose entire creative body of work was written for a single composer. And yet today his work has faded more drastically than that of any other major librettist, including Metastasio. This is partly the result of the complete change of taste which took place over the next hundred years, and which saw the inflated, aristocratic approach to opera give way to a more intimate and direct, middle-class one. What struck the audiences of the Quinault-Lully *Persée* and *Roland* as effective and even moving struck later audiences (and strikes current audiences) as pompous, overblown, and not a little ridiculous. Yet this fading also is owing to the lesser stature of Quinault as librettist and poet. He was certainly over-praised, except by those who rejected the *tragédie lyrique* as a vulgarization and debasement of the classical theater and by Boileau, who detested his soft-centered verses. But then, Metastasio, who has similarly suffered from the change of taste, also was overlauded. Any study of Metastasio's great librettos, however, will reveal power and control beyond anything Quinault produced.

Another factor should be emphasized: the importance of the total effect in this early French type of opera. To strip a Quinault-Lully work of its visual impact (not to mention the impact of the superbly rehearsed players, instrumentalists, and chorus on which Lully prided himself) is to judge on a partial basis. *Le merveilleux* is so integral to the Quinault librettos that the spectacle can be said to become poetry in and of itself: to consider it extraneous is to misunderstand what Lully and he were trying to achieve.[7]

The Lully-Quinault relationship is of further interest because it affords us the first glimpse of a documented collaboration over a span of works. Lully was an autocrat with fixed work habits that Quinault found congenial, so that the progress of each of their operas from idea to realization followed a stately and prescribed path as formal as a court gavotte. Essentially the progress went as follows:

> As soon as Lully and Quinault had assembled a number of subjects, they submitted a list to the King. He chose whichever appealed to him at that particular moment. Quinault then worked out a scenario, which he handed to Lully. The composer decided at which points in the story the divertissements, dances, chansonettes, choruses, etc., should appear, and Quinault then wrote the book in full. When it was finished, it was handed to the *Académie française* for approval, Quinault himself giving a dramatic reading of the entire text to the assembled Academicians. The fact that the book was approved did not prevent Lully from making alterations during the course of the composition; Quinault, in fact, had to alter one scene in *Phaëton* twenty times before Lully was satisfied.[8]

Notable in this progress is the circumscribed nature of the endeavor: a product directed toward a specific audience of one, the King, and on which there had to be the stamp of approval of a national cultural body. If the King was, as he considered himself, France personified, the Lully-Quinault operas were the lyrico-dramatic reflection of France. Librettists have been forced to fit themselves into more rigid straitjackets, but never again into any quite so political. After Lully's death in 1687, the King took less and less interest in opera (he had by that time moved from Paris to the newly finished Versailles), and no longer considered the

---

(7) "Completely in charge, as Wagner two centuries later, Lully oversaw the decoration, the direction, and above all that essential element that the opera of our day seems all too often to ignore; the coordination of all the artistic factors of which the synthesis forms the spectacle"; Marcel Doisy: *Musique et Drame*, pp. 51–2. The comparison with Wagner is particularly apt, as we shall see later, and the derivation is through the Scribe *Grands Opéras*, which must be similarly judged.
(8) Norman Demuth: *French Opera, Its Development to the Revolution*, p. 147.

tragédie lyrique an indispensable adjunct and promulgator of "*l'esprit de la gloire.*"

Lully as an autocrat demanded a great deal of his librettist, as he demanded a great deal of everyone who worked for him. Quinault's difficulties with him (the scene in *Phaëton* was far from being the only one that Lully made him rewrite) herald numerous others down the history of the libretto, and doubtless echo earlier contretemps that have gone unrecorded. The psychological fascination in a study of the collaboration of two independent yet dependent minds to produce a single work of art has led to reams of speculation and opinion. Yet it should not be forgotten that, even if Lully chose the spots for *le merveilleux* in the work, and even if he on occasion supplied Quinault with music to which the librettist was required to fit words,[9] the resultant libretto was the work of Quinault alone. A comparison of a Quinault libretto with that for *Bellérophon*, which Thomas Corneille and Bernard Le Bovier de Fontenelle supplied for Lully in 1679, when Quinault was temporarily in disgrace, shows a surface similarity but also reveals a difference: Quinault's works have more lightness and grace and a greater awareness of the scenic possibilities than *Bellérophon*; qualities that Lully must have comprehended.

Philippe Quinault was born in Paris in 1635. Although he dabbled with the law, his preference was clearly for the theater. He wrote comedies before he was twenty, and afterward turned to the type of tragedies then in vogue. His plays served to make him known in the artistic circles of Paris. After 1672, when Lully chose him as his librettist, he never again wrote a play. He died a year after Lully, in 1688. As Lully had carefully seen to it that all of the operas were successes, Quinault's literary career as a librettist can be said to have been happy save for the short period of his disgrace. The serene tenor of his life is reflected in his works.

------

(9) I was surprised to find, in the course of my research, how many opera lovers believe that the music of an opera is written first and the words are then fitted to it. I suspect that the musical dominance of the last century has fostered this notion, for even when people read that Wagner's poems were written well before his music, they persist in thinking that the music came first. In fact, well over ninety per cent of the words of a libretto precede the composition of the music. Although a composer often changes specific words to fit his musical line, the instances of whole verses being written for music already composed—an example would be the Scribe-Auber collaboration—are rare.

Although the heroes he created meet with all sorts of vicissitudes before finally triumphing, there is practically no feeling of anguish in the course of any of his operas. Such anguished moments as there are—most notably the very last scene he wrote, Armide's rage aria—stand out in contrast. Although Quinault uses many of the stock devices of the Italian seventeenth-century opera, he did not use the melodramatic *"Orride prigione!"*[1] Although Quinault shares with his Italian counterparts that separation from reality which fundamentally constitutes the aristocratic approach, his exaggerations and posturings are under far better control than theirs. He also has little use for euphuistic bombast: his language may be dull and clichéed with standard phrases, but it does not roll outward to the limits of risible metaphorics. Its artificiality and soft-centeredness[2] stem rather from the pastoral, whose vocabulary and conceits are reproduced with the trappings of the Louis XIV stage. Attention is always diffused, through emphasis on divertissements, machines, and scenery—and through characterizations that never cut too close to the bone.[3] A veil of charm surrounds these operas even at their most emotional moments, and this aura fitted in perfectly with the pattern of surface glitter and elaborate ritual of the court of Louis XIV. If the Lully-Quinault operas were meant as reflections of their age, they succeeded admirably.

The question of the influences on Quinault's work has always led to a certain amount of confusion for, as Quinault began his life as a playwright, some commentators have assumed that he

---

(1) Quinault saw the Cavalli-Buti *L'Ercole amante* and possibly several other Italian operas, but in sum very few. Nonetheless, the stock situations that appear in so many Italian operas were largely derived from Spanish and Italian plays of the late sixteenth and early seventeenth centuries, and there is every reason to suspect that Quinault was conversant with such works from his early youth.

(2) An excellent example of what I mean by "soft-centeredness," as well as an excellent example of unconscious humor in Quinault, occurs in *Alceste* after the heroine has been abducted. Lamentations are in order, but young Céphise can only opine: *"Au milieu des cris et des larmes,/l'hymen a peu de charmes;/attendons de tranquilles jours./ Le bruit affreux des armes/effarouche bien les Amours"* (II, i). "In the midst of tears and war cries, marriage has few charms; let us wait for quiet days. The horrible noise of arms scares away all thoughts of love.")

(3) In this sense, there is a direct comparison between the Quinault librettos and those of Scribe for the *Grand Opéra* of the nineteenth century.

owed a debt to the great French playwrights of the seventeenth century, Pierre Corneille and Jean Racine.[4] Although a certain amount of the "noble tone" of his heroes can be ascribed to Corneille, it is more likely that the influence is traceable to its immediate source, the Spanish play and the romantic novel, and to the general artistic temper of the Age of the Sun King, which encouraged idealized portraits of brave men as reflections of Louis XIV—and more particularly to a desire in both Lully and Quinault to have their sole patron recognize himself on stage. Racine's fame began with *Andromaque* in 1667 and did not crest until a generation or more later; moreover, his genius for psychological probing and revelation of character within a rigorously controlled framework of scene and word lies at the opposite pole from the effulgent *tragédies lyriques* of Quinault.[5] There are undoubtedly correspondences between the great tragedies of Racine and Corneille and the librettos of Quinault, but they are akin to the correspondences between the last two operas of Verdi and "Wagnerism." Indeed, quite the reverse influence is the actual case, for Racine's last plays, *Esther* and *Athalie*, use music and chorus in a manner partly derived from the Lully-Quinault operas.

In truth, the influences on Quinault's librettos, apart from that of the Abbé Buti, are generally the same as those on his earlier dramas: the plays of the generation before Corneille and Racine, which means those of Alexandre Hardy and the early works of Jean de Rotrou. Hardy, a playwright who was reputed to have written over six hundred plays in alexandrine verse (only thirty-four survive), is of cardinal importance in the history of French drama, for he single-handedly popularized the form that was to become the French classical tragedy. His plays combined high-flown poetry with improbable situations, plenty of action, and heavy use of machinery, thus combining the traits of the pageant plays and the

---

(4) As, for instance, Manfred Bukofzer's statement in his valuable book *Music in the Baroque Era*, p. 156: "The librettist Quinault provided Lully with tragedies in the manner of Corneille and Racine, whose works had received universal acclaim some years before Lully turned to the opera." A similar statement can be found in Leo Schrade's *Tragedy in the Art of Music: The Charles Eliot Norton Lectures of 1962–3*, p. 75.

(5) Some of the most stringent opposition to the *tragédie lyrique* came from lovers of the classical theater who saw Lully's operas as antithetic to their spirit. Although today we can note similarities that they could not, the differences remain great.

aristocratic tragedy of Étienne Jodelle. The novel of the time was also a fertile source, for its extremely complex mazes and its valiant heroes remained extraordinarily popular from the early seventeenth century, when Honoré d'Urfé's *Astrée* became one of the first runaway best-sellers. The preoccupation with idyllic love, so much a part of Quinault's librettos, was in all probability derived from the *salon* divertissements and ideals of such books and plays. Whereas Corneille and Racine purified, Quinault was content to borrow, selecting ingredients from all the artistic sources and combining them into the one *marmite* of the *tragédie lyrique.*

The success of Quinault's work lies in its ability to leaven the heaviness inherent in the alexandrine and tell a cogent, straightforward story despite the trappings of *le merveilleux* and the natural hyperbole of a *galant* style.[6] Quinault accomplishes the leavening by mixing alexandrines with eight- or nine-syllable lines and interspersing them with short lyrics. There are never the stretches of long speeches often found in the librettos, imitative of French plays of lesser French dramatists. Rhyme in French verse has much more power than in Italian, with its plethora of vowel endings and sounds, so that the lead-footed alexandrine can easily sound clumsy and end-stopped, and shorter lyrics with strong rhymes will stutter and gasp. Quinault's mellifluous handling of his lines mitigated many of the bad effects inherent in much French verse and showed his successors how to write for music without sacrificing everything to it. Indeed, this one trait, though perhaps essentially a negative one, was of value, coming as it did at the very beginning of French operatic history.

The clarity of a Quinault libretto extends from the story, which moves logically from point to point, to the verse, which is never obscure. Méduse's aria, which opens the third act of *Persée*, tells the audience who she is as directly as Figaro's *"Largo al factotum"* in *Il Barbiere di Siviglia* tells who he is, though with none of his panache:

> *J'ay perdu la beauté qui me rendit si vaine:*
> *je n'ay plus ces cheveux si beaux,*
> *dont autrefois le Dieu des eaux*
> *sentit lier son coeur d'une si douce chaîne.*

---

(6) I have consciously used an anachronism here to employ an apposite word. The *galant* in music history did not flower until a century later, but its attributes are precisely those of the Quinault librettos.

. . . .
Je porte l'épouvante, et la mort en tous lieux:
tout se change en rocher, à mon aspect horrible:
les traits que Jupiter lance du haut des cieux
n'ont rien de si terrible
qu'un regard de mes yeux.[7]

(III, i)

Pre-eminently a stage dramatist, Quinault uses visual means again and again to further his stories. Here once more is a distinction from Racine, who produces the action through the word. Quinault prefers to demonstrate it, thus linking the *tragédie lyrique* with the earlier *ballets de cour.* In *Alceste*, Apollon has decreed that Admète must die unless someone takes his place. At the beginning of the next act (III) the scene reveals an empty altar to be inscribed with the face of the man willing to die for Admète. Phérès, his father, refuses: he wants to conserve his last precious days. Céphise, too young, also refuses. Admète approaches the death rattle. Then: "The altar opens, and we see emerging the image of ALCESTE piercing her bosom." The chorus laments her death, tearing their hair and garments.[8]

Quinault took advantage of the fact that his audience knew the stories he was telling to present them in a flamboyant way. Scenes such as the one in which Persée slays Méduse were presented in pantomime, with balletic overtones (monsters are produced from her blood and fly about but cannot see Persée, whose magic helmet renders him invisible); later Persée flies through the air to combat the Monster, who is approaching to devour Andromède. The villain Phinée[9] is dispatched by Persée's giving him a look at Méduse's head, whereupon he turns to stone. It is simple to see why such scenes would captivate an audience.

---

(7) "I have lost that beauty which made me so vain. I no longer have hair so beautiful that once long ago the god of the waters felt his heart tied by such a soft chain. . . . I carry the frightful and death everywhere; everything turns to rock at my horrible appearance. The thunderbolts that Jupiter hurls from the skies have nothing so terrible as one look from my eyes."
(8) The inordinate number of altars and quasi-religious festivities in Quinault's librettos commences a tradition carried on with vigor throughout the French libretto. The French quickly perceived the essentially dramatic nature of such services. These scenes were largely impossible in Italy because of Church censorship.
(9) Phinée is one of Quinault's better creations: a fine stage villain full of derision and hate.

Notable in *Persée* and throughout Quinault's work is the interdependence of spectacle and story. Yet Quinault uses other, more compact, visual effects, and these too are closely allied to what is happening on stage. Metamorphoses play a great part in his librettos (not surprising, as seven of his subjects were taken from Ovid). In *Proserpine,* the heroine has been stolen away. Only Cyané knows who has taken her: she begins to tell: "It is ... it is ... " "Finish...." "It is . . ." "Ah! what new misfortune!" Cyané loses her voice, and turns into a bubbling brook. In *Thésée,* the King, misled by Méduse, is about to kill his own son, whom he has not seen since infancy.[1] As he gives his son the poisoned cup to drink, he sees his son's sword, which he had left with him in order to recognize him. Thésée is thus saved and Méduse foiled (she flees, returns in a chariot pulled by flying dragons, and is banished by Minerve). These two devices—the unfinished revelation and the inanimate-object prop—will remain staples of suspenseful stagecraft in both sung and spoken drama.

Despite the emphasis on action and the constant intervention of *le merveilleux* in one form or another, however, the binding element underlying all the Quinault librettos is neither of these, but rather the vicissitudes of love. Indeed, the reiteration of declarations of love, of the value of love, of the importance of love throughout the librettos by the members of the cast and the chorus was one of the features of Quinault's work most severely criticized both by his contemporaries and by later commentators. This "insipid cooing" seeped everywhere, disfiguring dramatic scenes (see footnote, p. 52) and weighing down the action with its pedal-point drone. "*Suivons, suivons l'Amour, laissons-nous en-flâmer,/Ah! ah! ah! qu'il est doux d'aimer*" ("Let's follow Love and let ourselves be inflamed, ah! it is sweet to love"), Cadmus and Hermione sing (I, iv), and countless other Quinault figures concur.[2] A saturation of love stained the Italian operas of the period as well as the plays and novels; this excess endured to dis-

---

(1) The situation of a parent unknowingly about to kill his offspring is an inordinately powerful one. We shall meet it again in its finest form in the various versions of *Mérope.*
(2) There are usually two classes of lover: the principals (who may expand to a triangle, or even a square) and the secondaries (usually servants, whose love is simple and idyllic). The chorus serves as commentary. The roots of this bifurcation go back beyond the seventeenth century, and can be evidenced in the works of Shakespeare and Molière.

figure the later *opera seria*, for although the eighteenth-century reformers attempted to purify opera of its useless appendages, the elaborate love chains survived to become a feature of Metastasio.

In Quinault the emphasis on celebration of love even outweighs celebration of *la gloire*. Yet this statement should be understood in a strictly circumscribed manner, for it refers only to the prevalence of the subject throughout any given libretto. Quinault appreciated love in its proper place, as a divertissement that in no way upset the individuals' status quo: if "love" became Busenellan passion, the matter had to be righted before the end of the opera.[3] In *Roland*, the hero has gone mad with love—necessitating the splendid scene-chewing *scena* that closes Act IV—but awakens to sweet reason. *"Sortez, pour jamais, en ce jour/des liens honteux de l'Amour"* ("Leave forever, today, the shameful precincts of Love") (V, iii), the chorus of heroes' shades sings, and he returns to his mission as hero in search of *la gloire*. The same happens to Renaud in *Armide*. He and Armide are shown as bewitched by Love rather than happily in love: when Renaud awakes, he tears off his garlands of flowers and declares for *la gloire*, at which time he is given a diamond buckler.[4]

In creating *tragédie lyrique*, Lully and Quinault created a genre entirely separate from the *tragédies* of Racine and Corneille and much closer to what was to become *opera seria*. Again, some confusion has arisen because of the terminology:[5] most of the operas culminate happily, in the traditional apotheosis ending with *dei ex machinis*, use of the full stage and chorus, and a plethora of extras; and all of them can be said to end in triumph for the Divine Order. Thus, though Phaëton, the headstrong charioteer, is blown from the skies by Jupiter's thunderbolt at the end of *Phaëton*, Quinault does not view this in Promethean terms as a personal disaster to be sympathized with: Man struggling to free himself from the yoke of the gods. As an obedient subject of Louis XIV,

---

(3) Here again is a fundamental difference between the librettos of Quinault and the plays of Racine, which focus on the characters' emotional stresses carried to their logical conclusions.

(4) Note once more the emphasis on the visual aspect of the scene: Renaud's acts symbolize his decision. Note also the resemblances to *Tristan und Isolde*—and the differences!

(5) French opera, with its passion for categorization, is replete with misleading terminology. Thus *Cadmus et Hermione* is a *tragédie* whereas *Carmen* is an *opéra comique*. It is vital to understand the context in which these labels are used.

he sides with Jupiter, who is outraged that Phaëton's incompetence has threatened the well-being of the world: "*Au bien de l'univers ta perte est nécessaire;/sert d'exemple aux Audacieux:/tombe avec ton orgueil, trébuche, Téméraire,/laisse en paix la terre, et les cieux*"[6] (V, last).

There is a remarkable homogeneity in the operatic work of Quinault, which stretches over fifteen years. Once he found his formula, he stayed with it (as did Metastasio), and although there are greater ease and freedom in his later works, their structure and ideas remain similar to those of the early ones. In the early operas, Quinault used alexandrines for recitative purposes and turned to the divertissements of Molière for his lyric meters,[7] but the two became assimilated quickly into the body of his thought. The subjects are practically all classical myths, and those which are not —*Amadis, Roland, Armide*[8]—maintain that feeling of distant lands and extraordinary happenings so essential to the Lully-Quinault ethos. As with the Venetian librettists, Quinault took advantage of the closed-end society to introduce a certain number of *à clef* characters—in addition to the hero (or Jupiter), who could usually be considered to represent the King. Quinault's disgrace came about because one of Louis' mistresses, Madame de Montespan, feeling that the imperious Junon in *Isis* was herself, successfully intrigued against the librettist.

The Prologue was one of the most notable features of the Quinault libretto. As in the Italian opera, it usually was divorced from the action itself and served as an opportunity to glorify the King.[9] Quinault wrote in the preface to the Prologue of *Cadmus et Hermione*: "The allegorical sense of the subject is so clear that it needs no explanation. It suffices to say that THE KING is placed above ordinary praise, and to form some idea of the greatness and éclat of his glory, it was necessary to elevate him to the godlike status of light, which is the materialization of his escutcheon." The Prologues are often set in the palace of Versailles or the Tuileries

---

(6) "For the good of the universe your death is necessary. Serve as an example to the presumptuous. Fall with your pride, rash bumbler, and leave earth and heaven in peace."

(7) Oliver: *The Encyclopedists as Critics of Music*, p. 8.

(8) From the Spanish novel, Ariosto, and Tasso, respectively.

(9) As with Italian opera, this was not always the case: the Prologue to *Amadis*, for instance, is directly connected to the opera and includes a character from the opera.

and reflect the historic times of the opera: if France was at war, the Prologue celebrated the glories of combat; if France was at peace, it celebrated the fruits of serenity. The action was usually simple: discord resolved into concord by an easily identifiable hero. Yet it is a mistake to consider the Prologues as monolithic: there is a great amount of variety in their approaches, and the later operas have shorter ones, with fewer characters.

A few words should be said about two works that lie on the periphery of the Lully-Quinault canon, for both have importance in the history of the libretto. The first is the initial work that the two collaborated on, *Les Festes d'Amour et de Bachus* [*sic*] (1672), a pastoral opera combining ballet and singing. The Prologue to it shows kinship with the bourgeois comedies of Molière, for it opens on a man giving out acting scripts while the chorus clamors for them. The opera is in three acts instead of the five traditional for the *tragédies*, and in the final act there is a change of scene: "The perspective opens, and there appears at the back of the theater an arbor in the form of a cradle. . . ." This scenic device—the opening out of the scene for a final pageantlike apotheosis, usually reinforced with machines—will remain a standard trait of the French libretto until the end of the nineteenth century, and will spread beyond the *tragédies* to all of French opera.

Le Triomphe de l'Amour (1681), an opera-ballet, is of interest because in it for the first time the ballet itself was integrated into the performance of the work and not treated as a series of *entrées*.[1] From that time onward, ballets formed an important part of all *opéras*, and their inclusion became hardened into canon law, much to the discomfiture of Wagner and other venturesome composers of the nineteenth century.

Variations can be detected in the homogeneity of Quinault. The middle-period librettos—notably *Atys, Isis, Persée, Phaëton*, and *Proserpine*—have a more mechanical approach: a succession of loose scenes bound together by the thread of action and of love and enlivened by *le merveilleux*. *Phaëton* could perhaps have been something more, for its hero is the only one not dominated by *l'amour*, but Lully cautiously saw to it that Quinault modified the character sufficiently to avoid any hint of royal displeasure. Lully did not mind his operas being attacked as trivial love games,

(1) Demuth: *French Opera, Its Development to the Revolution*, p. 124.

but he did not want them accused of being antimonarchical. His last three operas—*Amadis, Roland,* and *Armide*—are considered to have the most fluent and effective verse, and *Armide* has always been considered Quinault's masterpiece.[2] Yet for all the search for diversity within homogeneity, the distance from *Cadmus et Hermione* to *Armide* is minuscule compared to that between the worlds of Busenello's *L'Incoronazione di Poppea* and his *La Prosperità infelice di Giulio Cesare, Dittatore.*

Let us examine one of Quinault's librettos more closely—*Alceste* (1674), Quinault's second *tragédie lyrique,* which well demonstrates the wide-ranging, all-inclusive nature of his work. Charles Perrault[3] considered the libretto superior to Euripides' play because Quinault had the genius to go back to the wedding of Admète and Alceste and show their nuptial bliss, thus heightening the pathos of Alceste's sacrifice.[4] After the two marry, Licomède, a disappointed suitor, contrives to steal away Alceste in his boat, but Admète follows with the help of the wind god Éole. Licomède flings defiance from the ramparts of his castle (a touch *à l'italienne*) and a huge battle results in his defeat. Admète is left wounded and will die unless someone substitutes for him. Alceste volunteers, and is led to Pluton's realm. Alcide, who is also in love with Alceste, offers to fetch her. Act IV opens on the celebrated scene in which Caron is taking money in order to ferry shades across the Styx: those who cannot pay cannot cross. This scene both is typical of Quinault's approach to opera and foreshadows others later: an essentially extraneous moment memorable entirely on its own terms as a thumbnail portrait. Quinault has been rightly castigated for the shallowness of his heroes and heroines; in common with the later Scribe, he has far greater success with lesser characters and in marshaling scenic set-pieces. Al-

---

(2) As can be imagined, in a body of work as uniform as Quinault's, there is a considerable divergence of opinion as to the quality of any given opera. Thus, *Atys* is considered one of the best by several commentators. The opinion on *Armide* is general, however: both Quinault's contemporaries and succeeding generations have felt it to be his best work.

(3) The author and collector of folk tales, notably *Sleeping Beauty.* It was his son, however, who gave the world *Cinderella.*

(4) Of course, what Perrault does not say is that the diffused nature of Quinault's approach to Alceste's plight has weakened the force of the pathos far more than his inclusion of her earlier life has strengthened it.

cide can dominate Caron as easily as Caron can dominate the shades, and so gains access[5] to Pluton's court. Pluton agrees to give up Alceste. When the two return, Admète reluctantly admits that Alcide's bravery and effort should be rewarded with his heart's desire, and so offers to give up his wife. Alceste agrees: *"Il faut, dans les grands coeurs, que l'amour le plus tendre/soit la victime du devoir"* ("In all magnanimous hearts, the tenderest love must fall victim to Duty"). But Alcide has a *"grand coeur"* also, and refuses, paving the way to a *lieto fine*. Running parallel with the main story is a secondary love intrigue that also ends happily.

Quinault ended his libretto career with *Armide* in 1686: he had become increasingly religious and wished to cease writing secular works for the theater. The last scene he wrote, Armide's rage aria, has that quality of crackling fire which so much of his work lacks. The use of the halting line, rare in Italian opera, and extremely rare in French, heightens its paroxysmic nature:

> *Le perfide Renaud me fuit;*
> *tout perfide qu'il est, mon lâche coeur*
>   *le suit.*
>
> . . . .
> *Traître, atten . . . je le tiens . . .*
>   *je tiens*
> *son coeur perfide . . .*
> *Ah! je l'immole à ma fureur . . .*
> *Que dis-je? où suis-je? Hélas! Infortunée Armide!*
> *Où t'emporte une aveugle erreur?*
> *L'espoir de ma vengeance est le seul qui me reste.*
> *Fuyez, plaisirs, fuyez, perdez tous vos attraits.*
> *Démons, détruisez ce palais,*
> *partons et s'il se peut que mon Amour funeste*
> *demeure enseveli dans ces lieux pour jamais.*[6]
>
>   (V, v)

---

(5) This scene provides a good example of Quinault's crystal action-poetry:

     CARON: *L'eau nous gagne, ma barque crève.*
     ALCIDE: *Allons, rame, dépêche, achève.*
                        (IV, ii)

"We're foundering; my craft is breaking." "Go on, row, hurry, get there!"
(6) "The treacherous Renaud flees from one—as treacherous as he is, my cowardly heart follows him. . . . Traitor, wai— . . . I have it . . . I have your treacherous heart . . . Ah! I sacrifice it to my

It is easy to dismiss Quinault for the faults magnified in his successors and in the shapeless librettos provided Rameau almost a century later. It is easy to poke fun at the flatness of verse and thought and at the constant harping on pastoral love, at the flatness of characterization and the plethora of every aspect of *le merveilleux*. Yet Lully chose well, for Quinault's strengths as a lyric dramatist outweighed his faults, and he and Lully were able to create an iron tradition of French opera within the space of fifteen years. Because of it, the influences of Quinault's librettos pervade French operatic history until well into the nineteenth century,[7] and are reborn in *Grand Opéra*. Although the reform operas of Zeno and Metastasio take a great part of their esthetic from the *tragédies* of Corneille and Racine, their debt to Quinault is ever-present. Jean-Jacques Rousseau highlighted this connection when he contrasted the choice of subjects in the librettos of Metastasio and Quinault: whereas Metastasio chose subjects *"de ce que l'histoire a de plus illustre"* ("of what is most illustrious in history"), Quinault chose them *"de ce que la fable a de plus merveilleux"* ("of what is most spectacular in fable"). This brand of otherworldly fantasy, created out of the pastoral for the divertissement rather than the education of the aristocratic classes, and particularly for that of the King, was also to be promulgated in Italy in the *fiabe* of Count Carlo Gozzi in eighteenth-century Venice. It remains from that day to this one of the important though least discussed subspecies of the libretto throughout its history.[8]

---

fury . . . what am I saying? Where am I? Alas! Unfortunate Armide! Where is a blind error carrying you? The hope of vengeance is all that is left me. Flee, pleasures, flee: lose all your attractions. Demons, destroy this palace. We leave and it may happen that my doomed love shall dwell imprisoned in these precincts forever."
(7) One reason for this was that the autocratic tradition of a national opera saw to it that Quinault's works were kept on stage and that his librettos were read by succeeding generations.
(8) A further discussion of this point will be part of the consideration of Gozzi.

Chapter Five

The First Italian Reform

T HE IMPETUS TOWARD REFORM in the Italian libretto had emerged well before the end of the seventeenth century, the result of not one but a combination of factors. Most important of these was the wearing away of the novelty of the machines and extravagant displays of the seventeenth-century operas. Once the public had become accustomed to that type of opera, it began to see the more ludicrous aspects that had been disguised by the pomp, and to want something different. Impresarios, always alert to the possibility of saving money, began to reduce casts and machines. This change in turn played into the hands of those writers on opera, especially Frenchmen writing on Italian opera, who had long made brutal, satiric fun of the excesses and had contrived to make them appear even more ridiculous than they actually were. Their arguments against seventeenth-century Italian opera were based largely on intellectual snobbery. They said that these operas were a perversion of the Greek ideals as set forth in opera by the Florentine Camerata and as elaborated by the French classical tragedies. Opera should therefore purify itself and return to this One True Golden Path.[1]

It is interesting to note the extent to which the delusion of the Purity of Greece continued to operate through the years as a reform cry; it is amusing to note the various admixtures that were served up as representing "the Greek ideal." With the Camerata it had been the pastoral play, the influence of which extended to

---

(1) The pernicious effects of this blinkered criticism obscured the merits of Busenello's librettos for over two centuries, while exaggerating those of Metastasio because his works assumed all the critically acceptable postures.

the eighteenth-century reform as well. Yet the libretto had developed beyond the bounds of Rinuccini and Striggio, and particularly for the "aristocratic" opera, written for royal courts, a simple folk tale was not enough. Here the ideals of Corneille and Racine operated to the advantage both of "the Greek ideal" and of opera, for they provided rigid cohesion and concision within a scope far more inclusive than the pastoral ever afforded. Thus, what took place in the last two decades of the seventeenth century and the first two of the eighteenth was not a thoroughgoing housecleaning, but a pruning and repotting, accompanied by a great amount of philosophical flim-flam about Greece and the pastoral perfection.

One of the first demands was for a return to the Aristotelian Unities. This hoary excerpt from Aristotle's *Poetics* had been gaining immense power as a formulative principle through the seventeenth century. Aristotle had noted that the writers of Greek tragedy had observed the unities of time (all the action took place in the space of less than twenty-four hours), of place (all action took place in one locale), and of theme. Some critics, and the French tragedians of the seventeenth century, applied this observation as Mosaic Law, as an essential prerequisite not only for a logical continuation of the tradition of Greek drama but also for any meaningful tragic drama. The more the shoe pinched, the better is was for the soul. The absurd belief in a formalistic straight-jacket as necessarily producing an artistic work of value is patent to us, whose esthetic is almost diametrically opposed to it.[2] Yet the concept contained a grain of truth, for rigid order, in the hands of someone who knows how to manipulate it, does have a powerful effect upon pace and control, and the plays of Corneille and Racine stood testament to its dramatic value. The French, of course, were quick to codify, and the growing fame of their two great dramatists served to spread the Form as well as the Substance.

The Aristotelian Unities had of course been an ingredient of the Camerata operas, but largely because those operas were short works, in which a certain unity of time, place, and theme would be natural, and not because there was a conscious attempt to conform with an abstract rule. With the popularity of opera,

---

(2) Indeed, it could be argued that the exact opposite has been canonized.

64

indeed, all such philosophical niceties were quickly forgotten: as Ulderico Rolandi put it, "the public wanted to enjoy itself."[3] The importance of Aristotle, therefore, resulted directly from impatience with the swollen spectacle form of seventeenth-century opera and the success of the French *tragédie*, which trumpeted its adherence to the ancient virtues.

Yet the Aristotelian Unities will nowhere in opera be as rigidly observed as they were in French tragedy. One of the more bizarre practitioners of the librettistic art, Count Girolamo Frigimelica Roberti, who flourished at the end of the seventeenth century, made a practice of long introductions in which he detailed his adherence to the Aristotelian practices. But his librettos show the ordering influences only in contrast to the librettos of his most extravagant contemporaries: if he dispensed with magicians and concentrated on "the force of passions,"[4] he nonetheless uses machines, ballets between acts, euphuistic language, and the four- or five-act structure.[5] As later with Metastasio, the unity-of-place requirement was extremely loosely interpreted: Frigimelica's *Mitridate Eupatore* (1707) embraces an entire kingdom and six separate sets.

Frigimelica demonstrates the gap between theory and practice which is so much a part of the whole question of the Aristotelian Unities. What is important is that some librettists were turning to these outside ordering influences to justify a more logical product: if the product did not exactly reflect the Golden Age that it was supposed to reproduce, it nevertheless made an honest attempt to do so. The results of these efforts in pruning would be the reform libretto of the *opera seria*.

The other outside influence upon the reform was the creation, in Rome in 1692, of the Arcadian Academy, a gathering place for artists and intellectuals, formed by fourteen men, including Silvio Stampiglia, one of the first librettists of the "reform," and Gian Vincenzo Gravina, a wealthy lawyer and intellectual who would later find a young singer in the streets of Rome by the name of Pietro Trapassi, become impressed with his native genius

---

(3) Ulderico Rolandi: *Il Libretto per musica attraverso i tempi*, pp. 59–60.
(4) *Irene* (1695). He calls his libretto *"semplicissima."* Note the parallels, in philosophy at least, to the later Italian *melodramma*.
(5) The five-act structure was thought by the Aristotelians to be a particularly Greek feature.

for verse and song, adopt him, and change his name to Metastasio. As can be seen by its name, the Academy began with a certain set of preconceptions, which were developed into artistic precepts. The single most important word in the Academicians' canon was *"semplicità"* ("simplicity"), which in their minds was typified by the Arcadian pastorals. All members of the Arcadian Academy were required to take "Arcadian" names, which were in fact not simple at all but woefully overblown,[6] and were permitted to put the letters P.A. (for *"Pastor*—or *Pastorella—Arcade,"* Arcadian Shepherd—or Shepherdess) after these names. The virtues of the Academy were those they imagined to have existed in Arcady: the simple life, with simple, easily apprehended passions and tender resolutions.

The Academy was not so rigid an organization as the Académie française (although it had its own set of rules), but rather a social one: a gathering place of like-minded individuals for discussion and for company. Because the ideas it espoused appealed to others, branches of the Academy were quickly formed in other cities, and as the success of the *opera seria* spread, so did the fame of the Academy. It became fashionable among the patrons of opera to be "elected" and to take pastoral names.

The foregoing sentence gives a clue to one of the most important considerations in evaluating the impact of the reforms. Although their promulgators masqueraded under the aegis of the Arcadian Academy, with concomitant obeisances to the idea of the pastoral play, in fact the reforms were directed toward a purification of the high-flown "tragic" opera of the seventeenth century. The direct outgrowth was what has come to be called *opera seria*. The pastoral comedies, which would become so much a part of the later eighteenth century, gained their impetus not from the Arcadian Academy, but in opposition to the posturings of *opera seria*.[7] Thus the "reform" of opera was essentially an

(6) For example, the composer Niccolò Jommelli was known as Anfione Eteoclide. Women members were not unknown, but they were usually members of the nobility. Thus, Maria Antonia Walpurgis, Electress of Saxony, became Ermelinda Talea. Alan Yorke-Long: *Music at Court*, p. 54.

(7) There is some basis to the notion that by sowing the seeds of the Pastoral Ideal, the Arcadian Academy, despite its preference for *opera seria*, did contribute something toward the pastoral and bourgeois opera to be popularized in Italy and canonized by the Encyclopedists. Carlo Goldoni, the father of the bourgeois libretto and

aristocratic reform, taking as its inspiration the *"semplicità"* aspects of the pastorals, but having as its direct antecedents the rigidly controlled, élitist theater of the French tragedy. This aristocratic tradition would be continued in the works of Gluck and Ranieri de' Calzabigi, in what we could call the reform of the reform, and down into the nineteenth century. But even in the eighteenth century it was becoming of less importance. The growth of the "bourgeois opera" out of the fairs of Paris and the theaters of Venice and Naples served to undermine the reform as surely as the growth of the bourgeoisie undermined the aristocracy. The true reform came because of the changing tastes of the public, which came to care less and less for the posings of the *castrati* as supernoble, magnanimous heroes of yore.

Yet, in 1692, these developments were still a few generations in the future. The success of the French classical theater and its ideals of purity and nobility had made a lasting impression upon the Italian founders of the Arcadian Academy, and they too sought to purify their works. There should be no mixture of classes (except for the Confidant or Confidante, usually a private servant); there should be no miracles; there should be no comedy mixed with tragedy; there should be only the grandest themes and noblest passions, expressed with sentiment and effulgence, leading logically to a *lieto fine* in which all the knots would be untangled and the triumphal close could be effected.

One of the first reform operas was *La Forza del virtù*, given in Venice in 1593, with music by Carlo Francesco Pollarolo and libretto by Domenico David. The name of the opera gives a clue to its importance of a reform work, for the force of virtue was one of the prime themes of those librettists who wished their works to uplift and educate. As Apostolo Zeno was to write in the preface to his *Ormisda* in 1721, "In another of my dramas I showed the good effects of friendship. In this one I have sought to put before your eyes the bad effects of hatred." David's libretto was admired by both Zeno and Metastasio.

Another of the precursors of the two most famous reform

---

godfather of the eighteenth-century pastoral, was a member of the Academy (under the pastoral name Polisseno Fegeio), but then so were a good many other literary people. He, however, never used the Academy as a forum for his ideas, and indeed wrote *opere serie* as well as the bourgeois librettos for which he is remembered.

librettists was Silvio Stampiglia (1664–1725), who preceded Zeno as Caesarean Poet in Vienna (1705–18). Influenced by the ideas of the Arcadians, he began to refashion his librettos into shorter, more cohesive dramas. One aspect, however, remained unchanged and was to remain unchanged even in the librettos of the reform: love. Love was a staple demanded by the public, rich or poor, and its dovelike cooings, innocuous enough in the sprawling seventeenth-century operas, remained to disfigure the more rigidly laced works of the reform.

The librettist who laid the ground rules for *opera seria* was Apostolo Zeno (1669–1750), who held the post of Caesarean Poet from 1718 to 1729, when he was succeeded by Metastasio.[8] Zeno came from an illustrious Venetian family and spent most of his life in his native city. Primarily a critic and historian, he looked upon the writing of librettos as a sideline, undertaking it partly as a critical duty to purify the libretto along the lines suggested by the Arcadians, partly in a chauvinistic spirit to attempt to establish a counterweight in Italy to the artistic eminence and influence of France—and partly to make money. As editor of the *Giornale de' letterati d'Italia* from 1710 to 1719, he was acutely conscious of transalpine criticism of the dearth of artistic merit throughout Italy. His librettos, the first of which he produced in 1695, were written as much for the edification of his circle of friends as for production, and there is little question that most of them were intended rather to be read aloud (in sonorous and portentous voice) or read privately than to be sung. Zeno was indifferent to music—he was perhaps the most admittedly nonmusical of the major librettists[9] —but the cold, bookish quality that undoubtedly infests his works has been exaggerated. The early eighteenth century saw the final efflorescence of the power of the word over that of music and,

(8) The duties of the Caesarean Poet were roughly the duties of any of the court poets of the day: to provide one or two opera librettos per year, a varying number of texts for sacred works and whatever divertissements the royal household wished to perform, and to be on hand to versify for royal weddings, funerals, and the like. One of the last feeble remnants of the post is that of Poet Laureate in Great Britain. It is interesting to note that, in Zeno's time, the procedure for submitting a scenario to the Emperor, etc., copied that made famous by the French court. A recent article by Robert Freeman: "Apostolo Zeno's Reform of the Libretto," *Journal of the American Musicological Society* (1968), argues that Zeno has been overcredited for what was a joint effort of a number of librettists of the time.
(9) Other possibilities for the position are Scribe and Hofmannsthal.

because of the influence of the French esthetic, theory had come to dominate both; but Zeno's librettos have a good deal of dramatic viability, especially in comparison with those of his lesser contemporaries.

Zeno welcomed Metastasio's appearance, and surrendered the mantle of Caesarean Poet to him, after which he wrote only oratorio texts and returned to Venice in 1730 to live out the rest of his life.

With Zeno, the *opera seria* achieved a more or less stereotyped form that was further refined and made rigid by Metastasio. The cast of characters was reduced to six (or at most eight), who were interconnected by love chains. There was one main theme (always accompanied by the secondary one of love), upon which the librettist range changes for three, four, or five acts[1] in the form of dramatic scenes and confrontations of the characters, leading to a climax and a dénouement usually in the form of a triumphal scene. Each scene was contrived to end with an aria for one of the characters, who then left the stage. Concerted numbers and ensembles were few. The characters (with the possible exception of the villain) were motivated by the highest standards of noble and ethical behavior; the working-out of the story, though it might hinge on the inanimate object, was focused on the interplay of emotions from which the element of the miraculous was largely banished.

The setting, though it might be changed during the course of an opera, remained a backdrop to the action, as in the French tragedies, and was never manipulated as a concomitant of the plot. All *opere serie* share the element of otherworldliness and time-lessness,[2] no matter in which country and time they may be set: a quality that combined with the otherworldly attitudes of the protagonists and flattered the vanities of the ruling classes, who invariably saw themselves (as Louis XIV had done) in terms of the magnanimous heroes. It was this quality which most angered

---

(1) Zeno's librettos vacillate in the number of acts, but Metastasio's are all in three.
(2) The rigid limits of the Aristotelian rules were largely vitiated by this timelessness. Events occur, and if they are logically traced they can all be fitted into a day between sunset and sunset (most librettos conform to this pattern), but the impression gained from most of the librettos is that the action is spread over a good deal of time.

writers and thinkers attuned to the everyday virtues and vices of bourgeois life and led to the reaction away from *opera seria*, and, indeed, from "classic" opera.

Zeno's intellectually oriented nature is most in evidence in the foreparts of the librettos he wrote. Because they were meant for reading, Zeno was careful to delineate all the antecedents of the plot, as well as the historical sources for ideas and the changes he made. Zeno the careful scholar and follower of the rules is everywhere in evidence in his prefaces: "other characters and love interests have been introduced into the story for greater intrigue";[3] "it is true that the way in which Selearco comes to realize the affection of Antioco is told differently from the History mentioned above, but I thought I could take the liberty to change it, without incurring censure, because it is lawful to alter the middle parts, as long as the end remains the same";[4] "in order to satisfy the unities of time and place, I have made Quinto Fabio march to Rome with part of the army after the victory."[5] The sources of Zeno's librettos were always carefully specified, and included the ancients (Herodotus, Thucydides, Procopius, Cornelius Nepos, Plutarch, and Livy[6]) and the moderns, which generally meant the French dramatists (Rotrou, Thomas Corneille, Racine, Gauthier de La Calprenède, Houdar de La Motte[7]), as well as books of travel and memoirs (*A General History of the Mogol Empire*, by P. Francesco Catrou; *Memoirs of Niccolò Manuzio, Venetian; Voyages of Francesco Bernier*). The exotic, of course, continued to be sought after in *opera seria*, but here it was enveloped in a cloak of supposed historical accuracy: in the

---

(3) Preface to *Alessandro in Sidone* (1721).
(4) Preface to *Antioco* (1705). Note the discrepancy: often the end did *not* remain the same, because of the necessity for a *lieto fine*, although Zeno could usually find some other source on which to lean.
(5) Preface to *Lucio Papirio* (1719).
(6) Note the absence of any of the Greek dramatists. Zeno did compose an Iphigenia libretto which can be traced back to Euripides, but the immediate source was Racine.
(7) Houdar de La Motte was the author of one of the most famous plays of the eighteenth century, *Inès de Castro*. The situation was powerful: the King has arranged a *marriage de convenance* for his son, but the son is secretly married to (and has children by) the Queen's lady-in-waiting, Inès. The tragedy ends with the necessary death of Inès. *Inès de Castro* librettos were set well into the nineteenth century, and the story was used by Henri de Montherlant as the basis for his great twentieth-century play *La Reine morte*.

preface to *Teuzzone* (1706), a libretto laid in China, Zeno details seven "laws and rites" that govern the country.

Some of Zeno's librettos were written in collaboration with Pietro Pariati, and in the preface to the ninth volume of Zeno's collected works[8] there is a notice as to how the task was split: "The first [i.e., Zeno] did the sketch and the ordering of each subject; and the versifying was done alternately by one and the other." Zeno therefore was always in charge of the subject, form, and content of his works; Pariati now and then "filled in the background" of the words. Even in the eighteenth century, an era when the word dominated the music and librettos were meant to be read, the power of the word had been subsumed into that of the over-all form and dramatic moments—and the latter were considered paramount. It can be argued that Zeno gave up some of the versifying because he realized that he was an inferior poet and did not wish to waste his time unduly, but there is no doubt that the aspect of the libretto that he kept to himself, consciously or not, was the more important one, though, because of Metastasio, poetry would continue to remain a constant factor in any ultimate judgment of a libretto until the twentieth century.

Zeno's verse was indeed inferior: stolid, often end-stopped, and (particularly in the exit arias) abounding in diminutives and cliché-words of the later seventeenth century.[9] Because his librettos were written quickly—often in eight days or less—scenes are over-long, stories are unwieldy and complex, and the pacing is jerky. In extenuation it should be remembered that Zeno was working out of the inordinately bloated practices of the generation before him, and was to a great extent feeling his way in an unknown land.[1] Yet he managed his librettos so that their strengths

---

(8) Edited by Gasparo Gozzi, the brother of the playwright (Venice, 1744). Gozzi uses his introductory preface to decry the depths into which the libretto had fallen after Rinuccini. Zeno, of course, was its savior.

(9) "*Con fausti auspicii,/con Dei propizii/il nostro Marte/combatterà.//Giove è placato;/e debellato/il Sannio a Roma/s'inchinerà.*" ("With happy auguries and favoring gods our Mars will go to combat. Jove is placated and weakened Sannio will bow to Rome.") *Lucio Papirio*, 1719; I, i.

(1) Zeno employed arias at the beginning and in the course of scenes, although their use diminishes in the later operas. There are also occasional trios and quartets, never a feature of the "classic" *opera seria*. The usual seventeenth-century baggage of chains, prisons, letter-readings and portrait-lookings can also be found in abundance.

did not have to lie in the area of poetry and the exit aria, but in fast dialogue and action, solid set-speeches and emotional *scene,* dramatic confrontations, and clarity of thought and direction. Zeno's operas may lack grace (particularly next to Metastasio's), but he gets his message across, a rare enough accomplishment when he began to write.[2]

We remain constantly amazed by the quick-moving opening of *Don Giovanni* (albeit after the short hiatus of an opening aria), and yet the fast opening was a hallmark of the *opera seria* librettos, especially Zeno's. His opening for *Faramondo* (1699) has points of resemblance to the Mozart–Da Ponte opera, and that of his *Ornospade* (1727) must stand as an ultimate in compression and instant action: "PRINCESS: I am resolved. CONFIDANTE: To die? PRINCESS: Yes."—which in Italian totals four words ("*Son risoluto.*" "*Morir?*" "*Sì.*"). *La brevità, gran pregio,* even for the eighteenth century.

Any comparison with Metastasio, however, shows the superiority of Zeno's successor as Caesarean Poet, for Metastasio refined and idealized what Zeno had begun. A direct comparison can be made in the central scene of *Temistocle,* which both poets wrote, Zeno in 1700 and Metastasio thirty-six years later. Temistocle, an Athenian general, has gone into voluntary exile because his countrymen, fearful of his stature, have turned against him. Serse, the Persian King, takes him in, showers him with gifts, and appoints him to head his armies. He then orders him against the Greeks. Temistocle, in a memorable scene, refuses thus to betray his country, although its citizens have betrayed him. The power of Zeno's scene lies in the series of short sentences between the King and his general, but the scene is over-long and also involves other matters. Metastasio's scene is close to perfect in form and expression, using all the arguments found in Zeno, but organizing them with superb skill and dramatic force.

Much has been made of the rigid nature of *opera seria,* and

---

(2) Professor Robert Freeman believes that there were at least two quite different forces tending toward the positioning arias at the close of the scenes in which they occur. One was the singers' realization that an aria at the highpoint of the dramatic action makes for a better exit, and the other was Zeno's wish that his librettos be read as a kind of literature—but without reminding the audience that they were reading a libretto. I am indebted to Professor Freeman for several of the ideas found in the course of this chapter.

of its otherworldly qualities: glorifying heroics and magnanimous gestures. This entire armor was to peter out in the various attempts at "classic" opera, particularly in France, over the next century and a half. Yet underneath this armor plate of formalism there was a highly dramatic and pulsating core. The librettists of *opera seria* chose their sources as much for human interest as for patriotic or noble actions on the part of their fictitious characters, which is the reason why many of the stories retold by Zeno and Metastasio survive to be told again in the nineteenth-century operas of the *melodramma*,[3] which in most respects lies at the opposite pole from *opera seria*. Felice Romani's great libretto for Bellini's *Norma* can be said to represent the fusion of what was best in *opera seria* and those elements of directness and emotion which were to develop in contrast to it.

Although Zeno was only peripherally interested in the opera libretto, and although he depreciated it in his letters, he nonetheless had too much pride as a scholar to allow fifth-rate works to appear under his name, more especially as he wanted those works to be read as well as seen. He therefore made an effort to reorder the libretto and, indirectly, to put Italy once again on the literary map. Without Metastasio, he would probably have succeeded only in part: with Metastasio, he succeeded beyond the dreams of his wildest followers. For Metastasio became the poet and the dramatist not only of the age but of the ages, a writer who no less than Voltaire maintained was in certain respects greater than the ancient Greeks.

---

(3) To avoid semantic confusion, I use the Italian word *melodramma* to refer only to that period in the history of the libretto which encompasses the first half of the nineteenth century. The word itself was in constant use from the very first librettos, but in its restricted sense applies only to the Italian romantic operas of the nineteenth century.

Chapter Six

Metastasio

T HE STORY of the discovery of Pietro Trapassi is romantic enough to please the softest-hearted lover of the Horatio Alger myth, for the young boy, born in 1698, was found singing in the streets of Rome by Vincenzo Gravina, who later adopted him and, in keeping with his Arcadian predilections, changed the boy's name to Metastasio (i.e., using the Latin word, from the Greek meaning "change" or "transition"). Gravina saw to the young man's education, died when Metastasio was twenty, and left him his fortune. The next year Metastasio became a member of the Arcadian Academy under the name Artino Corasio. He proceeded to dissipate Gravina's money in general extravagance over the next few years, and later felt such remorse at the realization of what he had done that he set himself the penance of giving up poetry and articling himself to a narrow-minded lawyer in Naples. He stuck to the law for a few years, but his natural penchant for verse led him to write anonymously for the Neapolitan theater. At that time he began what is generally considered a liaison with the celebrated dramatic soprano Bulgarella, known as La Romanina. At her encouragement he wrote for her his first notable libretto, *Didone abbandonata* (1724).[1] The opera (which in this case meant the libretto, for no one thought much of Domenico Sarro's music) became as much of a sensation as his earlier *Gli Orti esperidi* (1721), which had audiences, especially Neapolitan ones, going to the unprecedented length of remaining hushed throughout the evening so that the poetry could be heard. Metastasio's reputation was made; he abandoned the law and returned in triumph to

---

(1) La Romanina is reputed to have suggested the idea for the last two scenes of Act II (which, to nobody's surprise, climaxes in a *scena*).

Rome. Each succeeding libretto enhanced his stature throughout Italy, and in 1729 he was invited to succeed Zeno as Caesarean Poet. He left Italy intending to remain in Vienna for only a few years, as Zeno had done, but, once settled in the Austrian capital, he remained there until his death in 1782, supplying librettos for *opere serie*, oratorios, *azione sacre*—whatever he was asked by the royal household to write. Year by year Metastasio grew in stature as poet, dramatist, and—most important—historical and ceremonial figure; so much so that, at the end of his life, the celebrated Enlightenment poet and dramatist Vittorio Alfieri, on visiting Vienna, refused to meet him, because to the younger generation Metastasio no longer represented any "reform," but rather the kept toady of a Divine Right despot.

Yet Metastasio's fame in his day (and that "day" was to last for roughly fifty years) was incalculable. *Opera seria* meant Metastasio librettos, at first-, second-, or third-hand, and practically every opera composer vied to set them.[2] Some of his works were composed by over twenty separate composers, and a single composer, in an age when music was far more perishable than words, would set one of his librettos two or three times. Metastasio naturally was as displeased as any latter-day Wagner by changes in his texts, but that availed him little outside his sphere of influence. His reputation was enhanced by a gentle, easygoing nature, which made him many friends throughout Europe; and the fact that he was a voluminous letter writer enabled him to spread his doctrines about *opera seria* to every European opera house. As well as an excellent poetic ear and organizational talent, Metastasio possessed a first-class knowledge of stagecraft, so that he often coached singers in their roles. What is less known is that he also was enough of a musician to be able to set his own verses while he wrote them, thus being able to judge whether or not they were sufficiently *musicabile*.[3]

The librettos of Metastasio represent the noonday of the

---

(2) Metastasio librettos were set until well into the nineteenth century. Meye beer even set one (*Semiramide*, 1819).

(3) This habit is not uncommon among librettists throughout the history of the form. Most recently W. H. Auden has written: ". . . Chester Kallman and myself always find it helpful to let our choice of words and style be guided by a sort of platonic idea of a suitable melody"; *Times Literary Supplement* (November 2, 1967), p. 1037.

power of the librettist over that of the composer, and that power is nowhere better revealed than in Metastasio's most famous letter, that to the composer Johann Adolf Hasse of October 20, 1749. Metastasio had been at work on the libretto for *Attilio Regolo* since 1740, and considered it "the least imperfect" of his creations. In the letter Metastasio, with conventional *politesses*, but as magnanimously as any of his fictional monarchs, proceeded to instruct the composer as to the characterizations and meaning of the work, and even suggested instrumentation and placing of orchestral interludes. A reading of the letter,[4] moreover, reveals the extent to which Metastasio as a librettist prefigured the contributions of Gluck and Calzabigi, and later of Mozart, in the vital area of the accompanied recitative, while his request for the orchestra to express the state of mind of the leading character is a direct antecedent of one of Gluck's most notable contributions to the "reform" of the Metastasian *opera seria*.

Given Metastasio's stature as librettist, poet, moral force, and cultural arm of a powerful monarchy, his advice to Hasse was likely to be heeded. The paradox—indeed, the underlying paradox of all of *opera seria*—lay in the fact that most if not all of this exquisitely crafted structure of both word and music was to be effectively vitiated by the singer's abuse of a single one of its elements, the exit aria. Any study of Metastasio's dramaturgy and his dramatic precepts will illumine the similarities with, rather than the differences from, the Gluckian reform that followed it.

Metastasio's great librettos present the ideals of *opera seria* as perfectly as is humanly possible: one can condemn the basic form, but never the means. All of his "tragedies" are variations on certain patterns, which more or less became codified through practice.[5] The operas were in three acts (very roughly one for exposition, one for development, and the last for climax and dénouement) and employed six characters, all balanced as to voices and including a hero or heroine, a foil (usually some sort of a tyrant), loved ones, and confidants. The chorus was reserved for act endings and triumphal closes, but often was absent entirely. The opening scene

---

(4) See the Appendix for the full text of this letter.
(5) Metastasio also wrote lighter works, such as *L'Isola disabitata* (1753). Some commentators maintain that these works are better tailored to Metastasio's abilities because they eschew the portentousness of his serious works.

or scenes laid out the background and set forth the situation. Metastasio was a master at setting up the story in as few words as possible—in fact, one of his major strengths lay in the extreme compression and directness of his language. His poetry may be flowery, full of metaphor, and elevated in tone, but it is never obscure. This was particularly valuable in the scenes of question and answer or debate, in which *opera seria* abounds.[6] Once the exposition is over, the development begins, and this section takes over most of the libretto. It consists in what could be termed elaborate minuets and gavottes for the six characters in pairs or in threes, all inexorably building to the climax, as in the French classical tragedies. The image of the minuet is apposite because of the stylized nature of these scenes: violence was often threatened in explicit terms, but swords rarely left the scabbard and the duels common in nineteenth-century opera were almost unknown. Movement was as severely restricted as in a Wieland Wagner production (or as in the Japanese theater), and each movement on the actor's part had a special meaning. As there were rarely more than three people on stage at one time, the actor who moved one step forward of the other two was the central figure; when a seated character stood, his words were thereby rendered more important.[7]

Mixed into all of the stories was the omnipresent theme of love, which needed not be the unitary theme of the work but was present either in the form of a love chain or of a counterpoint tandem of hero-beloved and a secondary pair. The secondary love interest, usually of confidants, of course carried over from the seventeenth-century librettos and plays, but in *opera seria* it assumed the function of "relaxation" that comic scenes had once afforded or that the intermezzos provided.[8] Comic scenes were banned from *opera seria* as vulgar and beneath contempt, and Metastasio

---

(6) This is one of the few traits of *opera seria* which can be traced back to the Greek tragedies, such as *Oedipus Rex*, through the French tragedies.

(7) Fruitful comparisons can be made here with the operas of Wagner, especially after the insights afforded by Wieland Wagner. Hagen's Watch is a splendid example of the "sitting" *scena*—and he should never stand during it (although some basses violate this). Hunding's rising from the table after he realizes that Siegmund is his mortal enemy (*Die Walküre*, Act I) is another example.

(8) There is therefore not as great a contrast in *opera seria* as the earlier opera provided, this exactly in keeping with the wishes of the writers. By narrowing the range they hoped to probe the depths, as Racine had done.

wrote no intermezzos after two in *Didone abbandonata*, which he included for his Neapolitan audience. These two, under the title of *L'Impresario delle Canarie*, are as wittily satiric a take-off on *opera seria* as Calzabigi's later libretto for Florian Gassmann, *Opera seria* (1769), or as Richard Brinsley Sheridan's play *The Critic* (1779); it is not surprising that as soon as Metastasio became the grand panjandrum of the form, they were quietly forgotten and omitted from many editions.[9]

The series of confrontations, debates, love declarations, and threats that make up the bulk of the *opera seria* libretto comes to a climax in most cases in one grand scene in which all is unraveled through some revelation, a magnanimous act on the part of the tyrant, or the triumph of a noble mind; and the opera ends with the chorus intoning a sententious homily, which is followed by a *licenza* (in the Viennese librettos) directed at the sovereign. Naturally, the operas end in a *lieto fine*—with the exceptions of *Didone abbandonata*, which culminates in a scene for Didone that Metastasio lifted from the already-quoted finale of Quinault's *Armide*, and of *Catone in Utica* (1728), whose ending Metastasio later modified.[1] The last scene, also, is most likely to employ some

---

(9) Indeed, their existence may have been forgotten by Metastasio—or he may in his mind have greatly altered their character—for on June 10, 1747, he wrote to Giuseppe Bettinelli: "I have never written satire in all my life and will never write it. I hate that type of writing, and am not gifted with enough black bile and bad taste to be able to sacrifice to it the sweat of my brow . . ." Already the poet was becoming marmorealized.

(1) It should again be emphasized, however, that the whole of the problem of the *lieto fine* needs a systematic reappraisal, for the question is not as simple as most commentators have assumed. In the first place, the *lieto fine* itself underwent several changes: the metamorphosis finale of the early librettos is different from that found in the reform period. It should not be assumed that audiences objected to an unhappy ending because they were escapist Pollyannas. The objection to the ending of *Catone in Utica* lay not in the fact that Catone (Cato) died, but that he died *on stage*. French classical tragedy had "ennobled" death by not allowing its grosser aspects to be seen on stage, and many critics felt as a matter of course that tragic stature demanded a certain austerity of presentation, which is why they considered Shakespeare an overwrought melodramatist. This attitude is captured in a satiric jingle on Metastasio's libretto for *Catone in Utica*: "Cruel Metastasio, you who have reduced all the Tiberian heroes to a band of pirates"; *Tutte le opere*, vol. I, p. 1399. Algarotti's comment is also to the point: the dramatic effect of the death of a great hero was bound to be lessened if that hero exited this life trilling and embellishing. It would be better to let him expire off stage, with a friend on stage giving his epitaph in *secco* recitative.

sort of mechanical device, although one of the "reforms" was to banish the machines almost totally from the other parts of the work.

The chief characters in the operas were not allowed to become complex, for complexity would lessen their stature as embodiments of one affect or emotion. Metastasio wrote to Signora Livia Accarigi (September 12, 1763): "It is true that nature is replete with devout rascals and blustering cowards, but we cannot bear portraits that express our bestiality, and the theater requires clear-cut characters." This precise point roused the antagonism not only of those who wanted to reform the reform, but also of those who rejected it entirely, for such mono-motivated characters, unless drawn with great skill and force, quickly became antihuman statues, an impression doubly reinforced by their "classical" garb, stylized poses, unearthly voices, fantastic embellishments of the vocal line, and (quite often) their ridiculous obesity.[2]

The most famous single attribute of the *opera seria*, however, was the exit aria, or short ABA lyric that one character sang at the end of a scene, just before leaving the stage. The exit aria, already common when Zeno began writing, reached its peak of perfection with the hundreds of examples that Metastasio provided. It became rigidly categorized and quasi-mechanical in application if the rules were adhered to. No one singer had two exit arias in a row; each had a total of five, no two of which could be of the same "character," and a few solo *scene* were included (usually just prior to a change of scene), with one for the titular character, who generally, but not invariably, appeared midway through the first act—the delayed entrance remaining constant through the centuries as both an organizational device to build suspense and, more realistically, as the prerogative of the "star."[3]

---

(2) This singleness of character could be used to advantage in librettos in which the central motivations depended less on character than on an abstract ideal or on twists of plot. It also serves as a major distinction from the works of Racine, whose characters, though sometimes superficially "simple" (e.g., Phèdre's lust), are in fact a web of conflicting psychological motivations.

(3) George Hogarth: *Memoirs of the Opera*, vol. II, pp. 62–8, details the various "characters" of the arias, which needless to say became a fierce battleground to the pedants. Briefly, they included the *aria cantabile*, for tender and pleasing sadness, with graceful ornamentation; the *aria di portamento*, for solemn dignity (no ornaments allowed!); the *aria di mezzo carattere*, a catch-all category; the *aria parlante*, for energy and force of passion; and the *aria di bravura*, for display purposes, and about which Hogarth dryly comments:

The form of the aria was also standardized. It consisted of two parts, or two thoughts, connected as similes, as oppositions, or as a syllogism, often using images from nature (animals, flowers, or the weather—particularly the weather on the sea) expressed in simple, "Arcadian" verse (which to lesser librettists, and at times to Metastasio, meant the use of diminutives or cute turns of phrase[4]) in, usually, an eight-line form whose length, in syllables, ran 7–7–7–6; 7–7–7–6.[5] The second half of the aria might well also include some moralistic tag.

One of the most famous of Metastasio's exit arias well illustrates that lotus-drugged, undulating line for which he was universally famous:

> *L'onda che mormora*
> *tra sponda e sponda,*
> *l'aura che tremola*
> *tra fronda e fronda,*
> *è meno instabile*
> *del vostro cor.*
>   *Pur l'alme semplici*
> *de' folli amanti*
> *sol per voi spargono*
> *sospiri e pianti,*
> *e da voi sperano*
> *fede in amor.*[6]
> (*Siroe*, 1726; I, ix)

Or this classically lovely one, which shows the value attached to the last lines of each part:

"Such airs too frequently serve no other purpose than that of astonishing the ignorant, while they make the judicious grieve" (p. 68). There were also sub-categories, which included the "imitation" aria (in which the singer imitated sounds of nature).

(4) As Nibbio says in *L'Impresario delle Canarie:* "And where could there be a better spot to put an aria with some sort of '*farfalletta*' or '*navicella*'?"

(5) These generalities about the exit aria apply in the majority of cases. Metastasio in his earlier librettos experimented to an extent with the number of lines as well as the number of syllables per line (as can be seen in the *Siroe* aria quoted in the next paragraph) and, although he largely stuck to the eight-line form in his later librettos, did continue to vary the syllabification now and then.

(6) "The waves that murmur between the shores, the air that trembles between the boughs, is less fickle than your heart. Yet the simple souls of those lost in love scatter sighs and plaints only for you, and from you hope for faith in love."

> *Senza procelle ancora*
> *si perde quel nocchiero,*
> *che lento in su la prora*
> *passa dormendo il dì.*
> *Sognava il suo pensiero*
> *forse le amiche sponde;*
> *ma si trovò fra l'onde,*
> *allor che i lumi aprì.*[7]
> (*Alessandro nell'Indie*, 1729; II, iv)

Or this highly compressed contribution:

> *Tardi s'avvede*
> *d'un tradimento*
> *chi mai di fede*
> *mancar non sa.*
> *Un cor verace,*
> *pieno d'onore,*
> *non è portento,*
> *se ogni altro core*
> *crede incapace*
> *d'infidelità.*[8]
> (*La Clemenza di Tito*, 1734; III, i)

The exit arias contain much of the poetry that Metastasio is remembered for, yet their value goes beyond the linkage of words. For Metastasio realized what Zeno and the earlier exponents of the exit aria had only partly apprehended: the dramaturgic function of the convention. Dramatically, the exit aria is a moment of pause and reflection, a summing-up of what has gone on before, in terms of an "affect," or emotion, or as commentary. Such a moment is by its nature indrawn and "implosive," in contradistinction to the explosive *scena*; such a moment must look backward and

---

(7) "Still in calm waters, the helmsman loses himself, as slowly, above the prow, the day drowses away. His thoughts wander, perhaps to friendly shores, but he finds himself amidst the sea swell once the day dawns."

(8) "How slowly does his generous heart/Another's crime believe,/Who ne'er himself with treacherous art,/Another could deceive!//No wonder he, whose honor tried,/From truth could ne'er descend,/Should think no treason could reside/Beneath the name of friend." I have used the late-eighteenth-century translation by John Hoole to point up the compression of Metastasio's verse, particularly next to the Drydenesque hyperbole then still fashionable in England.

never forward in time. With the termination of the expression, that particular moment is at an end and the character should leave the stage. The problem of the exit aria as it was used in *opera seria* lay not only in its rigid application, which was bound to result in a certain amount of contrivance and falsity even in so consummate a craftsman as Metastasio, but also, and primarily, in its monotonous overuse. Too many pauses for reflection engender a stop-and-go momentum that inhibits the gradual, inexorable rise to the climax of the *opera seria* libretto, and although this fact is only peripherally apparent when the eight short lines are read, or read aloud, it becomes evident immediately upon hearing the heavily ornamented vocal line to which the lines were inevitably sung.

The exit aria's function carries down through the history of the opera libretto, and "exit arias" can be found in operas long after *opera seria* as a codification of the set of rules had passed into history. A perfect, if flamboyant, example occurs in Wagner's *Die Meistersinger*, where five exit arias combine in a quintet (III, i) that is the essence of the reflective, "summing-up" nature of the form.[9]

Metastasio's dramatic use of the exit aria is evidenced throughout his works. In the great scene in *Temistocle* already referred to, Temistocle has refused to lead Serse's armies against his own countrymen and has given several ringingly patriotic speeches. The scene continues in one-line exchanges. Serse loses all patience and puts his general under arrest. "We shall see if that invincible cour-

---

(9) Wagner, as was usual with him, operated on a scale larger than that accorded to other mortals. Another good example of the exit aria function in later operas would be Renato's (Anckerstrom's) aria "*Eri tu*" in *Un Ballo in maschera*. This aria is of interest because the "scene" actually begins in the previous one, when Renato discovers that his friend the king's *amie* is his own wife Amelia. Scribe (and Somma) used the dramatic equivalent of a poetic enjambment to continue the action through the scene change to the point at which Amelia pleads to see her son before she is unjustly murdered. Renato sends her away; then, in a purely Somma-Verdi interpolation, which, as George Martin remarks in his biography of the composer (p. 345), "gives a depth to the story that Scribe did not plumb," he accuses the king rather than his wife as the prime cause of his misfortune, and goes on to lament his lost innocence. The first part of the aria is not strictly an "exit aria," but the passage from "*O dolcezze perdute*" on is, and the whole serves the function: to put a period to the scene and to reflect upon it. Of course, in both the Scribe and the Somma librettos the actual scene goes on with the introduction of the conspirators, but Metastasio (and the French classical tragedians) would have considered that a separate entity.

age can tremble," he says. Temistocle replies, *"Non è timor dove non è delitto"* ("Where there is no crime there is no fear"), a typical Metastasian conceit, and launches into his aria:

> *Serberò fra' ceppi ancora*
> *questa fronta ognor serena:*
> *è la colpa, è non la pena,*
> *che può farmi impallidir.*
>   *Reo son io: convien ch'io mora,*
> *se la fede error s'appella;*
> *ma per colpa così bella*
> *son superbo di morir.*[1]

(II, viii)

Donald Jay Grout, quoting from Willi Flemming's book *Die Oper*, says: "The recitative loads the gun, the aria fires it."[2] As long as the scene is considered the elaboration of one basic affect, or emotion, and the aria its expression, this is the case, but such a definition leaves aside entirely the dramatic movement interwoven with the characterizations, especially in Metastasio. Dramatically, the gun has been fired *before* the aria begins,[3] and the aria thus becomes a codification of what has just occurred. It cannot be emphasized too often that any considerations of the libretto which ignore its dramaturgic elements ignore the life-pulse of the work. Music can develop and strengthen that pulse, and in some cases even supply it when it is lacking in the libretto, but the basic drive must be found in the libretto.

Metastasio's favorite books were the familiar ones: Ovid, the Guarini *Pastor fido*, and Tasso's *Gerusalemme*; but the one he was said to reread before writing a libretto was Giambattista Marino's *Adone*. Marino (1569–1625), as famous a poet in his day as Metastasio became in his, saw his fame suffer a like eclipse. He wrote verse that took from every age and poet, and employed all sorts of poetic devices within a sweetly flowing line. *Marinismo*

---

(1) "Even in chains I shall maintain a placid repose: guilt, and not torture, can make me quail. I am guilty, and I should die, if honor is termed error; but for so glorious a crime, it is an honor to die."
(2) Donald Jay Grout: *A Short History of Opera* (2nd edn.), p. 187.
(3) Again, the usual disclaimer. At times during the course of an exit aria, the character makes a decision based upon the events of the earlier scene, in which case the dramatic movement extends through the aria itself.

is linked with euphuism in a general way, and can be noted in Metastasio's works in both his varied and mellifluous poetry and his use of metaphor, simile, and opposition.

Although Metastasio drew from classical sources and Italian poetry, his main dramatic inspiration came from France. Often he used the classical source as it was expressed in a French play by Racine or Corneille or by such lesser French dramatists as Crébillon, du Ryer, Lagrange-Chancel, and Houdar de La Motte. What he searched for was both a strong situation and a dramatic culmination that he could decorate with the usual trappings of love. Metastasio tried to regulate every aspect of the production, and his librettos give precise descriptions of the settings of each scene.[4]

His most productive years were those immediately following his appointment in Vienna (from 1730 to 1740), when he wrote as many as two or three librettos a year, plus assorted *azione teatrali*, oratorios, and whatever poetry needed to be produced. In these years he perfected the *opera seria* and produced what most commentators agree were his finest works. In 1740 he completed the first draft of *Attilio Regolo*, which he recognized as his masterwork in terms both of theme and of execution. Instead of allowing it to be set to music, he kept it in his study and spent the next ten years intermittently revising it. His output diminished after 1740, but he kept writing librettos until the *Ruggiero* of 1771, a product of his seventy-third year. The later librettos represent a falling-off of inspiration, although they include many fine arias and passages. As was partly the case with Quinault, once Metastasio had arrived at his formula, he was content to reproduce it and not enrich it further.[5] Exception can be made in the case of a few of his

---

(4) The scene settings were intended as backdrops to the action, a little more elaborate than the austere French classical tragedy settings, but nonetheless background. The exceptions were those scene changes which used machines—confined to the grand climaxes.
(5) As was also the case with Quinault, diversity can be detected within the homogeneity. Alessandro Donadoni, in his monograph *Dalla Didone all' Attilio Regolo* (Rome, 1897), divides Metastasio's production into four stages. The first he sees as the "tentative" stage, when the librettist was learning his craft (through *Catone in Utica* [1728]); the second, the intrigue melod amas from *Ezio* (1728) to *La Clemenza di Tito* (1734); and the third, the stage where one great figure, Attilio Regolo or Temistocle, was minutely studied. Donadoni does not discuss the librettos after *Regolo*, but it is assumed that he considered them a falling-off and a repetition of what had been produced before (pp. 13 *ff.*).

lighter works, such as the one-act *L'Isola disabitata*, whose charm and pastoral feeling, so beautifully expressed in Metastasio's verse,[6] not only look backward to the very dawn of the libretto, but also reflect the Arcadian ideal and, through that, the bourgeois village comedy librettos that were being popularized in Italy by Carlo Goldoni and in France by Charles Favart.

Any study of a Metastasian libretto, however, must place this pastoral feeling and verbal suppleness, both in his love strophes and in his exit arias, in the perspective of his organizational and dramatic abilities as a librettist. It is here that he sets himself apart from Rinuccini. Among his greatest librettistic achievements are two that he wrote in 1733: *L'Olimpiade* and *Demofoonte*. Both were originally set to music by Antonio Caldara, and the list from then on is practically endless.[7]

Metastasio derived the story of *L'Olimpiade* from Herodotus and Pausanius, but the greater part of the structure was his own invention. Licida and Megacle are friends; Licida has been in love with Argene, but his supposed father, the King of Creta, has forbidden the marriage. Argene has, in true Arcadian style, taken out her sorrow by becoming a shepherd, and Licida has, on the rebound, fallen in love with Aristea, the daughter of the King of Sicione. Now this king has made the error, like Veit Pogner after him, of offering his daughter to, in this case, the winner of the Olympian Games. Licida knows he cannot win, and so asks his

---

(6) As in this variation on the "*Ombra mai fù*" theme: "*Benchè di senso privo,/fin l'arboscello è grato/a quell'amico rivo/da cui riceve umor.//Per lui di frondi ornato/bella mercè gli rende,/quando dal sol difende/il suo benefattor*" (I, v). ("The shrub is grateful, albeit privately, to that friendly rivulet from which it receives its moisture. Covered with leaves because of this, it renders its thanks as it shades its benefactor from the rays of the sun.") Metastasio works in the "message" with his pastoral verse.

(7) In the notes to *L'Olimpiade*, Bruno Brunelli, the editor of the complete works of Metastasio remarks: "Many have considered it the most perfect of Metastasio's dramas both for the skillful handling of the story and for the nobility of its dramatic eloquence. Carducci wrote that 'all the eighteenth century joined in acclaiming the divine *Olimpiade*, in which the lyricism and the Italian songfulness joined in an unequalled and unattainable perfection'" (vol. I, p. 1496). *Demofoonte* was one of the favorite librettos of Charles Burney.

L'Olimpiade was also set by Antonio Vivaldi, Giovan' Battista Pergolesi, Johann Christian Bach, Tomas Arne, Domenico Cimarosa, and Giovanni Paisiello—to choose easily recognizable names from the list. *Demofoonte* enlisted Gluck and Paisiello.

friend, Megacle, a heroic athlete, to enroll under his name (Licida), win the games and the girl, and turn her over to him. The next twist is obvious: Megacle has long since been in love with Aristea (and she with him). The situation is thus alive with dramatic irony and all sorts of possibilities for emotion.[8]

Metastasio's opening puts forth all of this and more in his usual compressed, dramatic way. Licida, sick with impatience, is waiting for Megacle to arrive and enroll: time is growing short, and he can see the prize slipping from him if Megacle is late. In the third line, Licida's tutor exposes his student's ruling passion: "Moderate for once your violent, intolerant spirit." At last, after the two have recounted the story, Megacle appears and agrees to stand in for his friend. Megacle ends the scene with an exit aria on the merits of friendship, which have as a logical culmination the taking of a friend's name.

The scene then changes, and the two women in the libretto proceed to recount their woeful tales. Argene mentions that she was almost betrothed to Megacle; Aristea perks up at the name and admits that she has long loved him. Why can't he be summoned and win the games? asks Aristea, and both agree to try to get the King to delay the games. The King then enters and says that Licida is one of the entrants, news which makes Aristea and Argene despondent in different ways. Next Licida thanks Megacle for such a demonstration of friendship and offers him anything in reward. Embracing him,[9] he speaks the name of his beloved— and Megacle is aware of his horrible predicament. Licida exits, and, after a solo for Megacle, Aristea enters. She is overjoyed at seeing her beloved: he is torn with emotion. She senses his unease, but he cannot divulge his secret. The act ends in a duet as he departs for the games.

The two women are waiting for news of the games as the

---

(8) Notable here is the relative unimportance of the royal setting. The "aristocratic" nature of Metastasio's librettos has been overemphasized: these characters could just as well be highborn bourgeois landowners. The aristocratic elements of the libretto lie less in the fact that it involves kings than in the fact that, later, the characters will behave in a manner befitting royalty; that is, with nobility and magnanimity.

(9) Note again the stylized nature of the action: at the moment of greatest intensity in the scene the actor gives the gesture.

second act opens. In order to create suspense, Metastasio uses the fact that women were forbidden to attend the Olympic Games: when the messenger comes in, both pounce on him and interrupt him so that he can hardly stammer out his message—Licida has won. Licida's tutor tries to calm Argene, but does not succeed, and he has a pre-scene-change solo, similar to servant arias in most seventeenth-century opera, in which he comments on the vanity and instability of life.[1] The scene changes, and the King congratulates "Licida" on winning. "Licida" asks to be married in Creta, whither he wishes to return at once, leaving "Egisto" as his deputy. "Egisto" is, of course, Licida, and the King murmurs on seeing him: "What face is that? On seeing it, my blood churns in my veins"—thus giving a hint of the dénouement. Aristea enters, and is overcome with joy to find that Megacle has won, leading to the sort of cross-purposes scene which has long been the delight of playwrights. Licida wants Megacle to tell Aristea the truth, and, after sending Licida away, Megacle tells her that he is beholden to Licida, who once saved his life. He says to her, in a conceit typically Metastasian: "Haven't you said to me a thousand times that you love not my features but my greatheartedness, my sincerity, and that spark of honor which has guided all my thoughts?" It is precisely here, in the central scene of the libretto, that the difference between the *opera seria* and the middle-class opera that was to replace it is made manifest: these are people as they ought to be, not as they are, and they are meant to edify all those who watch or read of their exploits. Megacle is steadfast in his determination to sacrifice his love; womanish Aristea, distracted by passion and despair, swoons away. Megacle exits, leaving Licida behind; when Aristea wakes, she rounds on him thoroughly. Argene follows, threatening to tell the King of Licida's past love for her. Poor Licida is now himself in a state of emotion, and when his tutor comes in to tell him that Megacle has thrown himself into a river while crying his love for Aristea, Licida curses the gods. A messenger enters to inform Licida that the King knows all (Argene has made good her threat) and that he has been banished. This sets up a superb act-ending *scena* in

---

(1) The exit aria uses the image of ships abandoned to the capriciousness of wind and wave. Note again how Metastasio uses the conventions of the seventeenth-century libretto.

which Licida threatens to kill himself, the messenger, *anyone*—
the "violent, intolerant spirit" in magnificent poetry:

> *. . . Odio la vita,*
> *m'atterrisce la morte; a sento intanto*
> *stracciarmi a brano a brano*
> *in mille parti il cor. Rabbia, vendetta,*
> *tenerezza, amicizia,*
> *pentimento, pietà, vergogna, amore*
> *mi trafiggono a gara. . . .*[2]
>
> (II, xv)

The third act opens stormily, with Megacle threatening suicide and Aristea wailing to him, but the inevitable messenger
arrives to end the outbursts with news that Licida, in his madness, has attempted to kill the King, and is now a prisoner condemned to death.[3] Megacle at once decides to go to him (*"Lasciar
l'amico! Ah! così vil non sono"*—"Abandon a friend? Ah, I am
not sunk so low"). Another messenger shortly enters with the
news that Licida will be used as a sacrifice to the gods and that
Megacle has been seized and is attempting to die in his friend's
stead. Argene, who has previously been too jealous to care whether
her beloved Licida survived, is so moved by this evidence of
friendship that she resolves to emulate it. Metastasio uses this plot
twist as an example of good breeding good, central to the didactic
preoccupation of the *opera seria*. All the participants therefore
converge on the sacrificial altar, which will be the setting for the
final scene.

Licida terms his punishment entirely just, calling the King
"father" (Metastasio piles on the dramatic irony), takes leave of
his friend Megacle, and is preparing for the ax when Argene
rushes in. She has decided, she says, to substitute herself for her
husband, as Alceste did so long ago. "But you are not his wife—?"
"We were engaged—" "She is lying!" "Deny you gave me this
gold bracelet!" And the King, naturally (operatically speaking),

---

(2) "I hate my life, I am terrified of death, and I feel that my heart
is being shredded bit by bit into a thousand pieces. Rage, revenge,
affection, friendship, repentance, compassion, shame, love all vie to
torment me."
(3) Metastasio balances the scene in the accepted "classical" manner,
with Megacle being restrained at one side of the stage and Aristea
being restrained at the other. They meet in the middle.

recognizes the bracelet as the one placed around his son's neck so many years before, when he was set adrift. The mystery is unraveled: Licida is Aristea's twin, exposed because the Oracle ordered it; therefore (we are not in Wagnerian lands) he cannot marry Aristea, and is left with Argene. The King clings for a while to his upright decision that even though Licida is his son, that does not excuse his crime, but the priests open the way to a *lieto fine*.

This short recital of the details of *L'Olimpiade* glosses over the surefooted way in which Metastasio handles the story and its dénouement, and altogether ignores the poetry. The libretto well illustrates the many aspects of *opera seria*, which have been gathered under the roof of this tale of friendship. *L'Olimpiade* may seem, in its conceits and its noble approach to life, far both from reality and from our values, but it remains a masterful example of libretto writing at its most accomplished.

Demofoonte again shows Metastasio the libretto constructor at his peak. He has here joined two stories, a common one of a virgin sacrifice and that used by Houdar da La Motte in *Inès de Castro*, about the king's son who has secretly married and become a father. This conjoining adds depth to an already pregnant situation, for if the secret wife is chosen, her secret must be revealed, for it would be worse sacrilege to sacrifice someone impure. Metastasio adds the character of the girl's supposed father (unaware of his daughter's situation), who quite properly objects to putting up his daughter for sacrifice when the King's children are exempted, not by law, but because the King has contrived to keep them out of the country in safety. By objecting, the father brings down the wrath of the King, seizes the daughter as punishment and names her the sacrifice. Thus happenstance is forestalled by motivation. Metastasio's librettos have often been accused of being complicated,[4] but if they are heard or read, the complications reinforce and clarify rather than obfuscate the story. Metastasio can be justifiably accused of elaboration and of delay for the sake of emotional histrionics, but his sense of structure and his ability to characterize in pithy terms keep the audience's focus exactly where he wants it. His clear linear progression, moreover, in which one scene leads directly into the next until a

---

(4) Probably because they have been read in synopsis.

logical culmination occurs, aids this clarity. Not until Wagner would there be a librettist who could handle complexity with such assurance and dexterity.[5]

A glance at a portion of *Demofoonte* will illustrate this. The King (Demofoonte) has arranged for his son (already secretly married) to wed Creusa, and has sent another son, Cherinto, to fetch her. He, in constant contact with her, falls in love (*"Ti vidi,/t'ammirai, mi piacesti"*—"I saw you, I admired you, I fell in love with you").[6] She rejects him. Timante, the married son, tells Creusa he cannot marry her, but does not tell her why, and departs (without an exit aria). This news in turn offends Creusa's vanity and outrages her as a princess, and she demands that Cherinto be the instrument of her revenge, in return for which she will marry him. Cherinto in turn is now caught between two violently conflicting emotions. It is precisely this aspect of *opera seria* that will find its way unchanged to the *melodramma* of the nineteenth century.

Metastasio has all too often been confined to his greatest strengths, which are therefore seen as representative of his entire work: because he wrote the finest Arcadian poetry that has ever been produced for the libretto, and because he wrote it into every libretto he produced, the temptation is to consider him a happy hedonist unable or unwilling to express more than a narrow range of experience. While it is true that his placid nature and extraordinary fame led him to write too often from the top of his head, he was too great a librettist and thinker to straightjacket his poetic thought. His verse, besides having the virtues of pace and, often, nervous vigor (especially in the short-sentenced scenes of debate or question-and-answer), moved far afield from the pastorals of shepherds and their swains. Examples of his martial poetry abound in the *"all'armi"* exit arias that were staples of *opera seria;* and the following despairing cry of Timante, from *Demofoonte,* reveals the pessimistic side of Metastasio's nature:

---

(5) Beaumarchais' two great plays, both transferred to the operatic stage, are two of the very few, if any, that can approach this dexterous complexity.

(6) The Latin echo in Metastasio's verse is immediately audible. Like Marino before him, Metastasio lifted ideas and phrases from every age and tongue, much to the delight of his readers and hearers, who did not have our repugnance to what might be considered plagiarism.

Perchè bramar la vita? e quale in lei
piacer si trova? Ogni fortuna è pena;
è miseria ogni età. Tremiam, fanciulli,
d'un guardo al minacciar; siam giuoco, adulti,
di Fortuna e de'Amor; gemiam, canuti,
sotto il peso degli anni. Or ne tormenta
la brama d'ottenere; or ne trafigge
di perdere il timor. Eterna guerra
hanno i rei con se stessi; i giusti l'hanno
con l'invidia e la frode. Ombre, deliri,
sogni, follie son nostre cure; e quando
il vergognoso errore
a scoprir s'incomincia, allor si muore.[7]

(III, ii)

What is notable in this outburst is less the unexpected nature of it (if Metastasio be considered a seraphic librettist) than the limits within which Metastasio moved. He is a strong-enough librettist to be able to create and enrich the varying moods of his characters, but he remains bound inside the frame of his formula. For all the despair in the quote, the sentences are noble periods and the language remains flowing. Metastasio would never have broken up his line with sibilants or jagged sounds or imposed a pessimistic weight on it; he would never have fragmented his ideas into the, short, gasping sentences used a hundred years later by Giacomo Leopardi in his poem *"A se stesso."*[8] The limits

---

(7) "Why should we covet life? What are its charms, for all degrees are wretched? Every state partakes of misery. In infancy we tremble at a frown: in ripening youth we are made the sport of Fortune and of Love: in age we groan beneath the weight of years: now we are tormented with the thirst of gain, and now the fear of loss: eternal war the wicked with themselves maintain: the just with fraud and envy. All our schemes are shadows, vain and illusive as a sick man's dream! And when we but begin at last to know our life's whole folly, death cuts short the scene." (Hoole translation.)

(8) *"Or poserai per sempre,/stanco mio cor. Perì l'inganno estremo,/ch'eterno io mi credei. Perì. Ben sento,/in noi di cari inganni,/non che la speme, il desiderio è spento./Posi per sempre. Assai/palpitasti. Non val cosa nessuna/i moti tuoi, nè di sospiri è degna/la terra. Amaro e noia/la vita, altro mai nulla: e fango è il mondo. . . ."* ("Now you will rest forever, my weary heart. The last deceit, which I believed eternal, has perished. Perished. Truly in us not only the hope but the desire of happy illusions has disappeared. Rest forever. You have beaten enough. Your throbbings are worth nothing; neither is the earth worthy of sighs. Life is dull and bitter, nothing else, and the world is a sinkhole. . . .")

of possibility in librettistic verse had been defined by Rinuccini and Striggio: Metastasio perfected the basic musical line but never contemplated experimenting with additional concepts of musicality. Thus he bequeathed a monolithic staticity to the generations of librettists who succeeded him, and it was not until the verse of Arrigo Boito in the nineteenth century that the tyranny of the sweetly flowing line was breached, if not broken.

Metastasio's greatest achievement, his "least imperfect" libretto, is undoubtedly *Attilio Regolo* (1740–50). He realized, once he had begun work on it, that he had taken hold of a major theme that symbolized the stoic nobility of *opera seria*. He thus kept it back from production, revising and strengthening the verse for ten years until he was satisfied. The result is one of that small handful of great librettos that almost transcend the form: a work so strong in itself that it almost does not need music to accompany it. It is no accident that only four composers ever set the libretto, a minuscule number contrasted with the numerous settings of Metastasio's other works; it is also no accident that the libretto has been staged as a play—and remains in constant publication in Italy.

The question as to whether a libretto can be too strong for music is not clear-cut, although many believe it to be possible. It depends, in each case, on the librettist and upon the composer. Yet something in *Attilio Regolo*, perhaps the very quality of the poetry, made composers shy away from it. Certainly that libretto possesses throughout a measure of iron that is found only sporadically in other Metastasian librettos.[9]

---

(9) In my estimation, there is literally no work of art that cannot be effectively adapted for the operatic stage, given the understanding that great poetry will be in some sense lost when set against a musical line. Of course, certain types of librettos will always exist more as exceptions than as rules, for, although we have the example of Richard Strauss-Clemens Krauss (and others) producing *Capriccio*, the "talky" or debate libretto must remain an inordinately difficult subspecies to produce. It is also probably true that a libretto that "works" must by its very nature not possess the subtleties of a *Hamlet* or a *Lear* (or Part II of Goethe's *Faust*); yet Boito's libretto for *Amleto* is a highly creditable job and latterly even the composer Humphrey Searle has tackled *Hamlet*. No one who has the slightest knowledge of Verdi's genius with the father-daughter aspect of all his works can doubt that, had he written a Lear opera, its climax would have been as unbearable as the original. The problem is that we have not looked in the proper place for this "subtlety," which may exist in the music or in the dramaturgic handling of the themes. As far as the libretto is concerned, Hofmannsthal's dictum has a particular application: "Depth must be hidden. Where? On the surface."

The story hews closely to the Aristotelian precepts. Its single theme entirely dominates the action, and the decision of Attilio Regolo can serve as a paradigm for the entire *opera seria* preoccupation with idealized nobility. Regolo, the supreme example of Roman uprightness and virtue, has led the Roman armies in many wars and has eventually been captured by the Carthaginians. For five years he has languished in prison while Rome gradually forgets him. Only his children, Attilia and Publio, remain to prick the conscience of the state. Attilia puts it: "Carthage is not the barbarian. She only oppresses an ancient enemy, while Rome abandons a faithful citizen." Now news comes that Regolo has reappeared in Rome, brought by the Carthaginian ambassador, Amilcare. Publio recounts his arriving words: he had run up to him, crying, "*Ah, caro padre!*" Regolo had replied, "*Non son padri i servi in Roma*" ("In Rome captives are not fathers")—thus immediately establishing his incorruptible nobility. The city is wild with joy; the scene changes to the temple of Bellona.

The reason for Regolo's return is then revealed. Amilcare has brought him to help arrange an exchange of prisoners. But if the negotiations fail, Regolo has pledged his word to return to Carthage and be put to death. He arrives in the temple, and is greeted by Manlio, a consul: "Come, sit in your old seat." "But who are these?" "The elders." "And who are you?" "Have you forgotten the consul already?" "And should a slave take a seat with a consul and the elders?" "No, but Rome forgets the rigors of her laws for you, who have given her such manifold victories." "Rome may forget, but I do not." "(Who has ever seen a more rigid virtue?)"[1] Regolo then sets forth the terms, and closes by saying: "Refuse." He is an old man, useless, but Carthage would be getting back her warriors and, besides, Rome would lose honor by the deal. Let Rome arm instead and crush the Carthaginians, thus requiting his soul. Manlio says that the Senate will consider his advice.

The theme is thereby set forth: the second act will be taken up with attempts to subvert Regolo's determination. It is easy to see why the absolute monarchs of the eighteenth century would applaud such a theme, for its hero has the good of the state as

(1) The cool certainty of Regolo's questions has points of contact with the *Todesverkundigung* Scene in Act II of *Die Walküre*.

his primary concern. Yet this very attitude would go beyond the monarchic despotisms to the revolutionary governments of the next centuries, both Jacobin and Communist.[2] Napoleon may have demonstrated the essential falsity of Regolo's position, one man of genius being worth an army of foot soldiers, and Tolstoy may have demonstrated that both are irrelevant next to the irresistable forces of chance, yet Metastasio's insistence on the supremacy of love for country, not only in *Attilio Regolo* but also in other librettos, though derived from Imperial Rome cut through to the nationalistic movements that were beginning to rise. Thus, Alfieri's attitude in snubbing the old Metastasio, so correct when applied to the superficialities of Metastasio's house-dog life and to what most Enlightenment philosophers considered an archaic way in which to write operas, revealed the poet's ignorance of the substance of many of Metastasio's works. The surface foliage may have exuded a strong perfume of Watteau and Hubert Robert, but under the plains of Arcady lay veins of ore.

Regolo sets forth the theme to his son:

> *La patria è un tutto,*
> *di cui siam parti. Al cittadino è fallo*
> *considerar se stesso*
> *separato da lei. L'utile o il danno,*
> *ch'ei conoscer dee solo, è ciò che giova*
> *o nuoce alla sua patria, a cui di tutto*
> *e debitor. Quando i sudori e il sangue*
> *sparge per lei, nulla del proprio ei dona:*
> *rende sol ciò che n'ebbe. Essa il produsse,*
> *l'educò, lo nudrì. Con le sue leggi*
> *dagl'insulti domestici il difende,*
> *dagli esterni con l'armi. Ella gli presta*
> *nome, grado ed onor; ne premia il merto;*
> *ne vendica le offese; e, madre amante,*
> *a fabbricar s'affanna*
> *la sua felicità, per quanto lice*
> *al destin de' mortali esser felice.*
> *Han tanti doni, è vero,*
> *il peso lor. Chi ne ricusa il peso,*
> *rinunci al benefizio: a far si vada*

---

(2) *Attilio Regolo* was staged as a republican spectacle in Rome in 1799.

> *d'inospite foreste*
> *mendico abitatore; a là, di poche*
> *misere ghiande e d'un covil contento,*
> *viva libero e solo a suo talento.*[3]
>
> (II, i)

Regolo manages to win the consul over to his stern decision, but his children cannot accept it, and Attilia persuades the Senate to act against her father's wishes. In a long soliloquy, Metastasio allows Regolo to expose an uncertainty that his outward demeanor does not show, and which renders his character less severe.

The minor secondary plot is carefully linked with the main story. Publio loves his captive, Barce, who is also loved by Amilcare. Amilcare (acting as a barbarian should) accuses Publio of wanting his father to remain obdurate, for if Regolo were to remain in Rome, Barce would be returned to Carthage. Yet the *opera seria* conceit that good breeds good is employed to advantage: Publio, uplifted by his father's fortitude and rhetoric, magnanimously releases Barce: "Learn, barbarian, how we in Rome love!" Amilcare in turn converts to doing good; Licino (Attilia's suitor) runs off to stir up the people, and the second act ends on a note of expectation.

As the third act begins, Regolo is increasingly impatient to be gone. In a tender scene, he asks Manlio to act as father to his children.[4] News is brought that the aroused populace will not

---

(3) "Our country is a whole of which we form the part. 'Tis criminal in one that bears the name of citizen, to weigh his private weal distinct from hers. By him is nothing to be wish'd or shunn'd but what may harm or benefit that country, to which he owes his all. Whene'er he toils, or sheds his blood to serve her, from himself he nothing gives, but only renders back what he from her receiv'd. She gave him birth and nourishment: she rear'd his infant years to ripen'd manhood; with her laws protects from home-bred spoilers; with her arms defends from foreign insults: she on him bestows name, rank and honors: she rewards his merits, and vindicates his wrongs: a tender mother, she labors to procure him all the happiness which earth can yield. But blessings such as these 'tis true must have their claims, and who rejects them must give up every title to the advantage of law and social compact: let him seek the inhospitable woods, there feed contented on scanty acorns in some sordid sty, and at his will enjoy a life of freedom." (Hoole translation.)

(4) The scene provides a good example of that opposition word play which was always a part of the Metastasian libretto and which can be found in many exit arias: "You are going; we are losing you." "You should lose me if I did not go."

let Regolo leave,[5] and Manlio goes out to calm them. Amilcare, wanting to show that he can also be a hero, tells Regolo that, because of Publio's magnanimity he is prepared to turn traitor and allow his charge to escape. Being a benighted African, he does not realize that this is precisely the wrong type of magnanimity. Regolo replies: "Barbarian!" and proceeds to enlighten him on the meaning of honor and duty. Amilcare quite naturally becomes a little nettled. Attilia brings in the Senate's sophistic decision—an oath taken in captivity does not count—but Regolo makes short work of that. Barce is left on stage to voice the thoughts of the age that was succeeding Metastasio (but which Metastasio considered thoughts fit for a barbarian)—those of the man of reason: "What strange ideas does the love of praise excite in Rome! With envy Manlio views his rival's chains; while Regolo abhors the public pity that would save his life. The daughter glories in her father's sufferings; and Publio (this surpasses all belief), Publio, my beauty's slave, for honor's sake, resigns the mistress whom his soul adores." And she says in her exit aria: "But, thanks be to Heaven, I don't have a Roman soul."

The scene changes to the banks of the Tiber, where the ships are prepared to leave. The populace blocks the way, crying: "*Resti, Regolo!*" Regolo, entering, picks up their cry and flings it back to them, launching into a series of magnificent speeches to his countrymen. The cadences of these are as superb as the libretto has ever produced, as stirring as John of Gaunt's apostrophe to England in *Richard II*.

> *Roma rammenti*
> *che il suo padre è mortal, che al fin vacilla*
> *anch'ei sotto l'acciar, che sente al fine*
> *anch'ei le vene inaridir, che ormai*
> *non può versar per lei*
> *nè sangue nè sudor, che non gli resta*
> *che finir da romano.*
> . . . .

(5) The arousing of the populace was a common librettistic device in seventeenth-century opera as well as in *opera seria*, and it carries down well into the nineteenth century, especially in the *melodramma* works. It served two purposes: first, of using the chorus in a positive rather than in a mood-setting or "Greek chorus" way; second, to stir up action to prepare for the climax. In most cases, therefore, this device occurs at the end of the second act or in the first part of the third act, and sets up whatever will be the end of the opera.

Romani, addio. Siano i congedi estremi
degni di noi. Lode agli dèi, vi lascio,
e vi lascio Romani. Ah! conservate
illibato il gran nome; e voi sarete
gli arbitri della terra, e il mondo intero
Roman diventerà. Numi custodi
di quest'almo terren, dee protettrici
della stirpa d'Enea, confido a voi
questo popol d'eroi: sian vostra cura
questo suol, questi tetti e queste mura.
Fate che sempre in esse
la costanza, la fè, la gloria alberghi,
la giustizia, il valore. E, se giammai
minaccia al Campidoglio
alcun astro maligno influssi rei,
ecco Regolo, o dèi: Regolo solo
sia la vittima vostra, e si consumi
tutta l'ira del Ciel sul capo mio.
Ma Roma illesa . . . Ah! Qui si piange: addio![6]

(III, last)

Metastasio has here brought the *lieto fine* around full circle: from a god triumphing, to man triumphing, to man apotheosized and triumphing. For Regolo's final speech serves to elevate him to a godlike status of Protector of the Realm, as beneficent and omnipotent as any god in a chariot. His stage action reinforces this: he walks up the plank to the deck of the ship and looks down upon his countrymen. Metastasio's greatest contribution, however, may not be the lines themselves or the ideals they enshrine, but the one caesura in the last line. Here, Regolo is overwhelmed by emotion

---

(6) "Let Rome reflect that its father is but mortal; that now he stoops beneath the weight of years; that life creeps languid thro' his shrivvel'd veins; that he no longer now can shed his blood, or toil for her; that nought for him remains but, as a Roman ought, to meet his end. . . . Romans, farewell! and let our parting now be worthy of us. Thanks to Heaven! I leave you, and leave you Romans. Ah! preserve unsullied that mighty name, and be the arbiters of human kind, till all the world become, by your example, Romans. Guardian Gods! That watch this happy land; protecting Powers of great Aeneas' offspring! I instrust to you this race of heroes. Still defend this soil, these dwellings, these paternal walls. O! grant that valor, glory, constancy, justice and truth may ever here reside; and should some evil star, with adverse beams e'er threat the Capitol, see, mighty Gods! See Regulus—let Regulus alone be made your victim, and the wrath of Heaven be all consum'd on my devoted head: let Rome unhurt—but why these tears—farewell!" (Hoole translation.)

97

and breaks off his farewell with a short *"addio."* From being a god Regolo becomes a man; from being a figurehead he becomes human: the weight of his virtue has become literally unbearable and must be abandoned. The rest, quite appropriately, is silence.

Finally, this closing passage brings to the surface an element all too rarely visible in the work of Metastasio: a glimpse of the man himself. Whereas Busenello's works give us a portrait of him, we can grasp only the placidity and intellectual order of Metastasio —not the man himself—from his librettos. Yet Regolo's farewell to Rome is in a sense also Metastasio's: the librettist had lived twenty years in Vienna when *Attilio Regolo* was completed, and he was destined to remain there until his death. It is not far-fetched to see in Metastasio's nationalistic heroes not only a nostalgia for his native city but also a yearning to identify himself with his own, as yet unborn, nation through its Roman incarnation. Metastasio was always closer to the moral dramas of Pierre Corneille than to the psychological ones of Racine, but there is the knowledge that, even when Corneille wrote about the Cid or the Roman Horace, he was reflecting the later Sun King and the growing glory of France. The Austrian Court was content to believe that Metastasio was doing the same for the Hapsburgs, and the *Licenze* and effulgent letters of Metastasio would seek to bear this out; but the man himself was always an alien in a foreign land, fantasizing a return but not being strong enough to cut the silken cord. A portion of the unrepentant patriotism of his finest hero must be ascribed to this captive suffering.

With Metastasio's works the seventeenth-century libretto reached its own apotheosis. If *Attilio Regolo* and *L'Olimpiade* are at the opposite pole from the earthy and immediate realm of *L'Incoronazione di Poppea,* they are nonetheless the refinement and perfection of the uncounted other grandiloquent postures and multilayered bizarreries of a Minato or a Moniglia. "Perfection" was considered a measure of excellence by the eighteenth-century critics, and an attribute of perfection was to operate within a rigidly organized framework. Thus the formalities of the French classical theater were imposed upon the libretto to produce the *opera seria.* We today, not subject to the idea of perfection in art,[7] can judge much of that "perfection" more accurately as surface sheen that obscured rather than enlightened.

---

(7) The fall from grace of the painter Raphael is a good example of this change of taste over the centuries.

Yet the conventions of the *opera seria*, although removed in thought and feeling from the conventions of today, were not appreciably more rigorous in application than the conventions of the later Italian *melodramma*. The chief distinction lay not in formalism but in pace: whereas Metastasio preferred setting forth a situation and then pausing to reflect on its ramifications, the librettists of the *melodramma* concentrated on the strongly emotional moments and moved from one of them to the next with bold strokes. This brings them much closer to us; even though, in their extreme form, in some of Verdi's middle-period operas, almost all connective tissue is sacrificed to the "big moments."

The central paradox of Metastasio's career is that he was without doubt the most powerful librettist in the history of the form, in terms of influence as a librettist and as a moral force and in his commanding position vis-à-vis the composer, and yet it was during his years of greatness that the power of the librettist began to be broken. Flagrant embellishment of the exit aria by the singers antedated the librettos of Metastasio, and though he attempted to exert control over them he was largely unable to do so. Gluck and Calzabigi, realizing that reform in this area was impossible, went to revolution by excising the most flagrant violators, the *castrati*, altogether, by insisting on adherence to the notes and by hiring singers willing to take direction (to which the *castrati* replied by calling them "amateurs"). And yet, for all Gluck's good will in attempting to repurify the libretto, he accomplished its final decline from primacy by moving the focus of attention from the words to the words as defined by the music. If the singer attacked the word from one direction, the composer attacked it from another, and the librettist was forced to retrench.

All of this Metastasio never comprehended, for, having been brought up in the world of the emerging *opera seria*, he could not envisage the libretto outside its formalistic scope: even his light pastoral works reflect the conventions of the "tragic" librettos,[8] from the exit aria on down.

---

(8) Whether Metastasio's works are tragedies is open to question. George Steiner does not mention him in his discussion of tragedy in the *Death of Tragedy*, and René Guiet categorically states: "In a word, he is the author of dramas and not tragedies. For the librettos of Metastasio are, in effect, dramas on classical themes, because of their moralizing tendencies, because of their melodramatic complications, because their somber subjects carry with them happy endings;

Withal, Metastasio's astonishing achievement must be rated as the zenith of librettistic art. His body of work has been subject, over the years, to a close literary study that few other librettos, let alone librettists, could support. Certain aspects of Metastasio's works which have perforce been only touched on here could be examined almost endlessly: the variety and linguistic richness of his exit arias; his structural sureness and coiled-spring writing; the unerring dramatic instinct displayed in his reshapings of earlier librettos or plays on identical subjects. In the latter respect he is rivaled over a span of works only by Boito. Metastasio's faults unfortunately stand all too clearly etched today: they should not obscure an appreciation of his manifold qualities. He was a giant, and the libretto has only rarely seen his like since his death.

---

finally because of their grandiloquence." Guiet: *L'Évolution d'un genre: le livret d'opéra en France de Gluck à la Révolution,* p. 135.

Chapter Seven

The Eighteenth-century Italian Comic Libretto

ONE OF THE EFFECTS of the reform opera was to separate even more distinctly the comic from the serious aspects of opera. The early intermezzos and comic *lazzi*, which had grown up haphazard as offshoots of the *commedia dell'arte*, had been early incorporated into the opera of the seventeenth century. With the acceptance of the French classical esthetic, which banished all comic characters from works of "high purpose," the reform opera threw out the comic servants, venal old ladies, and all their bags of tricks, retaining only the chaste confidant, who was better able to breathe the rarefied air. Of course the *commedia* figures did not disappear any more than Zerbinetta and her gang disappear from the isle of Naxos just because Ariadne, wailing her fate, arrives. They returned to the intemezzos and short comic operas whence they came, and continued their merry existence, both in Italy and in France, developing more or less in conjunction with the continuing popularity of the *commedia dell'arte*.

This enforced separation served to accelerate the growth of a purely comic opera. In 1709, even before the reform opera had gained a prominent position, the Teatro dei Fiorentini in Naples presented a regular season of comic operas,[1] both in Italian and in Neapolitan dialect, and that practice spread to other Italian cities, particularly Venice. The reformers forbade intermezzos between the acts, but in the smaller cities there were almost certainly occasions when this rule was ignored. One of the few comic operas of the mid-eighteenth century that has survived to today, the

---

(1) Michael F. Robinson: *Opera Before Mozart*, p. 131.

Pergolesi-Federico *La Serva padrona* (1733), was itself an intermezzo, that could be given either with other comic operas or
between the acts of something more serious.[2] Notable about almost all of these productions was the quasi-amateur status of the
participants: all too often the singers were actors who could sing
rather than trained professionals (the similarity to American
musical comedy is evident). The emphasis was less upon the *fioritura* (which was left to the exit arias of the *castrati*) than upon the
freshness, comedic verve, and naturalness of the performers.

The great strength of *commedia dell'arte*, which undoubtedly
allowed the art form to continue to be popular and to develop
over the centuries of its existence, was the common touch of its
approach. Although it exaggerated all sorts of human foibles, its
situations were immediately understandable to the audiences of the
time as aspects of their own lives. The growth in importance of the
increasingly otherworldly heroes and actions of the *opera seria*
only accentuated this bond of immediacy, for whereas the seventeenth-century opera had become so preposterous that its audiences
went not to be edified but to admire the spectacle and glory in the
panoply, the *opera seria* demanded obedience. Even if the sum
total of the evening was a series of embellished exit arias, there was,
underneath it all, a lesson in the particular story which was meant
to be read at home and digested. Few would want to imitate the
castrato Farinelli, but Attilio Regolo was created to act as a model
for the reader/viewer, and such uprightness became increasingly
wearing. How nice it was to see people on stage that one knew!
How nice to laugh! And so the popularity of the comic pieces continued to grow, feeding on the backlash from the *opera seria*.

Opera buffa (which it came to be called in contradistinction
to *opera seria*) grew out of these intermezzos, parodies, and short
operas, and it grew without the focus of a single great comic composer. This was the case in both Italy and in France, where several
secondary composers contributed to the rise of comic opera but, as
was the case with *opera seria*, it was the librettist who did more
to focus attention on the form. Yet in Italy far more than in

---

(2) *La Serva padrona* achieved its fame because it became the basis
for the quarrel between the Encyclopedists and the lovers of *"tragédie"*
in France. Yet the situation of the opera was present in many intermezzos written before it, and derived ultimately from a *commedia*
plot.

France, the comic opera librettists were largely anonymous.[3] *Opera buffa*, growing as it did from the tradition-created *commedia dell'arte* and the intermezzos between the acts of more pretentious works, had always maintained a far greater degree of anonymity of authorship than *opera seria*, both because the actual "creation" was more a cobbling-up of various pre-existing situations than a work to which the author wished to perpetuate his name, and because the form itself was considered, by those who wrote about opera, to be largely beneath contempt. When Baron Grimm and Diderot turned the spotlight of intellectual appreciation on the Italian comic opera, they saw it as a triumph of the bourgeois taste for the immediate as opposed to the aristocratic taste for the pompous legendary, and in their writings on *La Serva padrona* did not bother to single out the librettist for praise. Indeed, it is doubtful if they ever knew who he was. What was being praised was the approach and the style, not the individual. This attitude toward comic operas persisted until well into the nineteenth century. Only recently, for instance, have we determined the authorship of one of the finest of the *opera buffa* librettos that is played today, *Don Pasquale*.[4] Although Metastasio's name appeared in large type on every one of his librettos offered for sale, the names of authors of comic operas of the same time only rarely appeared, and then most often through such pseudonyms as Polisseno Fegeio, Sogol Cardoni, Aldimiro Clog, Calindo Grolo, Loran Glodici. If these names did appear, they all led back to one name that many of them more or less anagramatically spelled: Carlo Goldoni, the father of the *opera buffa*.

In his time Goldoni had nowhere near the influence as a librettist that Metastasio or even Zeno did, because he was recognized primarily for his plays and his championship of reforms of the *commedia dell'arte*. He wrote fewer librettos because the pay

---

(3) As can be seen, there was a great amount of artistic communication between Italy and France in the comic as well as in the serious opera. Each country had its own distinctive flavor, but cross-fertilization was widespread. This was doubtless aided by the facts that French was spoken throughout educated Piedmont, in Bologna, and in Rome, and that, even despite Zeno's efforts at Italianization, France was still looked to as a cultural beacon.

(4) Giovanni Ruffini (as well as Donizetti himself). For a long time the libretto was thought to be by Michele Accursi (who still appears as author in the Ricordi score), or entirely by Donizetti (see Ernest Newman: *Opera Nights*).

was less, and many of those he did write he published under pseudonyms such as the ones above.[5] Yet we can now see that Goldoni stands at the threshold of the flowering of *opera buffa,* and that his personal imprint upon the form, in terms of both his librettos and his plays, was to effect comic opera until the twentieth century.

Carlo Goldoni may properly be called the first modern librettist, for, leaving aside the special case of Busenello, he is the first major librettist whose undiluted influence can be seen and appreciated today. His librettos do not appear in operas in the repertory, and none may be as accomplished as the finest which have followed his lead, but Goldoni stands as godfather to *Le Nozze di Figaro, Il Matrimonio segreto, Il Barbiere di Siviglia, L'Elisir d'amore,* and countless other works in the same genre.

Goldoni's fame lies almost exclusively in the realm of his Venetian comedies. Whether he consciously set out to reform the *commedia dell'arte* of his time—which had fallen into the decadence of excess and domineering actor-control—or whether his natural artistic taste led him to purge the theater of what may be called the "seventeenth-century operatic" elements is immaterial: what he accomplished in the city of Venice was little short of a revolution within the *commedia.* Like the *opera seria* reformers, he insisted on a greater adherence to a written text and a more logical coherence of the parts, and he tried to break the actors to the harness of the author's wishes.[6] The paradox was that although in his time Carlo Goldoni was considered the destroyer of the *commedia* tradition, particularly by the faction consisting of the Gozzi brothers, he today is seen as the embodiment of the *com-*

---

(5) Goldoni preferred using his "pastoral name," Polisseno Fegeio (or Fegejo), which appears on the majority of his librettos of the period and later. Vittorio Nivellini: "Goldoni," *La Scala,* Milan [November 1957]) suggests that he used pseudonyms in order to attack the opera of his time, but this seems unlikely, as the anagrams were easily decipherable and Goldoni never saw fit to hide his identity when he was attacking the mores of his time in his plays.

(6) Although Goldoni's insistence on adherence to the wishes of the playwright was considered radical in its day, we should not be tempted into the opposite position that Goldoni never allowed improvisation. In the libretto to *Il Ciarlatano* (1759; m., Giuseppe Scolari), there is a direction to one of the participants to do what must have been one of the standard *lazzi.* Indeed, without improvisation, the entire comic spirit would have been lost.

media, particularly in plays such as his famous *Il Servitore de due padroni* (1746).[7] This is because the *commedia dell'arte* as an art form had grown to encompass a wide variety of theatrical approaches, all of which rested on the improvisational abilities of the actors. Goldoni chose to institutionalize certain aspects of the *commedia*—particularly the human aspects—to curtail the improvisations, and to discard the elements of fantasy and magic, as well as the masks that contributed to its fantastic spirit. These in turn were championed by Count Carlo Gozzi, as we shall later see. Although there is little doubt that Goldoni was spurred on by the general reforming urge that was spreading from France through Italy, his reforms took another turn. Dealing in the less prestigious (and therefore less aristocratic) area of the comic play, he chose to return it to its own home: that of the people themselves. Thus he emphasized the human element in all of his comic works, in terms of characters who may reflect *commedia* types but were also portraits of "the person next door" in terms of use of local (i.e., Venetian) dialect and expression, sets that represented actual places and not stylized locales, and all sorts of touches meant to imitate the middle-class life of the period. All of this was in direct contradistinction, not only to the fantastic aspect of the *commedia*, but also to the aristocratic, otherworldly poses of the reform opera. Yet Goldoni was still not content: he went even farther. Applying himself to the world around him in Venice, he also began to comment on its faults, which was of course a Venetian prerogative dating back to Busenello and earlier. He wrote plays that leveled attacks on certain aspects of the social structure, such as the *cicisbeo* craze.[8] These moral overtones may be echoes of the

---

(7) Which was used as the basis for an opera libretto as recently as 1967 (m., Vittorio Giannini).

(8) A *cicisbeo*, or "gallant," was a man who escorted a married woman in public because it was considered unfashionable for her husband to appear with her. As can be imagined, this was only the minimum duty of the *cicisbeo*, who usually infested the house of his lady as well, and who had to ward off attacks from other aspiring *cicisbei*, all of whom operated on the brittle and superficial level of society badinage. Goldoni thoroughly detested the vogue, and returned to it constantly in his works, but in the nouveau-riche houses of Venice it was considered a trapping of elegance and style to keep such a butterfly. The craze spread from Italy, and is referred to by the revolution-minded servant Gérard as an aspect of 1789 France in Act I of Luigi Illica's libretto for Giordano's *Andrea Chénier*.

implacable moralities of *opera seria*, but they added an element of purpose to the comic play—and comic libretto—which was to flower with Beaumarchais and find a latter-day example in Giovacchino Forzano's libretto for Puccini's *Gianni Schicchi.*

Carlo Goldoni was born in Venice in 1707 and, although like Metastasio he studied law, was also early seduced by the attractions of the theater. He began his theatrical career by writing the French-type tragedies then in vogue, but they brought him little success. It was not until he turned to writing comedies that he became famous, and then his renown in Venice carried his name and his comedies throughout Italy. In one historic year he contracted with a theatrical company to write sixteen works for production and, although the effort almost caused a physical collapse, he kept his bargain, producing many of his best works in that one season. In 1762, for a combination of reasons (he had been offered a position in Paris, he had finished his pioneering work in Venice, and he was beginning to be outshone by the rival playwright Carlo Gozzi) he left his native city and emigrated to France, where he lived the rest of his life. He wrote several plays in French for the French comic theater, was pensioned by Louis XVI, wrote his memoirs (in French), and survived until the French Revolution cut off his funds. He died in penury in 1793, at the age of eighty-five, the day before the revolutionary Convention, at the instigation of the poet André Chénier, voted to restore his pension.

Goldoni's librettistic work is everywhere a reflection of his work for the theater. He reworked several of his plays as opera librettos—notably, his adaptation of Samuel Richardson's *Pamela: Pamela nubile* (1750), which became *La Buona Figliuola* (also sometimes *La Cecchina*). It was set by Egidio Duni in 1757 and forgotten; was reset by Niccolò Piccinni in 1760 to become one of the most popular *opere buffe* of the eighteenth century.[9]

As in his theatrical writing, which began with serious plays, Goldoni began his librettistic career with *opere serie*. In his memoirs he describes how he took his libretto *Gustavo Vasa* (1740) to Zeno, who had by then returned to Venice from Vienna, and how Zeno politely dismissed it with mild approval. Goldoni changed some specifics and the opera was given, but he notes that he told

---

(9) The seal of its success was set in 1771, when the opera was the subject of a parody in France.

himself: "This isn't my genre; I'll have my revenge with my first comedy."[1]

Goldoni drew extensively on the *commedia dell'arte* for his situations and humor as well as for the loosely strung-together structure of the comic form, which consists of the thread of a plot hung with the pearls of each comic situation. Goldoni was not, of course, the only comic librettist to glean from this fertile source, but his ability outshone all others. The popularity of his plays made him known, and his stated desire to revivify and prune the ancient art form served to fix his name (no matter how he chose to disguise it) in the minds of educated Italians. Most of the *lazzi* he picked up from the *commedia* found their way down through generations of comic operas, and can be easily recognized.

First are the various uses (or non-uses) of speech. The mute servant had always been a popular buffo character (he also appears in *La Serva padrona*). On the other hand, Goldoni used a variety of accents, as well as dialects, for comic purposes. Speaking Italian, a German could be counted on to bumble up the language with exquisite oafishness; Goldoni extends this through various dialects and baby-talk to writing stretches of a libretto in French, it being assumed that most of the audience either knew the language or could grasp the gist of what was being said.[2] There was also, predominantly, a calculated irreverence, usually centered on the servant Arlecchino (or Truffaldino), but also in all probability influenced as well by the free-and-easy atmosphere of eighteenth-century Venice.[3] One of Goldoni's most popular librettos, *Il Mondo della luna* (1750; m., Baldassare Galuppi, known as "Il Buranello" —also set, later, by Haydn), is in part a satire on *opera seria*, with its distant locales, grandiloquent costumes, and use of machinery.

The impact of *opera seria* had been too strong not to carry

---

(1) Despite what he said, Goldoni did not abandon the genre: he continued to write *opere serie*, though few in number, throughout his Venetian career. *Gustavo Vasa* was not his first libretto, which seems to have been *La Generosità politica* (1736; m., Giovanni Maria Marchi), and he wrote several more before 1740.
(2) It is possible that Goldoni realized what operagoers today take for granted: that it makes little difference to the grasping of the plot whether a majority of the words are understood or not.
(3) April Fitzlyon, in her biography of Da Ponte, *The Libertine Librettist*, says that the gondoliers of Venice were given all empty places free at the opera, and that they had the power to make or break an operatic performance. She says that Goldoni often wrote specifically to please them (pp. 30–1).

over to some extent into the Goldoni librettos (and other comic librettos of the time). The *commedia* itself had long made a distinction between the two "serious lovers" (usually of the upper class) and the rest of the buffo characters, and this distinction was transferred to the libretto, which, in the cast lists, separated the *parti serie* from the *parti buffe*. The love scenes of the serious lovers are couched in the Arcadian verse of the love scenes of Metastasio, though often with a touch of irony, and the two are often brought together at the end of the opera less by their own actions than by the machinations of a servant or some other buffo character.[4] The exit aria and the mid-act *scena* were also common, and although their use in comic opera is more flexible than in *opera seria*, Goldoni was careful to apportion the arias so that each character got no more than his just share, in rotation, just as Metastasio had done.

Yet comic opera was developing its own language in opposition to that of *opera seria*. Whereas the Metastasio librettos never used ensembles, comic opera depended on them, and they gravitated to the ends of acts. Often a Goldoni libretto would open with a chorus, a procedure very rare in *opera seria;* this trait would become a feature of the *melodramma* librettos. The cardinal distinction between the two types of libretto, however, remained the entire opposition of their worlds. Goldoni's world was the world of Italy of his time, and in re-creating it on stage—with actual Venetian streets reproduced in detail—he outraged not only the champions of the "classic" *commedia dell'arte* but also the champions of the "classic" theater, for the everyday was considered beneath the dignity of the theater. The same world can be seen in his librettos, which abound in such bourgeois characters as perfume and toothpaste sellers, custodians of public baths, peasants, workers, café owners, and hunters. The language they used was also more straightforward, being manipulated for comic purposes rather than for poetic similes of wind and wave. The *commedia* stock of bombinating epithets of insult—"*Birboncello!*" "*Bricconaccia!*" "*Furbacchiotto!*" and the like—was likewise transferred to the operatic stage.[5] Goldoni knew the value of fast give-and-

---

(4) A hundred years earlier Molière had made the same distinction.
(5) It can be quickly heard that the language of comedy is richer than the language of high-flown poetry, and this doubtless added to the musicality of the ensemble.

take for comic purposes, and his large and varied vocabulary provided as much amusement as the antics of his buffo artists.

Goldoni's characters, if exaggerated, were always entirely natural. The French comic libretto, as we shall see, tended toward the pastoral, especially in the portraits of the *soubrettes*, who seemed carved out of sugar; but Goldoni kept his young ladies closer to reality. Porporina, in *Il Negligente* (1749), refuses to float on a cloud of love:

> Io mi vuò maritar. Pasquino è vero
> e' un poco sempliciotto; ma tal volta
> un mezzo scimunito
> suol esser per la donna un buon marito.[6]
>
> (I, v)

Just as Goldoni kept his characters as close as possible to their everyday counterparts, he chose only those elements of the *commedia lazzi* and stock scenes which corresponded to recognized situations. In his memoirs he reminisces about one of his early loves: "I understood that she couldn't see me in her house without her parents' knowledge, and that if I wanted to speak to her from the street, at night, she would spend some time listening to me from her window. It was an old custom in Italy to pay court under the stars, and one had to conform to it."[7] The operatic equivalent of this courting is the night-time serenade under the balcony, and in Goldoni's librettos the serenade appears with regularity. One of its manifestations occurs in the beginning of *Il Ciarlatano*, where the lover has to pay off his hired serenaders: "Go! Oh? Aren't you satisfied? . . . I'm not going to give you any more! . . . Rabble!" This scene was neatly appropriated by Sterbini in his libretto for Rossini's *Il Barbiere di Siviglia*, although there the lover is more generous.[8] Another familiar scene that crops up constantly in

---

(6) "I want to get married. Pasquino, it's true is a little weak-minded, but often a half-wit could be a good husband for a girl." Note, however, that Porporina is a servant lover: Goldoni's "aristocratic lovers" generally breathe the Metastasian air.

(7) *Mémoires* (*Mercure de France* edn., 1965), p. 78. Casanova's memoirs, written at the end of the eighteenth century, also detail amorous adventures which in complexity seem derived straight from comic opera.

(8) Hired players do not appear either in the Beaumarchais play or in the Petrosellini libretto for Paisiello, which is a more faithful adaptation of Beaumarchais than Sterbini's.

Goldoni and other librettos of the time and later, both in Italy and in France, is the "heart like a clock" simile, in which the lover compares his beloved's heart to a clock which goes tick-tock, and then tries to feel it and listen to it.[9] Whether or not this grew out of a *commedia lazzi*, it was widely used in librettos because the composer could then "put the clock in the orchestra."

Goldoni's librettos were usually written in haste, often being adaptations of his own or other plays, and he was not above cobbling up his earlier efforts with bits and pieces from other work. The Venetian composer Baldassare Galuppi set about twenty of Goldoni's librettos, and some of them were set by more than one composer. Goldoni of course was not the only hand to change his librettos, for just as the *castrati* reserved the right (out of Metastasio's presence) to substitute or augment exit arias in *opera seria*, so the leading buffo player of the company reserved the right to include *commedia* scenes he was famous for, which would be set by the local composer. The pastiches that resulted would be pastiches of word as well as of music. Nevertheless, even in that time of laxity and freedom there was beginning to be a closer relationship between the composer and the librettist in the minds of the audience. Metastasio might consider Hasse his favorite composer, but that did not prevent other men from setting his works. Yet as the music grew in importance, so that it became identified with the particular libretto, such changes could occur less and less. Goldoni's *La Buona Figliuola* was famous throughout Europe in the Piccinni version, and Gluck's settings, especially of *Orfeo ed Euridice*, obliterated all others.

Goldoni's themes were those of the *commedia*, and were also known as comedies of intrigue. The generation gap figured largely, either between parents (grandparents or tutors) and their young, whom, the former thought, they knew best how to educate, marry, and provide for, or between old widowers and new wives. Other themes were: nouveau-riche merchants or landowners at the mercy

---

(9) The tick-tock scene is remembered because of its use in *Don Giovanni*, but it continues until the late nineteenth century. Henri Meilhac and Ludovic Halévy fashioned part of their play *Le Réveillon* around a man who uses his pocket watch to compare ticks with his inamorata's heart, and it triumphantly survives in Carl Haffner and Richard Genée's adaptation of the play *Die Fledermaus* for Johann Strauss.

of sophisticated charlatans; young minx servants with their eyes on the patron—the stuff of eternal comedy. Disguises were extremely popular (as they always had been) to gull the unwary: often disguise was used to invoke faraway lands and peoples— or to satirize the *opera seria*. All, of course, ended happily, in a grand ensemble, even when there seemed less to indicate a happy conclusion than in some "tragic" operas.

Whereas other librettists let these plots prescribe the limits of their possibilities, Goldoni constantly added to them his sharpened moral sense and view of society. His libretto for *La Contessina* (1743; m., Giacomo Maccari) not only attacks the insufferable *hauteur* of the titled aristocracy, but also takes a few swipes at Goldoni's favorite target, the *cicisbei*.[1] Count Baccellone Parabolano[2] has a daughter to whom the rich merchant Pancrazio wishes to marry his son Lindoro.[3] The Count is openly contemptuous of the suit: "*Rider mi fai, povero babuino. . . . Và, che il padre tu sei de Mamaluchi.*"[4] His daughter is a replica of her father, extraordinarily affected, attracted by titles, and, of course, ultrasensitive. Lindoro offers her his hand. "Excuse me, is your glove clean?" "I just put it on." "I have to confess to you that if I should touch a glove that was not perfectly clean, I would be seized with the vapors." She also avers that her nobility is offended if she allows herself to talk to the lower classes for more than a fleeting moment. Pancrazio disguises his son as the Marchese Cavromano, and when the little Countess asks him about *cicisbei*, he replies by castigating them. Once the Count has given his daughter to the supposed nobleman, Pancrazio gleefully uncovers the deception, upon which the Count, indignant, reneges. This gives Pancrazio the chance to refuse to demean *himself* by allowing his son to marry such a woman, which he does by using the same

---

(1) The fact that the aristocracy had less control over the affairs of Venice than they had in other cities probably allowed Goldoni to get away with more direct attacks on them. They revenged themselves by siding with (Count) Carlo Gozzi.

(2) Goldoni had as much fun with the names of his characters as he did with his own pseudonyms.

(3) Lindoro and Rosina were both popular names for young lovers and reappear throughout the eighteenth century.

(4) "You make me laugh, you poor baboon. Go! You are the father of mamelukes!" Note the use of the second person singular, reserved for social inferiors.

words as the Count. Goldoni tacks on a happy ending,[5] but
he has already had his fun at the expense of the aristocracy—and,
incidentally, with the idea of *l'amour raffiné*, which had been
satirized long before in France by Molière in *Les Précieuses
ridicules* (1659).

Goldoni's verse is undoubtedly the best comic verse written
for opera up to that time, and holds its own with any successor in
Italian. It is graceful, straightforward, and extremely fluent—almost
effortless—but its value lies less in its lyricism than in Goldoni's
constant felicitous turns of phrase. Goldoni realized that the spark
for comedic writing lay in outrageous ideas coupled with amusing
word-music (a recipe that was to be put to use by the nineteenth-
century French comic librettists and, quintessentially, by William
Schwenk Gilbert), but under the piquancy and élan of his words
lurks the constant comic spirit of irony and parody. Undoubtedly,
the basis for much of this parody has been lost, but the attitudes of
the time and the postures of *opera seria* provided ample targets
for Goldoni's wit. His imagination was constantly at work, as witness this excerpt, in which a miser speaks of his casket of valuables:

> *Il mio core poverino,*
> *che stà lì nel cassettino,*
> *mi trattiene, a se mi chiama,*
> *e il mio fegato, che l'ama*
> *senza cuore non può star.*
> *Anco l'ala de' polmoni*
> *voglion dir le sue ragioni,*
> *e i budelli, poverelli,*
> *fanno in corpo, gran rumore,*
> *perchè il cuore vuol cercar. . . .*[6]
> (*Arcifanfano*, 1750; m., Galuppi; I, i)

A closer look at one of Goldoni's librettos will reveal both
the extent to which its structure still looks to the *opera seria* and the

---

(5) Or, at least, everyone is seemingly happy. Query as to how happy
Lindoro will remain, married to a type like La Contessina, or how
happy the Count will be, having to contend with Pancrazio as an in-
law. There is an opening for a sequel: a fact Beaumarchais—and
others—took advantage of.
(6) "My poor little heart, which lies there in the casket, holds me
back and calls to me, and my liver, which loves it, cannot live without
its heart. Then my lungs clamor for attention, and my poor intestines
set up a howl inside my body because they want to search out my
heart."

extent to which the comic devices he used were forerunners of similar ones in operas that remain in the repertory. Indeed, the continued success of Mozart's operas and the comic operas of the early nineteenth century can mislead the unwary into assuming that Da Ponte and Romani invented when they were merely re-using clichés that had been worn thin over many generations. Goldoni did not invent them either, but he codified them and, be-cause of his wide reputation throughout Italy as a playwright, his works were read until well after his death. In all probability the works of Bertati, Petrosellini, and Da Ponte would not have been greatly different without Goldoni's example, but they certainly benefitted from his comedic and dramatic precepts.

Lo Speziale (*The Apothecary*), which Goldoni wrote in Bologna in 1729, and which was set by Vincenzo Pallavicini (first act) and Domenico Fischetti (second and third acts), begins with Mengone, the apothecary Sempronio's servant, bewailing his fate: *"tutto il giorno pista, pista,/O che vita amara e trista!"*[7] He loves his master's pupil, Grilletta, who loves him: she is the typical Goldoni minx. Sempronio, of course, is also in love with her, as is Volpino; while the "serious lover" Lucindo is in love with Sem-pronio's daughter, Albina.[8] Mengone, who now appears, delivers a "catalogue aria" of the remedies available in his shop. This type of aria was almost a standard occurrence in comic opera, and could either involve lists of faraway places[9] or catalogues of other kinds. Volpino is hanging around the shop hoping to see Grilletta, but hides while Lucindo and Albina have a tender love scene, which ends in a classic exit aria for Lucindo. Grilletta then straightens out Albina on the subject of love, and makes a pact with her: "You with Lucindo, and I with Mengone, will win the battle of Love, and the loser will be Sempronio." Albina sings an exit aria and leaves. Volpino immediately comes out of hiding, but Grilletta says that her tutor has forbidden her to talk with anyone. Volpino

---

(7) "All day mixing, grinding, mixing, grinding, what a sad and bitter life!"

(8) The involuted complexities of the lovers probably owes something to *opera seria* habits.

(9) There seems to have been a great interest in eighteenth-century Europe in the customs and habits of distant lands, which is reflected time and again in the libretto, both for *opera seria* and for *opera buffa*. Sempronio, for instance, talks of "an invention from the Mo-lucca Islands to make wigs out of wire"—an amusing conceit in itself, as if the islanders habitually wore wigs as the Europeans did.

113

works himself into a rage, and to an empty stage sings a *gran' vendetta scena*. This *scena* heralds, as it does in *opera seria*, a change of scene (to an interior room). Mengone delivers himself of a homely thought that is as inseparable a part of the bourgeois libretto as the magnanimous attitude is of the *opera seria* libretto: "*Ho fatto la fatica,/ho fatto le ricetta,/e poi non ho trovato più nessuno./Il cielo gli ha inspirati,/perchè se gli ammalati/prendean tai medicine, ho ben paura,/che andassero a guarire in sepoltura.*"[1] Grilletta enters, and tries to get Mengone to make love to her, but he is afraid of being caught by Sempronio. Just as she manages to get him to hold her hand, in comes the apothecary, and she pretends to be taking Mengone's pulse, as he looks ill. Sempronio comes over and also takes his pulse. Such a moment is probably directly taken from a *commedia lazzi*, and depends for its humor on timing and acting ability (Mengone's bashfulness, Grilletta's insistence, then her nimble transference of the hand-holding to a pulse-taking, while Mengone fumbles in terror). Sempronio puts them to work: there is a trio in which Mengone compares the powder he is grinding and Grilletta the leaves of the herbs she is cleaning to the amount of their love for each other,[2] while Sempronio dreams on about the division of faraway lands among the King of the Tartars, the King of the Indies, and the Prince of the Mogul Empire. Sempronio goes out to get a map, then a compass, and all the while the lovers edge closer to each other. Finally, of course, Sempronio catches them holding hands, and there is a fast finale.

Sempronio is now in a fury, and rejects the suits of both Lucindo (for Albina) and Volpino (for Grilletta). Volpino sings a witty cautionary ditty,[3] while Lucindo reacts with the vapors

---

(1) "I have done my job, I've made up the prescriptions, and now I can't find anyone. The gods have inspired them, for if the sick had ever taken such medicine, I'm afraid that they would have gone to their cure in the grave."

(2) The exit aria simile reduced to a plebeian level.

(3) "*Un certo Tuttore/in Francia vi fù,/che certa Pupilla/voleva far giù./E un certo amatore,/che amore ferì,/al caro Tuttore/diceva così./Se voi la negate/con tal crudeltà;/saran bastonate/ma senza pietà.*" ("There was a certain tutor in France who wanted to discipline a certain pupil. And a certain lover [whom love had wounded] said the following to the dear tutor: 'If you dare contradict her with such cruelty, you'll be roundly beaten, and without pity.'")

of *opera seria*,[4] which Sempronio says makes him laugh. Grilletta, disgusted with the fear-ridden Mengone, threatens to go off with Volpino, and Mengone in turn takes up with Cecchina (a passing herbseller). Grilletta is thereby made jealous, and Mengone becomes ever more distraught, giving vent to the standard "woman drives man mad" soliloquy as a *scena* before the scene change. Sempronio asks Grilletta to marry him, and she accepts—to infuriate Mengone further. Volpino enters disguised as a notary, and is followed by Mengone, who has found enough presence of mind to disguise himself as a notary also. They put their own names on the marriage document as husbands, which leads to the ensemble finale.

In the third act, Lucindo has concocted a letter which asks Sempronio to become Royal Druggist to the King of the Moluccas. Because Sempronio has always been fascinated by these distant lands, he happily accepts. Grilletta and Mengone are reconciled, but not before some additional fencing,[5] and the stage is set for the gulling of Sempronio, a scene that had long been a standard *commedia* laugh-getter. All of the cast enter, dressed *à la turque*, and there is a mock marriage ceremony in which both girls marry "Turks." In this pre-echo of *Così fan tutte* (as well as of *Falstaff*), those in disguise turn out to be the lovers, much to the fury of Dr. Caius–Volpino and the discomfiture of Sempronio, who had hoped to get rich in the Indies. The merry ensemble ends the opera.

The merits of the Goldoni librettos (of which there are over seventy), aside from their nimble verse and clarity of expression, lie in the vivacity and pace at which they move. The scenes themselves are as expertly constructed for comic purposes as Metastasio's are for serious purpose, and even at their most acerbic the librettos radiate a sunniness that would warm the Italian libretto for generations. Goldoni was incapable of not being funny, and his revivification of the *commedia dell'arte* spirit took root and flowered

---

(4) Goldoni neatly satirizes the hyperbole of the verse in one line: "*Cadere a' vostri piè morto, e svenato*" ("I'll fall at your feet dead, and in a swoon").

(5) Goldoni binds this scene with a visual aid, a ribbon (meant as a present from Mengone to Grilletta) which Mengone throws away. Eventually, both stoop to pick it up, and the libretto directs that this is to be done "with *lazzi*."

where Metastasio's attempted revivification of the "classic" spirit was doomed to eventual failure. Because Goldoni was the first of the modern librettists, his importance to the form cannot be overestimated.

This chapter would not be complete without a consideration of Goldoni's great Venetian theatrical and esthetic rival, the critic Count Carlo Gozzi (1720–1806). Although Gozzi wrote no librettos, he nevertheless exerted an influence on the form as long-lasting as that of his compatriot. As a literary critic, an aristocrat, and a conservative-minded artist, Gozzi was fundamentally opposed to Goldoni's systematic attack upon the *commedia* and his championing of the bourgeois virtues. What Gozzi saw in the *commedia* was precisely what Goldoni chose to reject. He liked its "mask" qualities: its fantasy and magic, its disjunct, often illogical pattern, the improvisatory nature of its comic moments—all the qualities that removed the action on stage from a picture of everyday life and transformed it into an illusory "diversion for an evening." He claimed that, far from being passé, this approach to the *commedia* could still bring in audiences—as many people as, or more, than flocked to see Goldoni's work—and to prove it he wrote what he called a *fiabe*, or fable, *L'amore delle tre melarancie* (*The Love of the Three Oranges*) (1761),[6] which expounded his theories while satirizing Goldoni and his followers by putting them on stage. Venice of course did fill the theater, and continued to fill it for Gozzi's subsequent *fiabi*, and when Goldoni left the city, Gozzi felt that his position had been vindicated.[7] Yet, as the history books of the theater are fond of saying, it was a Pyrrhic victory,[8] for Goldoni's plays and the ideals he espoused had swept to such success throughout Italy and beyond, that the bourgeois approach and not that of illusion and magic was to dominate the stage from then on.

Although Gozzi's fables did not serve to found a school of

(6) The title itself is part of Gozzi's satiric attack.
(7) The success of Gozzi's play was one of the reasons for Goldoni's departure from Venice, but it is inaccurate to say, as most books still do, that he was driven out of the city by Gozzi.
(8) A rather cattily extreme but representative opinion can be found in Vernon Lee's *Studies of the Eighteenth Century in Italy*, which as a book accurately reflects English nineteenth-century attitudes toward the Italian *settecento*: "[Gozzi's] plays have long since been forgotten, as a sort of posthumous retribution for his injustice towards a greater man than himself" (p. 45).

other fantasists, they remained in intermittent production, not in Italy but in Germany, where the blend of illusion and low comedy was always esteemed. Goethe and Schiller were among the Germans who early hailed Gozzi's genius; Schiller translated and adapted his works and the author of *Faust* himself directed a production of *Turandot*[9] at Weimar in 1804. As the century of enlightenment gave way to the age of Romanticism, the young Romantics began to see in Gozzi's work the type of unshackled imagination[1] that they themselves cultivated. These men were less interested in the puppet nature of the characters and welcomed the negation of real life that they found in Gozzi. The great German storyteller and opera-composer E. T. A. Hoffmann first saw the natural link between Gozzi's *fiabi* and the operatic stage. He puts in the mouth of the composer Lothar the following: "Think of the incomparable Gozzi. In his dramatized fairy tales he had succeeded perfectly in what I ask of a librettist, and it is incredible that this rich vein of operatic subjects has not thus far been exploited."[2] Hoffmann was prophetic, but not until the twentieth century did Gozzi's fables undergo a critical reappraisal and form the basis for an appreciable number of operas.[3] Yet even before this, the growth of a tradition of fairy-tale opera in Russia, and to a lesser extent in Bohemia and Germany, though it cannot be traced to the influence of Gozzi, must nevertheless invoke him as its esthetic forebear. In most adaptations, though the Gozzi play has been shortened and simplified, these operas reproduce Gozzi's anti-Goldonian world with surprising accuracy and fidelity,[4] almost as if Gozzi himself had adapted his own plays: thus demonstrating the inherent truth of Hoffmann's comment. It is symbolically apposite that Prokofiev's utilization of

---

(9) Italian spelling, *Turandotte*.
(1) Vernon Lee characteristically calls it "chaos" (p. 45).
(2) From the *Serapions-Brüder*, as quoted in Oliver Strunk: *Source Readings in Musical History*, p. 789. Lothar singles out Gozzi's fable *Il Corvo*, which has as yet not been made into a libretto.
(3) The nineteenth century saw an opera by Wagner (*Die Feen*), among others; the twentieth has produced operas by Busoni and Puccini (both *Turandot*), Prokofiev (*The Love of Three Oranges*), and Hans Werner Henze *König Hirsch*, i.e., *Il Re cervo*.
(4) The Puccini setting of *Turandot* (l., Giuseppe Adami, Renato Simoni, and Puccini) is appreciably different. Interestingly, Hofmannstahl used the names of several of the characters from Gozzi's *Turandotte*, as well as several of its situations, in his elaborate fairy tale, *Die Frau ohne Schatten*.

Gozzi's first fable should join the Russian tradition of fairy-tale opera and its spiritual source.

Venice in the seventeenth century had produced Busenello and Zeno, and in the eighteenth Goldoni and Gozzi. There are areas of libretto writing that none of these explored, but no other city produced representatives who divided so great a part of the world of the libretto among them. Comic and serious, formal and sprawling, aristocratic and bourgeois, worldly and fantastic, immediate and timeless—this is the legacy left by her sons. Florence may have been the cradle of the libretto, but if the art form has a home, it is Venice.

Chapter Eight

The Eighteenth-century French Comic Libretto

Lᴋᴇ ɪᴛs Iᴛᴀʟɪᴀɴ ᴄᴏᴜɴᴛᴇʀᴘᴀʀᴛ, French comic opera grew up apart from the world of serious opera, though it fed on that rich source for parodic material, but during the course of the eighteenth century it expanded and developed to a far greater degree than its transalpine cousin.[1] Its precursor, the various *vaudevilles* that played the fairs or were the repertoires of touring troupes, achieved a sort of permanence at the great Paris fairs (thus extending to comic opera the monopoly that Paris possessed over serious opera in France), the Foire Saint-Germain (from February to April) and the Foire Saint-Laurent (August and September). Because both of these fairs were visited constantly by all classes, what went on in them became as important to the intelligentsia as what went on at the State Opera, and reprisals for too great levity toward Authority were meted out there. Of course one of the sources of comedy, in France, as in Italy, had long been the *lazzi* of the *commedia* companies, which were as much in evidence, in both French and Italian versions, as they had been at the time of Molière two generations earlier.

The most famous Italian company in Paris played at the Hôtel de Bourgogne, but it was expelled in 1697, and at various

---

(1) Martin Cooper correctly remarks that the usage of the term *opéra comique* "has been such that even a Frenchman needs to know whether the date is 1715, 1775, 1825 or 1875 before he can be sure what to understand by the term" (*Opéra Comique*, p. 9). "Comic opera" as a term is inaccurate, but I shall reserve the use of the French term for its "classic" definition; that is, through-composed opera with spoken dialogue.

times in the early 1700's the French companies at the fairs were also banned for a collection of reasons, including licentiousness, audacity, and the jealousy of the entrenched bureaucracy at the Opéra and the Comédie-Française, who wanted no rivals, however distant. The resilient comedians replied by adapting and evading: if the ban forbade singing, a claque in the audience began the song (always a popular tune), which would then be taken up by the rest of the audience; if the ban forbade speaking, the actors mimed the story and then either pulled from their pockets rolls of paper on which their speeches were inscribed, and which they held up for the audience to read, or had placards descend from the ceiling (often framed by two children dressed as Cupids);[2] if the ban forbade more than one actor speaking or being on stage at a time, a single actor would stand stage center, deliver a monologue, then leap into the wings to be replaced by another.

The death of Louis XIV in 1715 improved matters, but still the companies were subject to sudden and often capricious edicts, as were the fortunes of the entrepreneurs who were given the right to run them. Very often bankruptcy was as hindering a force as bureaucracy.

These "fair" comedies employed music, only peripherally and most of that secondhand, so that the authors of the pieces were the only ones likely to receive credit. The singing was done by actors who happened to have voices rather than by trained singers. Not until Madame Favart in the middle of the century did French comic opera produce a famous singer, and even she was equally as famous, if not more so, for her acting abilities.[3] The aim of these works was gaily transient (in direct contradistinction to the *opéras*, which were written to endure): to poke fun, to have a good time, with a minimum of attention paid to plot or credibility. Indeed, most of the works were revues or sketches rather than single entities. The stock *commedia* figures were blended with allegory, mythology, fairy tale, magic tricks, "orientalia," society anecdotes, and intrigues, all making up the *drame forain* (fair spectacle).

---

(2) Lesage: *Oeuvres*, vol. I, pp. 34–5. Placard opera became such a novelty that it was exported to Venice—another example of the utilitarian developing into the artistic.
(3) The development of French comic opera has many points of contact with the development of the American musical comedy from comedy to "musical."

The most famous authors of these *drames forains* were Alain-René Lesage, Louis Fuzelier, and d'Orneval. They worked singly or in combination, but in any final estimate Lesage overshadowed his collaborators. When Lesage (1668–1747) turned to writing for the fairs, he was already famous as the author of *Le Diable boîteux* and of one of the best eighteenth-century French comedies, *Turcaret;* he would later produce one of the most famous picaresque novels, *Gil Blas.* He wrote about one hundred works, ranging from one-act parodies to full-evening revues for the fairs, and used his fame as an author and his ability to write a stage work to elevate the haphazard japeries of the fair comedies to a more ordered plane. He has been called the father of French comic opera;[4] certainly the form would have developed without him, but his contributions gave it needed respectability and cohesion. Yet it was in the person of Charles-Simon Favart that French comic opera found its first important voice.

Favart (1710–1792) is one of the few librettists to be perpetuated in a memorial: the Salle Favart in the Opéra-Comique building in Paris. The son of a pastry cook, he began by writing for the fairs, and by the time of his marriage to Marie-Justine-Benoîte Duronceray in 1745, was established as a leading comedy author. His wife, an accomplished singer and dancer as well as actress, also had a flair for writing,[5] and added immeasurably to her husband's works by playing the feminine leads. Favart became so famous that he aroused the jealousy of the rival Comédie-Italienne, which successfully intrigued against him and forced him out of Paris. He thereupon took a troupe to Flanders, where the French army was fighting, and proceeded to play to one side and then the other. The French commander, the Maréchal de Saxe, was captivated by the charms of Madame Favart and used the notorious *lettre de cachet* to rid himself of her husband.[6]

---

(4) Lesage: *Oeuvres*, vol. I, p. 44.
(5) She herself wrote a number of scenarios and collaborated on a few librettos, and there is reason to suspect that she had a hand in many more of Favart's librettos, particularly as regards the role she played. She and Favart also revolutionized the costumes worn by using more "realistic" peasant attire instead of the stylized dresses (an idea they derived from David Garrick).
(6) The Maréchal himself is a character in two later librettos: *Adriana Lecouvreur* (1902; m., Francesco Cilèa; l., Arturo Colautti) and *Madame Favart* (1878; m., Offenbach; l., Alfred Duro and Henri-Charles Chivot).

Favart was forced to flee, and Madame Favart spent the next few years in a series of adventures worthy of Alexandre Dumas in her efforts to dodge her aristocratic patron. Saxe's death in 1750 enabled Madame Favart to return to the stage and to her husband, and Favart himself was able to resume his career as a playwright-librettist. In 1758 he became the head of the Opéra-Comique, and held the post even after its fusion with the Théâtre-Italien in 1762. He retired in 1769 and, though he wrote a few librettos after that, his work for the operatic theater was finished. Like his good friend Carlo Goldoni, he lived on in retirement until after the French Revolution had put an end to the world he knew and described.

Favart is the first major French comic librettist, and, though his works do not show the penetration of Goldoni's, his great theatrical facility and comic verve, along with his luck in being able to reproduce what was most popular with the public as well as with the critics in the 1750's and 1760's, enabled him to achieve a position of dominance in France which Goldoni never enjoyed in Italy.

Favart's career as a librettist is divided into two parts: the works he wrote as *vaudevilles* or parodies of serious works, and those in which he developed a story on its own terms. Yet all of his works are adaptations to a greater or lesser extent of other sources: Italian librettos, French stories, or other material in which he saw comic possibilities. In the early 1750's he began writing story-librettos rather than straight parodies and *vaudevilles*, and these became increasingly his mode of expression. These story-librettos were known as *comédies mêlées d'ariettes* (comedies with arias intermixed), and their essential feature, as contrasted with the Italian comic librettos, was that the bulk of the written material was spoken rather than sung. This feature, which had always been a part of the *drames forains*, was thus carried over into the story-librettos and became a distinguishing mark of French opera until the twentieth century, although the amount of spoken dialogue was being whittled down as the years went by.

What is vital to recognize, and what becomes evident when the history of opera is seen from the perspective of the development of the French comic libretto, is that the codifications of Favart lead directly to the more highly dramatic works of Michel-Jean Sedaine and thence to the librettos of the Revolutionary period. The French "classic" opera, which developed from Rameau through the Gluck phase to the works of Spontini in the nineteenth century, although producing several excellent works, was always of less importance as an influence, and in the nineteenth century petered out entirely, save for the greatest example of classic opera which that century produced, Berlioz's *Les Troyens* (not given "complete" in Paris until 1921, and even then with cuts!). Appreciation of this logical development of the comic to the bourgeois libretto was to an extent obscured both by the noisy Piccinni-Gluck controversy, carried on by proponents of the *opera seria* and those who wished to reform it, and by the continual intellectual snobbery of those who felt that only operas produced at the Opéra were worthy of serious consideration as works of art. The contributions of Grimm, Diderot, Rousseau, and other Encyclopedists in breaking down this formidable barrier was of great importance in establishing the works of Favart and Sedaine in the minds of the intellectuals as preferable alternatives to the hieratic posings dictated by the Opéra.

Favart's parodies are representative of hundreds of others produced at the fairs over the years. In the eyes of the comedians, nothing was sacred, particularly if it was current news; and be it a scandal, a new opera, a play or book, a new social craze, or a fashion of dressing, it was certain to become the subject of one or more parodies.[7] Favart's parodies, reflective of the character of their author, were always meant as good fun, and were never vicious. The aim was, as with all of the fair spectacles, to give the public a good time and send them home laughing. It was also possible, of course, for parodies to educate and correct: *Arlequin-Dardanus* (1739), Favart's parody of *Dardanus*, an opera written in 1739 by Leclerc de la Bruyère and set by Rameau, impressed the librettist sufficiently so that in the next production of the opera he revised his libretto to conform with Favart's suggestions, as embodied in the parody.[8] All of the directness and verve found elsewhere in Favart's writing is evident in the parodies, which also have the advantage

------

(7) Comparison can be made with today's variety shows on television, which regularly parody popular plays, movies, and manners.
(8) Auguste Font: *Favart*, p. 224. Font also says that the librettist Le Noue played the parody of his own opera in the theater he managed.

over the later *comédies* of seeing things as they were, not as they seemed:

> ARICIE: *Ô chose surnaturelle,*
> *la lune tombe des Cieux!*
> HIPPOLYTE: *À l'aide d'une ficelle*
> *elle descend en ces lieux.*
> ARICIE: *Pourquoi donc ici la lune?*
> HIPPOLYTE: *C'est la voiture commune*
> *de Diane à l'Opéra.*[9]
> (Parody of *Hippolyte et Aricie,* 1742; xxi)

Favart parodied all aspects of the *tragédie lyrique,* as well as the *opera seria* elements that were being incorporated into it: the machines, the high-flown language, the diminutives, the de rigueur scenes,[1] the statuesque chorus, and, above all, the interminable *entrées* of the dancers.[2] In their irrepressible merriment and their use of verse for comic purposes—Favart liked to use strings of single-rhymed, short lines, preferably ending in hard sounds, such as *-oc*—these parodies look forward to those of Offenbach's librettists in the nineteenth century. Favart can also be said to have foretold the existence of aleatory opera: in his libretto *Le Supplément de la Soirée des Boulevards*[3] musicians fashion symphonies out of combinations made by throwing dice, and poets write librettos by putting pins in books to mark words.

By the 1760's Favart had turned from concentration on parodic material to adaptation of other works to produce comedies. This switch was undoubtedly influenced by the *Guerre des Bouffons,* which began in 1752, and the ceaseless efforts of the En-

---

(9) "O supernatural happening! The moon is falling from the sky!" "With the help of a string it's coming down to us." "Why is the moon here?" "Because it's the usual chariot used by Diana at the Opéra."

(1) As, for instance, the slumber scene. This was prime parodic material because one of the most famous scenes of the *tragédie lyrique* had always been the slumber scene from *Armide,* which had been parodied to death. Slumber scenes were so much a part of the essentials of the libretto, however, that they reappeared as normal parts of Favart's comedies (e.g., in *Les Moissonneurs*).

(2) "French opera is a spectacle in which the whole happiness and misery of people consists in seeing dancing around them"; Baron Grimm, as quoted in Romain Rolland: *Essays on Music,* p. 189. Favart entitled his parody of Rameau's *Les Indes galantes, Les Indes dansantes.*

(3) Sequels to popular works were as common then as they are today; this was one such work.

cyclopedists to create a French middle-class opera along the lines of the Italian *opera buffa*. Italian comedians had brought *La Serva padrona* to France in 1746, but it was not until the repeat performances in 1752 that the intermezzo became a *cause célèbre*. The group of writers and thinkers who helped Diderot produce his great *Encyclopédie* saw in the Italian intermezzo the alternative not only to the stilted *tragédie lyrique* but also to the ephemeral revues of the fairs. Diderot himself prosyletized for "drama," a category of stage work which he placed between tragedy and comedy and which he said should partake of the incidents of bourgeois life rather than of mythological, fantastic, or despot-oriented life. Characters were to be drawn from life, incidents from life, and the language, dress, and settings should also reflect what was going on at the time. Rousseau, who had seen opera in Italy, seconded this approach with even more vigor. Thus the middle-class movement that had already taken hold in Italy through the comedies of Goldoni and the Neapolitan intermezzos and *opere buffe* was transferred to French comic opera through the success of the Italian company in Paris and the polemic backing of the Encyclopedists.

The form in which "bourgeois opera" emerged in France, however, differed to some extent from that of the Italian comedies. Although the French works reproduced some of the moral strictures that Goldoni employed (particularly in respect to the worst features of the aristocracy, such as the *droit de seigneur* custom and the petty evil of the bailiffs employed to collect rents), they tended to gild the pill by emphasizing the pastoral aspects of the story. The early eighteenth century in France had seen a great vogue for the pastoral: that charming but fallacious idea that the country life was idyllic whereas the realities of the courts and cities were drudgeries, and that not only did aristocrats enjoy themselves in the country (as the canvases of Watteau and Boucher attested), but also the peasants themselves lived happy lives. This pastoral craze antedated Marie-Antoinette and her fake farm, but it gained force by being adopted, in part, by the Encyclopedists. Jean-Jacques Rousseau had come to the attention of Paris in 1750, two years before the success of *La Serva padrona*, by winning an essay prize in which he argued that intellectual disciplines such as science and art did not enhance but rather corrupted the basic moral health of Man. It was a short step from that attitude to one of glorification of those who had not been corrupted, i.e., the peasants, and Rousseau took it by writing the libretto for an intermezzo modeled on the Italian: *Le Devin du village*, which was presented at Fontainebleau in 1752 and in Paris the year later, at the height of the "Bouffons' War."[4] Rousseau produced a naïvely direct libretto, although it shows dependence on the standard French operatic devices of *le merveilleux* (the magician's tricks) and on dance.[5] Its two young lovers, however, came to represent the simple virtues of country life, and Rousseau's message—"*à la ville on est plus aimable,/au village on sait mieux aimer*"[6]—found echo in many Favart works.

The year 1753 also saw the production of *Les Troqueurs* (m., Antoine Dauvergne; l., Jean Joseph Vadé), which the *Mercure de France* considered the first "Italian" libretto in French, and which, in its theme of a pair of men switching sweethearts, was to be repeated down through the century, to culminate in Da Ponte's libretto for Mozart's *Così fan tutte*. Again the simplicity and immediate setting-forth of "honest" love formed the nucleus of the story.

But Rousseau had added another ingredient to the pastoral, and Favart was to gain fame through its development: that streak of sentimentality which centered around the leading female character. Favart is credited with the "invention" of the *ingénue*, but the type goes back to the *commedia dell'arte* and the *damigella* of seventeenth-century opera. What Favart did was to accentuate the sweetness in the character, making her into a girl of about fifteen or sixteen, to whom, as he said, "the declaration of love is sweet, the trial short, the pleasures gay, the end tranquil . . . never a passion, but an arrangement in which pleasure is the principle, the tie, and the object."[7] He was undoubtedly influenced in producing this

---

(4) It was immediately parodied by Madame Favart and one Marny (1753), and became one of her greatest roles. The German adaptation (by F. W. Weiskern) of this parody was set to music by Mozart as *Bastien und Bastienne*.

(5) Apparently the uncorrupted peasantry were immune from Rousseau's attack on the use of ballet in the *tragédie lyrique:* "priests dance, soldiers dance, gods dance, devils dance; there is dancing even at burials—in fact, dancing is seasonable with everything"; Rolland: *Essays on Music*, p. 189.

(6) A play on the word "*aimer*"; roughly: "In the city one is more (formally) pleasant, in the village one knows better how to love."

(7) Favart: *Prix de Cythère* (1740).

type of girl by the fact that his wife played it to perfection: the girl with childish manners, hovering between youth and maturity.[8] Yet just such a girl was also hovering on the edge of sentimentality, and when she began to cry, and wiped her eyes furtively on her apron (as in *Le Devin du village* and countless later librettos) she helped create the *comédie larmoyante* (tearful or three-handkerchief comedy), which was to typify French comic opera for the rest of the century. The development was natural, from the tugging of heartstrings at the sadness of a girl in love and unrequited to the tugging of heartstrings at any heightened emotional occurrence.

Favart's librettos for his *comédies* were notable for clarity and pace. Martin Cooper, in his book on *opéra comique*, quotes a definition of the essentials of a Favart *comédie*: (1) a swift and precise exposition, (2) closely knit intrigue of light-fingered love, in which the *couplets*, or ariettas, are inserted "whenever there is a moment of emotional expansion or when the situation threatens to become a little more than ambiguous."[9] What can be perceived immediately is how closely this definition of a Favart comedy structure parallels that of the Metastasio *opera seria*, and how they both reflect the structural nature of *commedia* works: the setting-forth of a situation and variations upon that situation. Slowly, the situation itself would expand to take over the whole of the story line, as would happen with the works of Sedaine.

Favart's pastoral comedies, such as *Ninette à la cour* (1755),[1] are the ones most directly associated with him, although two of his most famous works, which will be examined later, show that he was not limited to the Watteau-rococo. A parody based on a Goldoni work, *Bertoldo, Bertoldino e Cacasenno, Ninette* is an example of the increasing interchange of librettistic ideas between

---

(8) An additional consideration has not been given due weight in the assessment of Favart's work. Madame Favart, from reports of her acting, had the ability to suggest great sensuality underneath the apparently childlike exterior, and this undoubtedly mitigated a good deal of the sugary quality of the verse as well as giving it a depth of double-entendre irony. She would have made an ideal Manon.

(9) Cooper: *Opéra-comique*, p. 23, quoted from an article (by Lionel de la Laurencie) in the *Encyclopédie de la Musique*.

(1) Often a work was known under various titles, and often the author himself supplied two, the second of which became the more popular (e.g., Beaumarchais' *La Folle Journée, ou Le Mariage de Figaro*). *Ninette's* first title was *Le Caprice amoureux*, although when Egidio Duni set it to music it was called *Le Retour au village.*,

France and Italy.[2] If Goldoni concentrated more on satire and characterization and Favart more on gaiety and pastoral charm, nonetheless the Favart libretto preserves some of the cutting force of Goldoni's mind, such as Ninette's one-line comment on the arrival of the aristocrats in the village: *"Ce sont les gens du Prince, il faut bien qu'on endure."*[3] The situation is simple: a sweet country lass is seduced by the idea of courtly life, much to the distress of her village lover,[4] and "goes to Court." She is thoroughly dazzled (and a little disconcerted) by the glitter of the Court, but she remains pure in heart and body (even though pursued by the Prince[5]), and in the end returns to the village. This story was one of the century's most popular, and reappears in many guises, since it could be appreciated (for differing reasons) by both the upper and middle classes and was well calculated to flatter them both, as well as to pander to the Rousseauist ideals and giving the librettist ample opportunity to poke fun at the manners and morals of the artificial court life.[6] The seeds of many later eighteenth-century comedies can be found here: the Zerlinas and the Masettos (Colas, Ninette's sweetheart, is prevented by aristocratic hunters from following Ninette when she leaves for the Court, but Favart short-circuits a potentially explosive situation, reminiscent of both Masetto and Rigoletto, by having Colas give in and then having the hunters dance an act-closing ballet); the last act of Figaro (there is a countess, who is in love with the Prince, who is pursuing Ninette—and Ninette contrives a rendezvous in a darkened garden, supposedly with herself but actually with the

---

(2) It increased to the point at which Favart's comedy was adapted back into Italian in 1765.

(3) "They are the Prince's men; we must suffer them."

(4) NINETTE: *"Colas, je renonce au Village;/la Cour me convient d'avantage:/chacun viendra me rendre hommage"* ("Colas, I'm disowning village life: the Court suits me more; everyone will pay me homage"). COLAS: *"Hélas! ma pauvre Ninette,/la Cour te rendra coquette"* ("Alas! my poor Ninette, the Court will make a coquette out of you").

(5) He is listed in the libretto as the King of Lombardy, but is addressed as "Prince."

(6) Artificiality is indicated by the use of artificial flowers and euphuistic language, as well as by the Prince's cynicism: he will allow Colas to come to court to please Ninette, which will aid him in his conquest of her. The country-bumpkin-in-the-city situation had its opposite—or, in musical jargon, its inversion—the prince in disguise going to the country and finding true love among the simple peasants, which was equally Rousseauist and probably even more popular as a libretto idea.

Countess). If Ninette retains some of the saucy and worldly attributes of a Goldoni heroine, she nonetheless is first of all a girl "brought up by an old lady who was forced by circumstances to live humbly," but who formed the spirit of the girl by leaving in her soul *"une aimable simplicité,/une franchise honnête, et beaucoup de gaieté."*[7] The message is clear: *"La Cour n'est qu'un esclavage;/l'avantage/du village/c'est de vivre en liberté;/l'avantage/du village/c'est de suivre la gaité,"*[8] and this message, coupled with the many dances and the charm of the mise-en-scène[9] overrode all other aspects of the story.

Two of Favart's other librettos deserve mention. *Soliman Second* (1761), better known by its second title, *Les Trois Sultanes,* was based on a story by Marmontel. Essentially a verse play with interpolated songs, it was even closer to the spoken stage than any of his other work. In fact, it became so popular that the songs were dropped and it was "elevated" to the status of a verse play, in which guise it was regularly given at the Comédie-Française until the nineteenth century. The libretto thus has the distinction of being one of the extremely few examples of the genre which survived as plays in their own right. The verse (which combines alexandrines with shorter-length lines) is somewhat ponderous (as if Favart were aiming for posterity) in the accepted French manner,[1] but the story bubbles with such good spirits that it was assured success. It has maintained its familiarity through metamorphosis in such works as the Mozart–Gottlieb Stephanie *Die Entführung aus dem Serail* and the Rossini–Angelo Anelli *L'Italiana in Algieri.* Favart includes three women in the Sultan's harem: a Spaniard, a Circassian, and a Frenchwoman. The French girl, Roxelane, through her wit and verve outclasses the other two, much to the discomfiture of the Chief Eunuch, Osmin.[2]

---

(7) "A graceful simplicity, an honest frankness, and lots of gaiety."
(8) "The Court is nothing but slavery. The advantage of the village is that one can live in freedom; the advantage of the village is that one can pursue gaiety."
(9) Such as the opening of the first act: "Peasant men and women are occupied at their different jobs on their front stoops and in the fields."
(1) Perhaps the case because Favart was, consciously or unconsciously, competing with a famous verse play on a similar "Oriental harem" subject, Voltaire's tragedy *Zaïre* (1732), which was eventually adapted operatically as *Zaira* (1829; m., Bellini; l., Felice Romani).
(2) Roxelane is closer to Anelli's Isabella in spirit—another example of cultural interchange—but Mozart's opera includes the drinking scene and the character of Osmin.

Soliman Second, because of its verse pretensions, struck another blow in establishing the comic opera libretto on a footing comparable to that of the *tragédie.*[3] In the 1760's Favart expanded his territory with fairy-tale librettos, such as *La Fée Urgèle* (1765; m., Duni—later, also Grétry), and an attempt at "realistic peasant drama," *Les Moissonneurs* (1768; m., Duni). The story of *Les Moissonneurs* (The Reapers), loosely based on the Biblical book of Ruth, is one step removed from the pastoral, but the step is significant. A heavier dose of sentiment has been added, along with a greater emphasis on the actualities of peasant life. Favart indicates this by a fuller scenic description, which is in keeping with the scenic awareness of the French libretto. The reapers cut the grain upstage, the sun rises and beats down on them,[4] and at the lunch break the inevitable chorus is treated to a specifically detailed peasant lunch: soup with a bit of salt pork, bread, and cheese. If the peasants still express themselves in terms of what the middle class liked to think they thought—"our fondest hope is to be able to continue to glean"—Favart moved in the direction toward which Diderot pointed and a position that librettists such as Sedaine were to occupy.

Favart as a librettist has almost always been confined to his chief contributions: the *ingénue,* the sweetness of his verse, and the Boucher-like quality of his themes. Yet, though as a librettist he never showed as individual a mind as Goldoni's, his librettos, built up from a base of parody, moved in the direction of the "drama" that Diderot envisioned. If in the final analysis they rest more on the qualities Diderot rejected than on those he espoused, Favart's librettos nonetheless introduced some of the qualities—naturalness of dress, scene, and language (he copied Goldoni in using peasant

---

(3) The German playwright and theater critic G. E. Lessing devotes several articles in his *Hamburg Dramaturgy* to the Favart comedy and the Marmontel original. He writes, in Number 33: "I counsel all who desire to enrich the theater from similar tales to compare Favart's performance with Marmontel's original matter."

(4) Favart uses the sun not only as an almost physical component of the action but also as the Greeks used the sunrise to begin their plays. The first act begins at daybreak—one can still see the stars. He directs: "During the first act, the sky slowly brightens, the morning mists dissipate, and the sun rises; in the second, it is above the horizon, and at the beginning of the third it appears at its zenith, and declines until the end of the day. This progress should be effected imperceptibly, but its presence should be felt throughout the three acts."

slang and expressions)—that were to become integral to the dramas of his successors. Perhaps he does not deserve the accolade of a building in his name, but he certainly does deserve the memorial of the square in front of it.

With the advent of Jean-Michel Sedaine, the libretto was able to put into operation Diderot's ideas on drama. A self-educated stonemason, Sedaine (1719–97) became an architect, but as a part-time poet he also frequented the haunts of the writers of the *drames forains*, and he was persuaded by the director of the Opéra-Comique to write a few *vaudevilles*. He began writing for the stage after the "Bouffons' War," in about 1754, but his first success was *Le Diable à quatre* in 1756. He continued writing light *comédies mêlées d'ariettes* in the Favart manner (like Favart's they were adaptations from other sources), but paid more attention to the naturalness of the setting and the action. Thus, the comic by-play of *Blaise le savetier* (1759)[5] is set in motion because Blaise, a merry grasshopper of a fellow, has let his debts pile up so that, six months after his marriage, his creditors are repossessing all of his furniture. The situation of *On ne s'avise jamais de tout* (1761; m., Pierre Monsigny) was the main source of Beaumarchais' *Le Barbier de Séville*.

Sedaine quickly caught the attention of the Encyclopedists because of this naturalness coupled with a comic spirit, and capitalized on his popularity with librettos such as *Le Roi et le fermier* (1762; from an English play, *The King and the Miller of Mansfield*, by Dodsley; m., Monsigny). Favart's countryside was pastoral, with a few clouds of reality. Sedaine's was overcast, but with a final sunset: his story of the simple country farmer whose sweetheart is stolen by the local aristocrat borders on the unpleasant. Luckily the benevolent king, in this case Henry VI, is riding through the countryside and is forced to take shelter in the farmer's hut when he gets lost. Thus he is able to right the wrongs and punish the villain. As can be seen, Sedaine introduces a *rex ex machina* in this libretto (as in his later *Le Déserteur*): without that, the result would in no sense be lighthearted comedy.

Sedaine is the first major French librettist to write frankly in-

---

(5) Music by Philidor. The chief comic device, a man—in this instance, the comic villain—locked in a standing closet, is similar to Franc Nohain's libretto for Ravel's *L'Heure espagnole*, in which the man is trapped inside a grandfather clock.

ferior verse,[6] but he gained his fame through his sure handling of the story, his good characterizations, and his absolute sense of the theatrical. In this he is the direct precursor of Scribe and of most other nineteenth-century librettists. It is not coincidence that Sedaine's *comédies* were the first in France to be famous as much or more because of their music as because of their story, for with the establishment of the *opéra comique*, a single composer became linked with each libretto.

Sedaine's *Le Déserteur* (1769; m., Monsigny) is one of the handful of librettos that can be said to stand historically for a change in the history of the form, much as Stravinsky's *Le Sacre du printemps* can be said to do musically.[7] With *Le Déserteur*, the predominantly comic libretto becomes drama with comic undertones, and the *larmoyante* aspects, which had been reserved for the *ingénue*, spread through the entire libretto. *Le Déserteur* combines the austere nobility of Metastasio's *Attilio Regolo* brought down to a middle-class level with the comic characters of the fairs and the simple peasants of the pastorals. Out of it was to grow not only the "rescue operas" of the 1790's and early 1800's, but many later nineteenth-century works as well.

Sedaine based his libretto on an actual occurrence.[8] For reasons that are purposely left obscure, the father of Louise (who is affianced to the soldier Alexis) persuades her to consent to a fake marriage ceremony to play a joke on the soldier, who is coming home on leave. Alexis sees the merriment going on as he arrives, and assumes that his future father-in-law is being remarried. Upon being told that the wedding is Louise's, he crumbles completely. His only thought is to get away as far as possible. Some providently stationed soldiers ask him if he intends to desert ("No, I'm only leaving

---

(6) "It is too bad that Sedaine does not have a little more facility in his style. It is hard and knotty. All that disappears in the theater through the magic of the story and of the music." Baron Grimm, as quoted in Louise Parkinson Arnoldson: *Sedaine et les musiciens de son temps*, p. 102. Note that Grimm makes the cardinal observation that style becomes unimportant when set in the context of the music and the story.

(7) It should be unnecessary to emphasize that most of the "revolutionary" aspects of the libretto had been seen before, but Sedaine put them together with such dramatic force that *Le Déserteur* came to stand for the change in the approach to the libretto.

(8) "Actual occurrence" librettos were to become very popular during the Revolutionary period.

France") and they arrest him. The whole first act is thus but an excuse for the second.

The second act takes place in the prison: Alexis has been condemned to death for desertion. Sedaine now introduces a comic character, the drunken dragoon Montauciel, who shares the cell[9] with Alexis. This stroke of inspiration naturally raised a furor in the teacup of the French drama, for never before had the comic and serious been so openly mixed in one work. For this reason alone the work would have had a vogue, but because it was coupled with a suspenseful story and music which, by the standards of the earlier French comic operas, was gripping, the vogue quickly developed into a rage. The introduction of Montauciel constitutes an important advance in the history of the libretto, for it not only reintroduced the comic and serious in one work, but conjoined them. Where before there would have been a separate set of comic characters (usually of a lower class), here the (lower-class) comic character becomes a close friend of the hero and has most of his scenes with him. Montauciel, an actor's dream as a character, is extremely well drawn by Sedaine. His carefree, dissolute life at first repels Alexis, who, when Montauciel presumes too far, strikes him to the ground, thus arousing Montauciel to threats of vendetta when they both are released. When he finds out that Alexis is to be shot, however, his tone changes completely, and he becomes his fast friend.

Sedaine's purpose in creating the character was obvious: it gave exactly that relief from suspense which served to heighten suspense. Sedaine wanted his audience to think, "This man is going to die. Why are we being beguiled by this drunkard?" and then forget the death sentence while being beguiled, only to recall it with greater emphasis afterward. He succeeded.

Montauciel keeps up a constant banter—"I would only desert in order to drink"—until Louise arrives. She explains the misfired joke, finds out the severity of the sentence, and joins her father in despair. News is brought that the King is passing through the camp: Louise has an idea, and leaves. The act ends with another comic scene from Montauciel.

Act III demonstrates Sedaine's melodramatic skill in adding

---

(9) As usual with the French libretto, the cell is described in detail: water in a crock, stone table, stool, and bed.

twist after twist to the screws of suspense. Time is running out for Alexis; Montauciel is still gaily singing (he still does not know of the sentence). Alexis sits down to write Louise a letter;[1] Montauciel, now informed, takes the letter and promises to deliver it. Off-stage drums roll. Suddenly, in bursts Louise. In a typically realistic stroke, Sedaine has her enter barefoot: she has taken off her shoes so as to run better. She sees Alexis: *"Alexis, ta . . ."* she says, and faints from exhaustion. Alexis, happy to have seen her before he dies, exits with the soldiers. Louise awakens and tells us she has gotten the King to pardon Alexis—but it is too late! No: outside there are cries of *"Vive le roi!"* The King has providentially arrived on the execution spot, has seen that his pardon had not arrived in time, and has himself pardoned Alexis. With that, in typical French opera style (also typical of *opera seria*), the scene quickly changes to "a public place" where everyone is reunited and happy.

Le Déserteur can be seen as a synthesis of a number of the elements of the librettos that preceded it. The *opera seria* provided the over-all structure[2] and the rigid, Aristotelian time span and singleness of theme;[3] the earlier *comédies* provided the middle-class environment and the simple, natural language and direct emotions; and the exhortations of Diderot on the necessity for "drama" produced the overtly theatrical suspense and tear-jerking qualities that now suffuse the entire story. Yet *Le Déserteur* also looks forward to the close of the eighteenth century and to the nineteenth. The "rescue operas" of the Revolutionary and post-Revolutionary period followed its lead, and the "drama" that it initiated—that is, one of strong emotional involvement with the plight of the characters—was to be greatly heightened with the advent of the Romantic Age.[4]

---

(1) Reflecting the different sensibilities of two centuries, Alexis sings: "It would have been so sweet to kiss you (before I died)," whereas Cavaradossi in *Tosca* recalls "sweet kisses, languid caresses" in nights of love.

(2) Note, however, that the situation no longer gives rise to a number of variations leading to a climax: its force pushes the development along one line.

(3) Sedaine almost always observed the unities, particularly that of time, although (as usual) the unity of place was very loosely interpreted.

(4) A comparison of structure with the greatest of the "rescue operas" —*Fidelio*—will show how influential Sedaine's work was, for its basic form carried to the later French work by J. N. Bouilly and thence to Beethoven and Sonnleithner and Treitschke.

After *Le Déserteur*, Sedaine continued to work at both opera and ballet librettos, and even reworked a text for the Opéra, but it was not until 1784 that he was to have his second, and greatest, success. In 1780, he had written a libretto for Grétry on the fable of Aucassin and Nicolette which had taken advantage of a vogue for the Middle Ages and had enabled him to use strange words from that earlier time for purposes of novelty. It was not successful until reworked, but it laid the groundwork for further exploration. His next work, also with Grétry, took up the story of the imprisoned King Richard the Lion-Heart and of how Blondel, his faithful valet and minstrel, rescued him from a castle prison. Produced in 1784, the same year as Beaumarchais' *Le Mariage de Figaro*, *Richard Coeur de Lion* vied with Figaro as the most successful work of the year, and fixed forever Sedaine's pre-eminence as a librettist.

Richard joins *Le Déserteur* as a harbinger of the future, not only in areas that the earlier work had opened, but in new ones as well. The story, as can easily be seen, is another shy at the rescue theme before its time, but in this instance Sedaine has filled in the scene more than he had that of *Le Déserteur*. Blondel, disguised as an old, blind minstrel, arrives in the town under the castle at the same time as Richard's beloved, thus affording a totally *lieto fine* once Richard is rescued. There is also a standard love subplot involving the governor of the castle[5] and the daughter of a Welsh exile. Sedaine did some research into the period before writing the libretto,[6] and included genre elements that fleshed out the story. To audiences accustomed to the austerities of the classic opera or the pastoral pleasantries of most comic opera this was fascinating novelty; its great popularity would lead straight to the period settings of the French *Grand Opéra* of Scribe in the nineteenth century.

The structure of Richard is inferior to that of *Le Déserteur*, for its climax comes with the discovery of Richard in Act II, the rest being a long anticlimactic treatment of how to get him out.

---

(5) Named Florestan. The name had become popular during the pastoral craze, but now was gravitating to the local jails.

(6) Eighteenth-century research, particularly in the realm of the opera libretto, was not notable for its scrupulous accuracy. The novelty of period costumes and weapons was so effective that people forgot to question the anachronism of Blondel playing a violin. Also, Richard actually was ransomed, not released through assault, but the handing-over of money does not have great scenic éclat.

Yet Sedaine was adept at scene handling, and he held the attention of the audience with a dramatic assault on the castle by the supporters of Richard, which he choreographed for maximum effect. The opera was also noted for the novel device of the recurring theme, which became the most talked-of *coup de musique* of the time. Grétry invented a simplistic tune, supposedly written by Richard to his beloved, which is the tune that Blondel has been hawking around Europe, knowing that its composer will instantly recognize it. Grétry used the theme throughout the work, thus giving it a unity that was entirely appropriate musically and dramatically.

 Richard again demonstrates Sedaine's greatest strength: his scenic awareness. One of the reasons for the success of *Aucassin et Nicolette* had been its prison scene, in which Nicolette, at the foot of the prison tower, held hands through the bars with the incarcerated Aucassin. The "recognition scene" in *Richard* far surpassed this in stage effectiveness, and became one of the celebrated moments in French opera. The scene itself has already been mentioned in Chapter Four (see pages 48–9), but it should be given closer consideration, for this sort of scenic involvement always typified the French opera and would become even more powerful in succeeding years.

 Sedaine carefully describes the effect he wants.

> The theater represents a prison fortress; at the front is a terrace in front of a door; it is surrounded with an iron grille, and the terrace is placed so that Richard, when he is there, cannot see the back of the stage, which represents a moat backed by a parapet; it is on that terrace that Richard appears and on that parapet that Blondel is seen.[7]

As the second act opens, dawn is breaking, and when the King emerges he is in sunlight, whereas Blondel remains in shadow on the parapet. This effect was made possible by the use of the

---

(7) The "realism" preached by Diderot and the Encyclopedists is everywhere in evidence in Sedaine's librettos. In *Richard*, he used another novelty by having the peasants come on stage during the overture. He is scrupulous, however, to justify their movements: ". . . they cross the theater and, to have time to sing, they give the impression of waiting for their friends who follow."

newly developed smokeless Argand lamps in 1782. As the scene continues, the light strengthens, always putting Richard more and more in the sun while Blondel remains in shadow. Blondel begins playing "the theme" on his violin; then sings the ditty with it. Richard recognizes it and says: "What sounds! O Heavens! Is it possible that the air that I wrote for her has become known even here? Let's listen." Then: "Those accents! That voice! I know it!" He then starts the next verse, and it is Blondel's turn to listen, amazed. Finally, the two of them sing the theme. It is possible to sense the overwhelming effect that this scene, with its novel staging aspects, had on the audiences, but the actuality of the event must have been far more powerful. The raw stage power of Sedaine's achievement can only be felt in a parallel situation, such as Act II of *Fidelio*.

The libretto of *Richard* also continued another of Sedaine's strongest dramaturgic traits, that of the juxtaposition of opposing elements. In it, he placed the cloddish peasant's dance just before the assault on the fortress, thus setting the latter off even more dramatically. In his later *Raoul Barbe-Bleue* (1789; m., Grétry), he returned to all his familiar themes: "rescue opera," dramatic build-up to one central suspense scene, and yards more of medieval local color.[8] He also used a dramatic irony even more powerful than the scenic juxtaposition of the earlier opera: the young lovers, one of whom is betrothed to notorious *Barbe-Bleue* (Bluebeard), await with dread his coming and are forced to make merry at the wedding feast. Effective scenic juxtaposition, of course, had always been part of the French libretto, but Sedaine accentuated it and used it with such success that it was copied to become a fixture in nineteenth-century French opera. The central scene, of course, is the subterranean cavern scene at the end of the opera, with the rescue party battering at the door. With the coming of the Revolution and incarceration on a grand scale, repetitions of this scene would become commonplace.

Sedaine's final libretto of importance, written at the age of seventy-two, was *Guillaume Tell* (1791; m., Grétry). It openly pandered to the Revolution not only in its subject but also in the

---

(8) One of the features of Raoul's castle was an off-stage trumpet that signaled all arrivals and departures.

alternate ending Sedaine provided, in which the "brave *sans-culottes*" are heard singing in the distance, come on stage, and join Tell and his Swiss in a rousing rendition of *La Marseillaise.* The character of the tyrant Guesler was particularly well drawn by Sedaine, who brought out his sadistic tyranny (he blinds Melktal). Guesler joins the demonic Raoul as an evil force quite foreign to the earlier *comédies* and directly anticipatory of the romantic melodramas of the next century. The genesis of Scribe's *Robert le diable* can thus be traced to Sedaine.

Sedaine's two great librettos and his other work in the field changed the course of the French *comédie mêlée d'ariettes.* Although it was doubtless inevitable that the Favart type of light pastorals should run through their vogue and give place to a more honestly bourgeois drama along the lines advocated by Diderot, a turn toward "costume" melodrama could not have been foreseen. Works such as the A. A. Poinsinet–B. Davesne *Tom Jones* (1765; m., Philidor) and Jean-François Marmontel's *Le Huron* (1768; m., Grétry)[9] had served to expand the pastoral into the realm of the closer-to-real-life world of the eighteenth century. Yet Sedaine's contributions had added elements that the public would find habit-forming. He applied Diderot's insistence on seeing the specifics of everyday life on stage, not to the creation of the world of Enlightenment France, but to the evocation of a romantic and

---

(9) *Le Huron* had a tremendous vogue in France, because it shamelessly pandered to several popular conceits. Its basis was of course Rousseau's ideal of the Noble Savage, the hero being a Huron Indian imported into France. The Huron is contrasted to the French sophisticates: he likes constant action (hunts, etc.), and disdains repose. A sample of the dialogue captures the overpowering naïveté of Marmontel's writing, which reflected the popular conception of Rousseauism: "YOUNG LADY: Have you ever been in love? HURON: Yes, with the lovely Abucadaba. (He sings an air.) YL: What happened to her? H: A bear ate her. YL: That's too bad! H: I killed that villainous bear. But I still weep for her, after having my revenge."

Yet Marmontel cannot carry his story to its ultimate: he must return to the tidy happy ending of the earlier pastorals. Therefore, the Huron is discovered to be not a savage at all, but the long-lost nephew of a Frenchman ("Oh, what happiness! I am a Frenchman!") and thus easily able to be assimiliated into Society, which goes directly counter to Rousseau's theories (though, paradoxically, probably not, since Rousseau's ideas were to a large extent a fabric of conceits for the privileged classes, and thus a Savage who has the background of centuries of Civilization would be the ideal New Man).

mysterious past heightened by the adroit use of suspense and melo-drama. The novelty of this approach, coupled with its inherent dramatic power, disguised the essential abandonment of Diderot's bourgeois ideal.

Sedaine's work, however, cannot be seen merely in that con-text: if his re-creation of the Middle Ages led to the widespread use of escapist color in later operas, his emphasis on the rescue melodrama gave later librettists ready-made models for works which, in a time of turmoil and danger, would become the most contemporary of subjects during the Revolutionary and post-Revolutionary periods. Yet beyond that, Sedaine's importance as a librettist rests on a larger base. Always an indifferent and rather lumpish versifier,[1] he unconsciously moved the focus of the French libretto away from verse toward scene, situation, and char-acter. This was all the more interesting because France prided itself on its attention to good verse,[2] but the combination of Sedaine's making gestures toward verse, his writing for the lesser *comédie*, and his undoubted dramaturgic success allowed sharp-eyed observers such as Baron Grimm to gloss over the verse in-adequacies in favor of the assets. Although no one realized at the time the importance of such a choice, the result was that the verse elements of French opera became less and less of a factor (although they would continue to be discussed at a length far greater than their importance). Sedaine's other great contribution is that he continued and greatly implemented the work of Favart and the succeeding librettists of the *comédie mêlée d'ariettes* in establish-ing that once-vagabond offshoot as less an alternative to the Opéra than the mainstream of operatic progress, with the Opéra as an increasingly stultified and arcane backwater—to such an extent that, by the nineteenth century, the Opéra itself came to perform the direct descendants of Sedaine. This development, which was to effect the libretto from then on, places Sedaine in the proper

---

(1) Sedaine's most celebrated lines are some of his finest. Blondel's hymn to his master: "*Ô Richard! Ô mon roi!/l'univers t'abandonne;/ sur la terre, il n'est que moi/qui s'intéresse à ta personne*" ("O, Rich-ard, O, my king! all the world has abandoned you; only myself, of everyone on earth, remains concerned with your whereabouts"). *Richard;* I, ii.
(2) The French paid greater attention, of course, to the cadences of the *opéra*, which they did not mind emasculated as long as sonorous.

position of prominence vis-à-vis another librettist whose words, influence, and polemics commanded far more attention at the time: Ranieri da Calzabigi. Calzabigi may have thought he was reforming the libretto with his theories, but the more important reform developed outside his sphere.

Chapter Nine

The Second Italian Reform

THE IMPETUS toward the reform of Reform opera was essentially the same as the impetus that led to its creation: the abuses of the original intentions of the "reformers," leading to a greater and greater artificiality, added to an over-familiarity with the rigid nature of the structure of Reform opera, inevitably leading to a yearning for something else. Metastasio stood unchallenged as the greatest exponent of Reform opera, but after the middle of the eighteenth century the novelty of his works had worn off and singers were once more gaining control of the stage, as they had before he had appeared. The static, florid nature of performances of his librettos led to an undermining of one of his strongest attributes, the passion of his characters, all the more because that passion was expressed not in the exit aria but in the give-and-take of the preceding recitative. The *castrati* were uninterested in the *secco* portions: they tended more and more to hurry over them to get to the embellished aria, and the public, likewise uninterested in a part that may have been written as drama but was being ignored,[1] kept up their usual practice of talking during *secco* passages, being impatient for the fireworks. Such practices eviscerated the Metastasio librettos and transformed them into bravura

---

(1) Needless to add, in the hands of the lesser librettists these *secco* portions were often not drama at all, but mere connective tissue. There is also another factor to consider: it is probable that not many in the Viennese audiences could understand the Italian being spoken. *Secco* recitative, even in the best of circumstances, has a difficult life. In operas such as *Don Giovanni*, where it can add a great deal, it is almost always thoroughly butchered by being galloped through with minimal regard for the words.

concerts in costume, ever more unrelated to the stoic nobility of an Attilio Regolo or the sufferings of a Didone.

Thus once again the time-worn cry of "simplicity" and "return to nature" was heard: a cry made more urgent because of the success of the Italian intermezzos and other comic operas. Francesco Algarotti's celebrated *Saggio sopra l'opera in musica* (*Essay on Opera*) (1755) codified these complaints into a document that echoed the comments of the French Encyclopedists on opera and set the stage for the Gluckian reform.

Ranieri da Calzabigi[2] has come to be considered, along with Christoph Willibald Gluck, as the chief architect of this reform—a reform far more celebrated than its predecessor. If the Metastasian reform was quickly subsumed in Metastasio's own genius and was forgotten as his works lapsed into obscurity, Calzabigi rode the tide of Gluck's strong music, and on the strength of his championing of the reform and the maintenance in the repertory of at least one, and perhaps two, of his works—*Orfeo ed Euridice* and *Alceste*—continued to be remembered while Metastasio's many librettos gathered dust in the lumber rooms of the European opera houses. Yet Calzabigi's position in the librettistic hierarchy is the higher for being linked in his most famous works with a master of the dramatic moment and a musical force, whose precepts, though only intermittently applied in his music, were to remain as spotless ideals for the composers of the nineteenth century. Gluck, not Metastasio, meant reform to all who followed him; Calzabigi was but his literary adjunct.

Calzabigi's life and librettistic career were in some ways similar to that of his later compatriot, Lorenzo Da Ponte. Born in Livorno in 1714, he never restricted himself to the writing of librettos—or even to writing—but pursued several careers around Europe, including the running of lotteries. A scapegrace closely related to the self-portrait in Casanova's *Memoirs*, Calzabigi flitted throughout Europe, attaching himself in Paris or in Vienna, and died in Naples in 1795.

A touch of the charlatan infects all of Calzabigi's activities; yet it should not thereby be inferred that he was a fraudulent hypocrite of the Tartuffe species. In a society willing to lionize

---

(2) He Frenchified his name to Ranieri de' Calsabigi—in both languages, however, the "da" or "de" was spurious, added so that he could consort on a more equal footing with the aristocracy.

(or be amused by) the latest parvenu intriguer, nimbleness became a necessary skill to a continuing career, and Calzabigi no less than Casanova or Da Ponte reflected the practices of the time. When Calzabigi began his libretto career he unhesitatingly patronized Metastasio—his first libretto, *L'Impero dell'universo* (1745), was a direct imitation of the master—and while in Paris, he published an edition of Metastasio's works with a fullsome preface. But Calzabigi recognized those elements of Metastasio's librettos which went against his own feelings of how a libretto should be written and set out to correct them in a work of his own, which he would then use to become the "Metastasio of the reform." Opportunism and recognition of artistic worth were inseparably intertwined in these actions.

The eighteenth century, particularly in France, saw the emergence of a new approach to libretto writing, an approach influenced by both the example of Metastasio and the practices of the Encyclopedists. This was the libretto not written primarily for the sake of performance as part of an opera, but written to create one's own historical moment. Metastasio read his work to his admirers before permitting it to be set to music;[3] the Paris *salons* provided the same opportunities for those wishing to use them. Whereas Sedaine's *Le Déserteur* became a libretto classic by virtue of its novelties and its influence—which were not anticipated in advance—works such as Rousseau's *Le Devin du village*, Voltaire's *Samson*, and Beaumarchais' *Tarare* were written to serve as didactic tracts and only secondarily to serve as vehicles for music. The totally out-of-proportion success of *La Serva padrona* in France was constantly before both librettists and composers, who recognized the double advantage of a popular success and the triumph of an esthetic. Thus what emerged during the eighteenth century was the beginning of a conscious individuality in the libretto. If the librettos of Busenello or Goldoni at their best could not have been duplicated by lesser librettists, works such as *Tarare* bring such individuality clearly to the fore. This set the stage for the works of Richard Wagner, which are explorations of Wagner's psyche and of his conflicting feelings as much as they are librettos in their own rights. The godfather here is again Metastasio, despite the essential timidity of his approach and

---

(3) A practice adopted by Richard Wagner in the nineteenth century.

the veils of traditional pose with which he cloaked his works, for
he had sufficient stature as a librettist of power and as a writer
whose ideas could be expressed through the libretto rather than
through other channels to have his librettistic oeuvre stand for his
philosophical expressions. With the continued rise in importance
of music as the dominating factor in the collaboration, this librettistic individuality would become ever harder to express,[4] particularly when it is realized that the vast majority of all librettos
were at best considered occasional works. The librettos of Arrigo
Boito are an almost perfect expression of this dilemma of a first-
class mind channeled into becoming, to the detriment of his own
individuality, a first-class adapter of other men's works.

This digression is important in understanding Calzabigi's
method for publicizing his "reform" approach to the libretto, for
if neither *Orfeo* nor *Alceste* serves to emblazon the unique Calzabigi qualities on the map of the libretto, both were created in
order to exemplify and demonstrate a novel approach. Calzabigi
was also extremely lucky to find in Gluck such a perfect collaborator.

As has been emphasized before, the reform of the reform was
by no means limited to Gluck and Calzabigi. The presence of a
strong dominating force always creates a counterforce, and Metastasio was no exception. The distaste that many commentators felt
for the excesses of *opera seria* was compounded by the dissatisfac-
tion of those in Vienna not included in the Metastasio inner circle.
Thus Gluck, who set Metastasio's works but was notoriously not
on the great librettist's list of preferred composers, would naturally
tend toward a librettist who presented an esthetic diametrically
opposed to Metastasio's.

As had already become commonplace in the history of the
libretto, "reform" to Calzabigi meant simplicity, continuity, and
the Greek ideal hitched on to classical mythology, in this case the
Orfeo story with which opera had begun. Added to this was a
heavy emphasis on the naturalness and humanity of the characters.
Both Gluck and Calzabigi knew enough of the developments in
opera buffa and the nascent *comédie mêlée d'ariettes*[5] to appre-

---

(4) The essential conflict here expressed is at the core of Wagner's
insistence on the composer as librettist, a logical-seeming but in practice facile solution to an almost insoluble problem.
(5) Gluck had adapted a number of these French works in the late
1750's in Vienna and was thoroughly versed in their special qualities.

ciate the vitality of this one element, which was the clearest departure from the stilted figures of *opera seria*. Although Calzabigi laid special stress on the proper declamation of Italian poetry (as opposed to the breaking-up of the line by *fioritura* and orchestral *ritornelli* in *opera seria*) so as to bring the *dramma per musica* closer to stage drama with musical accompaniment highlighting its dramatic and characterizational aspects, the thrust of his reform was directed less toward the perfect wedding of word and music than toward the simplification and humanization of the classical operatic theater in terms of a series of dramatic scenes. As Gluck wrote in the famous preface to *Alceste,* which became the manifesto of the second reform:

> By good fortune my designs were wonderfully furthered by the libretto, in which the celebrated author, devising a new dramatic scheme, had substituted for florid descriptions, unnatural paragons and sententious, cold morality, heartfelt language, strong passions, interesting situations and an endlessly varied spectacle.

Calzabigi had effected this scheme even earlier, of course, with his libretto for *Orfeo ed Euridice* (1762). The striking features of that libretto are the twin constants of the Italian libretto, brevity and simplicity, here carried to their extremes, and the French feature of the ballet, which is intermixed with the action throughout. As Alfred Einstein wrote, the action of the myth is seen by Calzabigi not in terms of dialogues, as with Metastasio, but in terms of stage pictures,[6] in itself, as we have seen, a feature of the French strain and evidenced there from Quinault on. The emphasis is thus placed less upon the words themselves than upon the situation as intensified by the words—an emphasis further reinforced by the ruthless excision of "florid descriptions," similes, and metaphors, which in turn placed greater weight upon single words or short phrases that were in fact *parole sceniche.* And in contradistinction to the French drama, most if not all elements of *le merveilleux* were banished.[7] Thus Calzabigi eschews not only a resetting of the first great moment in librettistic history—the instant when Orfeo hears of the death of Euridice—

---

(6) Alfred Einstein: *Gluck,* p. 84.
(7) It will be recalled that this banishment is similar in intent to Zeno's and Metastasio's. *Le merveilleux,* however, constantly crept back through its exploitation in the French libretto, where, as has been shown, it was an integral part of the whole.

but also her burial ceremonies. He opens the opera with Orfeo and a chorus lamenting at her tomb,[8] and it is Orfeo's repeated interjections of "*Euridice!*"[9] which serve to heighten the impact of sorrow and loss. Orfeo then continues with a solo, which ends with his raging at the gods. Amor appears and tells him that Euridice lives on the other side of the Styx; Orfeo resolves to fetch her and the act ends.

The second act, which became universally revered as a "classical perfection," is constructed in two opposing parts. The first presents the gates of Hell, with the chorus, now transformed into Furies, attempting to block Orfeo's way. Orfeo uses his charms and persuasion to sway the chorus, and passes to the second scene, Elysium. He is immediately struck by the celestial bliss of the spot, which Calzabigi expresses in Arcadian poetic terms. A chorus of the happy spirits leads his beloved to him, and the act ends. Act III opens with a scene between the two lovers, in which the fatal necessity becomes ever more inevitable: Euridice cannot understand why Orfeo will not look at her; Orfeo wishes to get her back to the land of the living as soon as possible. She refuses to go, he must return ("*Più frenarmi non posso,/e poco a poco la ragion m'abandonna,/oblio la legge, Euridice, e me stesso! e . . .*"[1]), and, in his anguish, turns to look at her. She dies before his eyes, and he is left to sing of her loss. Amor then appears, and restores Euridice to him, and the ballets take over.

A more compressed and simple libretto can hardly be imagined. The actors are, in effect, reduced to two, and the story to its essence. The language, too, is kept simple and direct: Orfeo's thought after Euridice is taken from him a second time is "What shall I do without Euridice, where shall I go without my beloved?"[2] Calzabigi achieved with this one libretto an extreme position that neither he nor any other librettist could duplicate; his only failing is his mandatory bow to convention in the *lieto*

---

(8) In itself a French scenic device, the "*tombeau.*"
(9) The word "*Euridice*" could be considered the *parola scenica* of the opera: it reappears to overwhelming effect in the hands of a great singer—e.g., Maria Callas—in the "*Che farò?*" aria.
(1) "I cannot tarry any longer, little by little my mind fails. I forget the law, Euridice, and myself and . . ."
(2) The contrast to the French words is revealing, for when Gluck reset the opera for Paris Orfeo expressed himself in less human and more stage-posed terms: "I have lost my Euridice, nothing equals my sadness," which breathes the air of the *tragédie lyrique.*

fine.[3] This happy ending goes a long way toward undermining the noble ideals of which Calzabigi wrote, for, unlike Metastasio's "happy endings," this one is obviously tacked on and not an integral part of the whole.

Calzabigi's next work with Gluck, *Alceste* (1767), was the occasion for the famous *Manifesto*, but it also, and more importantly, demonstrated that Calzabigi, after *Orfeo*, was moving away from the extreme of simplicity toward a consciously "classical" libretto along the lines being followed in France. Although he is careful to keep the focus of the libretto on the humanity of his characters, especially Alceste herself,[4] his impatience to create a true "classic" work (as opposed to *opera seria*) led him to include that aura of aristocratic formalism which his French models typified. Thus he bargained away much of the strength of his earlier work and, although *Alceste* is a good libretto, it pales when set next to *Orfeo* or the more classically noble versions of Greek tales produced by the French librettists for Gluck. The most moving scene in the opera, the one between Alceste, who has resolved to give her life for her husband, and Admeto, contains an insistence of passion that recalls Busenello—but it also recalls certain Metastasian scenes, particularly in *Attilio Regolo* and *L'Olimpiade*.

> ALCESTE: *T'adoro;*
> *t'adorerò! La tomba*
> *il mio pudico affetto*
> *estinguer non potrà. L'anima mia*
> *seco trarrà nel fortunato Eliso*
> *questo tenero amor. Per la tua vita,*
> *mille vite lo darei.*[5]
>
>   (II, v)

Calzabigi's later librettos accentuate his weaknesses rather than his strengths. His last work with Gluck, *Paride ed Elena*

---

(3) A necessity, since the first performance took place on the name day of the Emperor Francis I, and a tragic ending was unthinkable.
(4) At the first performance, in Vienna, Alceste brought in her two children by Admeto, Eumelo and Aspasia (I, ii and iv), in order to reinforce this bond of humanity, but they were cut from the Italian performance in Bologna, 1778, and from the French version.
(5) "I adore you, I shall always adore you! The tomb will never extinguish my modest affections. My soul will carry this tender love with it to happy Elysium. In exchange for your life, I would give up a thousand of mine."

(1770), returns to the theme of young love and to the minimal cast, but its impact is dissipated over the "classical" five acts replete with choruses and ballets.[6] Because Elena, in this version, is not married, there is no opportunity for the dramatic accentuation implicit in illicit love, and thus the main interest lies in the question of when, if ever, Elena will give in to Paride's lust for her. Calzabigi was not dramatically adept enough as a playwright to be able to sustain such a slim plot through either witty verse or stage action. His post-Gluck librettos, of which *Elfrida* (1796; m., Paisiello) affords a good example, read rather like Metastasio in their straightforwardness, except that the obligatory exit aria has been omitted.

Calzabigi's importance as a librettist lies less in his specific works, aside from *Orfeo*, than in his being in the right place at the right time and having the foresight to persist in his beliefs and to find a composer who shared them. In his letters he constantly talks reform and complains of the problems that this novel course forced him to face. But the truth was that, although he was strong enough to impose upon the libretto a certain simplicity in language and story and a direct, heartfelt poetic language that was his one gift to the Italian nineteenth-century libretto, he was not strong enough to impose his own imprint, as Metastasio had triumphantly done, upon the "reform" opera. The paradox lay in the fact that the Gluckian reform ostensibly raised the librettist to new heights of importance vis-à-vis the composer, but actually placed the composer *acting as librettist*[7] in control. Gluck appropriated whatever Calzabigi had appropriated from Algarotti and others and made it his own, and although he paid tribute to

---

(6) Calzabigi begins most of his librettos with a chorus, a practice carried over to the *melodramma*.

(7) The moment when Oreste sings "calm re-enters my heart" in *Iphigénie en Tauride* but the orchestra reveals that he is deluding himself has been seized upon not only by Gluck but also by most historians of opera as the symbolic moment when music finally displaced the word as primary. From that time on, music would not necessarily serve to enhance and clarify the meaning of the word (most simply seen in a *faux-naïf tableau* such as Haydn and Baron Van Swieten's oratorio *The Creation*, with its depictions of lions roaring, etc.), but would act as commentary upon it. Although the music by and large did not use its newfound ability in a systematic way until Wagner, the possibility was now before every composer, and that possibility gave the composer a hand in the librettistic creative area. We shall note in succeeding chapters how the composer unconsciously used this power to the benefit of the resultant opera.

its source, he as composer took the credit. From that time on the composer and not the librettist would dominate the collaboration.

Calzabigi's lack of individuality crippled him in his relationship not only with Gluck but also with his fellow-librettists, for the precise elements that he attempted to inject into the classic opera were succeeding on the comic stages of both Italy and France, and with Sedaine's help would be transferred to the more pretentious realms of the Opéra, and his attempts at strictly classic works would be overshadowed by the French, who were steeped in the tradition. Even in the comic realm, aside from *L'Opéra seria*, the witty libretto in which he satirized Metastasio, he had scant success.[8]

Calzabigi therefore must remain a librettistic paradox: a reformer whose merits, in Einstein's words, "cannot be exaggerated,"[9] but a librettist whose merits were more severely circumscribed. This paradox would reappear more and more, as the composer continued to expand his sphere of influence beyond the strictly musical.

---

(8) He wrote a libretto for Pasquale Anfossi (1774) which, when further adapted by Marco Coltellini, was used by Mozart: *La Finta Giardiniera*.

(9) ". . . he it was who gave the decisive impulse by supplying the subjects in their proper form"; Einstein: *Gluck*, p. 80.

Chapter Ten

The Reform Libretto in France

THE DEVELOPMENT and assimilation of the effects of the two operatic reforms can be most clearly seen in the French classic operas of the eighteenth century, for the twin advantages of the Opéra—monolithic continuity and at least partial dependence on what was happening on the spoken stage—served as a focus for the reforming efforts of both Metastasio and Calzabigi.

French opera entered the eighteenth century still dependent upon the elaborate *tragédie lyrique* formula of Lully and Quinault, but without the control that the composer and his librettist had exercised over the form. The operas of Rameau, whatever their musical merit, were librettistically considered Quinaultism in decadence, with an ever-increasing reliance on disjunct scenes, interpolated ballets, *le merveilleux*, and splendid scenic settings. The last act of Rameau's *Zoroastre* (1749; l., Louis de Cahusac) gives a detailed description of the temple setting, with its twenty gold columns encrusted in rubies and carbuncles, its green-and-silver mosaic vault, its sanctuary protected by a gold balustrade, and its sacred fire burning on an altar banked with rare and exotic flowers. The Metastasio operas became known in Paris through their poetry rather than as staged *opere serie*, and several of their "reforms" became evident in the French classical theater, notably reduction to three acts and more logical construction. Yet the French adapted these works to their own taste, and thus all but eliminated the love subplots and replaced the short, nervous dialogues that Metastasio wrote so well with the alexandrine line and that staple of the French classical theater, *"le tirade,"* or the long-winded, high-flown

speech, usually bordering on bombast, which was the classical theater's equivalent of the *aria di bravura*.[1] There was a certain amount
of spillover into the French classic opera, but direct adaptations of Metastasian librettos appeared only at the end of the century.[2]

Developments in the theater and in the comic opera, of course,
found their way, slowly and piecemeal, into the spectacle and
long-winded vapidity of the Opéra. Certain melodramatic traits
of plays by Lagrange-Chancel and Crébillon carried over (especially because both playwrights wrote for the Opéra as well), and
with the emergence of the vogue for historical subjects, several of
these librettos were also seen on the classic stage. One of them,
Sabinus (1773; m., François Gossec; l., Michel de Chabanon) will
be mentioned again later.

Although Diderot had championed the cause of the *"drame,"*
which was to take the place of the outmoded classic opera, the
Enlightenment philosophers realized that the older form still could
be put to use. These men, Voltaire in particular, saw the national
theater as the ideal place for a patriotic and chauvinistic type of
"message play" (Voltaire called it *tragédie nationale* and du Belloy
tragédie patriotique), and they saw the Opéra as the natural home
for its musical counterpart. This chauvinistic development within
the national operatic monopoly was understandable: Lully and
Quinault had dedicated their works to the same proposition. The
difference lay in the fact that the Lully operas (larded with an
admixture of divertissement for the benefit of both King and
court) were directed at the glorification of the grandeur of the
king, who embodied the nation, whereas the Enlightenment philosophers sought to glorify the country and its people, to insist,

---

(1) *Le tirade* forms an important part of France's classical theater and
a good deal of her classic opera, and is a point of distinction from the
bourgeois drama and from the Gluck-Calzabigi reform operas. It
usually took the form of a long, sonorous speech by one of the leading
characters. It did not die with the eighteenth century: it is seen in
the works of Victor Hugo who, although considered anti-classicist,
was a master of this adjunct to the classic play. In watered-down form
(poetically speaking) it can also be now and then seen in the bourgeois drama: Figaro's great *tirade* in the last act of Beaumarchais'
Le Mariage de Figaro (which was toned down to standard buffo
proportions by Da Ponte for Mozart) became the most provocative
element of the play when it was produced.
(2) E.g., *Démophoon* (1788; m., Cherubini; l., Marmontel) and *Dé-
mophon* (1789; m., J. C. Vogel; l., P. Desriaux).

in a relatively more austere framework, on the primacy of humanity. This nationalistic spirit had been constant in the French libretto because of the historical importance of France as a nation in the seventeenth and eighteenth centuries. *Cassandre* (1706; m., Bouvard and Bertin; l., Lagrange-Chancel) ended with Apollon declaiming that Hector's son would live to found the French Empire. Similarly, in the historical opera *Sabinus*, there is a *merveilleux* scene in which the allegoric Génie de la Gaule shows to an amazed Sabinus the future glory of France. "The back of the stage opens, and we see Charlemagne on his throne, surrounded by the peoples of his Empire."[3]

This patriotism was expanded into a love of liberty by the Enlightenment, as seen in the final scene of Voltaire's libretto, *Samson* (1750, never set), in which the blind giant exhorts his people: "*Peuple, éveille-toi, romps tes fers,/la liberté t'appelle/tu naquis pour elle:/reprends tes concerts.*"[4] Such overt philosophizing, abetted by the Diderot-inspired penchant for "message" works,[5] led to various *opéras à thèse*, of which the most typical was Beaumarchais' *Tarare*, which serves (properly) as apotheosis for this chapter.

The impact of Gluck's reform, when presented in Paris in 1772 in the guise of his *Iphigénie en Aulide*, completed the shak-

---

(3) René Guiet disparages this scene as "regrettable" in his masterly *L'Evolution d'un genre: le livret d'opéra en France de Gluck à la révolution,* p. 47, and indeed it runs counter to the spirit of anti-spectacle which was prevalent at the time because of Metastasio and, more immediately, Gluck and Calzabigi's example. Yet Guiet ignores the vital, continuing importance of this type of apotheosis (or "*le théâtre s'ouvre*") scene, almost always a final scene (although the *Sabinus* example ends the third act of a five-act opera) in the history not only of the French classic opera but of French bourgeois opera as well, in which it was neatly metamorphosed. The final scene of both *Le Déserteur* and *Richard Coeur de Lion* is an adaptation of the apotheosis finale, and in the nineteenth century the form would continue to be used in a different way by Scribe. The influence on such classic masterpieces as Berlioz's *Les Troyens* is of course direct. Not to appreciate the power of the necessity of such moments, both for scenic and for epic purposes, is to shrink the scope of French classic opera.
(4) "People, awake, break your chains! Liberty calls you: you were born for her: take up once again your spirit of good will!"
(5) Which led Diderot to espouse the works of the genre painter Jean-Baptiste Greuze, whose insipid moralizings hung limp on the walls of fashionable Frenchmen.

ing-out of the lingering Lullian traces and later accretions in the French classic opera. The attaché at the French Embassy in Vienna, François du Roullet, had seized on the idea, already promulgated by Diderot and Algarotti, that Racine's play would make ideal operatic material, and had fashioned a libretto for Gluck.[6] In it du Roullet combined certain features of Metastasio (the nobility of the characters, the interrelation in increasing tension of recitative and aria) with "reforms" that the French classic opera had begun to anticipate (elimination of subplots, unnecessary divertissements, scenic opulence, and *le merveilleux*) and that Calzabigi had carried through (rapid pace and a language that was immediate and emotional); and Gluck set it to virile, rough-hewn music that highlighted the novelties.[7] Little wonder that Paris was bowled over. The magnificent humanness of the character of Agamemnon, pitted in impossible struggles against the decree of the gods that his daughter must be sacrificed, at once removed the libretto from the man-and-plot-oriented world of Metastasio and brought it as close to the great Greek tragedies as the libretto had yet come. "*Je n'obéirai point à cet ordre inhumain,*"[8] he sings.

Du Roullet added even more to the libretto: most importantly, the active participation of the chorus in the events. This again derived ultimately from the Greeks, although more directly from the Metastasian and other "revolt" choruses of the *opera seria,* but du Roullet developed the idea so that it became a vigorous counterpart to the action. Thus the soothsayer Calchas is bullied into providing a sacrifice to appease the gods by the rebellious anger of the chorus: "*Nommez-nous la victime et, prompts à l'immoler sur les autels des Dieux/tout son sang va couler!*"[9]

---

(6) Algarotti himself wrote an *Iphigenia in Aulis* in 1755 in imitation of Racine's, and du Roullet knew it.
(7) Gluck has suffered at the hands of most twentieth-century interpreters (except Toscanini), either because he is considered a "Baroque Classic" whose music must be played gingerly and with due regard for his genius, or because interpreters are misled by the sublime nature of the second half of the second act of Orfeo—and the pastoral nature of the whole—to think that all of his music should be treated as if fragile. The result is not re-creation but emasculation.
(8) "I will never obey that inhuman order." Note the strong anapestic rhythm of this famous sentence.
(9) "Give us the name of the victim and, ready to sacrifice her on the altars of the gods, (we shall see that) all her blood will flow" (I, ii).

The success of *Iphigénie en Aulide* led Gluck to recast *Orfeo ed Euridice* and *Alceste* for the Opéra, and also led to the creation of *Iphigénie en Tauride,* one of his greatest works and one of the great classic librettos. Nicolas-François Guillard, a Parisian poet, was its librettist, but almost certainly du Roullet had a hand in its preparation. The influence of Euripides' play on the same subject is evident—far more so than the influence of a prior treatment by the French dramatist Guimond de La Touche.

Iphigénie en Tauride seethes with emotion, although paradoxically it is one of the very few librettos without love interest. It begins with a storm scene, as Verdi's *Otello* does, out of which Iphigénie and her priestesses emerge. All of them are Greeks captured by the barbarian Thoas. The storm dies down on stage, but not for Iphigénie: "*Le calme reparaît, mais au fond de mon coeur, hélas!, l'orage habite encore*" ("Calm reappears, but in my heart's inner core, alas, the tempest still finds its home")—a telling use of the calm-versus-rage opposition that Gluck was to express musically later in the opera. She then tells the priestesses of a dream she has had, of the collapse of the palace of her father, Agamemnon, of her father covered with blood, pierced by wounds, and of the horrible specter of her mother Clytemnestre.[1] She implores the gods to join her with her brother Oreste, wherever he may be. Thoas, King of the Scythes, enters in a deeply troubled mood. He has been upset by the storm, and he wants his chief priestess to divine its meaning. She says that Heaven is deaf to her pleas: he replies that Heaven wants the blood of a sacrifice. She says: "*Quelle effroyable offrande! Apaise-t-on les Dieux par des assassinats?*" ("What a frightful offering! Does one appease the gods through murders?"), but he is too beset by unknown shadows to be convinced by reason. Thoas is a superb portrait of a barbarian caught in the mesh of his own superstitions and fears, yet yearning for the sophistication and learning that the Greek Iphigénie represents—and at the same time hating her for her knowledge and breeding. At this moment the chorus of Scythes informs Thoas that two Greeks have been shipwrecked in the storm, that one of the two is calling for death, and that obviously their sacrificial victims have been delivered up by the gods. Oreste

(1) A direct antecedent of Elektra's opening set-piece in Hofmannsthal's libretto for Richard Strauss.

and Pylade are brought in, and Oreste can only say: "*Ô mon ami, c'est moi qui cause ton trépas*" ("O my friend, I am the cause of your death").[2]

The second act opens on a scene between the two friends. In contrast to previous *tragédie lyrique* (and in contrast to Sedaine), the scene is very simply described: the interior of a temple, with an altar. Oreste is distraught that his misfortune has managed to entrap his friend as well—"*Je n'avais qu'un ami, je deviens son bourreau*" ("I had only one friend, and I now become his executioner"). Pylade is carried away by guards, and Oreste is left to sing the famous passage in which "*le calme rentre dans mon coeur*" ("calm returns to my heart").[3] Oreste, left alone on stage, is an ideal excuse for a ballet-*cum*-chorus of the Furies, with Oreste crying for pity—a fine example of ballet being interwoven with the action to the satisfaction of the Calzabigi reform principles. Iphigénie enters, and Oreste sees her in his delirium as his mother, but goes on to tell her that her dream-fantasy is true: her father killed by her mother, who was in turn killed by her son, who himself has gone off in search of death. Iphigénie is crushed by these revelations, sends Oreste away, and gives vent to her sadness. "*Ô malheureuse Iphigénie*" may in one sense be a Metastasian exit aria summing up the feelings aroused by the previous recitative, but it is also something different, for Guillard has opened the closed nature of the exit aria so that Iphigénie does not sing her sorrow to the winds (and the audience), but to her fellow-exiles, the priestesses, thus including them in her overwhelming grief: "*Vous n'avez plus de Rois, je n'ai plus de parents*" ("You no longer have kings, I no longer have parents"). Here as elsewhere the direct nature of the language is remarkable for its succinctness. The chorus in its absolute despair and Iphigénie in her personal sorrow interact to produce a far more immediate and compelling tab-

---

(2) The Furies are pursuing Oreste with ill fortune because he has killed his mother.

(3) This scene demonstrates another difference from the Metastasian *opera seria*: the stage directions call for Pylade to be torn from the arms of Oreste, whereas in *opera seria* the principals very rarely touched one another. The concept of fraternal friendship sprang from Metastasio's *L'Olimpiade*. A literal staging of this scene before today's audiences would give rise to an interpretation quite foreign to the intentions of Guillard and Gluck, which suggests that authenticity in matters musical may not be able to be extended to matters theatrical.

leau[4] which, combined with the directness of the speech, was precisely what Calzabigi had in mind when he set out to humanize *opera seria.*

Act III, which takes place in Iphigénie's quarters, finds her resolved to go through with the sacrifice, even though one of the victims reminds her of her brother. She summons Oreste and Pylade, and tells them that, although she must obey Thoas's command, she has it in her power to reprieve one of the two, in return for which she asks that he take a letter back to Greece. Confronted by the choice, she reprieves Oreste. She leaves, and Oreste begs Pylade to let him die in his stead: *"La mort de mes tourments est l'unique relâche,/je l'obtenais, Pylade me l'arrache"* ("The end of my sufferings is the only release possible: I could grasp it, but Pylade tears it from me"). Pylade refuses, deeming it an honor to die for his friend. When Iphigénie returns with the priestesses, Oreste informs her that he must take Pylade's place, and cannot carry out her wish to return to Greece. Iphigénie realizes that her ruse to confound the gods (i.e., the sparing of the youth who reminds her of her brother) was futile, but she persists. It is only when Oreste threatens suicide that she relents. She then gives Pylade a letter for Électre, and he resolves to go and return with help. The third act ends. Notable in the structure of this act is the close interweaving of recitative and exit aria forms, as if the Metastasian concepts had been telescoped and smoothed together, with the aria (here often *arioso*) not hermetically sealed off, but part of the action. Oreste determines to kill himself during an *arioso*, which brings about Iphigénie's change of mind, and Pylade resolves to rescue him. It is easy to see in this act both the antecedents of the Gluck reform as well as the influences of the reform on the *Gesamtkunstwerk* theories of Wagner.

The fourth act is set in the temple. Iphigénie does not know if she can go through with her task, and signals her weakness in the accepted *opera seria* manner, by falling in a faint in a chair. Oreste assures her that she is doing him no harm, as he seeks death. He is prepared by the priestesses; she steels herself and raises the knife. Oreste calls out: *"Ainsi tu péris en Aulide, Iphigénie, ô ma*

---

(4) The realization of this difference in approach should, however, not lead to an automatic deprecation of Metastasio, for he sought distance and idealization of emotion in his exit arias as consciously as the Gluck reform sought immediacy.

soeur!" ("Thus you perished in Aulis, Iphigénie, my sister!"). Iphigénie recognizes her brother, and the priestesses their king. The joyous reunion is interrupted by news that the aroused Thoas is arriving with his countrymen. Thoas insists on Oreste's death "no matter who he is," and will also include Iphigénie's. The execution is forestalled by Pylade's arrival with his own men (scrounged up no one says where). He strikes Thoas, and a general massacre is avoided by the intervention of the goddess Diane. Thus the *lieto fine* becomes a compound of the man-centered *opera seria* of Metastasio and the *deus ex machina* habits of the Opéra—although here the appearance of the goddess accords not only with French operatic practice but with Euripides' play as well.

Guillard's libretto is notable for its strength of character, simplicity, pace, and comparatively direct use of language. Yet it is true that all of these qualities were as well or better rendered by the type of libretto authored by Sedaine. What *Iphigénie en Tauride* claimed monopoly of was these qualities set within the limitations of Greek-revival opera: that is, austerity and an evocation of the spirit of the Greek tragedians. The success of the opera clothed in Gluck's music and the overinflated and theatrical "quarrel" between those French factions championing Gluck and those championing the more traditional approach of Piccinni served to turn the spotlight of notoriety back on classic opera—and probably popularized the "priestess heroine" theme that would bear further fruit in *La Vestale* and *Norma*—but it could not breathe new life into the stiffening corpse of the form. Diderot had been riding a rising wave when espousing the *"drame bourgeois"*; the effects of this bourgeoisation would spread to the classic opera and sap it from within while destroying it from without.

Thus Marmontel allied himself with Piccinni against Gluck, but sinned less through his inability to become a new Metastasio than in being a writer of bourgeois drama inflated into *tragédie lyrique*.[5] When Didon dies on her pyre at the end of *Didon*

_____

(5) Marmontel also was responsible for many of the librettos that updated Quinault (*Atys* [1780; m., Piccinni], *Persée* [1780; m., Philidor], etc.), reducing the five acts to three and generally freshening up the old poet for modern audiences. Interestingly, in the last scene of his *Roland* (1778; m., Piccinni), Marmontel deleted the appearance of a group of fairies and shades of former heroes and substituted a camp with a group of chevaliers and French ladies, this to take advantage of the vogue for the Middle Ages which Sedaine was to

(1783; m., Piccinni), the moment may be superficially "tragic," but the effect is intolerably *larmoyante: "Adieu, mon cher Énée,/ mon dernier soupir est pour toi."*[6] Similarly, *le merveilleux* itself undergoes a change. At the end of Marmontel's *Antigone* (1790; m., Zingarelli), the scene changes to represent a magnificent temple on which is inscribed "To the spirit of Mercy," and indeed the spirit herself descends in a cloud to crown Créon—who has spared Antigone. The cheapening not only of the Greek originals, but even of Metastasio's concept of the *lieto fine,* is manifest in Marmontel's sobbing verse and limited emotional scope.

Finally, one other classic French opera should be mentioned. Although as a libretto it stands as a monument of the Baroque, it restores to French classical opera much of the flavor winnowed out by the "pure" Greek-revival works, and it adds a strong dose of moral uplift (of the strangest kind) tapped from Metastasio and the Encyclopedists and Voltaire. This is Beaumarchais' *Tarare* (1787; m., Salieri),[7] his only libretto although *Le Barbier de Séville* was originally intended as a *comédie mêlée d'ariettes*—a rare example of a libretto that came into existence through being refashioned from a libretto into a highly popular success as a play. *Tarare* was written as a didactic exercise (a true *pièce à thèse*) several years before Salieri set it, and became as an opera almost as great a success as Beaumarchais' *Le Mariage de Figaro* was as a play. Beaumarchais had wanted Gluck to compose it, but the composer felt too old to tackle the subject and suggested his pupil. The libretto was already widely known in Parisian circles, for Beaumarchais had been reading it aloud at gatherings for three years before the première. This practice was common enough in eighteenth-century Paris, where *salons* were common in which *tragédies* or philosophical tracts (particularly by one or another of the Encyclopedists) were read and commented upon; but the aping of Metastasio the poet and reader of his works, followed by

---

develop into a craze. The success of *Iphigénie en Aulide* led to a spate of classic operas on subjects taken from Corneille and Racine. In one of them, *Andromaque* (1780; m., Grétry; l., L. G. Pitra), the librettist even used shortened versions of actual Racine verses for several scenes, thereby shocking the purists; Guiet: *L'Évolution d'un genre . . . ,* pp. 58 *ff.*

(6) "Goodbye, my dear Aeneas, my expiring sigh is for thee" (III, x).
(7) Da Ponte, wishing to duplicate his triumph with Beaumarchais' *Le Mariage de Figaro,* reworked *Tarare* into *Axur, re d'Ormus* (Prague, 1788; m., Salieri).

the insistence of the Gluck reformers on the importance of the libretto,[8] gained the libretto itself a pre-hearing on the same footing as the newest philosophical concept. This librettistic priority, both as separate work of art and as self-contained philosophical entity, would be picked up by Wagner in the nineteenth century, who was reacting against the hack writers and factory-tooled products of the "collaborative" school of librettists, such as the Italians and Scribe.[9]

Tarare is a heterogeneous farrago, today seeming more comic than serious, in which Beaumarchais tried to re-create standard French classic traits such as the allegoric Prologue, the five-act form, a melodramatically villainous tyrant, a complex plot with a number of changes of fortune, and a third-act ballet. The story revolves around the noble and valiant soldier Tarare, who is pitted against the tyrant Atar and his henchmen the High Priest Arthénée and his son, the commanding general Altamort. Atar has Tarare's beautiful wife Astasie abducted for his private harem, and the libretto details Tarare's efforts to find out who took her and to recover her.[1] The grand climax comes, naturally enough, in the fifth act. Tarare has been captured, and is ready to die (Metastasian magnanimity) because he has not succeeded in finding Astasie or killing Altamort. Note here that Beaumarchais, for all his revolutionary sympathies, refuses to take the final step and condemn the tyrant Atar directly, which, in pre-Revolutionary France, would have led him directly to jail. Instead, he has Tarare reply to Atar's question *"Qu'ai-je à craindre?"* ("What do I have to fear?") by saying: *"De te voir toujours obéi/. . . tu pourrais tout contre un seul homme; tu ne pourrais rien contre tous!"* ("Seeing yourself always obeyed . . . you can do everything [you

---

(8) To the extent of creating a vogue of considering the libretto superior to the music.

(9) The morass of paradox surrounding theory and practice in the debate of word vs. music ever continues: Metastasio wrote some of the finest poetry and became a powerful librettist, yet his singers transformed *opera seria* into *vocalises;* Calzabigi and Gluck tried to re-establish the importance of drama and the word, but in the process "drama" shifted to the music; Wagner insisted on the importance of his rhymed texts, and yet in the opinion of many they are redeemed and made viable only by his music.

(1) Several features of the plot of *Tarare* (Tarare's being named to lead Atar's forces against an invasion in an invocation scene, for one) suggest that Camille du Locle might have had more than Egyptian tales of Mariette on his mind when he sent Verdi the outline of *Aida.*

want] against one man; you cannot do anything against everybody.") The speech is but a phrasing of one of the Encyclopedists' contentions, namely that a tyrant will cause his own downfall by uniting the people against him. This was exactly what happened in France, although the aristocracy could not see in the kindly Louis XVI a tyrant like the raging Atar, and so refused to apply the lesson of *Tarare* to their own country. Atar relents enough to give up Astasie so that she may die with Tarare (the magnanimity of a tyrant), but at the fatal moment, Tarare's soldiers enter and deliver him. Does Tarare welcome them? Not at all: *"Oubliez-vous, soldats, usurpant le pouvoir/que le respect des Rois est le premier devoir?* ("Have you forgotten, soldiers, in your lust for power, that your first duty is to respect your king?") Then: *"Armes bas, furieux! votre Empereur vous casse/*(To Atar) *Seigneur, ils sont soumis, je demande leur grâce."* ("Put down your arms, aroused ones! Your Emperor cashiers you. Sire, they have submitted, I now ask their pardon.") Does this lead to evil triumphing? Not at all: Atar, furious that his countrymen dare prefer Tarare to himself, commits suicide: *"La mort est moins dure à mes yeux/que de régner par toi sur un peuple odieux"* ("Death is preferable to reigning through you over a hateful populace"). Does Tarare accept the offered crown? Not at all—until the people themselves force it upon him. The only possibility left is for the *deus ex machina*—here, divided in two and made into Rousseauist nature spirits as La Nature and Le Génie du Feu—to pronounce the moral of the tale:

> *Mortel, qui que tu sois, Prince, Brame ou Soldat;*
> *HOMME! ta grandeur sur la terre,*
> *n'appartient point à ton état;*
> *elle est toute à ton caractère.*[2]
>
> (V, last)

The "message," deriving from the philosophy of the Encyclopedists, was historically well placed—an idea whose time had come —but the convulsions of the Revolution itself would efface the moralistic pussyfooting of Beaumarchais' aristocratic characters, who still reflected the classic poses of Metastasio and the Opéra. The librettos of the next decade would be of a different order.

---

(2) "Mortal, no matter who you may be: prince, priest or soldier. MAN! thy grandeur on earth lies not at all in thy station: it is completely contained in thy character."

Chapter Eleven

The Fin-de-siècle Italian Libretto

THE *commedia* spirit as remolded by Goldoni continued to dominate the Italian libretto long after Goldoni went to France. This spirit was evidenced both in the loose construction of the story—an excuse for byplay—and in the *commedia* way of taking an idea and refashioning it. Thus, very few if any Italian librettos were entirely original, even in the sense that *Le Déserteur* was original: if the basis was not a French or English libretto, play, or story or an older work, the Italian librettists would take a Goldoni-like idea and let it blossom into *commedia lazzi*.

Another important aspect of the *commedia* continued to hang over the Italian libretto: the anonymity of its authors. Even Goldoni, as we have seen, was often ignored as the author of an opera libretto and, as the century drew to a close, it became more and more exceptional to see the name of the librettist upon his work. The name of the composer was far more likely to appear:[1] the very nature of the writing of most librettos was one of improvisation and haste. By and large, each Italian city opera house possessed its own company (as standardized as the *opera seria*, with its first and second *buffo*, its male lover, *ingénue*, etc.), and the texts, if not written directly for the theater by a local librettist (either in the pay of the impresario or residing in the city), were adapted from successes in other cities. Also, the growing importance of the music vis-à-vis the words, and therefore the growing importance of the composer, led to the librettist's being

---

(1) More often in Italian librettos published in Italy than in those published in Austria.

considered even more strongly as a necessary but strictly secondary appendage—necessary to put the *lazzi* into verse and give the action some sort of continuity, but at the mercy not only of the composer and the singers but all too often of the impresario as well. Now and then the composer dispensed with the librettist and wrote the text himself.[2] It is easy to understand this decline of the librettist, given the *commedia* context of the work: because the public was well aware of the stock scenes, whether of disguise in Oriental costume or of fathers lecturing daughters on marriage, it paid more attention to the newer elements, such as the music. The adaptive nature of these librettos greatly lessened the scope of the librettist's creative power. His major contribution lay in the quality of the verse and the novelty of language or approach to these scenes, which was rendered all the more difficult by the fact that in these areas Goldoni had already set a very high standard. Thus the librettist was left with acclaim as an adapter of stronger and more individual works, no mean achievement if successfully carried off, but far more neutral in tone than the achievement of a work such as *Tarare*. The librettist himself, then, hid behind his adaptations, and his individuality as a writer and a thinker had to be gleaned from the often meager evidences of departure from the original and from stock repetitions. This neutrality or blandness in turn encouraged the composer to fill the purely creative void, so that evidences of character and of pace shifted from the work of the writer to that of the notesmith.

It is no wonder, then, that, given these constricting circumstances, the libretto did not attract first-rate minds and came to depend upon the hack who could produce a serviceable work to order. Even those relatively gifted men who offered their services did not present themselves as librettists first and only, like Metastasio, but wrote poetry, sought sinecures, engaged in intrigues, and often traveled about in search of money and popularity. Giovanni Battista (also, Giambattista) Casti, who in a differing climate could have become a major librettist, and who even in the works he left demonstrates an individuality stronger than that of any of his com-

---

(2) E.g., *Il Conte di Bell'Umore* (1783; m. & l., Marcello Bernardini). It is also highly probable that in other cases composers tinkered with the libretto—Mozart was hardly the first, although one of the best, in collaborating with his librettist on the textual and scenic elements of the opera.

peers, expressed himself in barbed terms on the deflated status of
the eighteenth-century librettist in his work *Prima la musica e poi
le parole* ("First the music and then the words"—indicative of
Casti's opinion) (1786; m., Salieri). The poet proposes to the
composer that they divide their fee of one hundred zecchini
equally. The composer disabuses him:

> C: *Amico, l'interesse*
> *Non a la mia passion: ma pur dovreste*
> *pensar che la fatica è tutta mia:*
> *Onde parrebbe giusto,*
> *che la ripartizion far si dovesse,*
> *con un po' d'equità distributiva.*
> P: *Cioè?*
> C: *Per me novanta, e per voi il resto*
> P: *Cotal repartimento è troppo onesto.*[3]
>
> (I, i)

Casti adds that the Poet's reply should be spoken "*con ironia,*"
but the sarcasm is obvious. Or take this dialogue: COMPOSER: (reading out Poet's lines) " 'And this *castrato* will run me through!'
POET: *Castrato?* What the devil are you saying? C: I'm only reading what's written. P: Let's see. *Costato* [rib cage] was written,
not *castrato.* C: *Castrato* goes extremely well and I won't change it.
P: Eh? Are you making fun of me? C: What I wrote, I wrote. P:
Have you gone crazy? C: I wrote *castrato,* it will remain *castrato*!
P: And afterwards they will say, who was this poet who wrote
such idiotic tripe. C: You won't be the first or the last." (I, iii.)
Finally, the Prima Donna castigates the Poet as an insolent fellow,
and the Composer replies, with the languid assurance of a superior:
"Excuse him, he has the plebeian quality of feigning knowledge of
what he does not know."

The great majority of these Italian librettos were comic, as
the separation from the *opera seria* was still almost complete. It was
not until the *melodramma* period in the early nineteenth century
that the French concept of bourgeois drama would permeate Italy.

---

(3) "My friend, money is not my passion, but you should consider
that the labor is all mine, and thus it would seem fitting that the division
be made with a little fairness." "That is?" "Ninety per cent for me
and the rest for you." "Such a division is too fair."

At the first performance Michael Kelly, who played the Poet,
imitated the mannerisms of Da Ponte, which led to a widening of
the rift between Casti and Da Ponte.

Even themes with dramatic potential, such as Giovanni Bertati's one-act *Don Giovanni* (1787; m., Giuseppe Gazzaniga), the immediate source for Da Ponte's libretto, shied away from too overt dramatic power by interlarding the scenario with comic scenes and by providing a strict buffo ending that now would be associated with the Rossini operas, in which the lesser characters imitate musical instruments while singing "What happy craziness!"[4] Yet the Don does go to Hell, in a scene almost exactly like Da Ponte's.

The Italian libretto was not confined to Italy, for Italian had become the universal operatic language, and its practitioners therefore could be found all over Europe, from St. Petersburg to Esterháza to London, and most specially in Vienna. Vienna continued to be a center for operatic achievement and intrigue because the pay was better there than in Italy, and the other rewards immeasurably greater. An operatic "hit" in Vienna meant the establishment of a reputation and the chance to succeed to one of the two most prestigious librettistic posts in Europe, that of the Caesarean Poet (left vacant by the death of Metastasio in 1782) and that of the lesser Poet to the Imperial Theaters. Three Italian librettists vied in the scramble for these posts, and as they represent the late-eighteenth-century Italian libretto at its most characteristic, they will be considered at some length. They are Giovanni Bertati (1735-1815), Giovanni Battista Casti (1721-1803), and Lorenzo Da Ponte (1749-1838).

All three were great travelers and adept at connivance, and they all disliked one another (although for diplomatic reasons one in good fortune would cordially receive another temporarily out of favor): each had his own friends in the various cities, and particularly at the Viennese court, who would champion their candidate's cause. Da Ponte had been received by the aged Metastasio upon his arrival in Vienna, and the old poet had read out part of a Da Ponte poem, *Filemone e Bauci;* but on Metastasio's death, the post of Caesarean Poet was left vacant, Da Ponte being named Poet to the Imperial Theaters by his "friend," the Emperor Joseph II, who had acceded to the throne in 1780. Casti had arrived in Vienna in order to obtain the greater post for himself, but his maliciously

---

(4) This interweaving had the effect, of course, of heightening the drama, in the manner of Busenello, Shakespeare and latterly, Sedaine.

witty pen had placed him in disgrace, and in 1786, after several successes, he departed for Constantinople. With the early death of Joseph II in 1790, Da Ponte lost his patron—all the more ominous because Casti had been Court Poet to the new Emperor, Leopold, while the latter ruled only Tuscany. But, though Da Ponte lost his position as Poet to the Imperial Theaters, and left for Trieste, Leopold in turn died in 1792 and both Casti and Da Ponte returned to Vienna. There Bertati had taken over as Poet to the Imperial Theaters, and Da Ponte was further closed out when Casti was appointed by Francis II to Metastasio's post.[5] Da Ponte left Vienna for London and, eventually, New York, while Casti's irrepressible pen and tongue cut short his tenure of the Caesarean post in 1796. He went to Trieste and then to Paris, where he died in 1803.

Giovanni Bertati's work most clearly reflects the fin-de-siècle Italian libretto. Unlike the output of Casti and, to some extent, that of Da Ponte, Bertati's librettistic output was large. While never a strong versifier (in this resembling all the lesser Italian librettists of the time, such as Petrosellini, Mazzolà, and Palomba)—indeed, Da Ponte's partisan description of visiting him at work and finding the poet surrounded by rhyming dictionaries is probably accurate— Bertati could nonetheless order a story line with clarity and concision and stuff it with the requisite amount of plot intrigue and *commedia* business. His greatest success, *Il Matrimonio segreto* (1792; m., Domenico Cimarosa), is one of the better buffo works in the direct Goldoni tradition. Bertati's librettos have the lightness and a verve that characterize the *commedia*, and indulge in a high degree of *lazzi* foolery, such as disguise and the use of gibberish foreign tongues.[6] Bertati also made great use of the "catalogue aria,"[7] which was another staple of the libretto of the time. Almost all of his works had scenes or plot structures based on earlier Goldoni

---

(5) He was its next-to-last occupant, the last being one Clemente Bondi.

(6) Such as this, from *L'Avaro* (1776; m., Pasquale Anfossi), spoken by someone disguised as an East Indian: *"Salama mi lecca;/macacca rebecca,/urgasma ti kà,/houla babalà"* (II, x).

(7) E.g.: *"Voi sarete alloggiato/nelle stanze medesime/dove alloggiati furo ottanta re,/seicento trenta Duchi,/quindici mille ventidue marchesi,/Teutoni, Galli, Iberi, Itali, Inglesi"* ("You will be housed in the same rooms in which were housed eighty kings, six hundred and thirty dukes, fifteen thousand and twenty-two marquis, Germans, Frenchmen, Spaniards, Italians, Englishmen"). *L'Isola de Alcina*, 1772; m., Giuseppe Gazzaniga; I, vii.

texts or similar librettos; they were usually in three acts, of which the last was very short and was not uncommonly a merry free-for-all almost entirely without plot, played in disguise at night outdoors, in which couples paired and were parted, in variations on the last act of Beaumarchais, *Le Mariage de Figaro* (which in itself had drawn from *commedia* sources).

These librettos placed great reliance upon the abilities of the buffo actors, who were meant to embroider on the text and who doubtless made pointed references to local customs and/or individuals.[8] Yet, although Bertati's librettos follow by and large the slightly lunatic, humorous vein tapped by Goldoni, they also include a growing undertone of cynical protest at the license of the aristocrats. With Goldoni this protest had been aimed at specific customs, but with the influence of Rousseau and the French it had broadened to a protest against the system. This undertone is well disguised, for Bertati and his fellow librettists were at the mercy of the whims of the ruling class; but it is present in his work, in Da Ponte's, and in Casti's. Bertati's libretto for *Don Giovanni* is perhaps the best instance of this protest, for to Bertati[9] the Don was not the supra-human symbolic figure of freedom becoming license that the nineteenth-century Romantics were to make of him, but rather a portrait of a "modern" aristocrat, who could take and not have to pay back. Thus the Don's fiery end is less divine punishment than a just redressing of social wrongs.

Bertati's libretto for *Don Giovanni* has been attacked by those who recognize the superiority of Da Ponte's without a concomitant appreciation of its strengths (which Da Ponte largely appropriated). Bertati's verse of course has none of the elegance or invention of Da Ponte's, as is shown in a comparison of "catalogue arias." Here is a portion of Bertati's:

> *dell'Italia, ed' Alemagna*
> *ve ne ho scritto cento, e tante.*
> *Della Francia, e della Spagna*
> *ve ne sono non so quante:*

---

(8) The same is true, to a lesser extent, of Da Ponte's buffo works, but in them the conjunction with Mozart's genius (and, secondarily, the growing dominance of the composer generally) had begun to confine the libretto to the notes written for it.
(9) And, I strongly believe, to Da Ponte as well.

fra madame, cittadine,
artigiani, contadine,
cameriere, cuoche, e guattare;
perchè basta che sian femmine
per doverle amoreggiar.[1]

(I, vii)

Yet Bertati provided the framework of the libretto that Da Ponte wisely followed—with the exception of the Act I finale, which Bertati omitted because his libretto was written in one act. The one-act concept is also an asset, for, despite the opportunities for *commedia* foolery, Bertati keeps the pace moving inexorably toward the final supper scene. He is careful also to keep the idea of retribution before the audience and, although his characterizations have not the nuances that Da Ponte's have, the characterization of his Don is as ruthless as that of Da Ponte's.[2] Da Ponte realized the power of Bertati's graveyard and supper scenes, which alternate comic and intensely dramatic moments, and largely followed them: it is here that Bertati rises above his other librettos to show an intensity that Da Ponte and Mozart immortalized. Excerpts from the confrontation demonstrate Bertati's ability.

Commendatore: *Basta così. M'ascolta.*
tu m'invitasti a cena:
ci venni senza pena:
or io ti inviterò.
Verrai tu a cena meco?
Dammi la man per pegno.
Don: *Eccola—ohimè, qual gelo!*
C: *Pentiti, e temi il Cielo,*
che stanco è omai di te.
Don: *Lasciami, vecchio insano.*

---

(1) "From Italy and Germany I've written in more than a hundred. From France and Spain there are I don't know how many—ladies, city girls, working girls, farm girls, ladies' maids, cooks, and kitchen-maids. They only have to be women for him to start making love."
(2) In Bertati, Giovanni strikes the Masetto figure in his *first* scene with him—he has no truck with any of the lower class who disagree with him—and he comes to the graveyard to gloat over his triumph (in Da Ponte's libretto, he does not realize that the Commendatore is buried there).

C: *Empio, ti scuoti in vano*
pentiti, Don Giovanni.[3]
(I, xxiv)

The cardinal aspect of Giovanni's character in the Da Ponte libretto—his defiance of authority even at the cost of his soul— is carried over from the Bertati source.[4] The appearance of such a ruthless aristocrat was no doubt attributable to the increasing allowance of criticism of the *ancien régime*, which had been conditioned by the French philosophers (for Giovanni, *pace* nineteenth-century romantic enamelings, is essentially, in both the Bertati and Da Ponte librettos, a more compulsively active and oversexed Count Almaviva), but the vigor and clarity with which the portrait is drawn by both Bertati and Da Ponte points toward the changes that were imminent throughout Europe and were miles removed from the antic *commedia* japeries of the majority of Bertati's librettos—or the close of his *Don Giovanni.*

Casti was the opposite type from Bertati and Da Ponte: a highly individual mind who turned to the libretto at the end of his career and left very few works in the form (only three were published during his lifetime). He had high talent: a versifying ability as great as, if quite different from, Da Ponte's and an acerbic view of life, which is seen in a few of his librettos, at odds with the general temper of the form, but reflective of that strain of pessimism which reappears at intervals in the Italian libretto and was first noticed in the work of Busenello. Casti probably could not have lasted long as a librettist, for he did not have the overwhelming librettistic and poetic talents of a Metastasio, and possessed an independent character coupled with a highly satiric tongue and pen that would not only have alienated his patrons but would also have kept him from cranking out rewrites of Goldoni. He wrote his first-produced libretto, *Il Re Teodoro in Venezia*, in 1784 at the age of sixty-two; only a handful of his

---

(3) "C: That's enough. Listen to me. You invited me to dine; I have come of my own accord. Now I shall invite you. Will you come and dine with me? . . . Give me your hand as a pledge. DG: Here it is— ah! How cold it is! C: Repent, and fear Heaven, which has tired of you. DG: Let me go, insane dotard. C: Villain, I chastise you in vain. Repent, Don Giovanni."

(4) And from such earlier sources as Molière and Goldoni. The important fact is that the Don's character was in no way softened for the tastes of the *opera buffa* audience.

texts were set to music (he left several others in manuscript at his death). The bulk of his contemporary and posthumous fame rested on his poetic works, one written in 1783 (the *Poema tartaro*) and two written after he left Vienna and took up residence in Paris. These last two are the *Novelle,* or stories in poetry, and his greatest work, *Gli Animali parlanti (The Talking Beasts,* 1795), an updating of Aesop in verse, widely read and translated, which was a precursor of George Orwell's *Animal Farm.*[5] As with Da Ponte, Casti took minor orders and used the title "Abbé" to gain status and entrée into society.

If the history of the libretto is considered as a paradise of the journeyman and the graveyard of the talented, Casti must be one of the chief victims, for his voice, as shown in *Prima la musica,* intermittently in *Il Re Teodoro* and other librettos, and throughout *Gli Animali parlanti,* was strong enough to create a work in which satire and a moral tone could have blended to produce high art. Yet the constant attendant difficulties surrounding the libretto, plus the growing insistence of composers that the librettist be termed the "obedient handmaiden," necessarily blunted individuality. The days of Metastasian inviolability were over: the composer no longer took the finished work and set it to music, but wanted to collaborate on its creation.[6] As the composer arrogated an ever-greater amount of knowledge of the dramatic functioning and individual characterization of the work to himself, and as—more importantly —he came to have the power to compel obedience from his librettist, the indepedent-minded writer had the options of persuasion or knuckling under,[7] finding a more complaisant or understanding partner, slipping something through which the composer did not catch, composing the music himself, or leaving the field to others. The nineteenth century would see examples of all of these approaches.

---

(5) Da Ponte himself published the first English edition of the work. In *Gli Animali parlanti* Casti satirizes the source Prologues that Zeno and Metastasio had made a standard feature of *opera seria* by listing, *after* the poem, a long list of mythical "sources."

(6) Casti himself never really collaborated with a composer, preferring to send his finished work to be set.

(7) The scales were weighted more heavily than before in the composer's favor by the growing custom of publication of the musical score. With the libretto *as written in the score* being accepted as the final word, the composer could control the specific words to be written—as Casti said in *Prima la musica.*

Il Re Teodoro in Venezia (m., Paisiello) is important as a libretto largely because of its central character. Casti took the subject from Voltaire's *Candide*, basing it on a historical occurrence in which the King of Corsica, Theodore, Baron of Neuhoff (Westphalia), was overthrown by his adopted subjects and forced to flee to Venice (he died in London in 1756). Such contemporary history as the basis for a libretto was rare enough, even though Casti surrounded the King and his reduced court (a prime minister, who, like the King, travels incognito) with Metastasian exit arias, a love plot and subplot, and the almost-inevitable Ottoman potentate (also in exile)—the last of which would give rise to *buffo* scenes in the *Trois Sultanes* vein. Casti provides some "Goldonian" genre touches (notably a chorus of gondoliers); yet Teodoro rises above the merry antics, for Casti paints him as a humane but world-weary ruler, cognizant of the vanities of life but unable to affect or influence them: *"Senza soldi e senza regno/brutta cosa è esser re.*[8] He contrasts this sadness with a quixotic streak evidenced in a patter aria about a nightmare he had in which his debts appeared to him as a ghost—much like Gilbert's celebrated Nightmare in *Iolanthe.*[9] The poetry of this aria is in short, punchy lines of five or six syllables, which Casti often used in his work and which he is credited with reintroducing into the libretto. In fact, the King's debts do catch up with him, and he is thrown into prison —here, a prison far more real than the prisons in *opera seria*. The others incarcerated with him try to cheer him up, but he is inconsolable, and his final speeches are touching, as much at odds with the buffo gaieties of the *vaudeville* finale as the penultimate "scene" of *Don Giovanni*—too piercingly real even for the "real" middle-class world of Goldoni.

> TEODORO: *Questo squallido soggiorno*
> *d'ogni intorno*
> *offre immagini funeste;*
> *e fra queste—nude pietre*
> *scure e tetre—pien d'orrore*
> *sento il core—palpitar.*

---

(8) "Without money and without a kingdom, it is a harsh thing to be a king" (I, i).
(9) Which may have led Edward J. Dent to call Casti "the Gilbert of his day"; April Fitzlyon: *The Libertine Librettist*, p. 105.

> *Dunque questa catacomba*
> *e la tomba*
> *d'ogni mio vasto disegno?*
> *Questo è il regno—e questo è il trono?*
> *Questi dunque i Stati sono*
> *ove un dì credea regnar?*
>
> . . . .
>
> (To the others) *Finiscila una volta*
> *colle tue rancie istorie:*
> *non mi parlar di glorie,*
> *non mi seccar così.*
>
> . . . .
>
> *Giusto ciel! quanto nojosa*
> *e la gente virtuosa*
> *quando prèdica moral.*
>
> . . . .
>
> *In pace lasciatemi*
> *udir non vo' più.*[1] (He exits.)
>
> (II, last)

There is something symbolic about Teodoro turning his back on the *commedia* troupe as they sing the happy finale.

Casti's other work shows surprising range and unusual freedom. He did not, like Bertati and Da Ponte (and most other Italian librettists), readapt already-extant works but preferred to create his own from ideas or historical facts. He dabbled in history with *Cublai, Gran Kan de' Tartari* (1788; m., Salieri) and *Catilina* (1792; m., Salieri);[2] wrote a machine-and-magic comedy, *La Grotta de Trofonio* (1785; m., Salieri),[3] a sequel to *Il Re Teodoro* which was actually a preamble; *Il Re Teodoro in Corsica* (178?,

---

(1) "This wretched abode on all sides offers sad images, and among these bare stones, dark and gloomy, full of horror, I feel my heart beat. Then is this catacomb the tomb of all my vast plans? Is this my kingdom—is this my throne? Are these then the states over which I once thought to reign? . . . Stop your tired stories once and for all. Don't speak to me of glory, don't bore me like this. . . . Good Heavens! How tedious are virtuous people when they preach morality. . . . Leave me in peace—I don't want to hear any more." The English adaptation of the libretto (London, 1787) omits these speeches, as if they were too much in conflict with the buffo nature of the rest.
(2) In the latter, Casti sets Cicero's famous denunciation of Catiline to Italian verse: "*Fino a quando, O Catilina,/l'esterminio e la rovina/ contro noi mediterai? ecc.*"
(3) Which Rossini thought "a masterpiece"; Edmond Michotte: *Wagner's Visit to Rossini*, p. 40.

never set);[4] and a charming light comedy, *I Dormienti* (1793?), about two Crusaders who sleep for six centuries and awake to the eighteenth century, which carries the slumber scene to its final ludicrous extreme. All of these works are patchy, but the serious ones attempt to break out of the *opera seria* straitjacket that was still oppressing the Italian libretto. More testaments to a man than influences on the form, the librettos of Giambattista Casti stand as incomplete monuments to *une oeuvre inachevée*.

If Casti's librettos are signposts pointing to what might have been, the most famous ones of Lorenzo Da Ponte are signposts toward what would be. Da Ponte was born Emanuele Conegliano, of Jewish parents in Ceneda, north of Venice. He soon took the name of the local Catholic bishop, converted to Catholicism, and studied enough in the seminary to attach "Abbé" to his name. Left on his own at an early age, he lived by his wits in Venice and then, when he was expelled for proved adultery, moved on to Vienna, to which he went by way of Dresden.

Like Casti and many other Italian librettists, Da Ponte considered himself first of all a poet, and had no experience in writing for the theater other than a background of reading "great works." Despite this handicap, he obtained the appointment as Poet to the Imperial Theaters in 1783 before he had written a single libretto —testament both to the value of personal connections over ability and to the bureaucratic preference, in Italian-language operatic countries, for a poetic rather than a dramatic grounding.[5] Da Ponte's first produced libretto was a translation of Guillard's *Iphigénie en Tauride*; his first "independent" work was *Il Ricco d'un giorno* (1784; m., Salieri). The next few years were the heyday of Da Ponte's librettistic career, for they contained his collaboration with Mozart; in 1791, the year of Mozart's death, he was ordered to leave Vienna. He arrived in London in 1792, and in 1793 obtained appointment as Poet to the King's Theatre in the

---

(4) Goethe was a great admirer of *Teodoro/Venezia*, and Casti showed him the manuscript of the first act of *Teodoro/Corsica*, which he also enjoyed.

(5) The Emperor Joseph was supposed to have asked his young appointee how many librettos he had written. Upon being told none, he replied: "Good. Then we shall have a virgin muse." It is probable that the lack of dramatic fiber in many Italian "poets" led to the composer supplying precisely that ingredient, thus further reducing the librettist's role vis-à-vis the opera.

Haymarket. It was in London that Da Ponte was to write the rest of his librettos—in addition, he also set up as a publisher there. In 1805 he emigrated to the United States, where he lived the rest of his life, teaching Italian (at Columbia College), writing his *Memoirs*, and encouraging the development of the study of Italian literature. He died in 1838 an American citizen.

Da Ponte is typical of the fin-de-siècle Italian librettist not only in his restless traveling in search of posts and in his relentless involvement in intrigue but also, from a primarily librettistic point of view, in his semi-detached attitude toward the form. He considered himself above all a writer and a poet and he adapted or wrote librettos to order: if there was no demand, he turned to other means of making a living. What sets Da Ponte apart is not so much his dramatic ability or the quality of his verse as his good taste in subjects, his adaptive touch, and his conjunction with one of the greatest dramatic and operatic geniuses. It should not be forgotten that without Mozart, Da Ponte's work would bulk infinitely smaller, and that we are still unsure as to how much of the form and substance of Da Ponte's three complete librettos[6] for Mozart should be ascribed to the composer. The nineteenth century tended to dismiss Da Ponte almost entirely (he was known as D'aponte if he was known at all): if he deserves more, the limits of his abilities should be clearly defined.

A study of Da Ponte's non-Mozartean librettos will reveal a greater amount about his final stature as a librettist. They are either adaptations of *opera seria* subjects, done in the Metastasian exit-aria style with such "reform" overtones as shortening, elimination of amorous *longueurs*, and a tendency toward direct language,[7] or buffo operas, often also adaptations, in the Bertati or the Favart pastoral style, but with a pronounced accentuation of the lustful overtones[8] in keeping with the Casanova side of Da Ponte's nature. An allegoric libretto such as *L'Arbore di Diana* (1787; m., Martín) falls outside this categorization; it is nonetheless a type of the *livret d'occasion* or *livret à clef* that Casti and others wrote for the Viennese court. In common with all Italian and most French

---

(6) It is thought that Da Ponte also wrote the libretto for Mozart's unfinished *Lo Sposo deluso* (K.430) in 1783 (?).
(7) *Antigona* (1796; m., Bianchi), *Merope* (1797; m., Bianchi), etc.
(8) *Una Cosa rara* (1786; m., Martín); *La Scola de' maritati* (1795; m., Martín), etc.

librettists, Da Ponte shows little interior development over the course of his work (apart from a dramatic refinement that is almost immediately perceptible): a libretto such as *Le Nozze di Figaro*, even without Mozart's music, is as good a work as he would ever produce, and he wrote it in 1786. Moreover, apart from their overt enjoyment of sexuality, Da Ponte's librettos do not show the individuality that marks Casti's. Da Ponte was uninterested in being a moral force,[9] or even in seeking new forms of expression for the "standard" *opera seria* or *opera buffa* of his time, such as Metastasio or Sedaine had provided. He was hired to do a job, and he did it to the best of his ability.

The positive aspects of Da Ponte's work lay precisely there, and they were of importance because, as has already been stated, these qualities would come to the fore in the libretto of the nineteenth century. They influence the role of the librettist as adapter or "neutral" middleman between creator and audience. The adapter is of course not neutral, in the sense that he must of necessity add something of his own; and in most cases he is not neutral in that he effectively destroys the individual qualities of the original but does not replace them with anything comparable. Da Ponte's contribution was to demonstrate the power of the adapter, not only in organizing a work for the operatic stage but also in preserving as much as possible of the original in the adaptation, thus effacing himself for the benefit of the original writer and the composer. It is what the librettist did *not* do, rather than what he did, that affects the result, and in that result the original author must stand as co-librettist. *Le Mariage de Figaro* is a strong dramatic work of fascinating interrelation and subtlety, of which Da Ponte (and, we must add, probably Mozart) preserved the essence if not the totality. Bertati's libretto for *Don Giovanni* likewise was taken over and refined, and Da Ponte's treatment of plays such as *The Comedy*

---

(9) Although Da Ponte had Bertati's example before him in tackling the Don Giovanni legend, it took some moral courage to set the notoriously liberal Beaumarchais play in Imperial Vienna, even if it was somewhat watered down. But it should be seen in context: the work was notorious more for its reputation than for its specifics, which were grounded in the *commedia* tradition as interwoven with the Goldoni-Diderot contemporaneousness. What is more important, in considering Da Ponte as a librettist, is noting that he never (again?) attempted such a potentially provocative subject, even in the freer atmosphere of London, but relied on the tested *buffa* and *seria* formulas.

of Errors of Shakespeare (*Gli Equivoci*, 1786; m., Stephen Storace) and Goldoni's *Il Burbero di buon cuore* (1786; m., Martín)—or even his adaptation of Beaumarchais' *Tarare* as *Axur, re d'Oremus* (1788; m., Salieri)—show a translation into the spirit and the conventions of the time without loss of contact with the essence of the original.

This adaptive ability goes beyond the instances of reworkings of specific plays. Da Ponte's mind was exceptionally quick to grasp the essentials of anything he undertook, and he was widely read—certainly, in company with Boito and Hofmannsthal, one of the most literate librettists. He was thus able to synthesize; a quality evidenced in his last work for Mozart, *Così fan tutte* (1790). Unlike *Le Nozze di Figaro*, *Così* is not based on an original literary source, yet no aspect of it can be considered novel except the fact that it was one of the very rare operas of the period to be played in contemporary costume. The over-all idea of a light divertissement with strong pastoral overtones came not only from the pastorals themselves but also from numerous chamber operas, not least those of Metastasio. The basic plot contrivance of switching lovers as a joke had been used before in one of the first French comic operas in the Italian style, *Les Troqueurs* (1753; m., Antoine Dauvergne; l., J.-J. Vadé), as well as in *commedia* plots; the story follows the unities, and characters such as the cynical elder and the minx maid could be traced back to the earliest *commedia* days. The disguised "doctor," the fake poison and feigned marriage, the Oriental costumes, and the languishing-over-portrait-lockets are all drawn from the Italian theatrical stockroom. Da Ponte's poetry, likewise, has a feathery charm and simplicity reminiscent of the Calzabigi of *Orfeo* and of Metastasio:[1] indeed, Da Ponte cribbed an entire exit aria from Metastasio with the change of only a word (*"È la fede delle femmine"* [I, i] is the once-famous aria *"È la fede degli amanti"* from *Demetrio* [II, ii]). The organization of the libretto is close to perfect, being in complementary halves, each culminating in a ceremony. Without Mozart's music it would be a distinct, if small-scaled, achievement; with it, the opera becomes a synthesis of the pastoral-*cum*-buffo elements of the century, deepened and enriched with a humanness, as graceful and exemplary

---

(1) Exit arias and the Metastasian simile abound, here as elsewhere in Da Ponte (and other Italian librettists). Ferrando's aria *"Un' aura amorosa"* (I, xii) is pure Metastasio.

as a Watteau landscape with figures. The equivocal moral tone, a definite contribution of Da Ponte's, led to *Così*'s being ignored (or drastically altered) during the nineteenth century—but with the twentieth its qualities have come to be recognized.

The Da Ponte–Mozart collaboration brings up for the first time another aspect of the role of the librettist. It is generally thought that the ideal relationship between composer and librettist is one in which two minds function independently as one, each reinforcing the other. In the nineteenth century, Wagner was to feel so strongly that this ideal could not be achieved by two men that he championed the cause of a single one: the composer doubling as librettist.[2] Yet throughout the rest of libretto history we shall see not only this conjunction operating, but also its obverse operating—an obverse far from damaging to the work as a whole. For an apprehended dichotomy need not result in a pulling to pieces of the work: it can serve to deepen and enrich through ambiguity what should not be made finally explicit. The work as a whole— the opera—gains rather than loses. The obvious example of this in Da Ponte's work is the close of *Le Nozze di Figaro*. Mozart's intentions, interpreted through knowledge of his mind and, more to the point, through the fact of his score, are clear: the "magic modulation" that usually is discussed in terms bordering on mystic rapture before the Count's "*Contessa, perdono*" leads us to the certainty, in terms both of the outcome and of the musical power, that the Count has indeed reformed and will no longer be a womanizer. Yet it is equally clear from knowledge of Beaumarchais'[3] and Da Ponte's minds that neither of them thought for a minute that the Count was doing more than extricating himself from a particularly embarrassing predicament, and that the only "reform" possible for him would be the Don's punishment. The musical moment, of course, overrides the librettistic intention, but the general portrayal of the character throughout the opera pulls in quite another direction. The moment, then, though musically "resolved," remains ambiguous—to the benefit of the opera.

---

(2) Or, more accurately, as we shall see, the librettist doubling as composer doubling as librettist.

(3) Beaumarchais, in the final play of the trilogy, *La Mère coupable*, makes it clear that the Countess Almaviva had a child by Cherubino— a happening not inferable from Mozart's opera.

This dichotomy is apparent throughout *Così fan tutte*, for Da Ponte's lightly cynical, worldly libretto (even with its Arcadian overtones) was considered something far more serious by the composer, so that in a scene such as the one after the departure of the lovers (I, vi) we are torn between amusement and tears. And in *Don Giovanni* there is some debate as to whether Mozart wanted the opera a pure tragedy, whereas Da Ponte urged a greater emphasis on the comic aspects.[4] Certainly in Da Ponte's non-Mozartean librettos there is a clear separation of the comic and the *seria*; there is also little of the psychological depth of characterization that commentators have found in his Mozart librettos,[5] although his characters usually are well drawn. Nevertheless, we shall continue to note the presence of this opposition of intent in operatic collaborations—and even, Heaven forfend, in Wagner himself!—which will culminate in the fascinating push–pull relationship of Richard Strauss and Hugo von Hofmannsthal.

Next to his adaptive ability, Da Ponte's greatest gifts were in writing verse. He wrote light and graceful poetry that at its best had a measure of the élan and invention of Goldoni, the Arcadian grace of Metastasio, and the simplicity of Calzabigi. The best of it is found in his comic librettos and, like the comic libretto itself, tends to be repeated in variation. Thus, from *L'Isola del piacere* (1795; m., Martín) this echo of Leporello: "*Ogni colore ha un merto . . ./il bianco, ha l'innocenza,/il rosso, l'avvenenza/il bruno la fierezza: ma il nero ha la fortezza*"[6] (II, v). And from *Gli Equivoci* this echo of the Countess Almaviva:

> *Ah come in un istante*
> *speranza del mio cor,*
> *di tua bella alma amante*
> *è spento il caro ardor.*
> *Non son più questi i rai*
> *che tanto amasti un di?*
> *Chi t'ha cangiato mai,*
> *chi mi cangio così?*

---

(4) See Fitzlyon: *The Libertine Librettist*, pp. 141 *ff.*
(5) A recent example of this inflation by association is R. B. Moberly's *Three Mozart Operas.*
(6) "Each color has a trait . . . with a blond, it's innocence; with a redhead, allurement; brown is vigor; but black hair means strength."

Ah, se segue l'infedele
in si nera infedeltà
io saprò da quel crudele
imperar la crudeltà.[7]
(I, xvi)

He was equally adept at comic patter arias, of which this one, from *La Scola de' maritati* (also known as *La Capricciosa corretta*), is typical:

La prima notte del matrimonio
quel gran demonio, senti che fe.
Dopo la cena, seco mi guida
dentro una stanza, e chiusa l'uscio
con gran baldanza, cader dal manto
lascia un bastone, gettando un guanto
presso a miei piè.[8]

(I, iv)

Lorenzo Da Ponte the librettist, then, stands as a typical product of his nationality and his time, his greatest contribution being that of creative adaptive ability, his greatest fortune that of being placed in conjunction with Mozart. If his librettos are far above the average for their time, they nonetheless do not merit the distinction of being favorably compared, as products of an artistic mind, with the most distinctive and individual masterpieces of the great librettists. Yet this "mirror" quality which Da Ponte so well put forward—the quality that could turn Beaumarchais' play into a great libretto—would be enough to earn him a place of honor; for as the composer became ever more dominant, in terms of the opera as a whole, as well as in terms of the dramatic thrust of the work, such a role, secondary though it might be, was to become of vital importance. What it would necessarily mean was that from that time on such a librettist would need the composer

---

(7) "Ah, how in a moment, O hope of my heart, has the dear ardor of your loving soul cooled. Are these not the eyes which you once loved so much? Who then has changed you, who changed me like this? Oh, if the unfaithful one persists in such black unfaithfulness, I'll learn from this cruel one how to become cruel myself."
(8) "Listen to what that she-devil did on our wedding night. When the dinner was over, she led me into a room and, after boldly closing the door, drew a stick from under her dress, throwing her glove at my feet."

to achieve his fame: the finest adaptation of another source would be lost without the music, whereas an *Incoronazione di Poppea* or an *Attilio Regolo*—or even a *Le Déserteur*—is individual enough to exist alone. Da Ponte the librettist thus becomes godfather to Arrigo Boito, to the Debussy of *Pelléas et Mélisande*, and to the Berg of *Wozzeck* and *Lulu*.

Chapter Twelve

The French Libretto of the Revolutionary Period

IF THE RISE of the French bourgeois libretto as foretold by Diderot and initiated by Sedaine was confirmed by the upheaval of the French Revolution of 1789, the form it took was in a way somewhat different from what Diderot might have expected but logically consistent with the deepening of the *opéra comique* story line, the injection of suspense elements, and the immediate concerns of unstable times and a changing audience for opera. The state theatrical monopoly was abolished in 1791, and shortly thereafter a number of theaters sprang up to present patriotic screeds as well as plays and musical works more attuned to events. It was logical that, in such times, melodrama should play a more important role, both because Sedaine and others had prepared the ground and because the audience that watched could participate in spirit—having lived through the recent changes—and could appreciate the simplistic nature of the appeal since many of them were being exposed to theater for the first time. René-Charles Guilbert de Pixérécourt, who styled himself the father of melodrama though he popularized the form a decade or more after its appearance, put his finger on this change when he said that he wrote his plays for people who could not read. Previously those people had been spectators at the *vaudevilles* of the fairs, while those who attended the Comédie-Française either knew the plays given there or were expected to read them (or have read them) as well as see them.

Therefore, *mélodrame* became a part not only of the French theater but also of French opera with the coming of the Revolution. French *mélodrame* should not be confused with Italian *melo-*

dramma, which is a product of the beginning of the nineteenth century. Although the two forms share certain common traits—directness, an emotional distention, and an immediacy of appeal—they are quite different.

There are two aspects to *mélodrame*, one strictly dramatic and functional, the other broader. As a melodramatic tool, *mélodrame* is traceable to Jean-Jacques Rousseau's libretto for *Pygmalion* (1779; m., Jiři Benda). Rousseau was trying, in his words, "to join the declamatory art with the art of music," and used *Pygmalion* as a didactic exercise. Short spoken passages would alternate with passages of instrumental music. Rousseau insisted on the separation of the two, taking the idea from *pantomimes dialoguées* popular at the time, pantomimes interspersed with dialogue and music.[1] Rousseau's proselytization for the "new form" led to its use in French opera, and when it was found that this conjunction heightened the suspense elements of the opera stories, it became a French operatic fixture. Thus *mélodrame* (music-drama) became melodrama, and its original separation conflated into a unity of speech over a musical accompaniment. This device was widely used in the operas of the Revolutionary period and became a feature of French nineteenth-century opera. A prime example of *mélodrame* in its original form, including pantomime elements, is the digging of the grave for Florestan in Act II of Beethoven's *Fidelio*; a striking late-nineteenth-century use of the speech-over-music aspect of it occurs at the end of the Venetian act of Offenbach's *Les Contes d'Hoffmann* (1881; l., Jules Barbier). Passages to be treated in this speech-with-music way are always described as *mélodrames* in the libretto.

Mélodrame of course had, as well, a wider connotation, more akin to our notion of theatrical melodrama: the heightening of emotion through exaggerations of character, incident, and setting. The coming of the French Revolution accelerated the rise of an art form that had appeared because of a combination of factors: the general decadence of French classical tragedy (which itself had become more dependent on melodramatic elements), the efforts of Diderot and Rousseau, and the growing importance of the novel. In a time of upheaval and insecurity, it was not surprising

---

(1) Willie G. Hartog, in his *Guilbert de Pixérécourt*, argues that Rousseau's contribution to *mélodrame* has been overvalued.

that many theatrical subjects dealt with incarceration (usually unjust), escape, and rescue. The "rescue opera," as we have seen, antedated the Revolution, but "rescue opera" as a genre was a product of it. The first of them was *Les Rigueurs du cloître* (1790; m., Henri Berton; l., J. Fievée), which, quite naturally for the time, concentrated on the evils of clericalism. Other examples of this form are *Camille* (1791; m., Nicolas Dalayrac; l., Marsollier de Vivetières)—in which the recluse master of a ghost-filled semi-ruined castle has abducted a girl—and *La Caverne* (1793; m., Jean-François Lesueur; l., Palat Dercy)—in which a girl is held prisoner by brigands.[2]

Of course, the scenic reinforcements which had always been a part of French opera became indispensable aids to the impact of the *mélodrame*. Prisons usually took the form of subterranean dungeons or caverns; storms and other natural manifestations were in constant use. In the libretto of Cherubini's opera *Lodoïska* (1791; l., Fillette-Loraux) there is a detailed description of a fire that traps the lovers as they are crossing a bridge.

Although the themes dealt with characters and situations at some remove from the bourgeois surroundings of the hearth and yard,[3] another of Diderot's principles, that of homely sentiment and virtuous conduct, was a constant accompaniment to these tales of suspense. *Fidelio*, which has become the classic example of the "rescue opera"—it originated as *Léonore* (1798; m., Pierre Gaveau; l., J. N. Bouilly)—is an instance in which the sentiment and the "happy ending" finale were both raised to heroic and idealistic levels, here by Beethoven's concepts of the *Ewig-weibliche* and *Brüderschaft*. In Bouilly's workable libretto the

---

(2) These French prison scenes developed not only from the earlier prison scenes but also from the *enfer* scenes, or scenes set in Hell, which ran through French opera from its beginnings. Storm music was common in both Italy and France in the eighteenth and nineteenth centuries, although the French were probably more lavish in the use of accompanying stage effects. The Royal Hunt and Storm from the second part of Berlioz's *Les Troyens* is a continuation not only of this tradition but also of the use of pantomime on both the spoken and sung French stage.

(3) "It is rare that the heroes of melodramas are taken from ordinary life. They are princes, dukes, colonels in the Hussars or brigand chiefs —it does not matter—but always people who by their rank and above all by their uniform dominate and attract the common people." As quoted in Hartog: *Guilbert de Pixérécourt*, p. 61.

other prisoners and their plight are ignored, and the whole problem of freedom is secondary to that of the rescue of a hero by the heroine. What mattered to the audiences was the impact: the librettists skillfully conjured up the *marmite* that would provide it. In this process they continued to empty the libretto of the little social significance that it had achieved with Favart and Beaumarchais, and helped set the stage for the work of Scribe.

No consideration of the *mélodrame* would be complete without the mention of its "progenitor," the playwright Guilbert de Pixérécourt (1773–1844).[4] Pixérécourt began writing plays in the early 1790's, but did not write a success until 1800. Shortly thereafter, he realized that the type of play he was writing— usually a work based on a historical or literary source, with much flourish of source material, à la Zeno, but constructed to take advantage of every melodramatic possibility—was melodrama, and after 1802 he began calling his works by that name. By the end of his life, he considered himself the inventor of the form and the inheritor of the tradition of Sedaine. His definition of melodrama, although leaving out the suspense elements, underlines the "propaganda of virtue" that ran through all the melodramas of the time: "I understood that, to succeed [in creating something entirely new] in the theater, I had first of all and above all to choose a dramatic and moral subject, then natural dialogue, and simple and true style, delicate feelings, probity, soul, the happy mixture of gaiety united with interest, sensibility, the just rewards of virtue and the punishment of crime . . ."[5] This last was of prime importance: the villain at the end of Pixérécourt's melodrama *Le Chien de Montargis* (1814) says: "*Le Ciel est juste: il sauve l'innocent et frappe deux coupables à la fois. Je lui rends grâce de m'ôter une existence que je ne pouvais supporter, chargé de l'épouvantable fardeau d'un tel crime.*"[6]

Pixérécourt's influence on the theater of his time also extended to the libretto, for the emerging *opéras comiques* stood in the same

---

(4) Also sometimes spelled Pixerécourt.
(5) Pixérécourt: *Théâtre*, vol. IV, p. 493.
(6) "Heaven is just: it saves the innocent and punishes two guilty people at the same time. I pardon it for unburdening me of an existence that I could no longer support, since it was charged with the dreadful weight of such a crime." Note the similarity to the "confessions" of seventeenth-century operatic tyrants.

relation to the bourgeois theater as the American musical does to the American theater.[7] The proximity of the two spheres was further emphasized by the fact that all of Pixérécourt's melodramas used music (or *mélodrame*) to heighten suspense, and Pixérécourt himself headed the Opéra-Comique from 1822 to 1827.[8]

The rapport between the worlds of drama and opera had been enhanced by the Revolution, which, by abolishing the state monopolies—and, more importantly, by abolishing the rules that barnacled them—allowed opera, comic opera, and drama to develop concurrently. Thus each form was free to adopt features of the others. The "enhanced play" nature of the emerging *opéra comique* is clearly seen in these works, and stands in contradistinction to the Italian approach, which stressed an essential difference between play and libretto. Italian librettos were adaptations made for the through-composed operatic world, whose primary considerations were toward music, the voice, and the poetry. One of the reasons why the masterpieces of French opera of this time are so little known today is the "dramatic" orientation of the whole. That the music was not first-rate was less important, for it occupied a secondary position. Greater emphasis was placed on the spoken sections, and these demanded singing actors. French *Grand Opéra* would not only revive the dying classic opera form by transforming it with grafts from the newer forms, but also would dominate the stage as "French opera" in general until after the middle of the nineteenth century, by which time its resuscitation of the *opéra* mentality would have recreated that Lullian institution, re-encrusted with rules and snobbish prestige. Yet French *Grand Opéra* is more an adjunct to the development of French opera than the mainstream of its growth, for the developments of Sedaine, Bouilly, Scribe, and countless others in "legitimizing" the Favart *vaudeville* and making it respectable as *opéra comique* (which was often neither *opéra* nor *comique*) would provide the great majority of all French operas—including the great majority of all great and/or

---

(7) The difference lies in the fact that most French composers of these operas—Méhul, Dalayrac, Boieldieu, and Grétry—and the expatriate Cherubini were members of the French musical establishment and not considered tunesmiths. The comparison should be made with a work such as the Bernstein-Sondheim *West Side Story*.

(8) Reinforcing this proximity is the fact that most of these librettos were published by the French in collected volumes of the French *theater*, along with straight plays.

famous French operas—from Monsigny through Massenet. The most important aspect of this *opéra comique* esthetic was the alternation of stretches of spoken dialogue with music, either instrumental or sung—that is, the *mélodrame* inflated to encompass the entire work—and this aspect was sacrificed at the peril of the opera itself. The readiness to abandon the spoken-sung synthesis by composers in search of stature through a production at the Opéra brought forth the major French operatic tragedy of the nineteenth century.

The pure *drame bourgeois* of Diderot never had a great deal of currency in the libretto, despite the efforts of Sedaine and others. First it fell prey to the passion for the exotic or faraway; next it was adulterated by suspense elements, which developed into the rescue formula. Yet out of several post-Sedaine examples one libretto stands out, with all of its admixtures, as a summing-up of the more overtly melodramatic or spectacular works of the Revolutionary period and as an almost perfect example of the bourgeois libretto, in setting, action, and thought. This is Jean Nicolas Bouilly's only libretto for Cherubini, *Les Deux Journées* (1800).

Les Deux Journées was in its time extravagantly praised as a model libretto, by Goethe and Beethoven among others. In Germany the opera was known as *Der Wasserträger*, a title that carried over to England as *The Water Carrier*. Bouilly called it a *comédie lyrique*, by which he meant that it alternated spoken and sung passages. Yet, like *Le Déserteur* before it and many *opéras comiques* after it, the subject was comic only in the Gallic sense: the ending was happy and it did not conform to the rules of the Opéra. What happened during the course of the opera was not comic.

Goethe's comment on *Les Deux Journées*, contained in his *Conversations with Eckermann*, is worth quotation.

> If you ask what opera I consider good, I would name the *Wasserträger*, for here the subject is so perfect that, if given as a mere drama, without music, it could be seen with pleasure. Composers either do not understand the importance of a good foundation, or they have not intelligent poets who know how to assist them with good stories.[9]

I infer from this that Goethe is really saying two things: that when a subject is "perfect" and when the work is written as this

---

(9) Goethe: *Conversations with Eckermann*, p. 333.

one is, it can be presented as a straight drama, which is assumed
to be an advantage. Certainly *Les Deux Journées*, as a dramatic
work, is, like *Wozzeck* and *Pelléas et Mélisande* and a good number of the French spoken-dialogue operas, closer to the spoken
stage than to the sung stage. But this esthetic runs counter to the
Italian-influenced one, which holds that the great libretto need
not be "an enhanced play," but inhabits a world of its own lying
between straight drama and pure music and is necessarily incomplete without the music. Of course, the notion that a strong subject
can "carry" a drama—the notion underlying the *pièce à thèse*—
was particularly prevalent at the end of the eighteenth century.
Goethe certainly espoused it, as seen in music history by his admiration for the elevated hodgepodge of Emanuel Schikaneder's
(and possibly K. L. Gieseke's) libretto for *Die Zauberflöte*—an
admiration that he carried to the point of sketching out a sequel
to it which was never set to music.

Les Deux Journées is an opera with a moral, which is quoted
at the outset. It derives from Lucan: "The more that a good act
costs us, the more it is dear to us." The focus of the work is on the
family of Mikéli, a Savoyard water carrier, and although the
scene is carefully laid in 1647, at the end of the Thirty Years' War,
by implication the story is meant to be contemporaneous. The action takes place in twenty-four hours, as customary, over two days
(hence the title); it is in three acts, the first of which is laid inside
Mikéli's house in Paris at night. The well-described scene opens
with a fireside tableau highly reminiscent of Diderot's favorite
painter Jean-Baptiste Greuze, with Mikéli's father reading a book[1]
while Mikéli's son and daughter make bouquets of artificial flowers,
which they sell to earn money. This portrait of humble but
honest folk was precisely what the Encyclopedists meant by
bourgeois drama. Antonio, the son, is in love with Angelina, the
daughter of a wealthy farmer (Sémos) in the country at some distance from Paris, and he and his sister are going to go to her on the
morrow for the wedding. As the times are turbulent, they must
have *laissez-passer*s to leave the town, and they are about to go
out to pick them up. During the course of the exposition, Antonio

---

(1) Bouilly does not mind the anachronistic touch of the father of a
water carrier who, in 1647, is able to read.

gives out the information that when he was twelve he was saved from starvation by an unknown French stranger.

Mikéli arrives, tired from his day's work as a water carrier. Bouilly has him speak partly in the slang of the lower classes, slurring words together—a touch that was much commented on when the opera was presented, and which is also in complete accord with Diderot's ideas. After the children and their grandfather go out, Mikéli tells the audience of helping out a young couple he met on the streets. He knows that his first duty is to his aged father, but he also has a duty to aid his fellowman and save the innocent. The young couple, Armand and Constance, enter—Armand disguised as an officer. They are obviously of the upper class. Constance asks: *"Mais qui donc a pu vous intéresser à notre sort?"* Mikéli replies: *"Vous êtes malheureux, et ça me suffit."*[2] It seems that Cardinal Mazarin has abolished the Parlement and is hunting down its members. Armand was president of the Parlement, and thus would be a prize catch. The escape theme is now fully exposed as Mikéli vows to get them out of town. *"Je n'suis ni un dieu ni un prodige, mais un bon diable qui n'peut voir de sang-froid les braves gens dans la peine."*[3] Mikéli's plan necessitates Constance posing as his daughter, and he is reluctant to suggest this to a member of the upper class. But Armand assures him that it is an honor to be a member of his family.

At this point, Bouilly copies Sedaine by heightening the suspense. The ever-searching police arrive. Armand jumps into bed, feigning to be the old man, and Constance becomes Mikéli's daughter. Just as the police are ready to go, Bouilly, again following Sedaine, turns the screw. In walks Antonio. Who is he? Thinking fast, Mikéli says that he is a son living in the country. Where is his *laissez-passer*? Antonio produces it. The police are satisfied and leave. As luck would have it, the other two had stopped at the cloth merchant's before coming home. Armand is transported by Mikéli's benevolence: *"Ô céleste humanité! . . . si l'homme savait ce qu'il perd en désertant tes autels, il ne se trouverait bientôt*

---

(2) "But who was able to interest you in our fate?" "You are in trouble, and that is enough for me."
(3) "I am neither a god nor an exceptional man, but a good devil who cannot watch in cold blood brave people in pain." Again, straight Diderot, even to the note of condescension of the upper middle class's notions of lower-class virtues.

plus un méchant sur la terre."[4] Antonio now recognizes Armand, naturally, as the unknown stranger who saved his life. His sister will give up her *laissez-passer* to Constance; how Armand is to escape is left in suspense. The first act ends in rejoicing.

The second act takes place the next morning at one of the gates of Paris. The soldiers, who are portrayed as Italians in the pay of the Italian Cardinal Mazarin,[5] are exhorted to ever-greater vigilance and are told that Armand is known to be in the *quartier* and that there is a six-thousand ducat price on his head, dead or alive.

Antonio and Constance arrive at the barrier, and the commander of the soldiers asks for their *laissez-passer*s. He finds that Constance does not fit the description of her on the passport, and detains her. Antonio comes to her rescue, but trouble is averted by another officer who says that he recognizes them both. Mikéli enters, yoked to his water cart. He argues that the *laissez-passer* is false because it was dark when it was made out, and therefore the official could not see properly. The officer who recognized them offers to take whatever blame, and the two pass through the gate. Then Mikéli tries to get through but is stopped: no more carriages will be permitted without specific approval. Mikéli demonstrates that the cart is full of water by turning the faucet so that water runs out. One of the officers says he knows Mikéli, who is of course well known in the *quartier*, and asks him if, as an itinerant, he happened to notice someone fitting Armand's description. If he can locate Armand he, Mikéli, will get one thousand ducats of the reward. Mikéli describes the fugitive, and directs the officers to a house in the *quartier*. After the soldiers have left the scene, Mikéli opens the back of the cart, from which Armand emerges and escapes.

The libretto here details the construction of the water cart (the bourgeois adaptation of the seventeenth-century machines) so that it can both contain water and hide a man.

The third act is set in the countryside at a pleasant site that includes a bridge over a brook, a house, a path, and a large tree. The

---

(4) "O celestial humanity! . . . if Man only knew what he loses in abandoning your altars, there would no longer be found a single wicked man on earth."

(5) As we saw in Chapter Three, the French harbored no great affection for the Italian cardinal.

villagers have arrived to celebrate the marriage of Sémos's daughter. The officer from the exit gate passes by with soldiers; after him Antonio, Constance, and Armand arrive. Armand is conveniently hidden inside the large tree, and Constance tells him not to emerge until she has struck the tree three times. Sémos and his daughter arrive, followed by the officer, who demands quarters for himself and his soldiers. They all go into the house.

Armand emerges from the tree, and now begins the passage of *mélodrame*. Two soldiers come on stage with bottles and bread, forcing Armand to go back into his stuffy cell. They note that the disguised Constance is about to come out of the house, and resolve to waylay her for their pleasure. They hide in the underbrush as she arrives. She sees no one, goes to the tree and knocks three times. Dead silence. Again she knocks. Again silence. The suspense builds. Now the soldiers emerge and grab her: she promptly faints. Out of the tree comes Armand, brandishing his pistols, to save his wife's honor. Suddenly everyone is on stage and there is what is called *un tableau général*; that is, a statuesque representation of the climactic scene. Such tableaus were enormously popular in the French theater at the end of the eighteenth century and during the first half of the nineteenth, and were splendidly calculated to generate applause.[6] The officer asks who the unknown man is; Constance, awakening from her swoon, blurts out, "Armand!" The young man admits it, and says that Constance is his wife. At this point Constance gives the "Fidelio" speech: *"Oui, je suis attachée à son sort, et le partagerai jusqu'à son dernier soupir; vous savez tout ce que j'ai fait pour lui, jugez à quel point il m'est cher."*[7]

The officer is saddened that he must act, but he has his orders. Armand and Constance are separated. But, in the Sedaine tradition, rescue awaits in the wings. In comes Mikéli with a paper. Twenty thousand people have petitioned for the release of the innocents. Twelve were received by the Queen,[8] Mikéli among them. After

(6) Tableaus were also very popular as entertainments at large parties.
(7) "Yes, I am bound to his fate, and I shall share it until my last breath. You know all that I have done for him; judge to what degree he is dear to me."
(8) Contrast the uplift tone of this passage with the end of the nineteenth- and early twentieth-century cynicism toward such benevolence: Scarpia's taunt to Tosca that if she obtains a pardon for Cavaradossi from the Queen she will be pardoning a corpse.

hearing them, the Chancellor pardoned Armand, and Mikéli brings the pardon. Thus, in the Revolutionary tradition, the "classic" *lieto fine* has become a *populus ex machina* saving the innocent. Armand is overcome with joy, and offers to support the entire Mikéli family for the rest of their lives (they accept). The final chorus underlines the moral: *"Le premier charme de la vie/C'est de servir l'humanité."*[9]

Despite its melodramatic elements, the entire tone of *Les Deux Journées*, shot through with the ideals of the French Revolution, is similar to that of the lighthearted Favart pastorals: the idea that, although there is evil in the world, good will triumph because *the people* are basically good. But all this would be changed. The growing influence of overt melodrama, the traducing of the Revolutionary *esprit* by Imperial adventurism and pomposity, and, finally, the emergence of a romanticism oriented not toward the people or the state but toward the individual and his yearnings— which were grandly melancholic—would channel opera away from the pastoral spirit. The happy peasants would be removed to light comedy and operetta (with certain exceptions, of course), and the *opéra comique* would occupy itself with sterner, if not necessarily more profound, stuff.

---

(9) "The paramount charm of life is to serve humanity." Whereas the mid-eighteenth-century endings stressed happiness and gaiety, those of the post-Revolutionary period stressed serving higher virtues.

Chapter Thirteen

The Italian Melodramma

THE EFFECT of the Romantic movement on both French and Italian librettos was widespread. Coupled with the melodramatic devices that had seeped into the libretto from Sedaine and, latterly, from the works of Pixérécourt and others, the effects of Romanticism transformed the opera libretto into the entity that we today are most familiar with through the operas of Donizetti, Bellini, and Verdi. The Romantic movement did not accomplish this transformation overnight or in the space of a few years. The entrenched librettists, themselves not "Romantics," had to give way to a newer generation, while the often outrageous novelties of the new wave of literary thought had to become commonplace and assimilated to an audience unaccustomed to their audacities.

This slow process of assimilation was particularly evident with respect to the libretto in Italy. There, moreover, the fragmentation of the country into small entities hindered general acceptance.

Opera in Italy at the turn of the nineteenth century was very much a local affair, with each city opera house under the control of an impresario, who was in turn in some state of thralldom to the all-powerful singers, particularly the female singers. The impresario usually had under him the local composer and the local librettist, who produced operas on his commission (which was likely to be small). Because the Italian audience's only dramatic outlet was the opera—for, apart from various dialect troupes and what was left of the *commedia dell'arte*, spoken drama was less popular—and because that audience, though insatiable with opera, was also conservatively oriented, the impresario had to attempt to satisfy it with a constant run of new operas, which were in fact new music wedded to timeworn themes and situations. If the themes were too audacious, the impresario risked not only audience displeasure but also the displeasure of the Austrian, papal, or other censor. At stake was the impresario's job if he failed financially or ran afoul of the authorities. Thus the impresarios kept a sharp lookout for new operas which would pack in the populace without angering anyone. If that source failed, they cobbled up censor-approved themes with new music from their house artists. A great deal of the success of composers like Rossini and Donizetti can be attributed to this state of affairs, for what was wanted was lightning speed in composition and instant acclaim in presentation.

This very necessity also dictated to some extent the make-up of the opera. *Opera seria* dragged on in Italy, more as a duty than as a pleasure—especially with the disappearance of the *castrati*. The newer *opera seria* librettos tended to eliminate *longueurs* in order to tell the story with as much immediate effect as possible. Nonetheless, the twin forces of *brevità* and the power of the singers both interfered with the purity of the work. The one element of *opera seria* that the singers had liked was its emphasis on the vocal moment, which they had carried to extremes. Whenever possible, the singers tried to retain control over the creation of a new work so that they could plan their own showpieces; and the impresarios, mindful that a couple of show stoppers would bring in the public, acquiesced. Again, the comparison with the present-day Broadway musical is helpful in understanding the world of Italian nineteenth-century opera. Not until middle-period Verdi was there to be a composer who could break this control, although Donizetti and Bellini both fought against it. The librettist, of course, brought up the rear. Harassed by the impresario, the composer, and the singers, he had little room to maneuver, and if he happened to be either a city resident or a house poet, he also had to be careful not to offend the authorities. Impresarios, singers, and composers came and went, but if the librettist earned the stigma of *un uom sospetto, un volterrian,* his career could be permanently ended as librettist, as poet, and as whatever else he might be. Therefore the librettist did not venture far.

This combination of factors served to dictate to a great extent the form that the *melodramma* was to take. From the *opera seria* it appropriated a formal structure not as rigid as the Metastasian opera but definitely channeled. Most *melodrammi* began with a chorus; the entrance of the prima donna was delayed, and then highlighted by an elaborate *aria di sortita* in two or three parts: recitative, cavatina, and cabaletta. This last, the fast, ornamented portion of the aria, was usually reinforced by choral interjections to make a stunning climax. The intrigues of the plot would be told in arias, duets, and trios—and even sextets, as we know—with climaxes coming at the end of acts and a grand climax at or near the end of the opera. This last would center around the *gran' scena* for the prima donna: a scene which would call into play not only the vocal resources of the singer (as the first aria did), but her dramatic abilities as well.[1]

The approach to the subject matter was likewise derived, if at a greater remove, from the practices of the *opera seria* rather than from those of the Goldoni (and subsequent) middle-class librettos. If the Metastasian *opera seria* abstracted human emotions and viewed them from the empyrean plane of the exquisite poetry of the exit aria, those emotions were nonetheless separated from the story line and thus highlighted in a way that Goldoni, for all his use of the exit aria form, never aspired to. The *melodramma* carried over this emotional highlighting and made it human; made it human and, by the infusion of the French melodramatic and Romantic devices and postures,[2] made it as exaggeratedly human as the *opera seria* had been exaggeratedly ideal. The result was as unashamedly stagey as its predecessor, but whereas Metastasio had emphasized the supreme rationality of his characters, the *melodrammatisti* emphasized their human irrationalities. Thus, the neurotic, the febrile—and, pre-eminently, the outright insane—became an integral part of the stock operatic scene. Needless to add, these larger-than-life portraits were exactly calculated to rouse the audience to emotion. Here the essential distinction—apart from structural differences—between the French and Italian libretto can be seen: whereas the French approach operated from a base of plot intricacies and the importance of the setting (or the value of the

---

(1) As can be inferred, most *melodrammi* revolved around a female rather than a male lead, probably because the Malibrans and the Grisis were more famous than the Marios and the Rubinis—and also because the female voice was able to do more in the way of coloratura *cum* dramatic singing than the male voice. Yet the male roles, if subsidiary, were in no sense easy to sing.

(2) Including the Romantic device of separating the work into "parts" instead of "acts" and giving each "part" a title. This survived into the twentieth century (e.g., the librettos of Luigi Illica).

"message"), with the characters secondary, the Italian approach operated primarily from a base of the emotions of the characters themselves.[3]

The Italian preoccupation with *brevità* also influenced the form of the *melodramma*. The recurrent Italian criticism of the French sources for their librettos was the French tendency to prolixity. This was particularly true with respect to Italian attitudes toward French *Grand Opéra*. What in truth the Italians disliked was in part the instrumental interludes and *merveilleux* aspects of the *opéra*, but far more centrally the careful exposition of the story that was the rule among the librettos written by men trained for, or writing for, the spoken stage. Whereas the spoken passages in French libretto by and large revealed both story line and character, the Italians preferred to keep their *secco* recitative at a minimum and allow the characterizations to emerge in the sung portions. They realized (rightly, given the form of the *melodramma*) that the audience did not need to be told everything, and they therefore compressed or eliminated, often ruthlessly, in order to arrive at the vocal moment. The *melodramma* therefore often has a disjunct quality, especially in contrast to the smoothness of the French libretto, and this disjunctiveness would become even further accentuated in the Italian librettos of Verdi. Nowhere is the dichotomy of esthetics between the French and Italian approaches better exemplified than in this contrast, and any judgment of one form from the vantage point of the other necessarily obscures the merits of both.

Although the *melodramma* served to expand the scope of the stories that were considered *operabile*, and although it expanded the types of verse which were used, mixing long and short lines and making great use, in choral passages, of the *saffici* (broken lines), paradoxically the language itself suffered. If Metastasio used a limited vocabulary, he used it with consummate skill; by and large the *melodrammatisti*, either by inspirational mediocrity or, more likely, in fear of censorship, confined themselves to stock epithets and cliché responses to situations, to be repeated with

---

(3) Problems with censorship probably accentuated this tendency to dwell on the personal side of the characters, for a libretto that revolved around love and jealousy would be more likely to pass unscathed than one dealing with freedom or the evils of the aristocracy. Yet, freedom could not long be kept out of the *melodramma*.

minor variations in each libretto.[4] The standard opera Italian, which can of course be traced to Metastasio and even earlier, achieved full flower through overuse in the *melodramma;* such bromides as *"Vendetta!" "Che sento?" "Io son morto!" "Io tremo," "Oh rabbia!" "Numi, pietà," "Sciagurata!" "Gran dio!" "O cielo!"* became commonplace items. Professor Edward Cone has rightly remarked that this verbal limitation became in fact an unconscious abdication to the music, as the music could dilate upon the emotions of the character with far more freedom than the words could, and thus the words became less important in their own right than as signposts for the music. Concurrently, as the music expanded in scope, it could hardly avoid a physical domination of the word by its expressiveness as well as its sound, aided by the growth of the orchestra and the tremendously increased aural power and accuracy of its instruments. Thus the stock responses, whether of a line or a verse, were swamped by the music and became a jumble of sounds. Verdi found a partial way out of this verbal impasse in the use of the *parole sceniche,* or vital words that were highlighted by repetition or by being allowed to stand out from the instrumental fabric. Yet, of course, this attempt also treated the words as verbal translations of what the music was expressing (as well as destroying all semblance of meter and rhyme, as has already been stated) and, in effect, set into a bed of concrete the secondary position of the book vis-à-vis the music.

The development of the *melodramma* from the quasi-*opera seria* to the librettos set by Verdi was of course a process covering the first half of the nineteenth century, and all of the characteristics of the form discussed on the previous pages did not appear at once. There was a steady evolution as the attitudes of the Romantics—French, Spanish, English, and German—became assimilated into the opera of the time.

The first, and probably—in a breakthrough sense—the most important, change in the libretto was that involving the idea of death. The death of the hero or the heroine—usually in a melodramatic setting and involving some sense of failure, either un-

---

(4) The capriciousness of the censors, who varied from city to city and from year to year, added to this difficulty. In one city *"Gran dio!"* might be allowed; in another the name of God could never be invoked, and *numi* (heavens) had to be substituted. In many cities the name Maria could not be used, as it suggested the Virgin. The States of the Church were the strictest.

requited love or unrequited ambition—was a hallmark of the Romantic Age, reflected in the works of Sir Walter Scott, Victor Hugo, and (earlier) of Friedrich Schiller and Goethe. If the forces of evil or their allies, the powers or those in power, did not exactly rule the world, they consistently managed to outmaneuver and bring to defeat the often solitary heroes and heroines. These people, more often than not leaders of lost causes, whether personal (the love of someone unattainable) or political (a minority versus those in power), were marked for doom, and they went to it uncomplaining. Winton Dean's comment that the ending of an Italian *melodramma* "brings the action to a climax in which nothing is resolved"[5] is true insofar as those in power are concerned, but to the heroes themselves—the center of attention of the Romantic writers—there was a resolution, for the attempt rather than the success of that attempt was what mattered.[6] As with Shakespeare's *Romeo and Juliet* (a favorite of the Romantics), the fact that the Capulets and the Montagues might finally be brought to a grudging acceptance of one another by the needless deaths of their children is secondary to the fact of the deaths of Romeo and Juliet.[7] When they were snuffed out, the candle of the play was likewise extinguished.

This insistence on doom-laden death ran fully counter to the practices of both *opera seria* and its precursor, seventeenth-century opera, as well as to those of the Goldoni comedies. The *lieto fine* had for two centuries been a constant in opera, and when it was diluted, as in Metastasio's *Didone abbandonata* or *Attilio Regolo*, the clear implication was of a transfiguration—a triumph through death—rather than of a squalid end on the point of a sword. Even Don Giovanni had to meet his doom at the hands of higher powers. There was, moreover, the underlying assurance that, though some of the good men die, Good would breed Good and Good would

---

(5) Winton Dean: "Shakespeare and Opera," in *Shakespeare in Music*, ed. Phyllis Hartnoll, p. 164.
(6) This *echt*-Romantic conceit obviously had great appeal for the Italians suffering under Austrian and other tyrannical rule; and as the nationalistic spirit rose, so did their identification with any operatic underdog, be he Swiss or Scot. His inevitable defeat served to palliate the fears of the censors while massaging the *Angst* of the audiences.
(7) This is revealed, rather curiously, in Berlioz's loose adaptation of the play. He devotes the whole last section of his dramatic oratorio to this reconciliation; most commentators have found the passage musically weak, and even these who have not must admit that it is anticlimactic.

prevail over Evil: Attilio Regolo's shining example of sacrifice would better succeeding generations. This notion persisted in both Italian and French opera, and in the French theater down through the melodramas of Pixérécourt, but would disappear with the Romantic Age.

This gradual change can be seen by comparing the works of Simone Mayr and Rossini. Mayr's operas, written at the turn of the nineteenth century, look backward past *opera seria* in their use of the hoary figure of the repentant tyrant who cleared the way to a *lieto fine*.[8] Rossini's operas would inaugurate a change, but not without difficulties. In his *Tancredi* (1813; l., Gaetano Rossi) the second production of the opera, in Ferrara, saw the ending changed to a sad one, with Tancredi dying—but the original ending was restored for later productions. A more notable instance, that of *Otello* (1816; l., Francesco Berio di Salsa), saw the original sad ending changed to a happy one. By the time of *Semiramide* (1823; l., Rossi), the titular queen could die on stage at the end.

Yet this last demonstrated the way in which the "sad" ending would invade opera, for there was a good reason why she should pay with her life: she had killed her husband. Retribution was thus a justification,[9] and this justification could be, and was, widened in its scope as the years passed.

The *melodrammatisti* were careful, however, not to overdo the bloody aspects of their stories—at least not until the middle of the nineteenth century. The deaths would occur off stage, or else as close as possible to the final curtain. Thus, in one of the most famous of all *melodrammi*, *Lucia di Lammermoor* (1835; m., Donizetti; l., Salvatore Cammarano), the murder of Arturo by Lucia is accomplished off stage,[1] Lucia herself dies off stage, and Egardo kills himself just before the final curtain. An excep-

---

(8) E.g., *Ginevra di Scozia* (1801; l., Gaetano Rossi).
(9) The more justified since Semiramide in effect killed herself by interposing her body between the villain and her son, suicide being considered more leniently. Similarly, the ending of *Norma* (1831; m., Bellini; l., Felice Romani) could be "justified" because the end was a *Liebestod* transfiguration; and, besides, the harsh justice was meted out by pagans.
(1) Most people in the audience remain unaware of Arturo's death, especially outside of Italy, if the opera is performed in Italian. I remember the puzzlement of several people at Lucia's bloodstained nightgown during the Mad Scene, when Joan Sutherland sang the opera at the Metropolitan Opera in New York; they assumed she had somehow, in her madness, wounded herself.

tion to this would be the mass murder at the end of *Lucrezia Borgia* (1833; m., Donizetti; l., Romani) —mitigated by Henriette Méric-Lalande's insistence on a final cabaletta which would keep the focus on her rather than on the grisly events.

A concomitant of this increasing reliance on the bloodier side of human passions is the growing prevalence, throughout the *melodramma* and beyond, of the theme of hatred. Although on the surface most stories dealt with thwarted love, in fact the focus of most Italian librettos is less on love, which is often relegated to one duet and a few expressions by the tenor and the soprano, than on the hatred this love engenders. Jealousy, rage, and plain dislike are continually magnified in these works; words of hatred as well as situations of vendetta far outnumber expressions of any other passion. This hatred, moreover, is specifically directed at a single individual. Certainly this development was owing in part to the fact that hatred brought forth a heightened response that was not only in accord with the immediate emotional principles of the *melodramma* but also perfect for musical expression. Yet the widespread insistence on the theme suggests that it was basically far more appealing to the *melodrammatisti* than that of love. Hatred saturates the librettos of Verdi; Don Carlo's dogged, almost maniacal pursuit of Alvaro in *La Forza del destino* can be taken as symbolic of several generations of Italian bass and baritone roles, which may have had a pre-echo in the behavior of the seventeenth-century tyrants but which is wholly part of the Italian Romantic opera through Puccini. In this respect, too, the Italian libretto differs from the French, for hatred never played the leading role in French opera that love did, and when the theme did appear, as in Scribe's librettos for *La Juive* and *Les Huguenots*, for instance, it was likely to be generalized rather than specific—as well as being subordinated to the stage trappings.

The writers of the *melodrammi* differed in one important respect from Bertati, Casti, and Da Ponte: they were far less cosmopolitan. By and large, they stayed in their native places—Felice Romani, although he traveled, spent most of his time in northern Italy, Jacopo Ferretti lived in Rome, and Salvatore Cammarano in Naples. Although as librettists they had to hold other jobs in order to make a living[2]—the profession continued to be egregiously

---

(2) Ferretti held a sinecure in the papal tobacco monopoly, and Cammarano, with his family, ran a successful theater in Naples.

underpaid—they did not look beyond the borders of Italy for their fortunes. Vienna no longer held the attractions it once had, for the center of operatic endeavor had shifted to Paris and, besides, Vienna had become the seat of an "enemy": the Austrian oppressors. Romani for that reason turned down an offer to become *poeta cesareo*. Furthermore, whereas Italian *composers* could seek renown by journeying to Paris (as Spontini and Cherubini did, and as Rossini, Donizetti, and Bellini were later to do), the Italian *writers* could not, because in Paris most new operas were performed in French.[3] As a result, the Italian librettists, who still considered themselves, as Casti and Da Ponte had, primarily poets, chose to remain in their cities, remain "Italian," and adapt foreign works to the Italian taste as reflected in the *melodramma*. This parochialism, coupled with the omnipresence of the censors, who encouraged refuge in euphemism, served to give most *melodrammi* a strain of naïveté which emerges clearly when they are compared with the urbane work of French writers such as Scribe and Jouy.

Of the many Italian librettists of the first part of the nineteenth century, Felice Romani (1788–1865) stands out, although his Roman compeer, Jacopo Ferretti (1784–1852), also wrote librettos commendable for their literary taste, of which *La Cenerentola* (1817; m., Rossini—partly based on a Romani libretto, *Agatina*) is a good example. Ferretti, like Romani an educated man, labored to raise the general low tone of the libretto of his time, and his works are notable for smooth verbal felicity. He of course was hardly a full-time librettist: living in Rome and working for the papal government he also wrote extensively for the Church (epithalamia and the like) while maintaining a gregarious private life. His house was the meeting place for artists and visitors to Rome, and Ferretti prided himself on the breadth of his acquaintance. In keeping with the practices of the time, of course, he did not hesitate to tailor his works for the local theater, even if they were works by the master, Romani. In his preface to his reworking of Romani's *Il Sonnambulo*,[4] he states that the changes "have

---

(3) The exception was the very popular *Théâtre des Italiens*, which gave several world premières of famous Italian operas in the original language, such as *I Puritani* (1835; m., Bellini; l., Carlo Pepoli) and *Don Pasquale* (1843; m., Donizetti; l., Giovanni Ruffini).
(4) Not to be confused with Romani's *La Sonnambula, Il Sonnambulo* was written in 1824 for Michele Carafa. The theme has a lethargic hold on the libretto.

the only object of making the *melodramma* viable for the present acting company . . . and never through lack of deep respect for the renowned author who wrote the work in Milan."[5]

In the final instance, however, it is Felice Romani who represents the early *melodramma* and stands as one of the long line of premier Italian librettists. Romani is par excellence a transitional figure, for his poetic prowess looks backward to Metastasio, Goldoni, and the Favart pastoral, while his characterizational abilities and grasp of the *brevità* and directness of the *melodramma* look forward—albeit with some trepidation—to the full-blown Romanticism and melodrama of Cammarano and Piave. His artistic life well illustrates the vicissitudes of the Italian librettist, for in his years of fame he was so busy with commissions that not only his works but also his composers suffered. More and more wanting the librettist to be subservient to their wishes, the composers became restive when the required verses were delayed. Romani's renown throughout Italy as her finest poet-librettist did not improve matters, as the poet felt as a result that some attention should be paid to his demands because of his ability. But the age of Metastasio was over, as Romani ruefully learned: not only did Donizetti and Bellini turn to other collaborators rather than bow to Romani's vanity, but also the poet himself found it impossible even to arrange a publication of his own works in a collected edition—although everyone agreed on his eminence. The importance of the rupture with Bellini, for whom Romani had produced the librettos of all the mature works, and Bellini's acceptance of the inferior Carlo Pepoli to create his last opera, *I Puritani*, is indicative of the general increase in the importance of the music: valuable as Bellini found Romani, the poet was no longer indispensable. *Puritani*—or whatever the opera—could succeed through its music; as long as someone was on hand to give general order to the story, his ability was not of prime concern. The structure of the *melodramma* only aided this verbal and dramatic anonymity.

Romani was born in Genoa, and was forced at an early age to support his mother and younger brothers, his father having abandoned the family. He had a classical education, and was particularly impressed by the poetry of Metastasio and Vincenzo Monti, a "classic" Italian poet best known today for his translation

---

(5) Alberto Cametti: *Jacopo Ferretti*, p. 154.

LA DAFNE
D'OTTAVIO
RINVCCINI
Rappresentata alla Sereniss. GRAN DVCHESSA
DI TOSCANA
Dal Signor Iacopo Corsi.

IN FIRENZE
APPRESSO GIORGIO MARESCOTTI
MDC.
Con Licenza de' Superiori.

[1] Title page of Ottavio Rinuccini's *La Dafne*, 1600 (music lost).

L'EVRIDICE
D'OTTAVIO
RINVCCINI
RAPPRESENTATA
NELLO SPONSALITIO
Della Christianiss.
REGINA
DI FRANCIA, E DI
NAVARRA.

IN FIORENZA, 1600.
Nella Stamperia di Cosimo Giunti.
Con licenza de' Superiori.

[2] Title page of Ottavio Rinuccini's *L'Euridice*, 1600 (music by Jacopo Peri).

[3] *a. The Tragic Theater. b. The Comic Theater*. Engravings after Serlio.

[4] Gian Francesco Busenello
(1598–1659).

[5] Philippe Quinault (1635-
88).

[6] Metastasio (1698–1782).

CATONE
IN UTICA
Tragedia per Musica
DI
ARTINO CORASIO
Pastore Arcade

Da rappresentarsi nel Teatro detto
delle Dame nel Carnovale
dell' anno 1728.
DEDICATO
ALLA SERENISSIMA
VIOLANTE
DI BAVIERA
Gran Principessa di Toscana.

Si vendono nella Libreria di Pietro Leone a Pasquino
all'Insegna di S.Gio: di Dio.
IN ROMA, nella Stamperia del Bernabò, 1728.
Con licenza de' Superiori.

[7] Title page of Metastasio's *Catone in Utica*, 1728, using his Arcadian name, Artino Corasio.

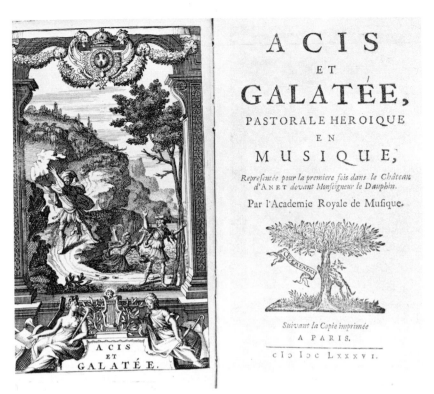

[8] Frontispiece and title page of Jean de Campistron's *Acis et Galatée*, 1686 (music by Jean-Baptiste Lully). From the Library of Congress.

[9] Set design for Alberto Vincina's *La Gara* (composer unknown), Vienna, 1652, showing typical seventeenth-century balanced approach and central perspective. From the Library of Congress.

[10] Carlo Goldoni (1707–93). From a pastel of the Venetian School in the Museo Teatrale alla Scala, Milan.

[11] Michel-Jean Sedaine (1719–97). From *Le Théâtre de Sedaine* (Paris, 1877).

[12] Architectural sketch by Giuseppe Galli Bibiena (1696–1756), showing increased complexity, use of oblique perspective, separately defined areas in forescene and mid-scene. From the New York Public Library.

[13] Lorenzo Da Ponte (1749–1838). From a painting by Samuel F. B. Morse in the Union Club, New York.

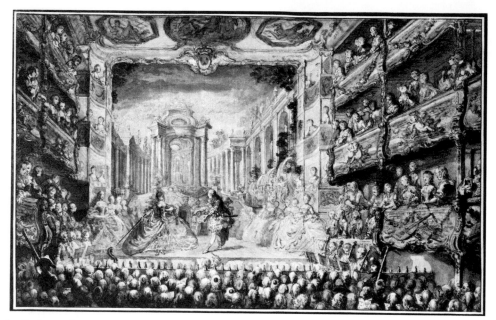

[14] A performance of the Quinault-Lully *Armide*. From a watercolor-and-gouache drawing over pencil by Gabriel de St.-Aubin (1724–80). Courtesy of the Museum of Fine Arts, Boston.

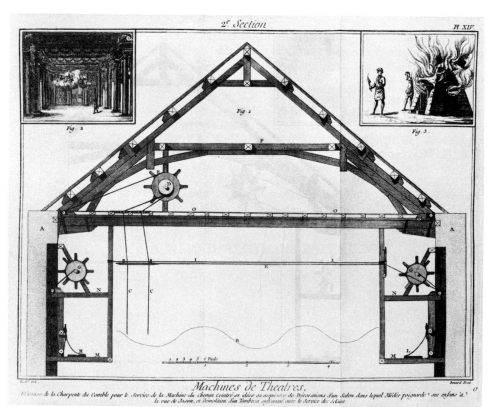

[15] Architectural plan of an opera theater (French, eighteenth-century), showing machinery. Inset top left depicts the set for a scene in which Medea kills her children in front of Jason. From the Diderot-D'Alembert *Encyclopédie*.

[16] Felice Romani (1788–1865).

[17] Title page of Romani's first libretto, *La Rosa bianca e la rosa rossa*, 1813 (music by Giovanni Simone Mayr).

[18] Eugène Scribe (1791–1861).

[19] Illustration from Scribe's *Gustave III, ou Le Bal masqué*, 1833 (music by Auber), Act II, scene iii. From the Library of Congress.

CARICATURES SUR BAYREUTH

Æschylus und Shakspeare, nach Porgès, die beiden einzigen Bühnendichter, welche Wagner an die Seite gestellt werden können, machen in vorschriftsmessigen Frack dem Meister ihre Aufwartung.

Eschyle et Shakspeare, les deux seuls auteurs dramatiques qui, d'après Porgès, se puissent comparer à Wagner, viennent rendre leurs devoirs au Maître en simple habit de cérémonie (1).

[Ulk, vers 1876.]

[20] "Aeschylus and Shakespeare, according to Porgès the only two dramatic authors to be compared to Wagner, come to render homage to the Master in simple ceremonial dress." From *Richard Wagner en caricatures* (Paris, n.d. [but 1891]).

à Philippe Gille
son ami
Emile Zola

MESSIDOR

DRAME LYRIQUE, EN QUATRE ACTES ET CINQ TABLEAUX

Représenté pour la première fois à Paris
sur la scène de l'Académie Nationale de Musique
le 15 février 1897.

[21] Title page of Zola's *Messidor*, 1897 (music by Alfred Bruneau), inscribed to Philippe Gille. From the author's collection.

[22] Arrigo Boito (1842–1918).

[23] Title page of Luigi Illica's *Germania*, 1902 (music by Alberto Franchetti). Published librettos of the late nineteenth and early twentieth centuries tended to decoration, in contrast to the utilitarian typography of earlier Italian librettos.

[24] Sir William Schwenck Gilbert (1836–1911). Caricature by Spy.

[25] Hugo von Hofmannsthal (1874–1929).

[26] Bertolt Brecht (1898-1956). Painting by Rudolf Schlichter, 1928.

[27] Gertrude Stein (1874–1946). Caricature by David Levine.

of the *Iliad*. He moved to Milan and began writing both poetry and librettos, the first of which was an adaptation of a Pixérécourt play, *La Rosa bianca e la rosa rossa* (1813; m., Mayr). His fame grew with each libretto, and attained its peak with his collaboration with Bellini in the years 1827–33.[6] The rupture of the two was a literary *cause célèbre* in Italy, as much because of the renown of the two men as because of the praise that Bellini had always given Romani's verses. Yet the rupture also coincided with the end, for all practical purposes, of Romani's librettistic career, for in 1834 he became editor of the official Piedmontese *Gazzetta* in Turin, a post he held until 1849, and in fact he wrote only sporadically for the opera stage after that (he wrote a total of about eighty librettos). Romani of course considered himself primarily a poet, and published several books of verse; as a journalist-critic, he reviewed both music and art, including on occasion an appraisal of his own literary work,[7] and even produced an article extolling the value of ladies' corsets.[8] Romani died in 1865, but his name was kept before the public through the determined efforts of his wife, Emilia Branca, who outlived the librettist and wrote an effulgent and unreliable biography of him.[9]

Romani is a transitional figure because he represents the values and attitudes of an older time within the framework of a very different age. He has been called "a classic writer who became a Romantic without knowing it,"[1] but in fact he merely aped certain Romantic conventions without fully believing in them. Trained as a classical poet, he never ventured far beyond classicism, and although he dutifully used the work of such poets as Victor Hugo and Byron, he never concealed his dislike for all the tenets of Romanticism they stood for. His greatest achievements in the libretto lie in the quality and "musicality" of his verse, itself slightly anachronistic in a time when verse was being crushed under the heel of music; in the directness and brevity of his storytell-

---

(6) For Bellini he wrote *Il Pirata* (1827), *La Straniera* (1829), *Zaira* (1829), *I Capuleti e i Montecchi* (1830), *La Sonnambula* (1831), *Norma* (1831), and *Beatrice di Tenda* (1833). Other heavy users of Romani's librettos were Donizetti (ten) and Saverio Mercadante (sixteen).
(7) E.g., a review he wrote of his libretto *Il Segreto* for the *Gazzetta* of November 16, 1833; in Mario Rinaldi: *Felice Romani* p. 355.
(8) Ermanno Loescher: *Romani—Critica aristico-scientifica*, p. 126 ff.
(9) Emilia Branca: *Felice Romani*.
(1) Rinaldi: *Felice Romani*, p. 389.

ing; and, primarily from a dramatic point of view, in the individuality and humanity of many of his characters. Conversely, when Romani was forced to enter the high-Romantic world of rampant passion and broad melodrama, his librettos ran to standard librettistic euphemisms of the *"Gran dio!"* stripe instead of convinced dialogue and invariably lack that gut quality which, for instance, Verdi obtained from his librettists. There is an element of parochialism coupled with chauvinism in Romani's dislike of non-Italian Romanticism, yet his distaste was innate, as is shown by his inability to appreciate the melodramatic middle-period operas of Verdi. At the same time, Romani's strengths as a librettist were of a much higher order than those of his compeers so that he nevertheless produced highly serviceable librettos on themes unsuited to his temperament.

Romani, in common with most Italian poet-librettists, had an adaptive rather than a creative mind. All his stories were cobbled up from other sources; reworked against a deadline for a specific set of circumstances which has already been described. What this meant in Romani's case was that many of his librettos suffer because of haste and overburdening, for he never could refuse a commission. His facility with verse and his immediate grasp of the dramatic essentials of the story led him to dash off works that would have been greatly improved by pruning of the clichés and deepening of the characterizations through the verse. For this reason, his Bellini librettos—and particularly *Norma*—benefitted through the constant rewriting that the composer insisted on.

A notable feature of the Romani librettos was the *avvertimento*, or author's preface to the reader, which introduced each work to its public. Romani's relaxed, informal little essays not only introduced the story but also commented on aspects of libretto writing, and contain perhaps more of the poet's thoughts and attitudes than all the rest of his work for the opera.

Romani's verse was the envy of his fellow-librettists. Supple, melodious, inventive—Romani was very free in his use of verse and meter, mixing long and short lines in one speech, using midline as well as end-line rhymes, off-rhymes, and assonance to give fluidity—his verse had the double value of illuminating character and existing as poetry. Its very musicality was its prime appeal to Bellini, who needed the catalyst for his own genius, but at its best

it is its quality of intense human warmth which is most important.
The lament of Giovanna Shore in the third act of his libretto of the
same name (1829; m., Carlo Conti) is one of many examples, in
which the onward-going quasi-musical period and the iteration of
the dolorous sound of "o" combine with this humanity to produce,
even without the aid of music, an exquisite portrait of sadness:

> *Nessun più veggo . . . De' miei gridi stanca*
> *si dileguò la turba, e sola io sono*
> *come in deserta spiaggia . . . E a me d'intorno*
> *profondo, spaventoso*
> *regna un silenzio che turbar non oso.*
> *Quanto sei lunga o vita,*
> *e tormentosa! Ardo di sete, e invano*
> *l'inaridito labbro all'aria chiede*
> *un umido sapor che lo conforti.*
> *Tutto è infiammato il ciel, l'aure son morte.*[2]

Similarly, the success of a character like Nemorino in *L'Elisir
d'amore* (1832; m., Donizetti) is owing in part to Romani's ability
not to let his balanced characterization fall into sentiment or village
idiocy,[3] but it is the sheer humanity of the hopelessly smitten
bumpkin which makes the character so unforgettable (and which,
it should be added, is almost never rendered adequately by the
tenor).

Two of Romani's librettos for Bellini highlight the backward-
looking orientation of the librettist. *La Sonnambula* is a slightly
modernized pastoral in the Favart vein, with happy peasants dis-
porting happily on a picture-postcard landscape. *Norma*, Romani's
finest achievement, is far more than a re-creation of the past—of
the French *tragédie lyrique*, with all its Greek overtones, in Italian

---

(2) "I no longer see anybody . . . the crowd, tired of my outcries,
has dispersed, and I remain alone as on a deserted beach . . . and
around me there reigns a profound, terrifying silence that I dare not
disturb. How long and tormented you are, O life! I'm burning with
thirst and my parched lips in vain ask the air for some humid substance to comfort them. The sky is all in flames, the air is dead."
(3) Romani's instinctive dislike of having to write the *romanza* "Una
furtiva lagrima" probably stemmed in part from his feeling that such
a moment would overly sentimentalize the character; thus the non-
sentimental words.

dress. Certainly *Norma* has as its precursors such *tragédies* as *Médée* (1797; l., François Hoffman),[4] and such Druid and/or errant priestess operas as Spontini's *La Vestale* (1807; l., Étienne de Jouy) or *Arvire et Evelina* (1788; m., Antonio Sacchini; l., Nicolas Giullard). The libretto of *La Vestale* is comparable to, if not the equal of, Romani's. Yet *Norma* plays precisely to Romani's classical training and temperament, and in so doing stands out as a splendid anachronism in the time of the emerging *melodramma*. In a sense it is the culmination of the pure Gluckian style which had invaded the *tragédie lyrique* but had never quite overcome the French insistence on divertissement and *le merveilleux*.

The first notable feature of the *Norma* libretto is the care with which it is written. Bellini rode close herd upon Romani, insisting that he rewrite until he, the composer, was satisfied. This imposed upon the librettist a discipline that resulted in a greater consistency of poetic style. The poetry of *Norma* is in that direct line of well-expressed, noble sentiment—slightly otherworldly— which can be traced to Metastasio, and it has little in common with the explosiveness of the later *melodrammatisti* poets or the sinew and immediacy of Boito's verse. The "*Casta diva*" reflects this empyrean nobility, and is a celebrated moment in which subject matter, verse, sentiment, and tone conjoin, for the moment is an invocation to the chaste goddess of the moon.

Casta Diva, che inargenti
queste sacre antiche piante,
a noi vogli il bel sembiante
senza nube e senza vel.

Tempra tu de' cori ardenti,
tempra ancora lo zelo audace,
spargi in terra quella pace
che regnar tu fai nel ciel.[5]
(I, iii)

---

(4) Which, as we shall see in the next chapter, was technically not a *tragédie lyrique*.
(5) "Chaste goddess, who ensilvers these ancient, sacred trees, turn your lovely face upon us, unclouded and unveiled. Temper the ardent hearts, temper the headstrong zeal; spread over the earth that sense of peace which you cause to reign in the skies."

Norma, however, is far from being a post-Metastasio *opera seria* or even a post-Gluck reform opera. The Romantic Age— which in Italy was inextricably bound up with the struggle toward nationhood—is emphasized by the fierce independence of the Druids and their hatred of their Roman oppressors, and the *melodramma* is perceived not only through the operatic gestures which stand for emotion but also through the continual insistence on the characters themselves. *Norma* revolves around three people —the hoary triangle situation—and Romani is careful to see that everything else remains ancillary. Norma's father, her confidante, even her children, exist only to heighten and make more expressive the emotions of the principals; in turn, the three principals exist only to heighten and make more expressive the emotions of one of them, Norma. The characterization of Norma—at once Druid priestess, leader of her people, woman in love, and mother, imperiously jealous yet forgiving—must stand as a major librettistic triumph and one of the great character portraits in all of opera. The difference from many other such portraits—and this again harks back to Metastasio—is its self-sufficiency; that is, its non-dependence on the music for complete realization. Bellini's long melodic lines stand not so much subordinate as apart, as pure music, yet paradoxically heighten the effect of the emotions themselves in a way that is in absolute opposition not only to the practices of Verdi but also to those of Wagner.[6] The *"Mira, o Norma"* duet exemplifies the unified dichotomy, and is almost unbearably poignant. Romani created other fine portraits, notably of a Spanish Joan of Arc in his libretto *La Solitaria delle Asturie* (set several times, but first in 1838 by Carlo Coccia), but he never surpassed his creation of Norma.

There is one more aspect of the *Norma* libretto which, finally, frees it of any dependence upon Metastasio, the French, the *melodramma:* which gives it uniqueness. That is the blanket of *caritas* which envelops the whole. Despite the conventional war choruses and the moments of angry jealousy within the libretto, this is not the hate-oriented world of the *melodramma,* but a world of understanding and forgiveness. Romani could have rested

---

(6) In Verdi the music dominates, the words become signposts; in Wagner, the music complements the words and must be considered in conjunction with them, but also dominates and takes over verbal functions.

his case on the obvious tear-jerking qualities of a mother with her children or of love thwarted, and could have ridden off on the conventional noble sacrifice of the sinner. Or he could have followed French practice by either producing a *lieto fine* through a *deus ex machina*, or by having Norma turn into a virago like Médée. He chose, instead, the most difficult path: to have her surmount her conflicting emotions, spare her children, ask forgiveness for her faithless lover, and go to her death. In so doing she reawakens Pollione's love, and he joins her in death. That this ending is so dramatically correct is owing to the spirit of *caritas* underlying all of the libretto. Verdi of course also worked with love in the sense of laying down one's life for a friend or lover (Gilda; Rodrigo in *Don Carlo*), but the scope and impact have shrunk because of the nature of the librettos. In fact, not until the librettos of Hugo von Hofmannsthal would this aspect—an understanding through love—become theme once more, and nowhere will he set it forth more triumphantly than Romani did in *Norma*.

Thus, the uniqueness of Romani's finest libretto transcends his strengths in poetry, in characterization and in structure, and becomes far more enduring a monument to his importance as a librettist than his versifying abilities or his knack of being able to organize a story to the taste of composer, singer, and impresario.

Chapter Fourteen

The French Grand Opéra

THE FRENCH REVOLUTION left its mark on the opera of the period from 1790–1800 both by the abrogation of the state theatrical monopoly and the creation of an audience highly empathic to the melodramatic excesses of the "rescue operas." The sequel to the Revolution—the Empire of Napoleon—also left its mark. That imprint, because of the publicity and propaganda demands of the government, would be found not in the *drame bourgeois* or the *vaudevilles* but in the realm of the *tragédie lyrique*. That development is of note in the history of the libretto (and of opera) because several of its aspects would be carried over through the Restoration to combine with what was left of the *drame bourgeois* and produce, in the reign of the "bourgeois" King Louis-Philippe (1830–48), the *tragédie lyrique bourgeoise*, or French *grand opéra.*

As detailed in Chapter Ten, Gluck and Calzabigi's reform of *opera seria* had had a great success in Paris and had inspired several French librettos in the reform spirit, which in fact outshone their Italian progenitor's efforts. Yet the victory of the *gluckistes* was Pyrrhic, for the Opéra was too encrusted with tradition to abandon entirely the beloved *merveilleux-cum*-ballet format in favor of something austere. Thus, a later Gluck-reform opera like Cherubini's *Médée* (1797; l., F. B. Hoffman) was relegated—even during the height of the popular Directoire—to the status of an *opéra comique* because of its spoken dialogue, omission of ballet, and non-*merveilleux* ending.[1] After the turn of the century a similar opera, Spontini's *La Vestale* (1807; l., Étienne de Jouy), was

---

(1) That is, non-*deus ex machina* ending; *le merveilleux* was well enough served by a final conflagration.

allowed in because of its lack of spoken dialogue and because it has a *deus ex machina* ending, but such works were exceptions rather than the rule. Another work that possesses this Gluckist directness of approach and lack of posturing, but which was excluded because of spoken dialogue, was the first unashamedly Biblical opera, Méhul's *Joseph* (1807), composed to a fine libretto by Alexandre Duval.

Yet the rise of Napoleon to First Consul and then to Emperor signaled the re-emergence of the *opéra* concept in its full Lullian, rather than Gluckist, robes. The freedom of the musical theater was gradually whittled down until the concept of the Opéra as a monopoly was again imposed: an Opéra with now an imperial patron. Napoleon, like Louis XIV before him, appreciated the glorification possibilities of the *tragédie lyrique* and encouraged that form which would give proper play to spectacle and pomp. The first such opera was *Ossian* (1804; m., Jean-François Lesueur; l., Palat [?] Dercy), about the legendary (and bogus) Gaelic poet, which was written on direct suggestion of Napoleon and dedicated to him. *Le Triomphe de Trajan* (1807; m., Louis Persuis and Lesueur; l., Joseph-Alphonse Esménard), dedicated to Napoleon's mother, set the seal on this neo-Lullian phase. In the time-honored *merveilleux* style, the opera ends with a chorus singing Trajan's praises, after which *le théâtre s'ouvre* and we see the Trajan Forum:[2] "In the middle the Trajan column rises, topped with a statue of the Emperor, holding in his hand a globe. We see around the base the eagles of his legions and the trophies taken from the conquered peoples. The populace crowns the portraits of Trajan with flowers and laurels. The soldiers place the crowns they have received at the foot of the column. The Dacian, Scythian and German prisoners come and heap on their chains. GENERAL BALLET."

Spontini's *Fernand Cortez* (1809, revised 1817; l., Jouy and Esménard) made a great show of putting horses on stage,[3] and thereafter horses were an almost indispensable part of any Opéra

---

(2) The description was meant to be "read" contemporaneously, for the Napoleonic copy of the column in the Place Vendôme had only shortly before been finished.
(3) Characteristically, Jouy wrote a prologue in which he stated that all the "spectacle" opportunities were founded on fact, and that the horses were not "a vain luxury designed to dazzle the eyes" but were used to approximate "the surprise and terror that their first appearance must have made on the Mexicans."

spectacle. Yet, if in this recrudescence of *l'esprit de la gloire* vocal standards were ignored and consequently the singing was third-rate, and if the Monsigny-Grétry stream of *opéra comique* was temporarily allowed to diminish, nonetheless the librettistic standards did not reach the depths plumbed by the Italians at the same time.[4] Alexandre Duval's *Joseph* has already been mentioned, but V.-J. Étienne de Jouy, who also provided criticism for the *Gazette de France* under the pseudonym of L'Érémite de la Chaussée-d'Antin, wrote a number of the major librettos of the period. *La Vestale* is his finest work and a notable achievement. If the sentiment and the language are reminiscent of the highblown periods of the Comédie-Française, the story is powerful and well told. The second act in particular has a master's touch. The heroine, Julia, is a vestal virgin given the task of tending the vestal flame. She allows her lover to enter the sacred temple, then allows the flame to go out. The plan of the act, with its build-up of emotional tension as Julia awaits her lover, its playing with the contrasts of light and darkness, its focus on the lovers while a guard watches outside, its final end-in-discovery, was of course taken over entire by Wagner for *Tristan und Isolde*. If Wagner emphasized the philosophic aspects while Jouy stuck with the immediate, the organizational shell was nearly identical, and in both cases the dramatic impact is strong.

The classically oriented grand operas were not in tune with the growth of the Romantic spirit, the popularity of the *mélodrame*, or the re-establishment of a less spectacular reigning body in France. But, given the fact that the state monopoly of *opéra* had been re-established, the *merveilleux-cum*-Gluck *tragédie lyrique* could have continued, insulated from the vagaries of public taste, much as the *tragédie lyrique* had continued in the decades after Lully's death. Several factors in addition to those referred to above conspired to prevent this. One was the great popularity of the Théâtre des Italiens, which presented the works of the early Italian *melodramma* to a French public, and which thus carried on, in an Italian disguise, the bourgeois tradition of Sedaine. Another factor was the importance of Paris as the world center of opera. After the Restoration, Paris solidified her position as the

---

(4) It should of course be constantly kept in mind that the number of French operas was much smaller than the number of Italian works in any given year.

focus of all new and interesting developments in opera, and she thus attracted the famous and the aspiring workers in that musical form. The arrival of Rossini signaled this development, which was to attract Donizetti, Bellini, Meyerbeer, Wagner, and Verdi to create operas in Paris. Furthermore, the Italian *melodramma* composers' general disdain for the Gluckian "Greek-type" libretto,[5] coupled with the continuing vogue for the historical, worked against any re-creation of the classic French opera.

In any final analysis, however, the death of the classic opera is attributable to the success of one man in the realm of the writing of *opéra,* and to one composer who worked in collaboration with him: Eugène Scribe and Giacomo Meyerbeer. What Scribe effected with his librettos for the Opéra was the triumph of the bourgeois precepts of Diderot, inflated by the demands of *le merveilleux,* heightened by the use of *mélodrame* exaggerations, and poured into the five-act framework of the Lullian *spectacle.* By thus tying *opéra* to *opéra comique,* Scribe destroyed the old-fashioned classic opera (except for certain isolated examples, such as *Les Troyens*), and it was not until later in the century that a different approach to *opéra* was attempted under the influence of Wagner's mythological approach.

Scribe's contributions to the libretto, both in terms of the works themselves and in terms of his approach to the writing of them, are some of the most far-reaching in operatic history. Not only did librettos that could be traced back to Scribe as an influence continue to be written for opera well into the twentieth century, but, although all of the operas composed to his most famous works are out of today's operatic repertory, nevertheless Scribe can be seen in more or less "pure" form in such diverse repertory items as *L'Elisir d'amore, Un Ballo in maschera* and *Don Carlo.*

The reason why this can be so lies at the heart of Scribe's importance as a librettist. That is, Scribe lives today not because of his specific excellence as a versifier, as a creator of character, as a creator of a work that can be traced only to him. In this

---

(5) French operatic history is a cosmopolitan affair: many of its famous composers were either Italian (Lully, Cherubini, Spontini) or German (Meyerbeer, Offenbach). In the decades after 1820, the only major French composer was Daniel François Auber, while the undoubted Voice of Opera in Paris was Rossini.

respect he cannot pretend to challenge such librettists as Busenello, Metastasio, Da Ponte, Romani, Wagner, Boito, and Hofmannsthal. But as a story planner and scene-and-act organizer—as a stage technician—and as a writer with a comprehensive mind and an endless facility for disguise he is without peer. The revivification of the French *opéra comique* (in its lighter, Grétry, style) and the establishment of *Grand Opéra* can be dated from three of his librettos: those for *La Dame blanche* (1825; m., François Boieldieu), *La Muette de Portici* (1828; m., Auber), and *Robert le diable* (1831; m., Meyerbeer). Rarely, if ever, has a single librettist been so successful in controlling history—Metastasio, after all, only perfected what Zeno had already created.

The paradox of Scribe's achievement is that, unlike Romani he appeared at exactly the right time to capitalize on his talents. Doubtless at any time his stage sense would have ensured success, but in the long run his deficiencies in verse and characterization would have relegated his works to a lesser place. But at a time when music was taking over the task of characterization and was ever more effectively blotting out verse qualities, Scribe's shortcomings could be minimized. And so it is: the reason that Amélie and Gustave do not possess the memorable qualities of Amelia and Riccardo lies less in the parallel efforts of Scribe and of his Italian adapter, Antonio Somma, than in the greater ability of Verdi compared with Auber. There is no doubt that had Verdi written the Meyerbeer operas (which he did with the *Grand Opéra* librettos to *Les Vêpres siciliennes* and *Don Carlos*) our appreciation of *Grand Opéra* would be quite different. In fact, it was left to Verdi and Wagner to bend the Scribean format to their own uses.

Scribe did not invent the historical libretto or invent the emphasis on spectacle. The legacy of *Richard Coeur de Lion* came down through the Revolution to such genre librettos, loosely based on history, as Jouy and Michel Dieulafoy's one-act *fait historique*, *Milton* (1804; m., Spontini), which presented the poet writing *Paradise Lost*, and the far grander *Fernand Cortez* of 1809. What is true of all these historical operas, down through the *Grand Opéra* librettos of *Les Huguenots*, *La Juive*, and *Le Prophète*, is not that they are scrupulously accurate—they are far from it—but that they are an attempt at a direct re-creation of a specific lost time. As such they are distinct from the "historical" librettos of the *melodramma*, like Romani's *Anna Bolena*, in which, for either censorship reasons or exigencies of the *melodramma,* the historicity was not stressed, and the figures could be kings and queens of any nameless country at any unspecified time. Scribe in these large-scale works emphasized bigger forces (religious hatred, power politics, and the like) within a larger framework, to the detriment of individual characterization. Wagner extrapolated exactly this epic quality from the surroundings of manufactured spectacle and plot complications and put it to work in a far more thoroughgoing way. But Scribe's widening of the horizon of the libretto was a genuinely novel contribution: one that had been seen sporadically before—Busenello's *Giulio Cesare,* for example—but had never been systematically explored.

Eugène Scribe was born in 1791 (thus being completely free of the *ancien régime* as an influence) into a middle-class family, and after a fine scholastic career took a degree in the law. As with Busenello, Quinault, and so many other writers for the stage, the lure of the theater tempted him, however, and he wrote his first produced work at the age of twenty, for the Théâtre du Vaude-ville. By 1821 he was well known as the author of "boulevard comedies"; that is, slender works depicting the foibles of the time much as the *drames forains* had in the eighteenth century. Scribe was not content with merely a career in light comedy: he also wrote for the Théâtre-Français, and began writing *opéras comiques* in 1813. *La Dame blanche* of 1825 assured his fame in *opéra comique; La Muette de Portici,* his first "grand opera" libretto, made him an instant success in the only remaining spoken theatrical area.[6] From 1830 on, the works of Scribe dominated the French lyric stage in a succession that included not only the great *Grand Opéra* librettos with Meyerbeer (*Robert le diable,* 1831; *Les Huguenots,* 1836; *Le Prophète,* 1849; and, posthumously, *L'Africaine,* 1865) but also those with Halévy (*La Juive,* 1835; *Guido et Ginevra,* 1838; *Le Juif errant,* 1852) and Auber (*Gustave III,* 1833; *Le Lac des fées,* 1839; *L'Enfant prodigue,* 1850), as well as such two- and three-act *opéras comiques* as *Le Philtre* (1831; m., Auber), *Le Domino noir* (1837; m., Auber), and many others. Scribe died in 1861.

The fact that Scribe's works for the lyric stage were only

---

(6) Scribe also wrote ballet scenarios.

one part of his output gives some idea of his large body of work, which ran to the hundreds of stage plays. He accomplished this output through a system of collaboration, organization, and diligence. He regularly began work at five in the morning in the summer, six in the winter, working until ten[7] and spending the rest of the time seeking out ideas for new works. He was a stage-oriented writing machine, ever at the ready to scribble down a new approach, a new snatch of dialogue, ever ready to incorporate ideas from others if they were of use in his work. He had little life apart from his work for the stage. As can be guessed, Scribe also possessed an uncanny instinct for stageworthy situations and for stage effects. He made full use of the newest technical devices (such as the development of the more reliable gas lighting) in planning his works.

Two aspects of his prodigious industry should be examined, for they are of importance to the study of the libretto. First of all, Scribe was not an adapter of other works in the manner of Italian librettists such as Romani. Although much of Scribe's output can be traced to earlier sources, either historical or written, Scribe himself thoroughly reworked the material for his own purposes so that it had only passing resemblance to the original. In this respect he followed the spoken-stage-oriented practice of Sedaine and other French playwright-librettists, and was in turn imitated by his successors. At the same time Scribe frequently used collaborators on both his librettos and plays.

There is an essential difference between Scribe's work with his aides and the usual practice of co-librettists. In his case the task can be described as a tandem, with Scribe always in the lead; this is reflected in the ascriptions in the works themselves, where Scribe takes full billing—in much smaller type appears the addition *"en société avec M. ———."*[8] Undoubtedly also many cases of touching up or additional help have gone completely unrecorded. According to one of his helpers, Ernest Legouvé, the practice was for both men to go through the idea for the opera in conversation and to reduce it to an over-all sketch. One of them

(7) Elizabeth Forbes: *Scribe.*
(8) E.g., *La Muette de Portici* was written with Germain Delavigne; *Le Comte Ory* with Delestre-Poirson; *Le Lac des fées* with "Joseph de Mélesville," who was Anne-Honoré Duveyrier.

would then write down the sketch and the other finish it (with sometimes each one taking on an act).[9] Rey M. Longyear, in a study of the Scribe *opéra comique* librettos, feels that the internal evidence of the works argues in favor of the conclusion that Scribe, in fact, not only reserved the over-all planning of the story and the stage effects to himself, but also wrote all of the verse and was responsible for the final literary style of the whole—a conclusion that I endorse.[1] In this sense, then, Scribe should be contrasted with librettists like Metastasio or Wagner in that although he wished final control, he was uninterested in sole creative credit. Rather like Rubens, he placed the stamp of his talents upon the work and left the minor details for others to finish.

The Meyerbeer-Scribe relationship can be instanced as an analogous example of this collaborative spirit. Meyerbeer, particularly after his success with *Robert le diable*, insisted on maintaining final control over the opera as it was presented on stage. Because Scribe was so powerful as a stage technician, Meyerbeer could not dispense with his services, and so accepted his treatments of the *Grand Opéra* subjects they created together. In the course of his composition of the libretto, Meyerbeer subjected it to various changes and now and then asked for new verses. If Scribe agreed, he provided them; if he did not, a "house poet" supplied them (without acknowledgment). But Scribe had one more weapon not possessed by the great majority of librettists, and particularly the Italian librettists: his collected works. In those he could include *his* versions of the libretto, which contained non-Scribean elements aplenty but could differ from the published score.[2]

Such a practice of collective libretto writing, endemic to the nineteenth century, is unthinkable to anyone concerned with the expression of his own talents, but to Scribe it was understandable, given his complaisant artistic nature, the volume of work he was

---

(9) As quoted in Rey M. Longyear: *The Opéra-Comique Librettos of Scribe*, p. 186.
(1) Ibid., p. 187.
(2) To select one example, in Act III of *Les Huguenots*, Scribe had Raoul learn of the marriage of his beloved from the lips of his sworn enemy, her father. Meyerbeer softened the impact by having him told by the Queen. I have considered the Scribe librettos as reprinted in his collected works.

called upon to provide, and, most importantly, his correct assessment of his own strengths. He realized that his forte was as a scenario writer and stage-effect planner, not as a creative genius, and he further realized that in *Grand Opéra* the words themselves were of far smaller import than the effect of the over-all design. Besides, the artistic value of the whole mattered to him less than its immediate success. Needless to add, such an outlook did not endear him to the young Romantic authors, to whom the public's taste counted for little and to whom personal expression was the highest of virtues.

Scribe was consistent in his approach. With Auber, he often supplied words to fit melodies already written. In his outline for his first work with Meyerbeer, *Robert le diable,* he had included the necessary ballet, but it was the usual Olympus-gods series of *entrées,* which had been a boresome standard since the time of Lully. The scene designer (and later director of the Opéra) Edmond Duponchel persuaded him to change the ballet to one involving defrocked nuns risen from their graves, an idea derived from the "boulevard plays" of the time and having the excuse of continuity, however slight, with the story line. This idea was so novel that it became notorious, and was one of the sensations of the opera. Scribe never forgot a lesson in stage impact, and his later librettos reuse similar ideas. There is a bathing scene for women in *Les Huguenots,* which is of course sheer erotic titillation, and before the première of *Le Prophète* in 1849, a skating ballet was inserted into the opera because of the popularity of roller skating in Paris at the time.

Scribe is likewise credited with the development, if not the invention, of the tableau curtain, in which the act climaxes on an unexpected twist of the plot or on a grand culmination. This upbeat finale, calculated to generate waves of applause, became a feature of the later well-made librettos and plays, and was known in England as the "tornado" curtain.

Scribe was always interested in stage novelty. In *La Muette de Portici* he had cast the titular role as a dumb girl who expressed herself through pantomime. Although the idea derived from the pantomime plays still popular in France, its usage in opera was apposite because it united in a particularly appealing way the talents of the ballet and those of the opera. Certainly Fenella symbolizes much of the French approach to the libretto, which, as has been emphasized, was far more strongly visual than was the case with the Italian libretto, and in which the talents of the ballet corps had habitually been used. But, as is also usual with Scribe, once the idea succeeded, it reappeared: thus we have a young dancer who pantomimes her way through *Le Dieu et la bayadère* (1830; m., Auber).

Anyone connected with the production was free to suggest improvements, and often these became part of the result. Thus the great tenor Adolphe Nourrit contributed a footnote to libretto history by suggesting the closing duet for the fourth act of *Les Huguenots* and by writing the words of Éléazar's most famous aria in *La Juive*. Scribe objected to the idea of the duet not, character- istically, because it was someone else's idea but because he felt that a duet at that point in the act would weaken its structure. He had planned the act to climax at the intensely dramatic blessing of the swords—the usual "tornado" curtain. Scribe, of course, was dra- matically right, but art has a way of confounding logic, and Nourrit's suggestion coupled with Meyerbeer's music capped the climax in an even more arresting way. Nourrit was allowed to write the *Juive* aria because Scribe was, as always, too busy and Nourrit offered to compose words that would lie easily for his tenor voice. Those interested in the problems of writing words suitable for singing should study the vowel and consonant place- ments of "*Rachel, quand du Seigneur*" for further enlightenment.

Scribe as a writer is a mirror of his age, and thus although none of his works illumines the depths of his thoughts or his soul— in this respect he is rather like most librettists—all of them reflect well his general liberal-bourgeois mentality, which was exactly in tune with the spirit of the age of Louis-Philippe. Scribe could never be a Victor Hugo, spouting radicalism and defiance and radiating genius, but in his watered-down way he sided with the weak against the strong, the underdog against the oppressors, and the good against the bad. Unlike the writers of the seventeenth-century hero-versus-tyrant librettos, Scribe softens the characters so that none of them is an idealization (again, the bourgeois ethic). Brogni, the implacable Cardinal and enemy of the Jews, is shown to have humanity, and even the outright fanatics, such as Marcel the Huguenot, Saint-Bris the Catholic, and Bertram the Devil, possess either a charm or a stage presence which is not wholly evil. The over-all tone of the librettos is that which would appeal most

strongly to a middle-class audience:[3] that is, one of strong sentimentality intermixed with pomp. The love story is central, but,
unlike the love chains of the *opera seria*, is usually a recipro-
cated love thwarted, Romeo-like, by incompatibility of back-
grounds (Jew and Christian, Huguenot and Catholic). The one
constant in the Scribe librettos—and in others of the period in
France—is the obsession with religion. Religious rites had always
been an integral part of the *merveilleux* aspect of the French
libretto from Quinault on. This continued, but added to it was
the theme of religiosity in its fanatic or traditional garbs. It is
almost as if the *deus ex machina* of the Lully spectacle could not
be banished entirely, but sat above, unseen, yet controlling the
action. Cathedrals, crypts, graveyards; Cardinals, Popes, friars,
inquisitors—all made their appearances. This religious streak can
be explained in terms of nostalgia, of facile dramatic device (much
as a courtroom scene is a facile way to write gripping drama, all
non-essentials being pared away), of the dramatic nature of the
Catholic ritual and so on: what is evident is the presence of the
Church on stage.

The essential difference in the "bourgeois" outlook of *Grand
Opéra* from the earlier Sedaine-Diderot works, aside from the
greater emphasis on spectacle, was the addition of the Romantic
element of the final sacrifice of the "good" to the more powerful
political forces. Although Robert le Diable is saved from his devil-
father Bertram by the love of a woman, Raoul the Huguenot,
Éléazar and Rachel the Jews, Masaniello and Fenella the oppressed,
and Jean the deluded prophet all die at the end, defending their
faiths. And they die not because—as in so many Italian *melodrammi*
—they are hated by a specific individual (because he loves the
heroine), but because the individuals arrayed against them are part
of an antagonistic system. This element, so much a part of the plays
of Victor Hugo (such as *Ruy Blas*), so much a part of the Romantic
esthetic, is clearly seen in the *Grand Opéra* librettos.

Yet *Grand Opéra* was much more than the story line. As
with so many ideas later adopted and adapted by Wagner, the
Gesamtkunstwerk notion that all parts of a production should be
consciously harnessed to produce a single entity known as "the

---

(3) Much as the Quinault libretto was written to please first the King
and then the upper aristocracy.

Opera" was first evidenced in *Grand Opéra*. Needless to say, the roots of this total organization go back to the Lully spectacles, but it should be understood that the impact of works like *Les Hugue- nots*, *La Juive*, and *La Muette de Portici* lay in the careful planning of their premières and in the total effect of the work, which inevitably surpassed the sum of their flawed parts. Each work, with all its novelties and its moments, stood apart from the others as a unique creation. Wagner of course saw the *Gesamtkunstwerk* as the creation of a single mind. In French *Grand Opéra* it was an extensive collaboration involving Scribe and whoever else con- tributed verses, the composer, the scenic designers (Pierre Cicéri and Duponchel), the director of the Opéra (Louis Véron at first; later Duponchel), and even the paid *claque* under the leadership of the genius-*claqueur* Auguste Levasseur. One problem with our understanding and therefore appreciation of *Grand Opéra* today is that the seizable elements of the production are perhaps the weakest—the music of Meyerbeer, Halévy, and Auber; the verse and shallow characterizations of Scribe. We can dimly envision the spectacle, but on the printed page the descriptions lack emotional impact and remain brummagem. *Grand Opéra* was meant to be experienced in a theater, as one experiences a circus: accepted in that spirit, the puppetry and pomp achieve the diversity to which they are entitled and a grandeur that they assume. Scribe never pretended to more: his detractors, such as Théophile Gautier and Wagner, saw the size of the framework and the paucity of what it contained, and cried out. Such a frame presupposed and deserved a more elevated esthetic approach and a more esthetically satisfying result. Wagner set about to achieve this within that expanded frame, while Gautier turned to the smaller-scale Italian *melo- dramma* to experience something of value.

Scribe's mirror can also apply to his artistic qualities, for the strengths and weaknesses of his oeuvre lie obvious on the surface of his writing. As a craftsman he is straightforward, setting forth the exposition immediately and proceeding in a clear progression from first to last. Although his "joinings" can lack plausibility— if a character is needed on stage he often appears, almost by chance —Scribe eschews the complex plot twists that are the mark of inferior librettists. He prefers an ongoing development in which interest is generated not by continual revelations of character or unlikely coincidences such as the poor boy turning out to be the long-lost prince[4] but in stage happenings that serve to change the course of the characters. Scribe's dramaturgy involves the audience in the story to a great extent: he wants them to know clearly what is going on. This clarity in turn simplifies the composer's task.

Throughout Scribe's work—be it *Grand Opéra, opéra comique, vaudeville,* or straight play—there is a remarkable homogeneity. The *Grands Opéras* differ from the others in being more fully stuffed with opportunities for stage spectacle, sequences of contrasting *coups de théâtre,* and a heavier dose of arias and ensembles,[5] but their distance from his *opéras comiques* is hardly as great as the distance between *Aline, reine de Golconde* and *Le Déserteur* of Sedaine or *Tarare* and *Le Mariage de Figaro* of Beaumarchais. In fact, this homogenization of opera as Scribe effected it brought a later *opéra comique* such as *Faust* or *Carmen* close enough to *opéra* so that it could gain admittance to the sacred precincts with only structural changes.

Stephen S. Stanton, in his *English Drama and the French Well-Made Play,*[6] gives six characteristics of a Scribe work, which apply to his librettos as to his plays. They are: (1) delayed-action plot, in which the hero overcomes obstacles; (2) increasing intensity of action and suspense; (3) alternation of focus between hero and opponent; (4) a logical order of the climactic scenes; (5) the use of misunderstanding; and (6) the fact that each act reproduces in miniature the play as a whole. Coupled with Scribe's straightforwardness and his reliance on Sedaine-derived genre elements, these criteria would more or less influence the history of the spoken stage through the nineteenth century, in the work of such playwrights as Alexandre Dumas *fils,* Victorien Sardou, Arthur Wing Pinero—and even their detrac-

---

(4) There are exceptions to this, more often in the *opéra comique* works. In *Les Vêpres siciliennes,* his libretto for Verdi, Scribe has the tenor hero revealed as the son of the baritone villain, but even here the baritone has been aware of this from the beginning.

(5) The even more inflated nature of Scribe's *Grands Opéras* for Meyerbeer led Wagner to state that those librettos were Scribe's worst. The statement contains some truth, both because those librettos stretch the *Grand Opéra* form to its absolute limits—a less "Grand" Opera such as Auber's *Gustave III* is much closer in spirit to *Un Ballo in maschera*—and because many of Meyerbeer's "improvements" on Scribe in fact weakened the causal structure of the librettos for the sake of other considerations.

(6) Unpublished work, quoted in Rey M. Longyear: *The Opéra-Comique Librettos of Scribe,* p. 180.

tors, Henrik Ibsen and George Bernard Shaw. Besides the French libretto, they would also influence the work of Wagner (note the importance of the sixth characteristic in his work) and Italian librettists down through those who worked with Puccini and Francesco Cilèa to *The Consul* (1950) of Gian Carlo Menotti. Even Metastasio, the most powerful librettist, never commanded that span of interest for his works.[7]

Scribe also must be credited with the bringing of the chorus downstage into an active role as participant. Certain earlier French operas, such as *Fernand Cortez,* had anticipated this expanded role of the chorus, and the Revolutionary period had popularized the notion of the emancipated people, which had been seen in *Guillaume Tell* and in Beethoven's and his librettists' reworking of *Léonore* into *Fidelio*. But *Grand Opéra* systematically highlighted the chorus as a force and a character in its own right, and Scribe, the cautious bourgeois, first saw the obverse of the joyous citizenry in *Fidelio*: that is, the chorus as mob. Particularly in *La Muette de Portici* and *La Juive,* but also in other works, Scribe demonstrates the volatility and power of this mob, and if he, because of the inanity of his choral verses and because of his essential timidity, never took the final step and transformed the chorus into a dominant force, he pointed the way to Mussorgsky and others later in the century.[8] Yet even in the *Grands Opéras* the chorus has a physical presence and weight that cannot help but be felt.

Scribe's chief weaknesses are his characterizations and his verse. His stage figures remain that—effective within the confines of the libretto but hardly rounded individuals—but certain of his portraits, notably those of Gustave III, Jean de Leyden, and Jean's mother Fidès, do aspire to more. His thumbnail sketches are almost always better done, because of their clarity and brevity: Marcel the Huguenot, or Urbain and Oscar the pages. His females tend to be the sentimental sweethearts so dear to the Romantic middle class. Scribe is also not very good at dramatic scenes involving the interplay of character, at which both Busenello and

---

(7) Metastasio's librettos were set well into the nineteenth century, but Mozart's failure with *La Clemenza di Tito* in 1791 is symbolic of the passing of the Metastasian form.
(8) Oddly enough, this is one aspect of *Grand Opéra* that Wagner did not adopt. His choruses remain in the background—even vigorous ones such as the vassals in *Götterdämmerung*—and never force or control the action.

Metastasio excelled: about the best of his scenes of that sort is the one (IV, iv) between Brogni and Éléazar in *La Juive*, but even that never penetrates the skin.

Scribe's verse, especially for the chorus, is at best hopelessly banal and at worse atrocious.[9] End-stopped and cliché-ridden, it never achieves any sort of life of itself, and the choral verses, as if copied from a third-rate Favart, are endlessly repetitive without the slightest merit of subtle variation that differentiates the great number of Metastasio's exit arias. The alexandrines that were necessary for the "recitative" portions of the *Grand Opéra* are almost always ponderous.[1] Scribe's indifference toward verse, as compared with his attention to the stage aspects of his librettos, is immediately evident on examining his works, and although his prose works are more comfortably written, even they do not flow gracefully.

Part of the secondary nature of the verse came from the nature of *Grand Opéra* itself. The vocal moments, of course, of solo (usually in ballad or romance form, or else a cavatina)—in keeping with the external nature of the *Grand Opéra* there were few soliloquies—or, of ensemble with or without choral backing, were considered moments of repose between the events. Except for the ballad, which may tell something germane to the story, these moments were analogous to the Metastasian exit aria in that they did not further the action on stage. Often they existed for themselves, shoehorned into the fabric without any regard for dramatic necessity, which enraged not only Wagner but also Italian librettists (to whom *brevità* was an article of faith). Yet there is no reason why such a looser form should be inherently bad; and indeed in the cases of *Grand Opéra* that survive today—the character of Oscar in *Un Ballo in maschera*, or the garden scene, with Eboli's Veil Song, in *Don Carlo*—this very diversity becomes an asset, for it opens up the work and suggests further vistas. It is, quite simply, more like life itself. Scribe used this general relaxation of tension through diversity to suggest the larger scope in which

---

(9) One example should suffice: "*Hosanna! plaisir! ivresse!/Gloire, gloire à l'Éternel!/Et que nos chants d'allégresse/retentissent jusqu'au ciel!*" (Hosanna! Pleasure! Drink! Glory on high! Let our songs of happiness resound up to the sky!") *La Juive;* I, i.
(1) The alexandrine never could shed that aura of French stage rhetoric which generations of *tragédies* had instilled into it; Scribe's limitations only accentuated the negative.

he was working, and its structural correctness was apprehended, if unconsciously, by the very same Wagner, who did not introduce irrelevancies but who expanded speeches into monologues of great length in order to achieve a similar relaxation and universality.

Scribe's *Grands Opéras* are all historically placed, as for example, at the Council of Constance in 1414 (often Scribe, in his librettos, included footnotes taken from history books as to the events). They climax around a specific historical event, be it the Saint Bartholomew's night massacre, the coronation of the Anabaptist John of Leyden, the Neapolitan revolt led by Masaniello, or the assassination of Gustavus III of Sweden. Even when the operas themselves are not re-creations of history Scribe tried to tie them to a specific place or date: thus *Le Lac des fées* includes the traditional Feast of the Magi at Christmas in Cologne and *La Part du diable* (1843; m., Auber) takes place on St. John's Day. The emotional and symbolic overtones of such placement were used by Scribe merely for stage purposes; again, the deeper implications were left to Wagner. Saint John's Eve and Day (i.e., Midsummer Eve and Day), Good Friday, the Song Contest on the Wartburg, all become in Wagner's hands not only specific events but events dovetailed into the opera itself, and therefore meaningful in terms of the work as a whole.[2]

The structure of the *Grand Opéra* libretto was loose, as it had to contain within its five acts one or more ballets or processionals as well as opportunities for other stage spectacle and vocal display. The operas (as with the *melodramma*) began with a chorus and the climax was usually achieved with the fourth act. The fifth, usually short, became a sort of apotheosis of the work—analogous to the seventeenth-century *deus ex machina* or *licenza* closes—which often contained the most spectacular stage display of the evening, but whose dramatic function was solely to ratify what had transpired before. Thus the fifth act of *La Muette de Portici* shows the final defeat of Masaniello's forces. We are told of the off-stage death of Masaniello; Fenella (his sister) half faints, then revives. In the distance Vesuvius begins to erupt. Fenella runs to the top

---

(2) A later development coupled this with a tie-in to a specific date and therefore added dramatic irony. The joyous Mardi Gras outside while Violetta lies dying within, or the joyous Christmas season outside while Werther expires in Charlotte's arms in his garret.

terrace and flings herself into the void as Vesuvius overflows with molten lava and flames.[3]

Because the rationale of *Grand Opéra* was so heavily in terms of spectacle, as many different—and differentiated—scenes as possible were included in each work. The opening act, with its necessary use of the chorus, was generally an outdoor scene; the third or fourth was another, if possible more spectacular. Scribe well understood the emotional value of quick contrasts within and between the scenes themselves. He liked to alternate closed-in scenes with open ones, or to have the first scene of an act an interior and then have the set "open out" into an outdoor one (*La Muette de Portici*, Act III; *Le Lac des fées*, Act III).[4] He also utilized the powerful device of having the chorus clamoring outside while a scene was going on inside (Nourrit's duet for Act IV of *Les Huguenots* made this even more dramatic).

The use of a multiplicity of strongly individual sets, coupled with the rest of the *Grand Opéra* ménage, was bound to change the Gluck reform esthetic in which the single thread of the story dominated everything. In Grand Opéra, the fragmentation was into tableaus, or scenic set-pieces, which duplicated on a visual scale the set-piece (or "number") of the ballad, cavatina, or ensemble. The story, important but secondary, wove its way through these tableaus. The difference from the Italian *melodramma* lay in the fact that, although there was a definite break after each act, each act was self-contained, with a greater amount of causal plausibility than could be found in the *melodramma*. Scribe gauged his effects well and paced them well, so that after the curtain fell there was meant to be a pause for reflection and refreshment. When the curtain went up again there would be a differing set and quite probably a goodly length of time would have elapsed. These self-

---

(3) Fenella does not, as many books, including the *Concise Oxford Dictionary of Opera*, assert, leap into the crater of Vesuvius. Scribe may have been a spectacularist, but he was no fool. The great popularity of this opera doubtless was the primary cause for the "leaping female finale," which appears again in Scribe *(La Juive)*, in Wagner *(Der fleigende Holländer)*, in Gounod *(Sapho)*, and in Puccini *(Tosca)*.
(4) These *Grand Opéra* stage setting practices can be seen today in Verdi's "Grand Operas." *Don Carlos* begins in a darkened outdoor scene (the Fountainbleau Scene), proceeds eventually to a *Grand Opéra* outdoor scene—the auto-da-fé, replete with obligatory cathedral —then moves inside for the dramatic fourth act. *Aida* employs the "opening out" device (Act II), as does Wagner's *Lohengrin* (Act III).

contained act-entities, then, served to break the long five-act form into seizable unities which, when put together, would combine into the totality that was *Grand Opéra*. The analogy to a group of short stories with a group of repeated characters is not inapt in suggesting the structural impact of tableau-opera. It is therefore vitally important that these operas be seen in their Scribean form—and this applies to any opera that follows the Scribean pattern.[5] When these spectacles are truncated, either by cuts or conflation of acts, they lose their chief assets, spaciousness and consequent grandeur. Within their large frame, these operas work, and the vindication of the value of the Scribe esthetic of richness in diversity can be found, not primarily in the Meyerbeer works, but in the continuing and growing popularity of an opera not written until after Scribe was dead, and yet which is thoroughly a memorial to Scribe, Verdi's *Don Carlos* (1867; l., F.-J. Méry and Camille du Locle).

The *merveilleux* aspects of *Grand Opéra* have been the ones most highly publicized. Scribe adapted the older *deus ex machina* notions to a middle-class setting—although spectacles like the erupting of volcanoes were standard Opéra crowd-pleasers from Rameau's time and before—and threw in the pageantry of coronations and the like. Yet he could also write a "classic" ending, such as that in *Le Dieu et la bayadère*, in which the god Brama ascends in clouds with the heroine.[6] In *Le Lac des fées* Scribe employs an arresting piece of technical artistry for the finale, which also serves to update the old machines. The story is the *Ondine* variant of the fairy who longs to exchange her status for that of a human because she loves a human. In this rendering, her wishes are granted, and she comes down from the clouds to her beloved:

> . . . we see her passing through the clouds which, tinted variously by the rays of the sun, continually change; finally, after several minutes of travel we see the earth appear, first the tops of mountains, then the buildings, the towns, the rivers, the prairies, the house, then the room that Albert inhabited in the third act.

---

(5) That is, five-act operas such as Gounod's *Roméo et Juliette*.
(6) One reason for this "classicality" may be that the opera bears great resemblances, unusual for Scribe, to an earlier opera, *Les Bayadères* (1810, revised 1814; m., Charles-Simon Catel; l., Jouy). Another "heavenly" ending occurs in *Le Juif errant*, in which the audience is granted a glimpse of the Heavenly Court in serried ranks assembled, while the poor Jew is told to keep on his weary way.

Albert, alone in his room and weighed down with despair, is about to kill himself—He raises his eyes and sees Zéila who is coming down on a cloud toward him, holding out her arms. He runs to her and the curtain falls.

Here, the sentimental and *le merveilleux* combine in a typically nineteenth-century approach to a standard French operatic device.[7]

A few words should be written about several of Scribe's *Grand Opéra* librettos for Meyerbeer, for their inordinate fame in their day led to their being used as storehouses of ideas for later librettos. This is particularly true of Scribe's first libretto for Meyerbeer, *Robert le diable* which, although it came after both *Guillaume Tell* and *La Muette de Portici*, was the work that ushered in *Grand Opéra*. Although some of the demonic traits of the story can be traced to earlier French librettos, there is no doubt that the influence of *Der Freischütz* (1821; m., Weber; l., Friedrich Kind)—seen in Paris in 1824 in the bowdlerized disguise of *Robin des bois*—is the controlling one. Scribe always took from wherever, whatever would be useful. Yet the German antecedent is less important, finally, than *Robert*'s influence on later French opera. The whole of the character of Alice, the sweet young peasant girl who loves Robert, runs down through French nineteenth-century opera. Her bringing of Robert's mother's will to him and reading it out to him in order to get him to forget his father (the Devil) will reappear in the character and actions of Micaela (the devil there being Carmen). Similarly, on reading Scribe's libretto, it becomes evident that Barbier and Carré's libretto for Gounod's *Faust* derives as much from *Robert* as from Goethe. The scene in Act V in which Robert listens to the chorus

---

(7) *Le Lac des fées* is interesting because of its relationship with the work of Richard Wagner. The influence of the final transformation is obvious enough; in the third act the Feast of the Magi is depicted by a very detailed description of the procession through the streets of Cologne, organized by guilds, each one preceded by its own standard. The opera was given in the spring of 1839, and was not a success, achieving only thirty-nine performances. (Incidentally, this fact is in itself revelatory: thirty-nine performances of a twentieth-century opera would class it as a major contribution to the genre, but thirty-nine performances of a Broadway musical would likewise be considered unsuccessful.) Wagner arrived in Paris in the fall of 1839. It seems evident that, if he did not see one of the last performances, he at least read and digested the libretto.

singing inside a church and tries to pray as Bertram attempts to drag him away is only slightly altered in the Gounod opera. The invocation of the absent mother reappears in the Munich scene of Offenbach's *Les Contes d'Hoffmann*.

Les Huguenots is a prime example of the Scribe five-act scenic form used to enhance the telling of the story: three widely varied locales for the first three acts—the Great Hall of a château, the exterior of the château of Chenonceaux (which is built over a river),[8] and the Pré-aux-Clercs in Paris—then the dramatic fourth act set in a closed-in room, and the fifth in three settings, first a brilliantly lighted ball, then a cloister, and finally a bloodstained street in which the massacre claims its final victims.

The libretto of *Le Prophète*, if containing nothing so intensely dramatic as the fourth act of *Les Huguenots*, nonetheless deserves to be examined as an example of Scribe's approach to *Grand Opéra*. It would be useful to sketch in the historical basis on which Scribe constructed the plot, because Scribe's adaptations for the taste of the nineteenth-century audience can then be more clearly appreciated. Scribe chose as his subject the second Anabaptist uprising, which convulsed Germany and the Low Countries from 1532 to 1535. Its leaders were a Haarlem baker, Johann Matthyszoon (Matthiesen), and a Leyden tailor, Johann Bockholdt (John of Leyden). These two men were out-and-out fanatics, Matthiesen believing that he was Gideon and Bockholdt convinced that he was the successor to the Biblical David. With their followers, they seized the town of Münster and held it for a year amid the most unbridled license: Bockholdt took four wives (one of whom he himself beheaded in the town square) and justified his arbitrary decisions as resulting from visions from heaven. The town was captured in 1535, and in 1536 Bockholdt was executed after suffering six months of torture.

In Scribe all of this is different. Jean becomes a simple innkeeper, in love with a local girl, who is manipulated by others who are less fanatics than opportunists in search of wealth and power. Because Jean is portrayed as a simplehearted, devout person, who throughout the opera is prey to doubts about his divinity and his mission (which he has undertaken because of justifiable anger

---

(8) Note the reasons for the choice of such a scene: the château is widely famous and would be instantly recognized by the audience, and its superfluvial location is ideal for the bathing scene.

against the social system), Scribe gains for him not only the audience's sympathy but also a measure of dignity and stature. To be sure, the underlying motivation—as in all Scribe—is love.

The first act opens with a pastoral scene in Holland. A castle stands to one side of the stage. Fidès, Jean's adored mother, has arrived to fetch Berthe, his fiancée. Berthe is somewhat dazzled to have been chosen by this handsome young man, whom she has long loved, but she cannot leave her home without the permission of her overlord, the Comte d'Oberthal. A shadow comes over the peace of the genre scene with the arrival of three Anabaptists, Zacharie, Jonas, and Mathiesen.[9] Scribe's portrayal of these three is not as fanatics but as opportunists willing to espouse a cause in order to advance themselves. They begin to work on the ever-present chorus, attempting to convert them. Oberthal now comes out of the castle with his friends; the chorus greets him as overlord. Oberthal sees the Anabaptists mumbling to one side, and recognizes one of them, Jonas, as a thieving servant he had dismissed. His attention is distracted, however, by Berthe, who tells him, in a *romance*, of how she is an orphan and was saved from drowning by Jean, whom she now wants to marry. Oberthal, taken by the beauty of Berthe, refuses her request, and has his men take her and Fidès into the castle while the chorus remains stupefied with fright and the Anabaptists gesture menacingly.

The second act is set in the inn of Jean and his mother in Leyden. The townsfolk are dancing,[1] and they call to Jean for more beer. The Anabaptists enter, and Jonas is struck by Jean's resemblance to the portrait of King David in Münster. They find out that Jean is a paragon—goodhearted, strong, brave, a man who knows his Bible by heart—and they resolve to make him their apostle. They approach him, and he tells them of a dream he had of being crowned king. The three are ever more convinced that Jean is their man, but Jean says he would rather marry Berthe "and have her reign in my heart." They leave, and Jean drives out his doubts by thoughts of marriage. Berthe now enters, disheveled, fleeing from Oberthal, and hides as his soldiers enter. Jean disavows knowledge of her whereabouts, but the Sergeant

---

(9) Scribe's spelling of the name.
(1) They dance a waltz, thus antedating the famous *Rosenkavalier* anachronism by more than a half-century and the *Faust* one by a decade. The verses are characteristically inept.

cannily suggests that, unless he tells them, his mother will be killed.[2] At this point there is an interesting stage direction in the libretto: "he [Jean] remains several instants with his head in his hands, while the orchestra expresses the tumults that are raging in him." Seemingly, the Gluckian use of the orchestra, continued in the French *mélodrame*, now appears in *Grand Opéra* on its way to Wagner. The irony is that Meyerbeer ignored Scribe's direction and the orchestra remains silent. Jean refuses to decide, his mother is brought in, and Berthe comes out of hiding and is carried off once more. Fidès is convinced that her son saved her; Jean on the other hand finds his thoughts turning on the injustice of society. As he remains in thought, he hears the Anabaptists outside intoning a Psalm and realizes that they have been sent by God to help him. He invites them in. The three feed his frustrated rage with visions of Joan of Arc. He continues to be torn—Should he leave his mother? He must forget her and go on to his glory, they tell him and, still unsure, Jean allows himself to be led away.

The third act takes place in the Anabaptist camp on the edge of a forest next to a frozen lake whose shores are lost in the mists. Prisoners are brought in while the chorus cries for blood. No, says Mathiesen prudently, ransom will bring more—thus underlining the tawdry nature of the heresy, which is interested more in material wealth than in spiritual salvation. Zacharie appears with booty, which affords a splendid opportunity for spectacle and a joyous skating ballet. The scene changes to the inside of Zacharie's tent. Mathiesen tells Zacharie that the elder Oberthal, Governor of Münster, still holds the city, although his son's château has been destroyed, and that the Anabaptists must take Münster because the Emperor is already on the way to crush them. But nothing can be done because the prophet, Jean, has shut himself in his tent. At this point young Oberthal is brought in, but the three do not recognize him, night having fallen. After they initiate him into the army, one of them lights a lamp and he is discovered. Zacharie orders him executed; Jonas asks whether the prophet should not be consulted; Zacharie tells him the prophet's approval is not required.

Jean enters and tells the rest that he has lost heart for the fight. He has liberated Germany: he does not need to go farther: he only wishes to go home and see his mother. Zacharie tries to in-

---

(2) In the opera Meyerbeer has Oberthal say this.

veigle him with visions of Joan of Arc, but he is obdurate. Oberthal is brought in; Jean is told that the man has been condemned. Jean's vanity is piqued because he has not ordered it, and he reprieves him. He then recognizes him as his enemy. He sends the others away, and Oberthal, now repentant, tells him that Berthe has disappeared. She threw herself into the river, but God must have saved her for she is reported to be in Münster. Oberthal asks Jean to kill him for his crime, but Jean is no longer interested. At this moment Mathiesen enters the tent to say that soldiers have come out of Münster and have put the Anabaptists to flight. We move outdoors again and Jean, after a prayer, rallies his men with a stirring address. Trumpets are heard off stage, excitement rises, a triumphal hymn is sung, and as the soldiers form into ranks and march off, the mists at the back of the lake dissolve and reveal the ramparts of Münster. Jean points to them, and the act ends on a tableau.

Scribe's handling of Act III is a masterful example of the wedding of spectacle and intimacy with the appropriate rising climactic close, which is exemplified scenically, musically, and dramaturgically. Despite the paucity of psychological depth and the abundance of nineteenth-century sentiment about mother love, Scribe's writing well delineates the captive nature of the prophet, caught between his own ambition and passivity and trapped in the coils of the three Anabaptists. The introduction of Oberthal is used to elaborate this dependence,[3] as well as to provide the basis for the change of heart in Jean. The Italian librettists would have excised ruthlessly in order to get from emotional moment to emotional moment—an analogy here would be to the *"Di quella pira"* scene in *Il Trovatore*, where the news of Manrico's mother's pending execution is brought in by a messenger without any folderol. Yet Scribe's insistence on this logical, if stage-oriented and sentimental, development of the story exemplifies that approach to history which has, since the nineteenth century, become controlling. Decisions like the taking of a city are made less because of idealism or grand-plan politics than because of the concatenation of trivial events, and if Scribe chose to symbolize this by the love of a woman, the underlying truth is nonetheless made evident.

---

(3) Even in Oberthal himself: in the scene he is shown as agreeing to anything the Anabaptists demand in the hope of not being recognized.

The fourth act is in two scenes, the first of which is a public square in Münster. The Anabaptists have captured the city, but its citizens remain unconverted. This day the Anabaptists will crown their leader as king. Fidès, now a beggar, enters, and (naturally) discovers Berthe disguised as a pilgrim. She tells the girl that her son is dead: she found his bloody clothes in the inn one morning. She is convinced that his death was the work of the prophet, and on hearing this, Berthe resolves to kill the man.[4] The scene changes to the Cathedral of Münster, and there is the grand coronation procession. Jean appears crowned, with a scepter in his hand, followed by the ever-present three. He is now almost convinced that he is truly chosen by God, but at that moment Fidès sees him and cries out: "My son!" The chorus shrink back from her as from a madwoman; Jonas whispers to Jean that one word means her death. Jean asks who that woman is; she replies indignantly. Jean again refuses to recognize her. The Anabaptists threaten to kill her; Jean stops them, saying she is crazy. Then he comes forward, has her kneel, puts a hand on her head and asks for divine help. If he is her son and not the prophet, he says to the populace, they can kill him. Then, he asks Fidès, "Am I your son?" She can only answer "No." Jean exits in triumph while Fidès can only imagine his coming downfall.

Act V is similarly in two scenes. The first is one of the subterranean cellars of the Münster palace. Jonas has found out that the Emperor is fast approaching the city, and has offered clemency to those who would hand over Jean. "It is the will of God," the three pragmatically decide. They go out, and Fidès is brought in by soldiers. She has time for two cavatinas before Jean comes in. She rejects him as her son, while he asks pardon; she wishes him to renounce everything; he finally assents. She tells him that Berthe is alive and still loves him; providentially Berthe now appears, having found a secret door that her grandfather, the Guardian of the Palace, had told her about. She sees Jean, but does not know him as the prophet, and Jean whispers to Fidès to keep his secret. The three sing of the joys of being back home. They are about to leave through the secret door when soldiers enter to tell Jean that the city has been betrayed to the Emperor's men.

---

(4) Of course psychologically Jean the innkeeper did die when Jean the prophet was born.

Berthe now realizes that Jean is the prophet, and, following another ensemble, commits suicide after cursing him. Jean, heartbroken, orders his mother taken to safety and resolves on his final act.

The scene changes to the grand hall of the palace. As in *Les Huguenots*, dancing and celebrating are going on while outside the world closes in. Jean gives his orders and tells the soldiers to go. He calls the three to sit beside him and drink. The imperial army enters: Zacharie delivers Jean over to them; Jean thanks his "new Judas."[5] Jean gives the signal: all doors are closed: he says they are all in his power. There is a great explosion—a piece of the wall falls in and flames jet out. Jean castigates them all—Oberthal included—as the catastrophe grows. Suddenly Fidès is in their midst, come to forgive her son and die with him. The palace crumbles in flaming ruin, and the curtain falls.

Wagner was largely correct when he called Scribe's librettos —particularly those for *Grand Opéra*—a series of effects without causes. Scribe first calculated the effect, then built backward to construct the cause.[6] In his better librettos, this causality persuades; in his lesser ones, and in certain portions of his major librettos, the bones of the dramaturgy glint bare. So little characterization was provided beyond the most rudimentary that any miscalculation as far as plot was concerned was disastrous to belief in the personages involved. The banality of the verse only added to this one-dimensionality.

Scribe's work for both the *opéra* and *opéra comique* illustrates in extreme form one of the underlying themes of this book: that the value and worth of any librettist cannot be limited to his handling of words in verse or for character portrayal. As long as these remain prime requirements Scribe must be judged by his weakest attributes, and will be summarily dismissed as a stage trickster. Similarly, as long as Scribe is judged from the vantage point of Wagner's librettos, particularly one like *Die Meistersinger* —which employs the Scribe method of construction but in a far more organically thought-through and realized way—his staginess will stand out. The value of Scribe's works, rather, lies in their merits on their own terms and in their own milieu and in the legacy that Scribe bequeathed to his successors. He not only pro-

(5) Not in Meyerbeer's setting.
(6) Wagner's obsession with cause led him to compose four operas to elucidate the cause of the death of one man.

duced major historical librettos in his own time but also influenced practically every subsequent librettist into the twentieth century. Indeed, it is not exaggerated to state that an appreciation of Scribe's strengths is a necessary prerequisite to the proper understanding of not only French nineteenth-century librettos or *Aida* but also the works of Richard Wagner.

Chapter Fifteen

The Later Italian Melodramma

THE EFFECTS of the Romantic Age, it is clear, settled rather uneasily upon the opera libretto. Carlo Pepoli but echoed many of his fellow librettists when he wrote:

> *In questo secolo del gran progresso*
> *se vuoi far l'opera di gran successo,*
> *fa in sette parti strano libretto*
> *ch'abbia terribile, strano soggetto:*
> *dagli più orribile, più strano il nome,*
> *ne curar l'epoca, nè il dove, o il come;*
> *sol fibbia e mescola cosa su cosa*
> *senza mai senso, nè ver, nè posa*
> *e sia qual nave che per vapore*
> *da spuma, sprazzi, fumo e rumore.*[1]

But the works, and more especially the attitudes, of the Romantics were shouldering aside the classicists and even the early Romantics such as Alfieri. The figure of Victor Hugo stood at the head of this movement, both because of his incessant polemicizing and because of his dramatic works. Hugo's plays—particularly his early ones—were theater pieces meant directly to make fun of the classical *tragédie* and calculated to shock, offend, and cause the utmost uproar. They did. Whereas "classical precepts"

---

(1) "In this century of great progress, if you want to write a smash-hit opera, write an outlandish libretto in seven 'parts,' which has a weird and terror-filled subject. Give it the weirdest, most horrible title, don't bother about the epoch or the whys and wherefores: only muddle up everything without any continuity, neither truth nor rest [this is a pun: it can also mean, "neither verse nor prose"], and it will be like a steamship which gives off spume, spray, smoke, and noise." As quoted in Mario Rinaldi: *Felice Romani*, p. 412. Note the entirely apposite use of the updated Metastasian exit aria simile.

held that the alexandrine could be split only at the caesura (after the sixth foot), Hugo often broke it up into five or six separate speeches (e.g., *Ruy Blas*, II, v). Whereas a masculine couplet was meant to be followed by a feminine couplet rhyme, Hugo ignored the convention entirely. Whereas a character was meant to make a chaste and dignified entrance upon the scene, Hugo thumbed his nose by having a character enter by coming down through the chimney and out through the fireplace. Many of his devices are today childish in their obviousness, but they served to cut through the artificialities of the form to its substance in one colossal blow. And the Hugo plays did possess vitality and kaleidoscopic brilliance that endowed them with life and zest.

What is obvious today about the Hugo plays is their operatic quality. This is evident from their melodramatic poses, their complex plottings, and their stagily effective climaxes, but it is also evident from their sound. One of Hugo's greatest assets was his full-throated use of the French language, so that the verses themselves gained power from their sonority. Hugo's plays abound in this "musicality"; and the peroration from Ruy Blas's *tirade* in Act III of *Ruy Blas* will give an inkling of the operatic quality of the speech in the mouth of a great French actor:

> . . . *Il nous faut ton bras! au secours, Charles Quint!*
> *Car l'Espagne se meurt, car l'Espagne s'éteint!*
> *Ton globe, qui brillait dans ta droite profonde,*
> *soleil éblouissant qui faisait croire au monde*
> *que le jour désormais se levait à Madrid,*
> *maintenant, astre mort, dans l'ombre s'amoindrit,*
> *lune au trois quarts rongée et qui décroit encore,*
> *et que d'un autre peuple effacera l'aurore!*
> *Hélas! ton héritage est en proie aux vendeurs;*
> *tes rayons, ils en font des piastres! Tes splendeurs*
> *on les souille!—O géant! se peut-il que tu dormes?*
> *On vend ton sceptre au poids! un tas de nains difformes*
> *se taillent des pourpoints dans ton manteau de roi;*
> *et l'aigle impérial, qui, jadis, sous ta loi,*
> *couvrait le monde entier de tonnerre et de flamme,*
> *cuit, pauvre oiseau plumé, dans leur marmite infâme!*[2]

---

(2) "It wants thine arm! Come to the rescue, Charles!/For Spain is dying, blotted out, self slain!/Thy globe, which brightly shone in thy right hand,/A dazzling sun that made the world believe/That thence

Curiously, Hugo's only attempt at a libretto—*La Esméralda* (1836), which he adapted from his novel *Notre-Dame de Paris* for the composer Louise Bertin—is a mediocre treatment in the accepted *opéra comique* form, possibly because he was afraid to let himself go in opera as he did in the theater.[3] He does make use of very short rhymed lines—a Hugo trademark—which was somewhat novel in the libretto,[4] but for the most part the verse reads as if he copied the lesser practitioners of the art.[5] Hugo's importance to the libretto lies in his plays, which were adapted into librettos not in France but in Italy, and in the influence his works had on other dramatists. His slam-bang approach to plot and incident, his heightened response to love and hatred, and his dislike of injustice were perfect tools for *melodramma* librettists, and what the librettos of his plays lacked through loss of the musicality and virility of the verse they made up with music— particularly the music of Giuseppe Verdi.

Hugo's plays were used by the early *melodrammatisti*, but as the *melodramma* developed, the later librettos came to resemble

---

forth at Madrid the day first dawned,/Is now a dead star, that in the gloom grows less/And less—is moon three quarters gnawed away,/ And still decreasing ne'er to rise again/But be effaced by other nations! Oh,/Thy heritage is now put up for sale./Alas! they make piastres of thy rays,/And soil thy splendors! Giant! can it be/Thou sleepest? By its weight thy sceptre now/They sell! A crowd of dwarfs deformed cut up/Thy royal robes to make their doublets, while/ Th'Imperial Eagle, which beneath thy rule/Covered the world, and grasped its thunderbolts/And darted flame, a poor unfeathered bird/ is cooking in their stew-pan infamous!"

I have used the fin-de-siècle translation of Mrs. Newton Crosland to give a flavor of Hugo's nineteenth-century rhetoric, although she hardly rises to the challenge of the splendid last line, which should read, "cooks, poor bedraggled bird, in their *marmite* of Hell!"

(3) A hint of this is given in Hugo's preface, when he says: "I only intend to offer . . . an operatic canvas more or less well constructed so that the musical work will fit on it happily . . ."

(4) E.g., Quasimodo's aria (IV, ii) "*Mon Dieu! J'aime,/hors moi-même,/tout ici!/L'air qui passe/et qui chasse/mon souci!/L'hirondelle/ si fidèle/au vieux toits!/Les Chapelles/sous les ailes/de la croix!*" ("Dear God, I love everything so much! The passing breezes that blow away my cares, the swallow, faithfully clinging to the old roofs, the chapels under the wings of the Cross!")

(5) E.g., Esméralda's first aria, sung as she dances: "*Je suis orpheline,/ fille des douleurs,/qui sur vous incline/en jetant des fleurs;/mon joyeux délire/bien souvent soupire;/je montre un sourire,/je cache des pleurs!*" (I, ii.) ("I am an orphan girl, child of sorrow, who begs your favor by throwing you flowers. My radiant happiness often sighs; I show a smile, but hide my tears.")

his plays more closely in terms of action and, more especially, in terms of directness of language and speech. As we have seen, the Italian librettists of the early nineteenth century were wedded to the classical concepts of longer, more leisurely lines and a measure of graceful poetic euphemism. Even the influence of Alfieri, with his short, nervous lines did not change the poetics markedly, for by and large his verse flowed in longer, more *tragédie*-influenced periods. But the *melodramma* gradually shed those eighteenth-century manners for the more violent and brutal world of the nineteenth, and the change that resulted in the verse can be shown in a comparison of two *Medea* librettos, *Medea in Corinto* (1814; m., Mayr; l., Felice Romani) and *Medea* (1851 m., Mercadante; l., Cammarano's adaptation of Romani). The comparison is unfair to Romani, as *Medea in Corinto* was but his third libretto, but his excessive reliance on older formulas is valuable in demonstrating the changes that took place in the *melodramma*. Medea's first entrance in the Romani libretto bears with it the weight of Metastasio and of Gluck, as well as the burden of the cliché. She says to the chorus (I, vi): *"Cessate . . . intesi . . . (oh mio furor!) . . . tremate . . ./partite, o vili; di mirare indegni/siete l'affano di Medea./* [Chorus exits.] *Son sola. Che penso? . . . a chi mi volgo? . . . ohimè! che sento/piangi, infelice! ah! si . . . piangi un momento./* [ARIA] *Sommi dei, che i giuramenti/de' mortali custodite:/disvelate e li punite,/il mia talamo oltraggiato/vendicate per pietà"*[6] She continues by invoking *"possente Amor"* to her aid. Cammarano's adaptation is far different (I, iv): *"Fia ver? . . . Giasone ritorna,/ed a me non ritorna! . . . Alto la Reggia/di letizia rimbomba,/e silenzio di tomba/Medea sol cinge! . . . Il dubbio in ria certezza/è volto! . . . io son rejetta,/traditta! . . . e qual sarà la mia vendetta?* [ARIA] *Presagio inesplicabile/il cor mi scuote in seno!/strisciar fra dense tenebre/veggio feral baleno!/qual nel' eterna pagina/eccesso ancor sta scritto?"*[7]

---

(6) "Cease . . . I have understood . . . (O fury!) . . . tremble . . . leave, cowards; You are unworthy of witnessing Medea's anguish. I am alone. What am I thinking? . . . To whom should I turn? . . . Alas, what do I feel? Weep, unhappy one! Ah! Yes, weep a moment. [ARIA] Supreme Gods, you who watch over the oaths of mortals, who uncover and punish them, avenge for pity's sake my abused marriage."
(7) "Is it true? . . . Giasone returns but does not return to me! . . . The palace resounds with great jubilation while the silence of a tomb surrounds Medea alone! . . . My doubt has turned into dire certainty! . . . I am rejected, betrayed! . . . and what will my vengeance

The confrontation scene between Giasone and Medea is similarly more directly and trenchantly treated in the Cammarano adaptation. In *Medea in Corinto*, the scene includes the inevitable Confidante, and Medea pleads in terms of: "*Mira, oh dio! Medea ti prega,/versa pianto a' piedi tuoi*";[8] the *Medea* scene is tighter, more to the point and—quite appropriately for a woman who has found out that her lover has arranged his marriage to another woman—seething with rage. Giasone asks for "*pietà*," and Medea shoots back: "*pietà soltanto?/amore io vo'!*"[9] The *Medea in Corinto* scene ends in a duet(!), while in the later opera Medea drives Giasone out with her scorn: "*Ahi! scellerata e fratricida/per te soltanto io mi rendea . . ./tu vuoi tradirmi, anima infida/tu vuoi tradirmi . . . e son Medea! ecc.*[1]

The developments in tautness and directness of language from the early *melodramma* librettos to the works of the middle of the nineteenth century cannot be better exemplified than through a consideration of the middle-period works of Verdi, who in the years from 1840 to 1860 came to represent Italian music to the world.

Verdi must be treated as a librettist in any study of the form. He had such definite ideas about the dramatic shape of his works and insisted so strongly upon obtaining what he desired that his influence upon the libretto was almost as direct as his poets', and in most cases was more important. Meyerbeer, as we have seen, also interfered with the libretto—as did many other composers in an age when the composer was dominant—but Meyerbeer had allied himself with a powerful dramatic force in Scribe, and, although he did effect certain changes within the context of the work,[2] he did not control the dramatic flow. Verdi definitely did, as can be seen in operas such as *Macbeth* (1847, revised 1865; l., Piave) and *Simon Boccanegra* (1857, revised 1881; l., Piave and

---

be? [ARIA] An inexplicable premonition rips the heart from my body. I see a deadly thunderbolt blasting through black clouds. What unperformed monstrosity can still be found in Heaven?"
(8) "See, oh god! Medea prays to you and sheds tears at your feet" (I, ix).
(9) "Only *pietà* you ask? *I* want love!"
(1) "*Ahi!* I, wicked, killer of my brother, merely surrendered to you. You wish to betray me, faithless soul: you wish to betray me . . . and I am Medea!" (I, vi).
(2) Quite often to the detriment of the work.

Boito), in which he began by giving his librettist a complete prose draft, and also in works like *La Traviata* (1853; l., Piave), in which he sat over every detail with Francesco Maria Piave, his complaisant partner. Verdi's difficulties with his French operas *Don Carlos* and *Les Vêpres siciliennes*, and his failure with his one collaboration with Scribe on the latter, can be traced in part to this arrogation of the one area which Scribe and other French librettists had jealously guarded: that is, the plan of the story and its outline.

Verdi's insistence on control over the general plan, moreover, worked toward ends far different from Scribe's. Both were interested in the Romantic concept of violent contrast and conflict within a scene and between scenes; both enlarged the canvas of the work to include greater spaces and longer periods of time. But Verdi was far more concerned with the reality of his characters than Scribe was. Verdi had to believe to be able to compose, and if that belief did not necessarily extend to the logical continuity of the piece—as *La Forza del destino* (1862, revised 1869; l., Piave) and *Il Trovatore* (1853; l., Cammarano and Bardare) demonstrate—it operated with force as regards the major characters, or those characters, like Azucena in *Il Trovatore*, who most interested him. Further, the belief that Verdi insisted upon had to be reinforced in the libretto, as finally written, by a certain directness of language and forcefulness of expression. Although Verdi used the words as metaphors for his music, he was not content with the empty phrases and conceits of Scribe: he wanted his characters to speak with enough distinction so that, when clothed in the mantle of the music, they could emerge as positive portraits.

The *parola scenica* operated here in two ways: to highlight the dramatic point of the scene and to throw light upon the character who speaks it. Thus, *la maledizione* (the curse), which was the original title of *Rigoletto* (1851; l., Piave), appears first in verbal form from the mouth of Monterone when he lays the curse upon the Duca di Mantua and then, more forcefully, upon Rigoletto in Act I, scene i. The curse haunts Rigoletto throughout the opera in various guises, but appears as *la maledizione* at the end of both the first and third acts as referring, respectively, to the exterior effects of the curse (Gilda's abduction and her invitation of death) and to the curse's effects upon Rigoletto (as a divine retribution for his baser nature and his alliance with the libertine Duca).

What Verdi asked of his librettist was the ability to order his ideas and/or scenarios into speeches and then to set them in verse, which should be competent but not necessarily first-rate. Verdi liked to read great dramatic verse, be it Shakespeare or Hugo, but he shied away from reproducing great verse in his librettos, possibly because he knew it would interfere with the music. Besides, he had already translated the "musical" qualities of the verse into music in his head. If the libretto he received from his poet was still in need of revision, and if the poet was unavailable, Verdi, like Meyerbeer, called on others to tinker with it further. He was not enough of a poet to realize that what he was doing by combining strong and varied situations with directness of speech and use of *parole sceniche* was undermining the verbal melody so completely that verse became secondary if not otiose, and could largely be discarded in favor of prose. In effect, however, this is precisely what he accomplished in his works. By the time that he worked with Antonio Ghislanzoni on *Aida* in 1870–1, he could write to him, "Abandon rhythm, rhyme, and stanza."[3] Verdi's own suggestion for the final duet of the opera may not be as polished as Ghislanzoni's revision, but it is entirely serviceable: "*O vita addio, addio terrestri amori/addio dolore e gioia/dell'infinito vedo già gli albori/eterni node ci uniranno in ciel.*"[4] Of far greater impact is his change of Ghislanzoni's words at the moment when Amneris discovers that she has Aida as a rival. Whereas the first change involved a smoothing out, this one involves a sharpening and heightening of the tension and, consequently, an intensification of the scene, which Verdi caps by the use of a whiplash phrase which becomes *parole sceniche*. Thus, Ghislanzoni: "AMNERIS: *Per Radames d'amore/ardo e mi sei rivale.* AIDA: —*Che? —Voi l'amate?* AMNERIS: *Io l'amo/e figlia son di re.*" Thus, Verdi: "AMNERIS: *Tu l'ami. Ma l'amo anch'io:*

---

(3) Letter of August 17, 1870. To quote the passage in full: "What if you ask me, 'And the verse, the rhythm, the stanza?' I don't know what to say, but if the action demands it I would immediately abandon rhythm, rhyme, stanza; I would write blank verse to put forward clearly and concisely what the drama requires. Sometimes in the theater it is only too necessary for the poet and composer to have the talent not to make poetry or music."
(4) "Goodbye life, goodbye earthly loves, goodbye earthly joy and sorrow. I already see the dawn of infinity. Eternal ties will bind us in heaven."

intendi? La figlia dei Faraoni è tua rivale![5] The final version
stays close to Verdi's, but with the line broken up, as it would be
in a moment of almost unbearable emotion, and with the guttural
qualities of the "a" and "o" sounds in the final word accentuated:
"AMNERIS: *(nel massimo furore) Si . . . tu l'ami . . . ma l'amo/
anch'io . . . intendi tu? . . ./son tua rivale . . . figlia de' Faraoni!*"

Verdi's insistence upon directness of language is far more
evident in the recitative portions of the libretto than in the arias,
particularly the love songs and duets. Yet the power that lingers
in the old-fashioned lyrics such as this one by Piave for *Simon
Boccanegra* (III, iii): "FIESCO: *Delle faci festanti al barlume/cifre
arcane, funebri vedrai./Tua sentenza la mano del nume/sopra
queste pareti vergò./Di tua stella s'eclissano i rai,/la tua porpora
in brani già cade;/vincitor, tra le larve morrai/cui la tomba tua
scure nego,*"[6] lies not in the words themselves but in the fact
that Fiesco is telling the Doge of his impending death. Out of this
a moving scene of reconciliation of two old men will develop.
This, again, is not far from Scribe in that the words themselves
are overridden by the strength of the situation. The difference is
that the constant attention given to the characterizations, especially
in the music, but also—largely because of Verdi's pressure—in the
text, adds a depth to the work that Scribe's surface texts lacked.
This can easily be shown in comparing the original Scribe *Gustave
III* with *Un Ballo in maschera*. To take one instance: Antonio
Somma, the Italian librettist, inserted into the text the *"Eri tu"*
aria for Renato. Leaving aside the value of Verdi's music as character portrayal, the words of the second portion, in which the
"villain" thinks back (III, ii) on his days of happiness with his
wife—whom he now considers unfaithful[7]—are set forth sim-

---

(5) "AMNERIS: I burn with love for Rhadames, and you are my rival.
AÏDA: What? *You* love him? AMNERIS: I love him, and I am the
daughter of the king!"

"AMNERIS: You love him? Well, I love him also—do you understand me? The daughter of the Pharaohs is your rival!"

(6) "By the light of the festive torches you will see strange and
deadly inscriptions. The hand of heaven has incised your sentence on
these walls. The rays of your star are eclipsed; your purple robes already fall in shreds; conqueror, among the ghosts that your ax has
denied their final rest you shall die."

(7) "*O dolcezze perdute, o memorie/d'un amplesso che l'essere
india!/Quando Amelia, si bella, si candida/sul mio seno brillava
d'amor,/si, brillava d'amor!*" ("O lost delights, O memories of embraces
that were godlike! When Amelia, so beautiful and innocent, burned

ply and naturally, but with a psychological correctness and a depth of emotion that humanize the character. The Somma ending of the opera, in which Renato repents his deed of assassination, becomes consistent with his earlier humanism and makes the King's forgiveness of his assassin more poignant.[8]

Those characters in whom Verdi was especially interested, such as Azucena in *Il Trovatore* and Amneris in *Aida*, reveal a greater depth not only in the music but also in the words they utter, giving further credence to the notion that Verdi "sat over" his collaborators in the strongest possible way. Yet, with certain limited exceptions, Verdi's characters reveal only that side of their character which is consistent with the story line. Their distinction from the Scribe characters is that in Scribe, the "side" shown is the only one. In Verdi, he and his librettists have suggested enough so that other sides are inferred, if not made manifest. Thus, we are shown Amonasro the revenge-filled Ethiop, whose paternity is used as a club on his daughter; Amonasro the revered ruler and beloved father can be comprehended, but remains off stage. The pirate nature of Simon Boccanegra, which probably led in part to his aspiring above his station for the love of a girl of the upper class (which led in part to the hatred of her father for him) is incidental to the plot, which focuses on Boccanegra the aggrieved lover, anguished father, and popular ruler.[9] In another vein, the nasty, fawning—even vicious—side of Rigoletto, which Hugo delineated in *Le Roi s'amuse*, is passed over briefly in the first scene of the opera, and is thereafter swamped by the "good" side. The courtiers of the Duca di Mantua were probably not as venal as the jester, and a few of them had good reason to hate him thoroughly, but they are cast as unremittantly cynical.

Again, it is not surprising that those characters Verdi invested with the greatest interest he set for baritones and mezzo-sopranos,

---

with love on my breast; yes, burned with love!") The Conte di Luna's aria, "*Il balen del suo sorriso*," similarly humanizes—at least a little—a far darker villain.

(8) Note here how *Un Ballo in maschera* works on the human emotions, while *Gustave III*, with its juxtaposition of tragedy downstage and merriment off stage, emphasizes the ironic.

(9) Not so strangely, the one scene that presents the Doge in a forceful light, as the ex-sea dog of redoubtable accomplishment, is the scene that Boito added: the Council Chamber. Piave's libretto showed none of this side of Simon's character.

and that the baritones with greatest interest were fathers. Further, it is of interest that some of the most complex of his soprano and tenor characters were derived from French librettos or plays— Riccardo (Gustave III), Don Carlo and Elisabetta, Violetta— which reinforces the contention that the oft-maligned French approach to the libretto was closer to life than has heretofore been admitted. Similarly, those librettos that were founded on French plays or French librettos—*Rigoletto, La Traviata, Un Ballo in maschera* (even *Aida,* from a French prose outline)—have a far greater coherence and organization than the rumbustiousness of the librettos based on Spanish Gothic melodramas: *Il Trovatore, La Forza del destino,* and, to a lesser extent, *Simon Boccanegra.*

Verdi's middle-period operas show other refinements of *melodramma* practices. In his insistence on getting at the heart at once, Verdi liked to begin a scene—particularly the beginning of the opera—in the middle of a conversation. This was also done to get away from the by-then hackneyed convention (of the early *melodramma* and of French opera) of the choral opening.[1] Even when he began matters with a chorus, as in *La Traviata* or *Un Ballo in maschera,* he wove it into the whole as soon as possible. As we have seen, in *Don Carlos* he used the French opening-chorus convention with great subtlety and imagination, and in *Otello* Boito transformed the commonplace into a dramatic moment of immense power.[2] Also in the middle-period works, Verdi used the dramatic device of the duologue to fine dramatic purpose. The duologue—a conversation of two characters not necessarily in opposition—was one of the cardinal features of the great *secco* portions of the Metastasio librettos, and was employed by Scribe in a far less effective way. Wagner would use this device so compulsively (the whole of *Siegfried* is constructed as a series of duologues) that it is a fingerprint of his dramaturgy as much as the diminished seventh is a fingerprint of his musical style. In Verdi, the duologue becomes the basis for some of his best scenes —Rigoletto-Sparafucile, Violetta–Giorgio Germont, Simon Boccanegra–Fiesco (Act III), Manrico-Azucena ("Part" II), Aida-Amonasro, Philip–Grand Inquisitor,[3] among many examples. What

---

(1) The Scribe librettos and the early *melodramma* were next door to this. All that was necessary was to cut the otiose chorus.
(2) As Berlioz would transform the French practice in *La Prise de Troie.*

this meant is that the dramatic node of the libretto, which in Metastasio was confined to the musically barren territory of the *secco* recitative, was now being infused with highly dramatic music so that it became a counterbalance to the immediate appeal and lyricism of the aria. Similarly, the aria[4] moved into the dramatic territory by not standing alone, as a vocal moment, but influencing the course of the action. Eboli's *"O don fatale"* is an excellent example: the *stretto* is dramatically justifiable because Eboli realizes that she has only a day to save him. In terms of the words, Verdi's contributions meant that the most poetic portions of the text—the "reflective" arias—were being ignored in favor of the more dramatic scenes in which the rhyme and meter were systematically undercut by the break-up of the line, so that the "verse" rapidly approached a sort of loose-metered prose sprinkled with *parole sceniche*. The *parola scenica* also appeared in the arias[5] generally as part of the *stretto*.

Verdi's greatest weakness as a collaborative librettist lay in his single-minded devotion to the achievement of strong situations, strong emotions, and strong contrasts. He compelled his librettists —Piave, Somma, and Cammarano—to give him work which was as accomplished as they could produce, but he did it by imposing himself upon them. Because they were lesser artists, the redirecting of their own talents into Verdian channels did little damage to their strengths; but it is easy to see why Verdi did not work with a stronger librettist, such as Romani.[6] Boito's success with Verdi lay in his genius as an adaptive librettist, his doggedness in ensuring the continuation of the collaboration—and his ability to give Verdi what Verdi wanted. Yet it was Méry and du Locle who presented Verdi with his most far-ranging libretto, *Don Carlos,* one which Verdi found distinctly less comfortable than his Italian librettos.[7]

---

(3) In fact, *Don Carlos* abounds in duologues, and the King's Closet Scene (IV, i) is in essence a series of them (Posa being negligible) framed by two arias.
(4) And, of course, the ensemble.
(5) E.g., *"O patria mia"* and *"mai più"* from Aida's Act III aria.
(6) Romani did provide Verdi with an early libretto, *Un Giorno di regno* (1840); its flat failure may also have contributed to Verdi's avoidance of further collaboration.
(7) Verdi was wary of French librettos for several reasons: he thoroughly disliked the practices of *Grand Opéra*, and he was conscious of the failure of his setting of Scribe in 1855.

Verdi's focus on the characters and the situation also led to that extreme compression of plot which is characteristic of the Verdi opera, in keeping with the Italian preference for *brevità* and at the same time damaging to the structure of the whole. Verdi was far less interested in the continuity of causal plausibility than in the psychological correctness of each dramatic moment, and therefore those librettos which have as their reference well-structured plays of the French theater—*Un Ballo in maschera, La Traviata,* and, to a lesser extent, *Rigoletto*—have more solid joinings than the Spanish-derived librettos, such as *La Forza del destino, Il Trovatore,* and the first version of *Simon Boccanegra.* Even in *La Traviata,* however, the jerky treatment of Alfredo throughout the opera may serve to make Violetta stand out the more clearly but sacrifices the equality of stature that the two should have. The too-fast comings and goings of the first scene of the second act further strain credulity by hyperactivity, although this highlights the "moment of repose" in the Violetta-Giorgio Germont duologue around which the scene revolves. Not until Boito was Verdi able to find a librettist who could compress not only without damage but with positive benefit; who could see the libretto as a work of art in itself and not as another work hacked down to fit Verdi's musical clothing. Boito was also able to prevent Verdi from committing excesses which, in the context of the final operas, would have been far more disastrous than in the context of *Il Trovatore.* Thus, he short-circuited Verdi's idea for an off-stage revolt to take place at the end of Act III of *Otello.* This revolt would have been used to build a brummagem ensemble of major proportions so that the curtain would be brought down on a "tornado" ending. Boito substituted the ensemble, then drained the stage—appropriately: the maddened Otello orders everyone to be gone—leaving the final tableau to Iago standing over the prostrate Otello while the crowd continues cheering Otello from outside; a tableau that Spike Hughes has correctly called "one of the most masterly strokes of pure theater in the history of opera."[8]

The practices of Verdi as a composer influencing his librettists have become the touchstone not only for composers but also for opera commentators since Verdi's time. Verdi carried the tinkering

---

(8) Spike Hughes: *Famous Verdi Operas,* p. 467.

of a Meyerbeer to its ultimate conclusion and, aided by the domination of the musical side of the collaboration and by the force of the music he provided, seemingly dealt a final blow to the autonomy of the librettist. The practices of Puccini in handling his librettists merely followed in the footsteps of Verdi's. Yet what is evident in the Verdi operas is that the music, although it can accomplish a great deal, cannot accomplish everything, and that what it cannot accomplish is the province of the librettist. Further, the composer, if he has a stage-dramatic flair, can improve what he is given and can certainly tailor the work to his own strengths as a composer, but unless he is a master of dramaturgy as well as of character and speech, he will not be able to create a first-rate libretto. That task remains with the librettist.

Chapter Sixteen

The German Libretto
to Wagner

GERMAN OPERA and the libretto of German opera have not
been dealt with until now, not because there was none or
were few of them, or even because what there was is not worth
discussion, but because the developments that opera and librettos
underwent in Germany in the seventeenth and eighteenth centuries
largely paralleled those in France and Italy without influencing
the form or creating something important enough to be examined
for itself.

Yet some sort of cursory consideration is useful, because
with the nineteenth century German opera would blossom into
European prominence both in terms of the music and the libretto,
and with Richard Wagner would attain major stature in both.

Opera in the loose confederation of small and large states
that made up the territory of Germany "began" only shortly after
the Florentine Camerata had presented its works, with an adaptation of Rinuccini's *Dafne* in Torgau (1627; m., Heinrich Schütz;
l., Martin Opitz),[1] but the fragmentation of Germany by the
Thirty Years' War (1618–48), plus the vogue for Italian operas
along the lines of the Roman and Venetian spectacles, severely
impeded the development of an indigenous form. There were
several notable exceptions to this acceptance of Italian opera
which spread through Germany during the seventeenth century.
Aside from certain towns that did present works in the German
language, the leading "German" house was the public opera house

---

(1) As the music has been lost, it is uncertain whether Schütz composed new music or merely arranged Gagliano's.

of the Imperial Free City of Hamburg, which flourished from 1678 to 1738. Yet, although the opera house employed German librettists (such as Christian Postel and Barthold Feind), the operas themselves followed the Venetian pattern in that they relied heavily on complex plots and the usual machinery displays. A measure of the nationality of the performances can be found in the fact that the operas were sung in an amalgam of German and Italian—the Italian being reserved, usually, for the exit aria.[2] This practice was also in evidence in other German cities. The impact of the Zeno-Metastasio reforms was widespread throughout Germany (one of Metastasio's most faithful composers was a Saxon, Johann Adolph Hasse), possibly because the combination of vocalism and nobility of sentiment fitted the operatic tastes of the German public. If the success of the reform opera prevented any concerted development of an indigenous form, it nonetheless influenced the creation of a series of librettos by Frederick the Great which are of more than routine interest.

The reform opera influenced Frederick only in a negative sense: that is, he disliked certain aspects of the form and wished to create something better for his own theater. His operas are also only peripherally "German," for they were written in French by Frederick and then translated into Italian verse by the court poet Giampietro Tagliazucchi. The impetus underlying all of them, and particularly the most famous—*Montezuma* (1755; m., Karl Heinrich Graun)—is less German than a combination of Metastasian moral uplift and Voltairean enlightenment philosophy.[3] Yet the attempt itself is significant, and the characterization that Frederick created of the Mexican Montezuma, the Noble Savage traduced by the fanatic and opportunistic Cortez, has regal stature. Held captive and about to die, Montezuma says to Cortez (II, vii): "Tell me, what do you want from me? Riches? Here are my treasures. Lands? You shall be satisfied. But what rights will you have on my life? If you have sensibility, if you have reason—if you have a heart—can you look upon me, in my unhappy state, without a feeling of pity?"

The German opera, however, which was the source out of which the later, true-German operas would develop, was not these

---

(2) A logical division, as the story line was contained in the recitative and the exit aria was famous for its verse.
(3) The opera was derived from Voltaire's play *Alzire* (1736).

lyrischen Trauerspielen but the singspiel. The growth of the singspiel parallels that of the French *opéra comique* in that the form
blossomed from the sung theater; that is, from troupes of actors
who could sing.[4] The first famous singspiel was an import from
England, where ballad opera had become popular after the success
of *The Beggar's Opera* (1728; m., arranged by John Pepusch; l.,
John Gay). The English ballad opera *The Devil to Pay* (1731),
adapted by Charles Coffey from Thomas Shadwell's play, became
Der Teufel ist los, was first given in Berlin in 1743, then was
revised by Christian Felix Weisse to new music and given again
in Leipzig in 1752, and finally had its greatest success to music
by Johann Adam Hiller in 1766.[5]

The singspiel operas followed the outline of the Favart
comédies mêlées d'ariettes (indeed, many Favart librettos were
adapted into German): they were lighthearted folk pastorals with
sentimental stories and happy endings. The German libretto had
no counterpart to either Favart or Sedaine in terms of accomplishment or influence—Weisse was the nearest it came—though no
less a personage than Goethe contributed examples. Judging from
some of his light lyrics for *Erwin und Elmire* (1775; m., Johann
André), he saw the libretto in the same inferior light as Hugo:

> *Liebes Kind, was hast du wieder?*
> *Welch ein Kummer druckt dich nieder?*
> *Sieh! wie ist der Tag so schön;*
> *komm, lass uns in Garten gehn.*[6]
>
> (I, i)

Yet the German libretto, very like the French, was influenced
more by the playwrights of the language than by the poets. Weisse
himself was a playwright and a noted tragedian (as well as an
editor), and Christoph Martin Wieland, another fine dramatic
poet, collaborated on the first "German" five-act opera, *Alceste*

---

(4) As with *opéra comique,* the term singspiel was not used until
later, and came to have its precise meaning of an opera including
spoken words and songs at a later date. Some early singspiels were
sung; others were called "*Schauspiel mit Gesang,*" i.e., "play with song."
(5) The opera also appeared in France under the title *Le Diable à
quatre* (1756; m., arranged by Philidor; l., Sedaine).
(6) "Dear girl, what is the matter with you? What sorrow weighs
you down? See! how beautiful the day is: come, let us go into the
garden."

(1773; m., Anton Schweitzer), albeit the result was more Italian than German. Likewise, the plays of Lessing and Schiller and the influential dramatic criticism of Lessing had an impact on the libretto, but in a roundabout way. The school of the *Sturm und Drang*, exported to France by the publication of twelve volumes of the German theater in French in 1781–2, went into the "rescue operas" and the Pixérécourt melodramas and thence returned to Germany. The genesis of an opera like *Fidelio* can be traced back to Germany through its immediate French source.

Mélodrame also had a German root, one that was probably more important than the Rousseau opera and was pervasive in the German singspiel after its first appearance in *Ariadne auf Naxos* (1775; m., Jiřì Benda; l., Johann Brandes). Goethe was one of its chief advocates. Interestingly, it developed for the same reason that the French *mélodrame* did, and in the same way. Because the singspiels were oriented toward acting rather than singing, spoken words could be expressed more effectively in them. Similarly, the genesis of *mélodrame* as a clear separation of word and music, in the "pure" Rousseauist style,[7] developed into the word-over-music amalgam, which was far more emotionally powerful and consequently was overused in the early Romantic German libretto.

These supposedly German developments made history, not in the German libretto, which continued to languish, but in the French. Not only was the level of German librettistic poetry low, but also the quality of the singspiels was not appreciably more distinguished. *Undine*, La Motte-Fouqué's adaptation of his tale of the water spirit become human, was an exception in that it contained better poetry than the German libretto usually produced, besides serving as the first of many Undine operas (its most notable successors were works by Lortzing and Dvořák).

The German libretto contains several examples of librettos that were not in themselves notable but had an extensive influence on later librettos written in Germany. Mozart's music provided the ennobling element for two of these, *Die Entführung aus dem Serail* (1782; l., Gottlieb Stephanie) and *Die Zauberflöte* (1791; l., Schikaneder and Gieseke). The first is traditionally considered

---

(7) E.g., *Undine* (1816; m., E. T. A. Hoffmann), written to a libretto by the Frenchman F. de La Motte-Fouqué.

the starting point of German operatic music of consequence, as well as being a representative example of the singspiel, although it is librettistically surpassed by one of its ultimate sources, Sedaine's *Les Trois Sultanes*. Schikaneder's farrago, which without Mozart's music would have passed into oblivion, became a far more important progenitor becasue of its great success as a singspiel and by bringing forward that mystical side of German thought which was to be revisited in German operas from Wagner to Hofmannsthal. This mystical element differs from, yet in a curious way combines, two strains from earlier libretto history: the god-cluttered works of the seventeenth-century and the rational, Enlightenment *opera seria* librettos. The godlike, otherworldly aspect is seen in the mysticism in which the whole is wrapped, and the concentration upon the individual within the framework of this mysticism introduces the personal element. This was expressed, in *Die Zauberflöte*, in the Masonic ethos that transfers the godhood to mortals in the sense that a human being, be he prince or pauper, could attain Enlightenment by a progress involving not only "good works" but also a higher, inexpressible union of some vague sort. The ethical base of *opera seria* was thus mixed with a philosophy of less intellectual and more emotional and subjective cast, a philosophy that tended toward the inexpressible. It is no accident that Goethe was impressed by the libretto of Mozart's opera, wrote a sequel to it, and used its regenerative impulse to return to work on his *Faust*. Part II of the great epic, largely ignored by the more literal-minded to whom Part I was a self-contained, graspable entity, foreshadowed in its mystical yearning spirit the later works of Wagner, and was the immediate vision behind many of the symphonies of Mahler and the thoughts of Boito and Ferruccio Busoni. If the works of Wagner would bring into the corpus of the libretto a thoroughgoing philosophical world-view, which was a definite addition to the dramaturgy of the form, the roots of the development lie in Schikaneder's naïve poetastry, and in the Sarastro side of it rather than the Papageno.

The appearance of a full-blown approach to stage mysticism had other concomitants than merely a visionary push toward the Ideal. The more mundane side of the mystic is the supernatural, which had been amply evidenced in the magic tricks of the wizards who had infested seventeenth-century opera, only to be cleared away by *opera seria*. In an esthetic that once again sought the unattainable, the supernatural was bound to return, and in German opera it took a form that differed greatly not only from the earlier magic tricks but also from the stage-bound melodramatic shiverings of the French Revolutionary-period works. This approach to the supernatural is evidenced in one of the most powerful scenes in opera history from both a historic and a scenic viewpoint, which brings the German libretto to the Romantic Age: the Wolf's Glen Scene of Weber's *Der Freischütz* (1821).

Der Freischütz, and the other two of Weber's most famous operas, *Euryanthe* and *Oberon*, illustrate the continuing application of the theory that in German opera the lesser librettos have had greater impact than in either French or Italian counterparts. *Freischütz* is incomparably the best of the three librettos, although it is an ordinary literary work in many respects; and though the nonsense of *Euryanthe* and *Oberon* is consistently overshadowed in libretto history by several librettos set by Marschner and several set by Lortzing, these two also contributed to German libretto history.

Weber always had trouble in finding librettists, and as early as 1813 had resorted to advertisement to find suitable material. The following appeared in the *Allgemeine Musik-Zeitung*:

> The undersigned wishes to come into possession, as soon as possible, of a good libretto, which he wishes to put into music and pay for suitably. He invites the poets of Germany who wish to undertake this task to send their manuscripts in a parcel with care. He guarantees that, in case of non-acceptance, the manuscript will be returned to the author, without the least damage.
> Prague, 12 March 1813   Carl Maria von Weber
> *Kapellmeister*
> Opera Director of the
> Royal Theater of Prague

Friedrich Kind, the librettist of *Der Freischütz*, produced a serviceable tale of good and evil heightened by adroit use of the supernatural. Reduced to its essentials, it told of the young Max, in love with Agathe, who was forced by a literal "trial by fire" (i.e., a shooting contest, the prize being the hand of Agathe) to put himself in league with the powers of evil, represented by Caspar, agent of Samiel (the Devil). The powers of evil could be well enough represented on stage with the usual magic, but Kind wanted to balance this by first presenting the power of good on stage, in the person of the Hermit, who at the end of the opera acts as a *deus ex machina* to bring all to a happy close. He wanted to begin the opera with two short scenes in which the Hermit is granted a vision of the evil befalling Agathe (and, by implication, Max) and his attempt to protect her by a blessed gift to her of roses from Palestine. Unfortunately, the weakness of the scenes, coming at the beginning of the drama, led Weber to agree with his wife Caroline (then his fiancée) to cut them and open on the more directly stage-worthy and traditional choral scene. This excision not only led to the truncation of the role of the Hermit, who now shrinks to a *deus ex machina* instead of a force for good in the Sarastro sense, but also deprived the libretto of an opening that could have been even more effective, and certainly more audacious, than the choral one.[8]

Yet the libretto contains a good deal more that explains the cause of its celebrity in its day and its fame as a historical work. If the rollicking gaiety of its hunting and drinking choruses infected German opera—and even French opera—for generations, the very setting of the opera itself had a profound effect upon the libretto.

The setting was, nominally, a Bohemian forest, and the personages of the story were the inhabitants of the territory. But these inhabitants, though rustics, were of a very different order from the rustics of Favart or Goldoni, and the world in which they lived, albeit country, was very different from the cleared fields and villages of French and Italian *opéra comique* and *opera buffa*. The heavily wooded forests of Germany and Bohemia impose a somber cast on the stage and on the story. The trees, rocks, and infinite green depths of the German forests (the most famous of which is aptly called the Black Forest) reinforce the claustrophobic feeling that serves to shut out the sky and vista—and even man himself. In turn, this feeling of aloneness and beetling natural forces engenders awe in the face of nature which can quickly be transformed into awe of the supernatural. Precisely this feeling is at the heart of *Der Freischütz*, and that is why the Wolf's Glen Scene, the node of the entire opera, represents more than a piece of superior stage trickery. When Max ventures into the darkest part of a forbidding forest in order to attend the rite of the casting of the magic bullets by night, he is at the same time venturing back into primitive

---

(8) A recent production (Berlin, 1966) partly restored these scenes.

savagery and primitive ritual (the Jungian interpretation is un-avoidable). The mumbo-jumbo involved in the rite and the weird apparitions that accompany it therefore become logical and, more important, frightening, and this primitive terror in turn raises the "magic trick" level of the other manifestations (the portrait falling off the wall, the magic shooting of the eagle, the equation of Agathe and a dove, the appearance of a funeral wreath) in the opera.

This Germanic apprehension of a link to the dark recesses of ages past in the history of man is entirely foreign to the French or Italian libretto, both of which are organized along more direct and more sophisticated lines. Bertram the devil in *Robert le diable* may be first cousin to Caspar and Samiel of *Freischütz* but is none-theless closer in spirit to *le parfait gentilhomme* who is Méphistoph-élès, simply because Scribe was too much of a man of the world to make him otherwise. Similarly, Berlioz's Méphisto and Boito's Mefistofele accent this cynical worldliness, and even in scenes such as the Walpurgisnacht seem to stand apart and look on the demonic revelry with a jaundiced eye. Caspar, in the Wolf's Glen Scene, cannot do that—he is as terrified as Max[9]—and Samiel does not, because, like the overlord characters such as (partly) Sarastro and, later, Keikobad in *Die Frau ohne Schatten* of Hofmannsthal, he *is* the terror incarnate.

Wagner, of course, grasped at once this cultural continuum and translated it into a call for operas based on myth, thus con-sciously divorcing the past from the present and allowing it to stand as its own justification and as a comment upon the present. In the narrower sense of the supernatural powers latent in the forest, both *Die Walküre* and *Siegfried* are strongly dependent upon *sauvagerie* as a contributing element of the whole,[1] as is, to a lesser extent, *Parsifal.*

If the supernatural element in *Der Freischütz* brought to the libretto something distinctively different from the magic trick, its product, the "villain" Caspar, reinforced this novelty. As with the tentative attempt of Schikaneder and his star-flaming queen, Caspar

---

(9) He is probably more terrified because Max is an upright hero and Caspar is fully aware that, should he fail, his life is forfeit.
(1) Certainly the character of Hunding is an extension of this forest *sauvagerie*, while the Forest Bird in *Siegfried* represents the benign side of the forest. Humperdinck's *Hänsel und Gretel* (1893; l., Adel-heid Wette), which, paradoxically, is musically very Wagner-influ-enced, also displays this notion of the terror-filled forest.

is bound up with a "higher power" which, unlike the French adaptations of the gods, is felt as an immanent presence. His antecedents can be easily traced to Sedaine's Barbe-Bleue or Fillette-Loraux's Dourlinsky in *Lodoïska*, but the added element transformed the "villain" into an agent and not an evil man acting in his own right.

Der Freischütz as an opera is one of the landmark contributions to the form, more because of Weber's musicalization of Kind's libretto than for what Kind produced. Yet Kind did provide a serviceable base for the composer, with one great opportunity, the Wolf's Glen Scene, and this was more than Weber encountered again. *Euryanthe*, a libretto by Helmina von Chezy, is one of the worst experiments in the form, not so much because of its complexity of plot and vicissitude of event but because of the librettist's thoroughly fifth-rate dramatic mentality. *Oberon*, by J. R. Planché, may be marginally superior but still falls short of minimal librettistic standards.[2] Several separate points may be gleaned from these two works. First and most obvious is the fact that the setting forth of a libretto for musical clothing is not so simple as it may appear. Conversely, writers able to set forth clearly such works deserve the credit for being the dramatic tailors and fabricators and not opprobrium for failing to be geniuses. Related to this is the second point, which has never been answered (and probably never can be). Why did Weber never find adequate librettists for his mature works—except, perhaps, once—and why was he not able, although he had a dramatic flair, to work with his collaborators as Meyerbeer and Verdi did? Certainly several of the librettos that were provided to Marschner, as well as Lortzing's own texts, were of a high order. Finally, the renown of the composer and the quality of his music even for these heavily flawed works led to their being influences on later German opera librettos. The character of Eglantine in *Euryanthe* descends to that of Ortrud; the chivalric Romanticism of the opera was reflected in Marschner's *Der Templar und die Jüdin;* and the fairy orientation of *Oberon*[3] continued that preoccupation with the fairy tale which was so much a part of German dramatic history.

---

(2) The best case for these two works may be found in John Warrack's biography of Weber.
(3) Planché's libretto, incidentally, was written in English.

What Weber did—specifically in *Der Freischütz* but also in his other operas—was to turn the key on the lock which confined German opera, and his greatest opera accomplished the same for the libretto. Heinrich Marschner's work can be instanced as witness, for his melodramatic singspiels—more dramatic, in the manner of Sedaine, than light—encompassed a large range of subject matter and treatment within the framework of the spoken-dialogue-and-number formula, which incuded the obligatory choruses direct from *Der Freischütz* as well as the alternation of comically rustic scenes with melodramatic ones—a facet of the German libretto that differed markedly from the more homogeneous French examples.

The problem with any consideration of Marschner's librettos, and even with those of his contemporary, Albert Lortzing, who worked in a more traditionally light singspiel vein (and who wrote his own librettos), is the difficulty in assessing them within their own context. At every turn the librettos invoke those of Richard Wagner. Wagner pillaged Marschner's work and turned its ideas to his own use, which was occasionally different in intent from Marschner's but which today effects any consideration of the work of the earlier man's librettists.

For instance, Marschner's librettos are notable for their subtilized handling of the role of the villain. His first great success, *Der Vampyr* (1828), to a libretto by Wilhelm Wohlbrück, who happened to be Marschner's brother-in-law, brings to the libretto an original idea in keeping with the melodramatic Romanticism of the time: the study of a vampire, Ruthven. Wohlbrück[4] makes it clear that Ruthven is an agent by beginning the opera with a chorus of witches and ghosts whose Master holds Ruthven in thrall. He is sent to earth for a year, in which time he must marry three times and kill his brides in the accepted manner or suffer the consequences. Ruthven accomplishes two thirds of his task before the *deus ex machina*, in the form of a lightning bolt, destroys him and allows a *lieto fine* of sorts. Not only the idea but also the telling of it were novel for 1828: Ruthven bleeds his first bride to death in a cave, is himself killed by the grieved father (over the tooth-marked corpse), but is resuscitated by the light of moon-rays. This was

---

(4) Marschner doubtless also had a hand in the structure of the opera.

heady stuff for a public accustomed to the singspiel, even when it was mixed in with the usual gaieties. But equally as interesting was Wohlbrück's portrait of Ruthven. Ruthven is seen as basically a good man who has been captured by the Evil Ones and forced to do their bidding: throughout the opera he struggles against them to free himself but cannot—he is up against too much. This portrait of an unhappy man battling against his destiny can be immediately seen as a sketch for Wagner's Holländer, which in a certain sense he is. Yet the later incarnation should not blot out the earlier, for Ruthven is a quite different man. His tragedy is at once more personal and more limited and smacks of jobbery on the part of the librettist, who wished to make Ruthven both a vampire and an appealing character, thus gaining both worlds. Wagner's character is far more universal and poignantly human, very differently oriented, and he also includes an element from a later titular hero-villain of Marschner's, Hans Heiling.

Hans Heiling (1833), to a libretto by Philipp Eduard Devrient, was Marschner's masterpiece, and well demonstrates the scope of his operas. Where *Der Vampyr* was a Romantic melodrama of the most extreme sort, *Heiling* worked the fairy-tale vein. Heiling is the son of the Queen of the Earth Spirits, who live underground. He falls in love with a mortal and gains permission from his mother to woo her. In the end the girl rejects Heiling's jewels and riches for the love of one of her fellow-men, and Heiling is stopped from taking revenge on all of the wedding party by the intervention of his mother. Heiling is portrayed, as Ruthven was, as neither all good nor all bad, but as a mixture: as a prince and as a non-mortal, he is quick to anger and terrible in his punishment, but as a man in love he is "only human." Wagner studied the character of Heiling and used it in various guises in the *Ring* librettos; he also adopted for his Dutchman the aspect of Heiling which demanded absolute obedience to love.

Marschner also wrote historical operas, *Der Templar und Die Jüdin* (1829; l., Wohlbrück), derived from *Ivanhoe*, and *Adolph von Nassau* (1845; l., Heribert Rau). The range of his subject matter shows the range of the German libretto of the first part of the nineteenth century. Those elements which found their way into Wagner were not only the characterizations but also the scenic devices which Marschner's librettos used so well. *Heiling*, for instance, opens on a scene in the Kingdom of the Earth Spirits, the description of which foreshadows Niebelheim almost exactly.[5] Marschner had used this choral opening scene in *Der Vampyr*— as we have seen, the choral opening ran through all librettos of the early nineteenth century—but here he uses it as a Prologue to the opera, and has the overture follow it: an excellent dramatic stroke not lost on Wagner. Interrupted wedding processions, the sudden appearance of a *deus ex machina* to halt catastrophe, the preparation for sacrifice of the heroine unless a champion will come within a set time, an opening address by a leader to his knights— all of these were reused by Wagner. Their adaptation, however, should only reinforce what is obvious: that Marschner and his librettists possessed a first-rate sense of the theatrical. Wagner purloined only what was best.

Even without overshadowings by the Master, the post-*Freischütz* German libretto is of interest both because of its espousal of the Romantic postures and because of its scope. This scope is best evidenced in Marschner's operas, but Marschner himself stood between the more tradition-minded singspiels of Lortzing and the fully sung opera, of which the first in German was Ludwig Spohr's *Jessonda* (1823; l., Eduard H. Gehe). The arrival of Wagner preempted the stage and effectively obliterated what had come before, except as reflections of his glory.

---

(5) "Underground, deeply vaulted cavern, whose exits lead off into other side caverns, lighted by a dim reddish glow. Dwarves clamber from the jagged walls and polish the ore, busily bring specimens and jewels, which they present kneeling to their Queen and to Heiling . . ."

Chapter Seventeen

Wagner

THE WORKS of Richard Wagner have, since the nineteenth century, been wrapped in layers of writings compounded of his life, his own writings on his works, his writings on opera, the writings of his followers and detractors—and the general pendulum swing of taste, which moved strongly in his favor in the generation after his death and has been moving as strongly away from him in the twentieth century. The hope that time would grant a perspective of distance on the obfuscations, polemics, and confusions that his works engendered was partly dashed by the application of facets of his esthetic to contemporary political events and their consequent relevance backward to his works, so that Siegfried the young hero became a paradigm for the Aryan *Übermensch* and the whole of Wagner's last opera could be judged as a Nazi allegory.[1] Yet if Wagner the creator cannot be restored to the pedestal he occupied at the turn of the century, certainly some of the more pernicious canards that have been mindlessly reiterated over the past years should be cleared away. Many people have fervently wished that Richard Wagner the man and the artist would just go away and not be heard from again, but because of the scope of his achievement, this has not happened. Nor will it. Any student of opera, and particularly any student of the opera libretto, must come to terms with Wagner's work for any understanding of the history of the form, for Wagner stands as one of the major librettists in its history. André Gide's celebrated quip when asked to name France's greatest nineteenth-century poet—"*Victor Hugo, hélas*"

---

(1) Robert Gutman: *Richard Wagner*, pp. 421 *ff.*

—might be applied to Wagner. With that said, the task of consideration may be undertaken.

What becomes clear when Wagner is viewed from the perspective of his librettos is that the dramatic node of the opera—that is, the aspect that may be contained in the music but springs initially from the story—is absolutely controlling.[2] Because Wagner was his own librettist, this could be assumed to be the case, but the immense power of his music *qua* music has tempted commentators to dismiss not only the specific words but also the dramas themselves as secondary constructions, scaffoldings for musical genius. Precisely the opposite is true, and in a far more comprehensive way than with other great opera composers. In the operatic work of Mozart, Verdi, Richard Strauss, and Alban Berg there is more absolute music than in Wagner; in Wagner, despite seeming evidences to the contrary,[3] the librettist guides the musician at every step.

Wagner as a librettist belongs to the genre of works written primarily for self-expression and self-gratification and as such he is listed with Metastasio, Calzabigi, Busoni, and Hofmannsthal, and such isolated other writers as Beaumarchais in *Tarare* and Boito in *Nerone*. The vast majority of librettists have either reworked other immediate sources or written for specific conditions and/or specific composers with little thought beyond immediate success. Wagner wrote for the ages, and with a vengeance born partly out of his need to create a seamless corpus of work and partly out of revulsion from the low grade of hackwork that resulted from immediate librettistic tailoring. One result was that as a librettist he created a corpus that can be examined as a literary progress.

This idea was all but unknown in the history of the libretto.

---

(2) This is the case as long as his works are the basis of examination. Care should be taken not to read his statements on his works back into them, for although those statements are often helpful in understanding the works, they also often obscure them.
(3) E.g., the "Ride of the Valkyries" Scene, which can be said to be extraneous, but which is structurally apposite because it roils up the scene in a tremendous burst of energy out of which will develop first the Sieglinde Scene, a moment of repose, and then the Wotan-Brünnhilde Scene, in which this energy will be internalized and then transformed into compassion. The "Ride," moreover, continues and carries through the excitement of the opening of the first and second acts.

Metastasio "developed" as a librettist; but within a far narrower range and, beyond an early grasping of the essentials of dramaturgy or the addition of one or another element to an already set dramatic pattern, no other librettist even began to approach Wagner's achievement. The development of Wagner's mature librettos from the *Grand Opéra-cum*-Marschner orientation of *Der fliegende Holländer,* through an addition of mythic elements (*Lohengrin* stands at midpoint, containing an admixture of both), to heroic myth on an epic scale, to heroic myth on an epic interior-psychological scale, and, finally, to symbolic myth, represents a progress comparable to the strictly literary progress of writers such as Tolstoy, Goethe, and Ibsen. This progress, besides, leaves aside the creation of what is certainly one of the greatest examples of the Scribe-Dumas-Ibsen-Shaw—and purely nineteenth-century—"well-made play" structured works, *Die Meistersinger,* which can lay strong claim to being the greatest libretto ever written. Only the work of Hugo von Hofmannsthal can show a similar developmental progress over a span of works. For the first time in its history, then, the libretto itself served as reflection of the range of a man's mind and his deepest thoughts.[4]

Wagner's method of work was at the opposite pole from that of the traditional librettist. Time was no object with him: the thoughts, gathered around the germ of the story, were allowed to grow and develop into the final work. Signposts along the way were prose sketches, or lengthy verbalizations of the dramatic continuity of the piece; these were constantly refined into the "poem," or verse rendition, of the libretto. As the final step, the music was added, in a similar layered way: first the piano score, which incorporated the musical ideas Wagner had jotted down while working on the sketches, then the short score, and finally the full score.[5] This gestation period, coupled with the difficulties that production of the operas presented, meant that the

---

(4) Metastasio and Goldoni may be cited as possible instances of earlier librettists who projected themselves into their librettos, but neither of them committed himself as deeply as Wagner. Helping the later librettist, of course, was the Romantic precept of self-identification with one's works.

(5) Wagner was hardly rigid in this sequencing of composition, and at times wrote out the music and then fitted words to it later. The poem, however, was the general basis, and would be read out to his friends before the music was completed.

dates of production were often unrelated to the dates of composition. This had not been the case with most earlier operas, which saw production within a year at most after completion of the score (and, more likely, production *before* the score was complete); the Wagnerian model, founded on the idea of the work-for-itself, became a feature in the later history of opera and the libretto. To a far greater extent works were written and productions were arranged afterward—a practice that continues to the present.

Wagner's music was of course a totally interdependent part of the libretto. His esthetic pre-ordained this, for the function of the music was further to illumine the words, which by their nature were cramped in expressive content. He talked of the orchestra as a Greek chorus commenting on what was being said on stage, and he regularly invoked the famous Gluck example in *Iphigénie en Tauride*. Yet, as is commonplace with any aspect of Wagner's art, the reality of the scores is far richer than the dogmas. The music indeed performs the ironic function of the chorus, but it also is fully characterizational on an internal, personal level, and not infrequently on a psychological level that Wagner himself doubtless had not apprehended—and it could also be irrelevant. No composer before or since has managed to bind together the librettistic aspects of the opera collaboration with the musical in such a thoroughgoing way; the necessary omission of discussion of the librettistic functions of the music in order to concentrate on the librettos themselves should in no way imply that the music was considered separate, or was separated in the final result. The entire structural concept of the plastic leitmotif, which underwent changes as the on-stage situation warranted, is primarily librettistic. A moment such as the one in the third act of *Die Meistersinger* when, after the citizens of Nuremberg have hailed their beloved Hans Sachs by singing his composition "*Wacht auf!*" and the strings plunge into a statement of the *Wahn-motif*, is not only overwhelming in its emotional impact of heartsickness piled on joy but also gives an ironic depth to all that subsequently transpires on stage.[6]

---

(6) One of the very real problems of this linkage of the music with the libretto is Wagner's silence on the exact meaning of his leitmotifs. If, as William Mann believes, what I have called the *Wahn-motif* is nothing more than a musical tag associated with Sachs and not with

What Wagner brought to the libretto, in his usual doggedly comprehensive way, was a philosophic and psychological approach that dominates all of his mature work. The psychological aspects were largely latent, yet they fitted in so perfectly with the mythic philosophical orientation that they were elaborated on by Wagner and have come today to have far more importance in his operas than the consciously applied philosophy. Instances of the insights of each of the great trio of psychological discovery, Freud, Jung, and Adler, can be found in the later works of Wagner, particularly in the epic *Ring* cycle, and this is so in part because Wagner's movement toward myth, a much-belabored tenet in his writings, freed the stories from their dependence on the immediate. Wagner, the idealizer of the "classic" opera of Gluck and its Greek antecedent, combined it with the scope of French *Grand Opéra* and the mysticism of German opera, added a philosophical underpinning, and produced an entity that was thoroughly of its century[7] and yet reached out to the past and to the future.

Philosophy as a librettistic ingredient was nothing new; in its ethical guise, it was vital to the work of Zeno and Metastasio, and, mixed with the Enlightenment philosophy of Diderot and Voltaire, it could be evidenced in the work of Frederick the Great and Beaumarchais. Wagner's approach to philosophy was characteristically more thoroughgoing, but differed radically from the earlier attempts in that, unlike them, it reached toward the mystic. Schikaneder's Masonic libretto for Mozart and the mumbo-jumbo of the Wolf's Glen Scene in *Der Freischütz* had formed the background for this departure, which Wagner further heightened by Romantic nineteenth-century postures of death-as-triumph and redemption-through-death. The central character of the earliest of Wagner's great operas—the Dutchman—commands attention because his suffering is legendary: like the Wandering Jew, he has been condemned to traffic through the world to seek his salvation.

his despair, the moment is far more prosaic in its import. I can only say that the theme has never had that limited association *emotionally* for me—that is, has always represented something more than a mere one-for-one correspondence (in common with most of Wagner's leitmotifs)—and that the ambiguity of the musical language was a vital part of Wagner's dramatic esthetic, and one that works to splendid effect here.

(7) Note that the first two of these roots were combined to produce a work which in many respects is the direct antithesis of Wagner's: Berlioz's *Les Troyens*.

Whereas the Jew, in Scribe's hands, remained a mortal limited in time and place (and an excuse for a final tableau in which the Heavenly hosts reject him and compel him to continue his travels), the Dutchman looms huge over the mortals Daland, Erik, and even Senta. The magnitude of his suffering thus works in favor of the story, for it serves to justify his instant acceptance of the idea that Senta has betrayed him, however circumstantially this is presented.[8] The ending also—a surcease of pain: and more, a triumph through the sacrifice of a woman—if it contradicts the ongoing nature of the myth (that the Dutchman can by his very nature never find salvation) is purely of the nineteenth century, derived primarily from both parts of Goethe's *Faust*.

Wagner's "discovery" of the philosophy of Schopenhauer and, through him and other writers, his contact with the Far Eastern philosophies, particularly that of Buddhism, underlies *Tristan und Isolde*, the *Ring* cycle, and *Parsifal*. Though its importance is major,[9] Wagner's writings on its influence and the commentaries of others on its presentation in his works—coupled with Wagner's stirring in of Romantic ideas of the nineteenth century—have caused the contribution of philosophizing to be overvalued. Wagner was always, first and foremost, a stage dramatist, and his use of philosophical concepts or Romantic notions was tempered both by his grasp of the symbolic meanings of the myths themselves and by his knowledge of what he wanted on stage.

The single element of this mystically oriented, myth-wrapped philosophy which was vital to his works was its yearning away from the realities of this world toward a nirvana beyond it, be it Valhalla, Monsalvat, or transfiguration through death. This is of course a form of religious teleology, but unlike the one religion it most closely resembles—Buddhism—Wagner's concept of it left out the quietism. The necessary admixture of the ancient myths, all of which emphasized strife and violence and outsized heroes, moved the myth-operas (with the exception of *Tristan*) away

---

(8) The Dutchman's motivation is far stronger than that of Hans Heiling, who demands absolute obedience not because of love but because he is a prince; it is also superior to that of Mandryka in Richard Strauss's and Hofmannsthal's *Arabella*, whose rejection of his beloved under similar circumstances smacks of pique (and inferior stagecraft) rather than of genuine distress.
(9) Wagner through much of his life toyed with the idea of an opera on Buddha, *Die Sieger* (The Victors).

from passivity and *caritas* and left Wagner's works open to the interpretations of Houston Stewart Chamberlain and the later National Socialists, who needed this combination of mythic joy and primal strength surrounded by vapors. Peter Gay[1] has mentioned the importance of the divorce of ethics from German historical thought in the nineteenth and twentieth centuries and the contribution of this to the disaster of Germany in the thirties. This divorce can be seen in Wagner's operas, and through its mystic yearnings it grew out of the still ethically centered world of *Die Zauberflöte*.

Wagner's librettos in their philosophic aspect play *schwarz*-Metastasio to those of the earlier librettist, but the two great librettists have much in common. The range of Wagner's work and its development are more extensive than Metastasio's, while Metastasio's poetry (within its narrower range) is superior to Wagner's and his sense of elegant nuance more assured. Wagner received his "classical" training and his ideas of a Greek revival in opera[2] at the fount of Gluck rather than of Metastasio, but many of his ideas, particularly as expressed dramaturgically in his librettos, go back past Gluck to Metastasio.

The underlying similarity in Metastasio and Wagner is their demand for a conscious frame of reference in which to judge their work, a frame more stylized than that of Gluck. With Metastasio the frame was externalized in the traits of the *opera seria* form, while in Wagner's librettos the frame was internalized and amorphous, adapting itself to the needs of each specific work. Yet this frame had its postulates, the chief of which was the postulate of time. Wagner demanded a breadth of time in which to reveal his characters and have them interact, and this breadth of time is inseparable from the specifics of what Wagner is trying to say. Form and content are inextricably bound together in Wagner's artistic whole, and particularly the leisurely span of time is central to his esthetic methodology. This length of "actual" time is directly related to that sense of mythic time or "timelessness-in-time" which is also an integral part of the librettos. The love duet from Act II of *Tristan und Isolde* takes x minutes to sing depending on the artists and the conductor; the time it takes in terms of the myth can be ten seconds or ten thousand years. Wotan's monologue in

---

(1) *Weimar Culture*, p. 89.
(2) Not, alas, the last backward look to Greece for operatic refreshment.

Act II of *Die Walküre* is another instance where the actual length of time span invokes a timelessness.

Wagner's use of compression and excision in the shaping of the myths for the operatic stage can also be traced to Gluck, but again is in fact more characteristic of Metastasio's dramaturgy. Berlioz's *Les Troyens* follows more clearly in Gluck's footsteps (albeit with French *tragédie lyrique* additions), whereas Wagner remakes the myths to his own demands, much in the way Metastasio recast history into the *opera seria* mold. Like Metastasio, Wagner was a master of knowing what to leave out and what to concentrate on in order to tell the story in a wholly personal way, and his differing treatments of the Tristan and Nibelung myths demonstrate his flexibility of approach. Certainly the reduction of the *Nibelungenlied* to the operatic stage, even within the span of four operas, is a colossal logistic feat, and superficial comparison with another attempt, such as Ernest Reyer's *Sigurd* (1884; l., du Locle and Alfred Blau) will reveal Wagner's superior organizational powers.[3] Other Metastasian traits that Wagner reused because of their dramatic viability were the emphasis on contrast in dialogue, typical of the *secco* portions of Metastasio's librettos; the use of opposition of image or figure of speech within the speeches themselves, which was a feature of Metastasio's aphoristic and metaphorical style;[4] and reliance on soliloquy. The soliloquy and its adjunct, the narrative pause, are both integral to Wagner's librettos and will be discussed later; in their structural aspect they are often related to the exit aria as a summing up of what has transpired before. Wotan's narrative in Act II of *Die Walküre* both stands at the center of his linear development as a character in the *Ring* cycle and, in terms of the specific opera, is an elaborate exit aria that sums up the immediately preceding "*secco*" conflict-duologue of Wotan and Fricka—in fact, sums up everything preceding it in the cycle.[5] The French and the Italians generally

---

(3) Reyer and his librettists were apparently unacquainted with the specifics of Wagner's libretto when they wrote their opera.

(4) E.g., Siegmund's narrative in Act I of *Die Walküre*, the import of which is that as much as he, Siegmund, sought happiness in life, he achieved woe.

(5) As can be seen, Wagner's use of the "summing-up" qualities of the exit aria was far more complex than that of Metastasio, whose librettos are both linear and compartmentalized. In this instance, the addition of Brünnhilde, both before the Wotan-Fricka scene and after it, gives further dimension to the narrative.

shunned the soliloquy in favor of the ensemble, and restricted the narrative to its smallest confines, the ballad. If they used the extended solo, they concentrated on its musical features (i.e., a "mad scene" or a musical moment whose spotlighting purposes are better served by having everyone off stage). The logical antecedent for Wagner's amalgamation of drama, musical form, and over-all structural envelope is less the immediate precursor, the Scribe *Grand Opéra*, than the Metastasian *opera seria*.

Wagner was hardly the first librettist to have a close working knowledge of theater, but he certainly was one of the most thoroughly schooled in it. His contemporaries repeatedly wondered at his innate abilities as actor and stage director; it seems likely that he received more professional training as a stage technician than as a composer.[6] Wagner's total mastery of the devices and possibilities inherent in the form that the dramatic spectacle assumed during the nineteenth century, the proscenium-arch stage, is everywhere evident in the librettos he wrote. Indeed, his genius in adapting the framed and closed-in area not only for the well-made play form (for which the proscenium arch is ideally constructed) but also for the timeless myth-tales is rivaled in scope only by the works of Ibsen; and it is not going too far to say that Wagner's stage grasp of the proscenium esthetic is as comprehensive as Shakespeare's of the Globe Theater thrust stage with balconies. We are lucky that the continuity of opera in the Bayreuth Festspielhaus, which was built to Wagner's specifications for Wagner's operas, has allowed us to recognize the correctness of this evaluation. Despite changes in production approach, the essentials of the proscenium concept remain static. The hooded orchestra damps down the sound so that it becomes homogeneous yet distinct, and so that at all times the words sung on stage will be heard; and this aural clarity is reinforced by the excellent acoustics. The severe framing of the playing area confines the action to a lighted rectangle enclosed on both sides by the dim light reflected upward from the orchestra pit and then by the blackness of the hall. The spectator's attention is thus focused solely on the stage: on the visual scene, the words themselves and, only secondarily, on the orchestral sound. This concept, which is the proscenium-arch esthetic reduced to its essence, should be con-

---

(6) The idea that Wagner was a musical amateur on a gigantic scale can be placed in understandable perspective when he is seen as primarily a professional playwright and librettist.

trasted with that of French *Grand Opéra*, which is similarly oriented toward the visual as well as the aural. Yet *Grand Opéra* demands for its full effect as spectacle an interrelation among the opulences on stage and the visual opulences of the instruments in the orchestra pit, the chandeliers in the auditorium, and the light from the boxes. Wagner's organizational puritanism, which has been amply documented in its musical application in his distaste for artistic license, particularly of the Italian vocal sort, subjects each of his works to the strongest creative control.

The technical virtuosity that Wagner commands is amazing: the use of height and depth—upstage, downstage, and off stage—; placement and inter-relation of characters, movement, and climax; manipulation of lighting, machinery, and moving scenery; and constant awareness of new developments in stage technique and their incorporation in his work. Wagner's librettos are a primer for playwrights no less than the works of the great dramatists. The orchestration of the stage for the climax of the second act of *Die Walküre* is only one of countless examples of Wagner's absolute control of stage dramaturgy.[7]

George Bernard Shaw and others, relying on Wagner's writings about the *Gesamtkunstwerk* and the creation of an all-new operatic form divorced from existing opera (save possibly Gluck), had great fun pointing out how Wagner "returned" to opera with *Götterdämmerung*—and even held this return against the composer. In fact, although some of Wagner's music dramas are more rigorously organized than others, Wagner never left the confines of opera. He continually used its theatrical devices and, when it suited him to open the form, did so. The *"Rache"* trio in Act II of *Götterdämmerung* may be more obviously operatic than the use of the *aubade* in Act II of *Tristan*, but both are extracted from usages in previous operas and used in ways similar to those of other librettists and composers.

The delineation of Wagner's riches in terms not only of stagecraft but also of recurring themes would entail a volume as long as the present one, and has already been detailed in numerous other works. I shall choose certain aspects of his librettos and comment on them, perhaps omitting some of the important ones,

---

(7) The power of this climax is such that it "works" even when shorn, in modern productions, of many of Wagner's specifically called-for dramatic aids.

but hopefully implying the further richnesses that his librettistic work contains.

The one great feature of all of Wagner's librettos is their organic unity. This organic unity, unlike that of Metastasio—and such nineteenth-century examples as Romani and Scribe—derives not from an outside formula to which the works have been tailored but from a self-contained entity. Metastasio was able to use the *opera seria* form so expertly that he personalized it, but in the works of a Scribe, however well he adapted his skills to the setting forth of the story within the framework, the "number" structure existed apart.[8] This organic concept can be seen in all of Wagner's works; it is operative on all levels, from the immediate effect-with-cause to the encompassing structure. *Lohengrin* is an interesting example, for in that opera Wagner stood between the *Grand Opéra* trappings of the divided chorus, King Heinrich, Elsa, and Friedrich von Telramund and the myth-figures of Ortrud (in part) and Lohengrin. The myth dominates, and for that reason the opera suffers, because Wagner at that stage of his development had not made the conscious transition from one milieu to the other. The important theme of the Saxon Heinrich commanding obedience from his Brabantine vassals, led by Friedrich, is necessarily swamped. It is essential to understand this theme if the political motivations of Friedrich and his countrymen (as opposed to those of Ortrud) are to be appreciated, and if Friedrich is to be seen as more than a creature of Ortrud's will. Wagner clearly outlined his wishes in the text, which not only calls for a visual distinction between the two peoples but also is highlighted dramaturgically by the use of horses.[9] Hippophilia had become a staple of *Grand Opéra*, but Jouy had justified the use of horses in *Fernand Cortez* by the notion that their appearance would cause the same surprise in the audience as it had to the horseless Aztec society. Wagner, in the third act of *Lohengrin*, had the Brabantine nobles arrive on horseback. Superficially this may be a carry-over of the *merveilleux*

---

(8) At the risk of boredom, it should again be stressed that this does not mean that the formula itself is "wrong." Indeed, it is becoming increasingly evident that the disjunct nature of the number tableaus of the nineteenth century prefigured the disjunct—even random— dramas of the mid-twentieth.

(9) One of the many strengths of Ernest Newman's discussions of Wagner's operas is his constant awareness of the stage orientation of Wagner's works. The discussion of the horses is further elaborated in his *The Wagner Operas*, p. 115 *ff.*

habit; in Wagner, however, nothing is superficial, even if its significance would escape 99 per cent of the audience. The Saxons were noted as horsemen, and their cavalry was the finest part of their army: for the Brabantines to appear on horses meant that they had acquiesced to Heinrich's call to arms and were ready to contribute to his strongest weapon. Wagner the historical dramatist was merely showing Scribe how it should be written, if it were written.

Another great feature of Wagner's librettos was his contemporaneity. Wagner's works, both musically and librettistically, breathe the nineteenth century, and some consideration of them is indispensable for any understanding of nineteenth-century modes of thought. This contemporaneity is one of the chief reasons why Wagner is downgraded today, for the Romantic ideals of triumph through death and the sacrificing female (so much a part of Goethe's *Faust* and other works), plus the emphasis on overt self-pity and mystical yearning, have placed a distance between Wagner and us. *Lachender Tod*[1] and *Verklärung in Liebestod* are worlds away from Wozzeck passing out of the world-picture unnoticed except as a child's diversion or an anatomic study[2] or Alwa making love with his stepmother on the blood-stained sofa where his father was shot—by her. Yet if the heroine was the one element of Wagner's esthetic which he treated with absolute reverence, he was only following the lead of Goethe with his *Ewigweibliche* and echoing one of the germinal myths of the Western world.[3] Beyond that, only one of Wagner's operas, *Der fliegende Holländer*, revolves around the semi-deity of the female; the others, including the *Ring* cycle, have other themes as well. Brünnhilde's death is not necessary for the climax of the myth—despite its necessity as a *grandissima scena*—nor is the ending her triumph alone. Similarly, the mystic yearnings are carefully presented so that they can be seen and explained in purely human terms. Wagner was too great an artist to be bound by the conventions of his time, and though he reflects them, they do not overwhelm him.

---

(1) This can be translated in various ways: laughing death, laughing at death, laughing in death.

(2) Ironically, a product of the nineteenth century, though spiritually of the twentieth.

(3) As is evidenced not only in Shaw's *Man and Superman* but also in the Don Juan myth—and in *Lulu*!

Wagner's organic concept can be evidenced in his employment of a simple technical device such as the narrative ballad.
The narrative ballad was a commonplace in *Grand Opéra* and the
melodramma as a direct method of conveying the essentials of the
story in a musical frame. The strophic structure reinforced this
"storytelling" aspect. *Robert le diable* contains a classic example,[4]
as do *Lucia di Lammermoor* ("*Regnava nel silenzio*") and several of Verdi's operas, notably *Il Trovatore*. As its purpose was
expository, it almost always appeared in the first scene of the opera.
But Wagner, in *Der fliegende Holländer*, sensed the inherent
power that the narrative ballad could have but which lay dormant
in its previous use. He saw that it contained not only expository
power, but characterizational and structural power as well. He
could have introduced the legend of the Dutchman on stage through
the voice of one of Daland's sailors, perhaps in a steersman's song at
the opening of the opera, but he deliberately eschewed that effect
by having the steersman sing of his loved one.[5] The sailors well
knew the timeworn story of the Dutchman. But Wagner had a more
comprehensive plan.

He moved the ballad to the second act. It therefore appeared
after the introduction of the Dutchman on stage and *after* the
Dutchman had characterized his sufferings in his agonized monologue, "*Der Frist ist um.*" Superficially this might seem to have
blunted its expository purpose, but in fact it accomplishes the exact
reverse. The dramatic value of an early use of the narrative ballad
is to whet the audience's appetite while giving them information;
Wagner put the man and his sufferings on stage, thus whetting the
audience's appetite for the reasons behind the suffering, and *then*
explained them in the ballad. The explanation thus refers not to
something that has happened and therefore is prelude but to something that has happened to someone already known to the audience.
Thus the moment is far more "active" and powerful dramatically
than the passive recitation of prior events.

But this is hardly all. Wagner puts the ballad in the mouth

---

(4) Meyerbeer used the ballad theme as a recurring Devil's motif.
(5) Wagner does not let the "number" stand alone, as Scribe would
have done, but ties it in to the action by having the steersman go to
sleep while singing, which leads to the appearance of the red-sailed
Dutchman's ship. In *Tristan*, the sailor's song is similarly tied in to the
action: the song triggers Isolde's rage anew, she thinking that the
sailor is mocking her.

of Senta,[6] whose obsession with the legend of the Dutchman is well known in the village. She would logically be the one to tell the tale; moreover, her telling of it would be more alive and passionate and more meaningful than in anyone else's mouth. The ballad therefore becomes symbolic of Senta's obsession with the Dutchman and his tragic story, and this symbolic obsession is reinforced *musically* by the repetitious strophic form, *visually* by having Senta sing it while staring at the Dutchman's portrait on the wall. The ballad thus becomes the structural node around which the opera revolves, and in its telling gathers up a motive and emotive force that is dispelled, not in the immediately following scene between Senta and Erik, but in the appearance of the Dutchman in the doorway and in Senta's scream of recognition. No more comprehensive illustration of the dramatic possibilities of a simple stage device can be imagined.

Wagner did not use the ballad only to perform the functions of exposition. Unlike Metastasio and Scribe, who preferred to use dialogue to set the scene, Wagner turned to the "messenger" device of the Metastasian and other early operas: that is, the person charged with coming on stage and detailing what has occurred before the curtain rose or during the earlier course of the action. This use derived ultimately from the Greek tragedies, and was ubiquitous in the French classical theater. By Wagner's time, however, the messenger (and, to a great extent, the confidant) had passed off stage, and so he transferred their duties to the leading characters. This explains the narratives that are so much a part of Wagner's operas—the Dutchman's *"Der Frist ist um,"* Tannhauser's Rome journey recitation, Lohengrin's revelation of his identity, David's delineation of the rules of the Meistersinger, Loge's account of *his* travels, etc.—and are usually the first parts to be cut in performance. Yet these narrative pauses—and in stage terms they are exactly that—perform a vital function in Wagner's works. First, they are not all alike. Loge's recitation has much more movement than Wotan's monologue in Act II of *Die Walküre,* and David's speech is the sprightliest of them all. Lohengrin's *"In fernem Land"* is a semi-ecstatic vision, structurally balancing Elsa's Dream in the

---

(6) After Wagner teases the audience with the suggestion that Mary sing it, in which case it would be traditionally employed. Mary refuses, in horror at the thought of singing about that *"gottverdammt"* soul.

first act, whereas the Dutchman's hopeful yet tortured entrance *scena* reveals him and his plight at the outset of the opera.[7] Their length is necessary for several reasons: in some cases as a summing-up, and also to allow the music to embroider on the words and events described. Wagner as a librettist who wrote music wanted the music to have as dramatic a function as possible. By binding it up as counterpoint and expansion of the words, he could create another dimension of dramatic depth, a process integral to his dramaturgy. The narration pauses are the inner lair of the perfect Wagnerite, for they express in the most stylized way the approach that Wagner took to opera.

This stylization extends from the narratives to the soliloquies. The greatest of them, Hagen's Watch, becomes all the more chillingly menacing because of the night pall of the stage, the character's aloneness in a great hall, and the stillness of the moment. Wagner knew, as Metastasio knew, when to move his characters and when to keep them from moving: the demonic intensity of Hagen's words is crippled if he blinks an eye. The pause has here become a suspension of time itself; a suspension that is not timeless, as the others are, or as such moments as the quintet in the first scene of the third act of *Die Meistersinger* are, but a suspension *from* time.

Wagner also knew how to use silence on stage. His librettos mark silences between speeches like the *Luftpausen* of Bruckner symphonies, but he also manipulates silence for dramatic purpose. The shattering nothingness that follows the Dutchman's appearance in Daland's house is magnified by the echo of Senta's scream; its lyric counterpart is the silent intensity of Eva and Walther in the scene i of Act III of *Die Meistersinger* while Sachs, all-knowing, chatters along in frivolities. Wagner, in his passion for layers of dramatic counterpoint, liked to juxtapose silence with sound. Thus the silent wonder with which Parsifal stands and watches the Consecration service is vital to the stage picture as well as to the meaning of the scene,[8] while Ortrud's silence in the first act of *Lohengrin* symbolizes the evil latent on the stage and in the action:

---

(7) Its structural use is similar to that of the Agamemnon monologue Hofmannsthal wrote for Elektra.
(8) The physical demands this standing-in-silence makes upon the Parsifal leads tenors to exit during the scene (as Melchior regularly did.)

an evil combatted visually by the entrance of Elsa and her retinue clad in white.

Wagner's movement to myth and legend freed the libretto of its dependence upon the immediate, and consequently opened up the world of what has come to be called the subconscious. His dependence upon the power of dreams in his librettos is almost chronic, and, as is characteristic of him, the dream is not a mere theatrical device; nor is it the same for Elsa as for Hagen or Walther. Linked with this is Wagner's hero's dependence upon his father and, more importantly, upon his mother. Siegfried's cry of help to his mother upon first seeing a female form is symbolic of similar parental preoccupation in other librettos. These psychological manifestations have been commented on at length elsewhere;[9] today Wagner's obviousness in his approach is more evident than it was to the nineteenth century. Yet never has another body of librettistic work been subjected to such close scrutiny and yielded such rich rewards.

The aspect of this psychological dependence which is most interesting is the *ex nihilo* quality of Wagner's work. The arrival of the stranger is a classic dramatic device, used from Sophocles to the movie *Shane;* Wagner coupled it with the Unconscious from which so many of his strangers come and to which they return. Lohengrin may describe Montsalvat, but it is a never-never land directly related to the unknown shores to which Tristan and Isolde sail. It is this *ex nihilo* which gives to the myths their disturbing otherworldliness and to the characters a dimension not so much larger than life as apart from it. To compare the arrival of a stranger from a never-never land in the Gozzi-based libretto to Puccini's *Turandot* with the appearances of Lohengrin and Parsifal is to appreciate the existence of that dimension. The *Ring* cycle, of course, brings this Unconscious onto the stage in the characters of the Norns and Erda.

The use of the Norns is typical both of Wagner's layered structure and of his philosophical unity of word and music. *Götterdämmerung* is, structurally, a vast recapitulation of the cycle as well as its culmination; thus the Norn Scene, called the Prologue, both echoes *Rheingold* and, in putting on stage the creatures of the void, visually echoes the *ex nihilo* E-flat chords that inaugurate

(9) E.g., Robert Donington: *Wagner's Ring and Its Symbols.*

the cycle. Erda, as a character, is an updating of the seventeenth-century *deus ex machina*, and is so employed in *Rheingold* in the sense that her intervention changes the course of events. But Wagner, as usual not content with mere reuse, develops the *deus ex machina* idea into something more. When Erda is summoned from her sleep by the Wanderer in *Siegfried*, she admits her powerlessness to cope with the situation and her fears at the world's course,[1] and only wishes to be left to sleep. This attitude parallels that of Fafner, but for differing reasons: Fafner wishes to sit on his ill-got fortune in a paroxysm of inertia; Erda wishes to escape into the nothingness of sleep. Wagner cruelly exposes the underbelly of the *deus ex machina* idea: the fact that gods can no longer control events (if they ever did), and that the realm from which they come is an escape *from* life and not a nirvana. Tristan and Isolde must go through life in order to reach nirvana, and thus the sacrifice of their struggle leads to their "triumph over death"; for Erda the choice has never been made, and she remains a pathetic figure wanting release in forgetfulness. The contrast to Wotan deepens both characters.

Contrast is a decisive weapon in the hands of Wagner as a portraitist of characters. He uses contrast on stage in much the way that Metastasio used it, by pitting conflicting characters against each other. It is a personalization of the *Grand Opéra* device of juxtaposing strongly contrasting scenes, and as such creates emotional tension in the same way that Verdi's scenes do. Because a great part of Wagner's dramatic methodology was conceived in terms of the duologue, contrast of character became the one essential way to bring the debates to life. Wagner's characters are strengthened in their forcefulness by the power of their wills. In this respect his personages keep their distance from the anti-heroes of today's drama, as typified by Wozzeck, in that they exude power and an ability—if not a wish—to control events which is totally foreign to today's esthetic. In the nineteenth century, this behavior, carried to its extreme in the person of Siegfried, was looked upon favorably; in this century it is not. Because Wagner drew his characters with large brushstrokes, they lack the subtlety of the creations of a librettist like Hugo von Hofmanns-

---

(1) ERDA (after a long silence): "*Wirr wird mir,/seit ich erwacht:/ wild und kraus/kreist die Welt!*" ("I am dazed since I awoke: how wild and wobbly is the world's course!")

thal,[2] and this fact is reinforced by the movement to myth and the consequent universalizing of the characterizations. Yet Wagner did not put cardboards on stage; indeed, his tenor roles, especially those of Tannhäuser, Tristan, and Parsifal, are some of the most rewarding in the repertory in terms of acting opportunity for that voice. The dramatic possibilities inherent in any one of Wagner's great roles is never farther than the portrayal by a great singing actor, and though Wagner's motivations may at times appear elephantine, they conceal layers of subtlety which can be revealed with as much finesse as those in *Le Nozze di Figaro*.

The universalization of the characters by the mythologizing of the story gives Wagner another weapon not granted those who operate in a more genre-oriented frame. This is the symbolic power of the figure independent of his characterization. The tragic figure of the ever-seeking Dutchman is one such portrait; even more powerful is the figure of Amfortas, who because of his own weakness has been dealt both a real and symbolic wound from which he suffers terribly and from which he cannot obtain surcease through either death or cure. Even the unseen figure of Titurel possesses this power, which is that of image: the ageless king being kept alive solely through ecstatic sustenance. The character of Kundry, on the other hand, is the most complex web of symbolism, motivation, and psychological penetration which Wagner created, so that any realization on stage of her totality as a character is necessarily impossible.

Yet, as is always the case with Wagner, one facet of his genius cannot be divorced from the rest. The characters in his operas gain stature not only through the standard dramatic devices or through the music but through Wagner's use of even another layer of visual and emotional dramaturgy: irony. Wagner used irony to some extent in almost all of his librettos; he used it extensively in the *Ring* cycle. He used it in several ways. Most directly, in its sarcastic guise, he allowed villains like Ortrud and Telramund to use it to cut down the heroes somewhat to size (the Dutchman also employs it in this way, but against himself); in the later works he broadens its implications. The standard definition of dramatic irony is a situation on stage about which the audience knows something one of the characters does not (i.e., that the

---

(2) The exception would be *Die Meistersinger*, in which the characters, and particularly Hans Sachs, approach this degree of subtlety.

water in the cup is poisoned, as in *Simon Boccanegra.*[3] Yet there
are extensions of this, both the obverse and the layered. The
layered, or box-within-box, idea is endemic in Wagner's librettos;
it results when someone else stands between the audience and
what is happening on stage, also "knowing" more or less what
will happen but watching it, while being watched by the audience.[4] This feature of Wagner's dramaturgy is acutely stage-conscious and designed for the proscenium "box"; it is derived from
the overtly stagey works of Scribe. Its use as a positive force
and not merely for effect prefigures the works of Luigi Pirandello
and other dramatists of the twentieth century, who have gone a
step further in manipulating these conventions for dramatic purposes. Thus, in the second act of *Die Meistersinger* the audience
watches the stage, on which Sachs watches the stage, although
Walther—in hiding with Eva—feels *he* is alone in watching everyone (Eva is aware that Sachs knows she is in hiding, but does not
tell Walther); while Beckmesser, looking at Magdalene (whom
he supposes to be Eva), actually sees nothing and is watched by
everyone, is directly criticized by Sachs, will soon come under the
gaze of David, who, understanding only a portion of the events—
he thinks Beckmesser is serenading his sweetheart—acts, and thus
destroys the staticity of the situation, which then devolves into
frenzied (but totally choreographed) action and is resolved in
silence with a visual symbolic reinforcement (the light of the
"chaste goddess"). The clarity with which Wagner handles this
extraordinary complexity is testament to his dramatic skill; moreover, each of these layers of consciousness carries its own ironic
import.[5] The importance of Parsifal's watching of the Grail consecration can now be more fully understood, for Wagner here
employs an obverse by which the "pure fool," knowing nothing,
learns literally and emotionally while he watches, only to have
this enlightenment misunderstood, so that he is driven from the
hall and is forced to learn through his deeds.

The *Ring* cycle, however, offers the most thoroughgoing

(3) The addition of that example of dramatic irony was owing not
to Piave but to Boito in his revision of the libretto. When Piave
originally wrote the story, the impact of dramatic irony was not as
important, and so Paolo poisoned the cup off stage.
(4) Another layer, of course, is the irony of the music.
(5) And affords a glimpse of the opportunities for actors which Wagner's operas offer—if the singer is interested.

use of this technique. Beginning with the straightforward use of sarcasm which sets the half-god Loge apart from the gods, who are heady with imagined power, Wagner systematically displays the possibilities of stage irony. He can use it comically, as in the first act of *Siegfried*, when he balances Siegfried's reforging of Nothung with Mime's boiling up of poisons for Siegfried.[6] The scurrying figure of Mime, cooking and chattering away, makes the sword forging a shade less heroic, but gives it a depth that the rigorously exclusive heroes of Metastasio were denied; likewise, the utter futility of Mime's desperate efforts are under-scored by the ease and command of the young man's actions. But it is in the figure of Wotan that Wagner developed this ironic overview to its ultimate, for the character of Wotan is one of the greatest achievements in all of opera. Wotan grows in stature throughout the cycle in direct proportion to his loss of power to control events, and with *Götterdämmerung* achieves a tragic omniscience that is powerful precisely in its lack of omnipo-tence.[7] The Wotan of *Das Rheingold* seeks to control events, and in the end of that opera is partly stymied by Erda. He sets out on a second tack in *Die Walküre*, and in the scene with Fricka realizes the impossibility of that course. From that point on, he begins to withdraw from the direct action (the point is marked by the hurricane-eye quietness of the Monologue), and at the same time begins to become the watcher of events. When Sieg-mund is about to kill Sieglinde, the emotion of the moment is reinforced by Brünnhilde's presence, and her development as a person is hastened because of the possibility of that sacrifice, but it is doubly reinforced by Wotan's unseen but felt despair over an event involving his children which he cannot control. Yet this despair is still tinged with power lust, for should Sieglinde die, Siegmund would still be slain and the way would again be open for Wotan to scheme anew. Brünnhilde's action prevents this (and part of Wotan's rage at her must be understood as thwarted power lust), and Wotan is forced by the end of the opera to part not only from his earth children but also from his favorite Valkyrie

---

(6) The contrast in character is very important here: short, nervous, evil, old Mime; and tall, serene, good young Siegfried. The gestures and the presence should reinforce this contrast.

(7) Comparisons with other operas are unfair because Wagner gave himself the space of four operas in which to develop the character.

as well. In *Siegfried*, Wotan has become an old man, capable only of riddles, threats, and one final act, the outcome of which he already knows (the breaking of his spear). In *Götterdämmerung*, Wotan does not appear physically, except at the very end, but his presence overshadows the whole opera, and to consider *Götter-dämmerung* without Wotan is willfully to shrink its significance. It is not too strong to say that the whole of the action of the opera takes place in Wotan's mind, and everything—every development —must be appreciated relative to the watching eye of the old man, all his dreams shattered and his hopes ground down, sitting in Valhalla surrounded by his gods and the branches of the world-ash-tree, itself long dead, awaiting the end. The end of the opera is often seen as Brünnhilde's sacrifice in order to join her beloved, but Wagner was too great a dramatist to return to the Tristan theme or to narrow his epic into a love story.[8] Siegfried's murder has "opened her eyes"—she has moved through self-pity to wisdom[9]—and she knows that her duty is to return the Ring to its rightful owner. The key passage of the final scene is not her encomium to Siegfried but the moment in which she tells her father he will now rest, as is shown by the care with which Wagner set the words *"ruhe, ruhe, du Gott!"* The fact that Wagner specifically wanted the gods to be seen in Valhalla by the audience at the end of the opera carries this profound irony to the close of the cycle. Seen through Wotan's mind, the intensity of his suffering contributes to the epic quality of the whole.

The structural qualities of Wagner's operas have been referred to throughout this work. There is no doubt that Wagner as a musical architect was one of the most powerful ever; there is also no doubt that this musical architecture is intertwined with the specifically dramatic. Extensive consideration of specifics has

---

(8) Wagner realized this when he revised his original poem for the last opera, first called *Siegfrieds Tod*. Yet care should be taken not to believe all of what he wrote about the perfect unity of the *Gesamtkunstwerk*, for if the *Götterdämmerung* libretto is read without the music, the impression is overwhelming that Siegfried is the center of attention. By the time that Wagner came to the music, however, he recognized the fallaciousness of this use of Siegfried as cornerstone, and so instead of changing the poem, blandly composed largely Brünnhilde music, giving his hero a magnificent musical tribute once he was dead.

(9) A particularly nineteenth-century method of operation. It is when the self-pity became divorced from wisdom that it became so objectionable.

already been attempted in other books, of which Alfred Lorenz's[1] four-volume work can stand as symbolic. What should be noted in terms of Wagner's librettos is rather the hierarchy of structural levels always at work, beginning with (1) the immediate organization of the scene (quite often in terms of a duologue), then (2) the next higher organization in terms of the total stage picture—which includes not only the structuring role of the music but also the ironic depth and the full use of scenic *merveilleux* manifestations—and finally (3) the complete act structure and the over-all structure of the work as a whole. In the *Ring* cycle, this achieves the complexity of a macrocosmic overview of a cosmos of which *Das Rheingold* is a microcosm—the whole standing as a staggering tour de force, by far the greatest structural achievement ever carried to fruition by a librettist. All of this dramatic structuring can have its correspondences to "pure" musical form (e.g., sonata form),[2] and it can everywhere be carried to explanatory *reductio ad absurdum* extremes that Wagner never envisioned, consciously or subconsciously, but the organizational genius of the man was so far-reaching and comprehensive that commentators can be forgiven for becoming blinded by awe. There have been numerous other librettists whose structural powers were great, most notably Metastasio, but Wagner's scope and diversity compare with theirs as Bach's fugues compare with those of Buxtehude.

The poetry of Wagner's librettos has always been the most criticized element of his artistic make-up. Even in his own time it did not escape censure, and today it is virtually dismissed as pretentious, dull, and obscure. But his verse should be placed in perspective. Verse today is largely out of fashion,[3] and particularly out of fashion is the overt use of alliteration and word-assonance which Wagner relied on heavily in his later operas and which is evidenced in English poetry by the once-popular and now-scorned verse of Swinburne. Added to this the very nature

---

(1) *Das Geheimnis der Form bei Richard Wagner* (1926).
(2) George Bernard Shaw's conscious use of musical form in some of his plays is derived less from the works of Mozart than from those of Wagner.
(3) Much modern verse, at least in English, consists in attempts, often highly stylized, to hide the versicality of the poetry. The work of T. S. Eliot, W. H. Auden and, latterly, John Berryman are instances of this.

of the German language itself, which tends to heaviness in its guttural sounds and agglutinative proclivities, works against all but the finest poets. As Metastasio (in part) and countless other lesser Italian poets have shown, the Italian language can sound beautiful while holding no meaning and little true beauty of expression; similarly the French language can mask paucity of thought with ringing rhetoric. The German language (at least, to non-Germans) cannot hide behind these titillations, and therefore only in the hands of great dramatic poets like Bertolt Brecht and Hugo von Hofmannsthal has its power been released for the musical stage. Wagner was never on this plane, and indeed never achieved the plasticity of alliterative expression which Swinburne did. What he is reproached for is that he held himself forward as a major poet and as a poetic genius comparable with himself as musical and dramatic genius. Yet this very position, far from condemning his poetry, is its justification. For Wagner was a poet and not a poetaster, and the power of his will forced him to develop his verse as he developed his music.

That a librettist's verse should change during the course of his artistic life was totally unthought of. A writer was assumed to possess a style that would gradually become refined with time, and that was the extent of any change. Certainly none of the great poetic librettists—Metastasio, Goldoni, Romani—who preceded Wagner ever shifted gears as radically as Wagner did from *Lohengrin* to *Rheingold* to *Tristan*.

The poetry itself, of course, was considered organically as part of the whole. In this way it is loosely similar to Verdi's *parole sceniche*, in which the words stood as signposts for the dramatic action of the scene. But there are key differences. In Verdi the words act as a musical trigger, whereas in Wagner the words and the music are interdependent, and quite often to be considered, not as single words or short phrases, but in greater agglomerations of speeches. The awakening-of-love duet which is the climax of *Siegfried* is an example. It is, in fact, a shorthand version of a ritual courtship dance which, in a novel, could take up the entire book. The eager male and the reluctant female—tied to her past, yearning for union, yet afraid of its sexual as well as its emotional implications—reproduce the theme of many ballads, poems, and the like; but the very psychological complexity of the ritual negates its being expressed in one scenic word or even several scenic words. The allusiveness of Wagner's verse, particularly in *Tristan*, also works against this signpost rationale, for where "*Vendetta!*" or "*Mia patria!*" refers to concrete ideas, "*Wonne-hehrstes Weben,/liebeheiligstes Leben,/nie-wieder-Er-wachens/wahnnlos/hold bewusster Wunsch*"[4] manifestly moves in the opposite direction, and must be further elucidated by the music. What is more, Wagner varies his verse to suit the libretto, so that the compressed quality of the *Tristan* poem gives way to a more traditional approach in *Die Meistersinger*. In the narrative portions the verse can be straightforward, even in Wagner's last opera, as in Gurnemanz's Good Friday Spell:

> *Des Sünders Reuetränen sind es,*
> *die heut mit heil'gem Tau*
> *beträufet Flur und Au:*
> *der liess sie so gedeihen.*
> *Nun freut sich alle Kreatur*
> *auf des Erlösers holder Spur,*
> *will ihr Gebet ihm Weihen.*[5]

Wagner, as a poet, knew the possibilities of compression, but, beyond that, gloried in the musical side of his poetic gift. His librettos abound in word-plays and puns, which are demonstrated in two ways. One is the strictly literary, as in "*Freia, die Holde,/ Holda, die Freie*" ("Freia the fair, Holda the free"—Holda being another name for Freia) from *Das Rheingold*, and the other the more directly musical. There is little doubt that much of Wagner's fooling around with word-sounds—and even his development into alliteration—was intimately connected with the musical aspect of his artistic make-up. Just as he played with the variations in sound of his leitmotifs so he played with words. Thus, in *Das Rheingold*, the Rhinemaidens sing "*Rheingold, Rheingold, reines Gold*" (Rhinegold, Rhinegold, pure gold"). *Reines* is but a variation on *Rhein*: characteristically (whether intentionally or not) the Rhinemaidens only use the variation at the end of the opera,

---

(4) "I engender sublimest bliss, I live for holy love, nevermore to waken, illusionless, sweet, conscious desire." (Translation by William Mann.)

(5) "The tears of the repentant sinners are moistening meadow and field with a holy dew, which causes them to thrive. Now all creatures rejoice in following the Saviour's footsteps and will consecrate their prayers to Him."

after the gold has been stolen (and thus, dramatically speaking, when its purity has become all the more evident), so that the variation becomes a dramatic intensification of the moment, as well as an ironic comment upon it.

Wagner's use of *Stabreim*, or alliteration, is closely bound up with this word-play, but has other roots as well. He was the first librettist to discern the effects of the de-poeticization of verse at the hands of music, and instead of reacting by abandoning verse for prose, he took the opposing tack and actively sought to enrich it. By insisting on strong, repeated sounds, by stressing sound further with the use of interior assonance and variation rather than leaving it entirely to the end-rhyme and by shortening the line and making its effect more punchy, he hoped to build up the power of the verse vis-à-vis the immense strength that music had achieved, especially in his operas. The additional argument that *Stabreim* was a favored poetic method of the old sagas was used to bolster this usage: by reinvigorating the old, Wagner linked his day with the early history of his peoples while giving his verse the timelessness of myth-poetry.

Yet this reinvigoration of verse had side effects. The old sagas had employed *Stabreim* and assonance to give their work strength and a virile musical quality, and it was precisely this strength which had been transferred to the music in opera. Scribe's poetry was feeble but, apart from certain howlers, could be ignored: Wagner's poetry could not. Its very verbal power could be held in check only by music as strong as Wagner's, and even then at times its sounds overwhelmed the accompaniments. Further, Wagner's infatuation with the musical side of the verse—that is, the variations possible with the word-sounds—tended in its extreme compression to push the words past the bounds of meaning into something bordering on pure sound for its own sake:

> *Des Schweigens Herrin*
> *heisst mich schweigen:*
> *fass' ich, was sie verschwieg,*
> *verschweig' ich, was sie nicht fasst.*[6]
> *(Tristan und Isolde;* I, v)

---

(6) "The queen of Silence commands silence from me: I understand what she wrapped in silence; what I wrapped in silence, she does not understand." Note the resemblance to Metastasio's antitheses.

The verse thus takes on an abstract quality responsive to its own inner world of assonance and alliteration as well as, and perhaps more than, remaining a tool for understanding the story or the characters. In this sense the verse foreshadows the "abstract poetry" fragmentation of Gertrude Stein in her librettos for Virgil Thomson, which derived directly from Dada, but which, in libretto history, had, like Siegfried, another unknown but powerful grandfather.

Tristan is, of course, the opera in which this abstract approach is most clearly revealed—and in which it is most in keeping, for the solipsistic world of Tristan and Isolde finds perfect reflection in solipsistic verse. *Tristan und Isolde,* in the history of opera as well as of music in general, has always held the position of a landmark. Although the libretto does not attain this primacy of importance in the history of that form—it must be considered in conjunction with *Die Meistersinger* and the *Ring* cycle—it nonetheless possesses a forward-looking quality that the others, by and large, do not have.

The great quality of the *Tristan* libretto is its interiorization. Wagner seized on the theme of eternal love, which was hardly new and which had been reflected, in opera, in the "mad scenes," and developed it so that the very act of reciprocal love not merely blotted out the world but removed the world from consideration. The only objects of interest were the interior feelings of the two participants and their progress toward a nirvana of death, in which the world and its petty vanities would finally dwindle away. His conception of timelessness fitted in perfectly with this interiorization, for although in *Lohengrin* the immediate political theme had been uneasily conjoined with the mystic one, in *Tristan* the emphasis had decisively shifted. Ireland, Cornwall, Kareol, feuding kings, and trucial weddings may enter into the first act and lurk off stage throughout, but they are unimportant: to call *Tristan* an Anglo-Irish opera in the sense that *Die Meistersinger* is a German opera is to realize the absurdity of the comparison. Just as *Götterdämmerung* can be understood as a visualization of Wotan's suffering, so *Tristan* can be understood in the souls of its two participants. Not only the timeless quality of the last two acts and the *Verklärung* close, but also the *ex nihilo* feeling of the whole libretto drives the opera into the trackless expanses of the inner life. Isolde begins Act I by being jolted out of a deep reverie (by the sailor's song) to ask where she is; Tristan begins the third act by doing the same, and meets his end in a moment of *Verklärung* after he has finally gone completely mad. Wagner's obsessive elaboration of this internal vision is reinforced by the highly compressed and allusive verse, which twists and turns in upon itself, playing not only with the day–night symbolism which had been for centuries a constant in Western literature, but also with words such as *Licht, Leuchte, Liebe, Leiden.* The final blending together of the two at the climax of the love duet, when Tristan calls himself Isolde and she calls herself Tristan, and the blending of disparate elements before Tristan's death, when he says that he hears the light, establishes that nirvanic unity out of which the two have emerged for a time, only to be swallowed up once again.

Yet, by the same token, the importance of these developments, which would have a great effect upon the librettos that followed Wagner, should not obliterate the more narrowly formal dramaturgic evidences in the libretto. It has come as somewhat of a shock to twentieth-century observers that Wagner's operas, underneath, are much like those of his contemporaries, and, at the risk of further shock, it should be said that even *Tristan* does not present an entirely new face to the world. The madness and death of Tristan, for instance, are fully consistent in tone and result with the classic "mad scenes" of Romantic opera, from Lucia to Ophélie,[7] and would be repeated in Wilde's Salomé and Hofmannsthal's Elektra. Brangäne's *aubade*, during the love duet, has numerous structural felicities, not the least of which is the introduction of a consciously archaic set-piece into a fluid and emotional scene. The sudden strictness of the verse adds to this contrast.

The first act of *Tristan* may not be as obviously well made as that of *Die Meistersinger,* but nevertheless it is a classic example of dramatic exposition and development of character, and the use of the love potion as a visual and symbolic focus merely demonstrates how much better Wagner could handle the "inanimate object" prop than did his French and English counterparts: Scribe, Sardou, Dumas *fils*, Pinero, etc. Mention has been made of Scribe's handling of the contrast between the "open" and "closed" scene: Wagner, in *Tristan*, perfoms his usual Lisztian pyrotechnics with

(7) To the extent of being left alone on stage, which was always the prerogative of the prima donna, allowing her to make the greatest possible effect.

the device, but keeps it so unobtrusive that it passes almost unnoticed (to the extent of being dispensed with in modern productions). The opera opens on a "closed" scene, with the outside suggested by the singing of a sailor off stage; it is opened to reveal Tristan, then once again closed. Finally, it is completely opened, *but at the same time totally closed;* for although the scene is replete with people, banners, and joy, the focus is entirely on the two lovers, who remain transfixed by one another. Thus the exterior and interior aspects of the opera are set forward simultaneously.

Die Meistersinger and the *Ring* cycle are both as important librettistically as *Tristan und Isolde. Die Meistersinger*'s relationship to the well-made play of the nineteenth and twentieth centuries has already been mentioned; it stands as one of the finest examples of its kind and as one of the great humanistic librettos. The combination of complexity and underlying simplicity,[8] denied most well-made plays (except in a derogatory sense), give the libretto a perspective of the universal within the particular, while the surface busy-ness of the story provides a richness of texture which is always handled with clarity and dexterity.

The achievement of the *Ring* cycle, so utterly different, is far more encompassing. To undertake such a vast canvas is to move to the forefront of the field in terms of vision and daring; to have succeeded so amazingly is a justification and a vindication of that daring. That the *Ring* cycle is an epic work there is no doubt: it is, moreover, an epic responsive to the artistic current of its century, which cements its significance. The nineteenth century saw the greatest flowering of the opera art form in terms both of popularity and of artistic influence beyond the realm of pure music; this is reflected in both the expression of the *ur*-themes of Western culture in operatic terms and in their widespread philosophic and cultural import. The endless commentaries on *Don Giovanni* and *Die Zauberflöte* and the conscious embroilment in philosophy of Wagner's work led to Nietzsche's involvement with the art form, his famous break with Wagner, and his espousal of the "Mediterranean" approach to opera as symbolized in Bizet's *Carmen.* The epic form, therefore, which in its greatest manifestations had provided the summation of an age of history within the formal context of verse, had passed from verse to the poetic stage

---

(8) Represented in microcosm in the finale of the second act.

work as its expressive form—as Goethe's *Faust* (Part I) had in-dicated—and from the stage had passed, in Part II, to the intellect, albeit preserving the envelope of the dramatic method. Wagner realized that the perfect expression of the epic in nineteenth-cen-tury terms was no longer poetry, or even stage poetry, but opera. His achievement in the *Ring* cycle was manifold: the apprehension of the formal context, the grandly simple yet complex teleology of the specifics of the tale, the layers of the structure from im-mediate to universal—and the contemporaneity of the themes[9] and the specifically local import of the work. The subsequent history of Germany has turned this last—the nationalistic facet —into a grave fault, but Wagner's nationalistic pride was nowhere conceived as a justification of tyranny or genocide. At a time when the German states were, like their Italian counterparts, struggling toward nationhood and the whole of the German-speaking people was searching for an artistic heritage, works like Wagner's *Lo-hengrin, Die Meistersinger,* and the *Ring* cycle provided the con-temporary link with the German classics of the past, both by their own artistic worth and by their retelling of German tales. The *Ring* itself was conceived in the same spirit as Vergil's *Aeneid,* and was thus irrevocably linked to the national pride of the German peoples.[1] This was in its time an aspect of its triumph, and has now become, in part, its tragedy, necessitating the "cleansing" that Wieland Wagner performed on it after the Second World War. Yet, as with all great works of art, the *Ring* is hardly limited to a single one of its facets. It is of its time and it is universal.

Wagner's achievement in his three greatest librettos almost prohibits comparison with any other librettist. Simply to have been able to conceive and carry through two works as diverse as *Tristan* and *Die Meistersinger* within the same creative period is proof of genius; to add to that the germination and flowering of a cycle of four operas in yet a different direction is staggering. Wagner further limits the areas of comparison because he was never, except in the broadest possible sense, a re-creative librettist as Da Ponte, Romani, or Boito was, and thus their particular strengths in

---

(9) Those who would consider dated Shaw's socialistic interpretation, or even Donington's Jungian one, should read the librettos straight and then look at the headlines. The recent gold crisis, and the policy of the South African government in hoarding its gold off the world market have points of reference with Fafner—and Alberich's curse.
(1) Which is untrue of Berlioz's *Les Troyens.*

adaptation, however important they were to the libretto, have little application to him. Wagner must be compared to librettists such as Metastasio or Hofmannsthal, as creators of a self-defined librettistic world.

The twentieth century has seen a movement away from the Wagnerian esthetic, in terms both of the ideals that lay behind the works and of the specifics of the dramaturgy itself—particularly its lengthiness. The febrile, the fragmented, the understated, and the disjunct are values today where they were faults in the nineteenth century.[2] Yet Wagner's formal structure, if at times stylized and always leisurely, is an integral part of his esthetic make-up, and to attempt to separate it from the works is to damage them and willfully to denigrate him. As with the *opera seria* of Metastasio or the *tragédie* of Racine, we must accept Wagner as an artist fully aware of what he was trying to do and fully in command of the means he was employing to set forth that awareness.

Wagner as librettist explored a greater range of the possibilities of his craft than any other librettist, preceding or following him; as his own composer, he was able to reconcile those possibilities with the fact of the musical envelope and to produce an amalgam that was to a great extent an interrelation from a librettistic, and not a musical, standpoint. Wagner as librettist possessed a greater command of the stage, from both the point of view of technical knowledge and that of intuitive sense of the dramatic, than any other librettist. As a creative artist Wagner in his librettos breaks free of the inherent limitations of the form and can stand in comparison to artists working in other disciplines.

Richard Wagner, as librettist, is the greatest the form has produced, and if the libretto needs justification in terms of an artistic identity in its own right, Wagner will stand advocate of its strengths and its possibilities. There will always be disagreement

---

(2) These traits may not be as alien to Wagner's music and librettos as we may think. Pierre Boulez, in an interview with Roland Gelatt in *Harper's* Magazine (June 1969), says about causality in Wagner: ". . . the first act of *Götterdämmerung*, for instance. Nobody can really say where it's going. I'd like to do an experiment with that act some time, making an aleatory piece of it by cutting it up into various sections and reassembling them in a different order, just making sure that the modulations are still all right. I'm sure that many listeners would never know the difference" (p. 100). The first act, although it does recapitulate the *Ring* in one structural sense, nevertheless is disjunct enough to support Boulez's contention.

on which libretto is the finest the form has produced, and perhaps the ones chosen will not, for a variety of reasons, be authored by him, but those who would come forward with another candidate for premier librettist will have to dispose of his presence as dramatically as Siegfried disposed of "the old man" who stood in his way.

Chapter Eighteen

The Nineteenth-century
Opéra Comique *and* W. S. Gilbert

EUGÈNE SCRIBE (helped by Rossini and Meyerbeer) not only created the form of *Grand Opéra* but also managed to revitalize that of *opéra comique*, which, if hardly dormant, had been in a state of semi-eclipse since the Revolution. Scribe wrote a libretto for Auber, *Leicester*, in 1823, but the appearance of *La Dame blanche* in 1825, to music by Boieldieu, signaled the revival of *opéra comique*. The fantastic popularity of the opera led to numerous other Scribe efforts in that genre, mostly to music by Auber, and their popularity in turn led to the vogue for the *opéra comique* which would continue into the twentieth century. Among the Scribe librettos for Auber were *Fra Diavolo* (1830),[1] *Le Cheval de bronze* (1835), *Le Domino noir* (1837), and *Les Diamants de la couronne* (1841). The popularity of the form also attracted Italian composers, notably Rossini (*Le Comte Ory*, 1828; l., Scribe and Delestre-Poirson)[2] and Donizetti (*La Fille du régiment*, 1840; l., Vernoy de Saint-Georges and Bayard).

Scribe's *opéra comique* librettos in general contain better dialogue and more arresting characterizations than his *Grands Opéras,* as well as a welcome lack of pretension, but they lack such brilliant touches as Sedaine provided with the character of Montauciel. The emphasis is on the usual *commedia*-derived comic devices of disguise, misunderstanding, and surprise, the whole en-

(1) This *opéra comique* is notable in that it has an unhappy ending—in its first version.
(2) Technically, this opera was through-composed, but the subject from a Scribe *vaudeville*) and tone are comic.

wrapped in that aura of Favartian romantic sentimentality which was inherent in Scribe.

The story of *Les Diamants de la couronne* is a typical example, involving a heroine who is the leader of a band of brigands but is also the Queen of Portugal in disguise. She has taken to life in the rough not through whim but (by an entirely acceptable Diderot rationale) to save her country. Portugal is bankrupt and has been run by a regency. The young Queen now has come of age, and has made use of the "ancient custom" of royal retreat before coronation in order to spirit away all the crown jewels and have them copied by her brigand friends (who are all goodhearted souls). They then dispose of the originals, thus providing the Portuguese treasury with cash; and La Caterina can ascend the throne of a solvent country, while the brigand chief, her erstwhile "uncle," is made a count. She also gains her beloved, who is, naturally a bit nonplused. "Is all this true?" he asks her. "Yes," she replies and, pointing to her magnificent jewels, adds, "Only these are false," and the chorus swings into the usual Scribe doggerel as the curtain falls.

The cardinal aspect of *opéra comique*, as distinct from *Grand Opéra*, has always been noted, but its importance has not been sufficiently emphasized. The alternation of stretches of spoken dialogue with ensembles or arias was vital to the structure of the libretto and of the opera. In an atmosphere as sentimentally charged as that of nineteenth-century opera, the opportunity for expansion in dialogue was necessary: it not only fleshed out the stick figures of the arias but also provided a measure of Gallic irony in the give-and-take of the conversation, which undercut the moonings of the verse. Whether Scribe actually wrote all the dialogue in his *opéra comique* librettos is uncertain;[3] he certainly sketched in the essentials of each scene. The importance of the spoken dialogue in *opéra comique* is revealed whenever Bizet's *Carmen* (1875; l., Meilhac and Halévy) is correctly performed, but it is even more essential in a work like Gounod's *Faust* (1859; l., Barbier and Carré). Gounod was persuaded to inflate his work for the stage of the Opéra, but its first incarnation, with spoken dialogue, brings out better the characterizations of all three principals and ties the

---

(3) Of the Scribe *opéras comiques* that have been mentioned, *La Dame blanche* and *Fra Diavolo* were written by Scribe alone and *Les Diamants de la couronne* "en société avec" Saint-Georges.

work securely not to the world of Goethe but to the world of Sedaine and Scribe.[4]

The use of prose dialogue and its emphasis on the singing actor rather than the acting singer was reinforced by the theatrical devices of *mélodrame* and pantomime which were an integral part of French nineteenth-century opera. This in turn led to a further refinement of the habit: the actual singing of dialogue rather than speaking it over music. What this development accomplished was to soften the staticity of the "number" arias and ensembles and give them a measure of musical drama. Jules Barbier and Michel Carré's libretto for Victor Massé's *opéra comique Les Noces de Jeannette* (1853) contains such examples, and this refinement reached its expressive peak in the final scene of Bizet's *Carmen*. The great confrontation between Carmen and José is, in effect, sung *mélodrame*; although Nietzsche may talk of the work's "Mediterranean" qualities in order to set it against Wagner's Germanic ones, the roots are Parisian and not Italian.

Prose dialogue, of course, reduced the already shrunken role of the poet in the French libretto vis-à-vis the playwright who could scribble verse, and also served to move the form of the *opéra comique* closer to the *vaudevilles* and music-hall entertainments from which it had originally sprung in the eighteenth century. Thus, although the operatic categories can be defined in terms of structure and intent, there is some overlap in all of French opera of the nineteenth century. *Grand Opéra* was more akin to an inflated *drame bourgeois* than to *tragédie lyrique*,[5] and the "classic" *opéra comique* moved closer to it, not only in the works of Gounod but also in those of Massenet, while the lighter aspect of *opéra comique* shaded into operetta and the *opéra bouffe* of Jacques Offenbach.

Another feature of nineteenth-century *opéra comique* and lighter librettos was their dualistic creation. Scribe's "factory" had

---

(4) The demands of the Opéra were not the only pitfalls in the way of the "purity" of the *opéra comique*. Any *opéra comique* that went south to Italy lost all its dialogue, and not infrequently reappeared in France—in French—in a bastard combined version.
(5) When the Encyclopedists argued for a *drame bourgeois*, it was as an expression of the rising middle class against the dominant upper-class *tragédie*. With the nineteenth century, the bourgeoisie was the dominant force, and thus a *drame bourgeois* in the Diderot sense was not the *Grand Opéra*, which preserved much of the shell without the force, but a work such as Charpentier's *Louise* (1900).

included a number of collaborators, named and unnamed, but all of them had worked in tandem fashion with the master in terms of credit for the finished work. Yet the librettos of many other, contemporary and later, works were signed by two men working together. There were a number of reasons for this proliferation of duality. Certainly several duos, such as Barbier-Carré and Meilhac-Halévy, worked well together and, in the less importantly considered area of tailoring sources to a musical form (or of writing "boulevard comedies" aimed at instant success), two did not mind sharing the rewards of creation. In some cases—Puccini's librettists Luigi Illica and Giuseppe Giacosa are a good example—one provided the structure and prose form (Illica) and the other was the versifier. Most arrangements, however, were not subject to such simple division, for not only did both men work on the entire libretto, but so did the composer, and quite often unrecorded contributions were made by others. The libretto of Gustave Charpentier's *Louise* is credited to the composer, but was actually the work of numerous hands.[6] The dual-librettist form was also a perfect arrangement for the composer, because it effectively divided responsibility for the libretto and thus weakened each librettist's hold on the work. Composers took advantage of the situation by playing one librettist against the other, shuttling verses back and forth until the composer—not the librettist—was satisfied.

The team of Barbier and Carré was most typical of the French opera libretto of the mid-nineteenth century, and the two were in constant demand, both together and singly, for librettos for the major composers, as well as for "boulevard comedies."[7] Their work represents the "number opera" in its standard form, in which the polished technique and the careful three- or five-act tailoring—in themselves solid achievements—were outweighed by

---

(6) Virgil Thomson maintains that about twelve people had a hand in the libretto. The libretto of Richard Strauss's opera *Capriccio* (1942) is another example of an uncredited librettistic *marmite:* Clemens Krauss receives credit, but contributions to it were made by Strauss, Joseph Gregor, Stefan Zweig, Hans Swarowsky, and Rudolf Hartmann.
(7) E.g., *Faust* (1859; m., Gounod); *Roméo et Juliette* (1867; m., Gounod); *Mignon* (1866; m., Thomas); *Hamlet* (1868; m., Thomas). Carré also wrote *Mireille* (1864; m., Gounod) and Barbier *Les Contes d'Hoffmann* (1881; m., Offenbach), the last adapted from a play by the two.

the emotional blandness of the situations and characters. Their adaptations of Shakespeare and Goethe have done much to earn them lasting critical enmity, although close inspection reveals that their librettos for *Faust, Hamlet,* and *Roméo et Juliette* are only superficially responsive to the originals, and are in truth emotionally tied much more directly to the French operatic tradition of Scribe and, in the case of the Shakespeare restatements, to the popular bowdlerizations still current and exemplified in the works of Jean-François Ducis of the late eighteenth century.

One of the better examples of the art of Barbier and Carré is the libretto for *Les Noces de Jeannette* (1853; m., Massé), a light comedy in the peasant, pastoral vein of Favart. The simple Jean loves Jeannette and they have set their wedding day, but Jean cannot face marriage, and so reneges. Jeannette, in despair, persuades him to sign the marriage contract in order to save her reputation in the village, vowing that she herself will not sign it, and thus the wedding will be null. Jean signs, but Jeannette is too weak and affixes her signature as well. When she tells Jean, he becomes enraged and tears up the house. While he sleeps off his torment, Jeannette replaces the broken furniture, sews his clothes, and cooks his dinner. Jean cannot help but be impressed when he awakes, and cannot help but be flattered despite his discomfiture. The villagers then arrive to tell him that the contract is void because the mayor was not present at the signing, and thus Jean is freed of the bargain; but by this time the joys of wedded bliss have so infected him that he once again—and this time happily —consents to marriage. The whole is a trifle, but a trifle carried off well.

It was in this lighter vein that the French libretto of the nineteenth century made its greatest impression. It made it not through the reuse of the Favart sentimentalities, but in a return to the out-and-out farce *vaudevilles* that preceeded him. Offenbach's *opéras bouffes* were the rage of Paris during the years of the glory of the Second Empire, and the librettists for the finest of his works were Meilhac and Halévy.

Louis Meilhac and Ludovic Halévy were friends who worked well together, and they possessed verve and sauciness that fitted in perfectly with Offenbach's ebullient music. Besides writing for Offenbach, they produced "boulevard comedies," one of which

served as the basis for *Die Fledermaus*.[8] Among their works for
Offenbach were *La Belle Hélène* (1864), *Barbe-Bleue* (1866), and
La Vie parisienne (1866), while Halévy collaborated with Hector
Crémieux on *Orphée aux enfers* (1858).

All of these works sprang directly from the *vaudeville*
parodies of the previous century, repeating their lighthearted
burlesque of the manners and morals of contemporary society. The
method that the librettists used was to take an accepted myth-tale
and update it with a vengeance. By doing this, they not only
satirized the *tragédie lyrique*, with its insistence on subjects drawn
from myth, but also used the myth to poke fun at current figures
in the news while hiding them behind fictional characters such as
Achille and Ménélas. The general tone of burlesque was directly
aimed not only at French society of the fifties and sixties but also
at the pretensions and charades of the court of Napoleon III, and
a good many of the specific thrusts have been lost to history. But
even granted that their impact at the time must have been greater
than it can be now, the best of the Meilhac-Halévy *opéras bouffes*
—and *Orphée*, which may be the best of them all—still hold the
stage. This is so pre-eminently because of Offenbach's music, but
the librettos themselves have not died. The collaborators were not
tied to political and social satire; they also took on additional elements which continue to be universal (vanity, lust for power,
love) or which continue to be presented on stage, such as in opera.
Thus, men and women were shown in the full stature of their
foolishness while the exaggerated conventions of a stylized form
were mercilessly exposed. The addlepated choruses of *Grand Opéra*
were parodied to death just as Favart had parodied Lully—and had
himself been parodied—and the *mélodrame*, the *tableau vivant*,
le merveilleux, and the slumber scene were all held up to ridicule.
The whole was encased in a form which, in the myth-based
librettos, was travesty rather than parody, for its object was to
debase.[9]

---

(8) The play was *Le Réveillon* (1872), which was itself adapted
from a comedy of Roderich Benedix called *Das Gefängnis* (1851).
Johann Strauss's librettists were Carl Haffner and Richard Genée.
Meilhac also collaborated with Philippe Gille to write the libretto
for Massenet's *Manon* (1884).
(9) Dwight Macdonald, in his anthology of *Parodies*, defines travesty
as "putting high, classic characters into prosaic situations, with a
corresponding stepping-down of the language" (p. 557).

A fine example of the use of *mélodrame* in its pure, Rousseauist, guise occurs in *Orphée aux enfers*. The Orpheus legend has here been turned upside down: Orphée, an itinerant violin player,[1] cordially detests his wife Eurydice, who reciprocates this dislike, considering him a boring musical pedant. He is only too happy that Pluton has taken a fancy to her, but is persuaded by *l'opinion publique*—the *bourgeois* equivalent of a *dea ex machina*—that to preserve his reputation he must present her infidelity to the gods and demand redress. He therefore journeys to Olympe and, before the assembled gods, renders Gluck's most famous aria on his violin. The humor is manifold: to French audiences *"J'ai perdu mon Eurydice"* was considered little short of perfection as an aria and as musical expression, and thus it was close to sacrilege to use it to sway a crowd on behalf of someone of definitely easy virtue—whom the protagonist does not want in the first place.[2]

Meilhac and Halévy's comic librettos are similar to those of Scribe and others in that the verse is generally inferior, in style and content, to the prose—although their verse has a gaiety and a flexibility that Scribe's lacks. Yet the comic talents of the two are most evident in the spoken sections. The éclat of a scene such as the one between Popolani and Comte Oscar in *Barbe-Bleue* (III, ii), for instance, is specifically provided for in the directions: "The scene should be played with the fastest possible exchange of speeches, in a breathless and precipitous tone"—and reminds one of the comedy of Groucho and Chico Marx. Similarly, as with the rest of *opéra comique*, because most of the action took place in the spoken portions, the opportunities for comedy lay largely there. The sung parts have their share of humor, particularly in the music, but it is not in them that the contributions of the librettists are seen to best advantage.

Meilhac and Halévy—and others who worked with Offenbach—used a standard tool of broad comedy with which to construct their stories. This consisted in the setting up of a situation bordering on the absurd and then, entirely logically, letting it

---

(1) Readers of this book may notice a parody that was perhaps unconscious: the anachronism of the violin-playing Orphée and of the earlier violinist, Blondel, in *Richard Coeur de Lion*.
(2) Offenbach's powerful use of *mélodrame* in the Venetian Act of *Les Contes d'Hoffmann* demonstrates his ability to handle the device in both serious and comic contexts.

grow ever more absurd. This absurdist tone is heightened not only when the material used is "epic" or legendary, but further when such material is treated contemporaneously by using the language of Paris of the 1850's and 1860's and the slang expressions then in vogue. The logicality of the absurd can be instanced in the case of the notorious Bluebeard (Barbe-Bleue), who is what he is because his family motto is "Always a widower and never a widower," and thus he is condemned to marry and kill in order to keep up appearances. Being somewhat kindhearted, he leaves the killings to his pocket magician Popolani, who of course has not the heart for the tasks and so puts the wives to sleep just long enough to satisfy Barbe-Bleue—and then, in classic French farce style, keeps them for his own use.

The everyday dialogue between Hélène and Pâris in *La Belle Hélène* (II, iv), is more appropriate to a farce of the nineteenth-century Noël Coward–type than to the language of a daughter of Zeus[3] and a Trojan prince. "Pâris slouches in, as a young man today would enter a salon. 'Good evening, prince.' 'Good evening, madam.' 'Are you looking at the way I am dressed?' 'Yes.' 'It looks well, doesn't it?' 'Yes, very well.' 'What's new in the fashionable world?' 'Nothing I know of.' (Silence.) 'You're not being very likeable, this evening.' 'You think so?' 'Are you mad at me?' 'Mad at you—why?' 'Because I made you wait.' 'No, I'm not mad at you.' 'Ah.' (Silence.)"

The absurdist orientation is very much a part of the whole of *La Belle Hélène*, which, with *Orphée aux enfers*, belongs to the genre of the mock-epic. All the characters, with the possible exception of the lovers, are seen from a farcical point of view. Ménélas is an addlepated elder surrounded by bores, including the twin Ajax brothers, the boasting and vainglorious Achille (who nevertheless cautiously encases his vulnerable heel in armor for protection), and the fraudulent prophet Calchas, who gets spending money by cheating at dice. Small wonder that Hélène is restless— a condition that is aggravated when the handsome Pâris appears. Pâris of course uses logic to win her over. Reports of his famous Contest of the Golden Apple have already reached Sparte; everyone knows that Vénus was the winner and promised the young man the love of the most beautiful woman in the world. When Hélène

---

(3) Who, in the guise of a swan, raped Leda.

resists his advances, Pâris tells her that, because she rejects him, she cannot be that woman—which brings about a change of heart that is described by the librettists as *"la fatalité"* ("the will of the gods").

The absurdist invention of the plot is continuous. Here are several examples. The Kings engage in various parlor games (very popular in Second Empire France), all of which are won by Pâris. This gives the librettists a grand chance to satirize. The first answer is "Locomotive." Pâris opines: "Yes, locomotive . . . and it's marvelous to have thought of that four thousand years before the invention of railroads." The third game consists of making verses out of rhyming words. Ajax II comes up with a verse, but Agamemnon says: "It sounds fine, but it doesn't mean a thing. You should be teaching school." In the third act, the Kings are counseling poor Ménélas to give in to the will of the gods. Agamemnon says: "Certainly, I love my daughter Iphigénie . . . but the gods will ask me for her . . . well, I would say to them, 'You have her . . . take her!' " Ménélas replies: "But if they asked you for Clytemnestre?" "My *wife?*" "Yes." "Ah, that's something else again!"

Act III takes place at the seaside—i.e., at one of the summer resorts so fashionable during the Second Empire, such as Deauville[4] —and culminates in a classic *deus ex machina*. A galley from Cythère arrives, carrying in it a *"grand augure"* who is none other than Pâris in disguise. He carries off Hélène and laughs at his triumph, as the Kings shake their fists at him in a final tableau.

Meilhac and Halévy's librettos for Offenbach possess not only a wealth of verve and invention, but also a feeling for human nature and foible which is largely absent from the conventional "number operas" of the mid-nineteenth century. It would be too much to say that this humanness was conscious, but it reflected a movement away from the reliance on scene and vocalism which had seeped down from *Grand Opéra* to *opéra comique*. Absurd as these characters were, they did behave like actual people (a trait doubtless far more evident at the time the works were presented); as such, they performed the timeless comic task of returning the overblown and/or the stylized to the populace through recognition and laughter.

---

(4) The act begins with a parody of the "We're all gay" chorus of *Grand Opéra*.

The team of Meilhac and Halévy, however, has another distinction in the history of the libretto, for their example—and that of their confrères—was the immediate forerunner of the work of the finest comic librettist of the nineteenth century, William Schwenck Gilbert (1836–1911). Gilbert, who wears one of the rare and supreme librettistic honors in music history—the privilege of first billing over the composer—collaborated with Sir Arthur Sullivan to produce a series of comic operettas which dominated the English stage of the 1870's and 1880's and have been regularly revived to this day. Further, Gilbert and Sullivan's operettas revived the tradition of the English comic opera, which had earlier flowered with the Gay-Pepusch *Beggar's Opera* and numerous other ballad operas of the eighteenth century.

Gilbert's librettos owe a great debt to those of the French comic librettists.[5] He took over both their subject matter—the satirizing of society and its mores—and their familiar tone, as well as the necessity for "numbers" that would also serve to satirize the operatic elements. He also relied on the formula of absurdity logically compounded, which he carried to even more logical extremes because of his training in the logical profession of the law.[6] And, as is true with the best French examples, his better works continue in viability long after their original targets have faded into history.

Yet Gilbert's debts to the French *opéras bouffes* were but a starting point for his own talents. Apart from his earliest collaboration with Sullivan, *Thespis* (1871), which draws on both Heinrich Heine's theme of the Greek gods grown old and on the French penchant for classical themes, Gilbert manufactured all his librettos without recourse to a primary source, although all of them more or less derive from aspects of Victoriana.[7] The

---

(5) The Offenbach *opéras bouffes* were popular in England in expurgated form, and Gilbert and Sullivan's first triumph, *Trial by Jury* (1875), which was incidentally the only Gilbert and Sullivan operetta to contain no spoken dialogue, was paired with Offenbach's *La Périchole* (l., Meilhac and Halévy) when it was first staged.

(6) Another of the rare examples of the theater influenced by the libretto may be noted here, for a large measure of the logical absurdity of Oscar Wilde's masterpiece, *The Importance of Being Earnest*, is owing to the Gilbertian examples.

(7) There was also a good deal of satire of opera contained in the works, which Gilbert generally handled far better than in his obvious, elephantine attempts at direct parody, collected in *New and Original Extravaganzas*.

facility and ingenuity of his comic invention are shown both in the plot developments and in the characters he created. Besides the usual heroes and heroines—who are in Gilbert less interesting than in the French operettas because Gilbert's Victorian sentimentality and shunning of overtly sensual aspects of love led inevitably to blandness of feeling—Gilbert created at least one comic type that has come to be identified irrevocably with his name. This was the figure of the middle-aged, at best plain and at worst ugly, spinster —Katisha in *The Mikado* (1885) is the best example: a woman *"who may very well pass for forty-three/In the dusk, with the light behind her"*[8]—and who is still very much on the lookout for a husband. Gilbert has been censured for his handling of this character in his librettos, for the character not only reappears constantly but also is treated with a roughness that borders on cruelty; but what is evident is less the cruelty than the pathos that he (unconsciously?) creates as a concomitant and, more important, the vividness of these portraits as contrasted with the heroes (and even with the straight comic characters). The Italian and French comic librettos derived from the *commedia dell'arte* also contained strong comic characters who now and then achieved a measure of pathos (although the chief example, Don Pasquale, is from the nineteenth century),[9] but Gilbert, in his Katisha-figures, created rather than developed a type.

As the Gilbert and Sullivan operettas, with the exception of *Thespis*, were written for Richard D'Oyly Carte and, beginning with *The Sorcerer* (1877), for the D'Oyly Carte company, Gilbert provided roles for the voices in that company, in keeping with the Italian *opera buffa* tradition. The Katisha roles went to a contralto; stolid, dignified ones to a bass; and the main comic parts to a baritone. This last person did not have to have a beautiful voice, for his task involved not singing so much as expression. Gilbert entrusted to his baritone what are called "patter songs," which again have come to represent Gilbert in music. Patter songs, or lengthy explanatory arias dependent on vocal agility and usually involving verbal dexterity, may be looked upon as the comic counterpart of the operatic *scena* (or the Wagnerian narrative pause), and they go back to the eighteenth century. Leporello's "catalogue aria"

---

(8) *Trial by Jury*.
(9) Falstaff, another example, does not derive from the *commedia*.

or Figaro's *"Largo al factotum"* are instances of a very popular species of patter song. But Gilbert in his librettos went beyond what had theretofore been accomplished with the patter song, and he set a standard that has not been met since. This was because he was as good a comic poet as the libretto has produced.

The advantage of this ability is that, in the Gilbert librettos, the poetic portion is not the artistic and developmental wasteland that to such an extent it is in the French examples. Not only can Gilbert use the spoken dialogue to further his story, but he can further it in the sung portions as well. Beyond this, the invention that he displays in the spoken dialogue, which is as fertile as that of Meilhac and Halévy, is even more profligate in terms of sheer verbal magic in the poetry. Gilbert could produce the standard love-ballad rhymes, but beyond them he could twist and turn verse and line into ingenious combinations and outrageous rhyme (*"you shun her"*–*"executioner"*; *"lottery"*–*"terra-cottery"*; *"lot o' news"*–*"hypotenuse"*). The patter songs contain some of the finest of this dextrousness, and an example such as the Lord Chancellor's Nightmare Song from *Iolanthe* (1882) can stand—for ingenuity, flexibility of line and rhyme, and onrushing momentum —with any piece of comic verse ever written for opera. And it is only one of many Gilbertian patter songs. Perhaps the most characteristic part of it comes at the very end, when in effect Gilbert mocks his own creation: *"And the night has been long— ditto ditto my song—and thank goodness they're both of them over!"*[1]

Gilbert not only varied his verses, but also never lost sight of the metrical and aural reinforcement of the moment or the characterizational necessity. In *The Mikado*, which is perhaps the most profligately rich libretto he penned, this can be shown in two "trio" situations. When the Mikado arrives in Titipu, he expects to find that an execution has taken place; but there has not been one, so one has to be invented. Thus Ko-Ko, the Lord High Executioner, Pitti-Sing, a ward of Ko-Ko, and Pooh-Bah,[2] the

---

(1) Gilbert here writes extremely long lines with internal rhymes which must be delivered with speed and crystalline clarity to achieve the best results.
(2) The word itself has largely passed into the language to denote a pompous, self-important nonentity.

Lord High Everything Else, describe the death to the ruler. Ko-Ko begins, using both alliteration ("*frightful, frantic, fearful frown*") and word-allusion ("*squirmed and struggled*"; "*gurgled and guggled*") to enhance his tale, while the chorus comments in the background. Pitti-Sing now takes up the tale, and tells it from her womanly, vain point of view: that the prisoner left this world happy because he saw her the instant before he died (Chorus: "*Her taste exact/For faultless fact/Amounts to a disease.*") Finally Pooh-Bah rounds out the story in more sonorous lines, telling the really quite gory but somehow entirely proper incident of the head standing on its neck and bowing three times at the Lord High Everything Else ("*This deathly bow/Was a touching sight to see;/Though trunkless, yet/It couldn't forget/The deference due to me!*"). Earlier, Ko-Ko and Pooh-Bah have joined with Pish-Tush (a Noble Lord) to try to find someone willing to have his head chopped off. Ko-Ko demurs at being the victim, because, as Lord High Executioner, his reputation is at stake "*and I can't consent to embark on a professional operation unless I see my way to a successful result.*" Thus, he appoints Pooh-Bah Lord High Substitute. Pooh-Bah demurs: "*Such an appointment would realize my fondest dreams. But no, at any sacrifice, I must set bounds to my insatiable ambition.*" They thereupon begin a trio, in which Ko-Ko says that to kill himself would be to deprive Titipu of all his new ideas, and so it would be a social disaster for him to die; Pooh-Bah claims that he would like nothing better than to volunteer, but that there can be too much of a good thing (insatiable pride) and he must discipline himself, while Pish-Tush urges them on. The trio ends in a splendid *cabaletta*, which all three sing at once, and which gathers together alliteration, onomatopoeia, and end-line accents depicting the fall of the ax, which is Gilbert at his finest:

> *To sit in solemn silence in a dull, dark dock*
> *In a pestilential prison, with a life-long lock,*
> *Awaiting the sensation of a short, sharp shock,*
> *From a cheap and chippy chopper on a big, black block!*

Indeed, Gilbert's handling of the difficult poetic nineteenth-century habit of alliteration should be contrasted with Wagner's, for Gilbert manages to keep the use from becoming overly obtrusive even when he uses it for other than comic purposes. In his most ambitious libretto for Sullivan, *The Yeomen of the Guard*, he created the character of Jack Point the jester, who almost runs away with the operetta. The bittersweet quality of Jack Point's hopeless love for Elsie is thoroughly in keeping with the pathetic nature of clowns stretching back to Shakespeare and the *commedia*. His duet with Elsie, *"I have a song to sing, O!"* so beautifully partnered by Sullivan's bittersweet music, is not only the central song of the operetta, reprised at the end, but also recalls (quite consciously) the great Shakespearean fool's songs, such as Feste's *"For the rain it raineth every day,"* from *Twelfth Night*. In its original form, in Act I, the song, which is an agglutinative ballad, picking up lines that change and develop the story, ends happily, with the merrymaid rejecting the "peacock popinjay" for the love of the merryman. At the end of the operetta, however, Elsie has chosen Fairfax, and Point can only reprise the song in its pathetic aspect, with a comment by Elsie that clouds over the finale and gives the operetta that curious incompleteness which is both its strength and its weakness:

> POINT: *For I have a song to sing, O!*
> . . . .
> *It is sung to the moon*
> *By a love-lorn loon,*
> *Who fled from the mocking throng, O!*
> *It's the song of a merryman, moping mum,*
> *Whose soul was sad, and whose glance was glum,*
> *Who sipped no sup, and who craved no crumb,*
> *As he sighed for the love of a ladye!*
> . . . .
> ELSIE: *I have a song to sing, O!*
> . . . .
> *It is sung with the ring*
> *Of the songs maids sing*
> *Who love with a love life-long, O!*
> *It's the song of a merrymaid, nestling near,*
> *Who loved her lord—but who dropped a tear*
> *At the moan of a merryman, moping mum,*
> *Whose soul was sad, and whose glance was glum,*
> *Who sipped no sup, and who craved no crumb,*
> *As he sighed for the love of a ladye!*

ALL: *Heighdy! heighdy!*
        Misery me, lackadaydee!
    He sipped no sup, and he craved no crumb,
       As he sighed for the love of a ladye!
(Fairfax embraces Elsie, as Point falls insensible at their feet.)

Gilbert's taste and grace in his handling of alliteration is equaled by the flexibility of his verse, in terms of line-length and assonance. In his librettos Gilbert showed the uses to which poetry could still be put, at least in comic opera, and his dazzling success ushered in an era of fine comic verse in the operetta, as well as in its Anglo-Saxon offshoot, the musical comedy. Superior versifiers such as Noël Coward, P. G. Wodehouse, Cole Porter, Ira Gershwin, Lorenz Hart, and Alan Jay Lerner would have appeared without Gilbert, but he must stand godfather to their achievement in the same way that Goldoni stands godfather to the comic-opera libretto.

Aside from the verse, the single quality that is most striking about the Gilbert librettos is their contemporaneity. The idea of making fun of the foibles of society was hardly new with Gilbert —or with Meilhac and Halévy—but where Gilbert differs from his French (and even from his English sources, in *The Beggar's Opera*) is in his essential wholehearted embracing of the political and social structure. *Patience* may satirize the Pre-Raphaelite movement, *H.M.S. Pinafore* the Royal Navy, *Ruddigore* the landed aristocracy and the Gothic tale, *Princess Ida* the feminist movement, and *Iolanthe* the House of Lords, but what is being satirized is the excesses, never the system itself. This is emphasized again and again:

>   *For a British tar is a soaring soul*
>   *As free as a mountain bird!*
>   *His energetic fist should be ready to resist*
>   *A dictatorial word!*
>   (*H.M.S. Pinafore;* I)

>   *He is an Englishman!*
>   *For he himself has said it,*
>   *And it's greatly to his credit,*
>   *That he is an Englishman!*

. . . .
For he might have been a Roosian
A French, or Turk, or Proosian,
Or perhaps Itali-an!
But in spite of all temptations
To belong to other nations,
    He remains an Englishman![3]
(*H.M.S. Pinafore;* II and finale)

Similarly, the victorious pirates in *The Pirates of Penzance* are persuaded to surrender because of the majesty of Queen Victoria. "*We yield at once, with humbled mien/Because, with all our faults, we love our Queen!*" There may be an air of satire in the statement, but the undertone, as throughout all of Gilbert's work, is favorable to the continuation of the status quo.

Gilbert's librettos, then, are an almost ideal portrait of Victorian England in its eclectic dynamism as well as in its smugness and insularity. Part of the immense popularity of his operettas is owing to this very fact: that he was able to tweak noses while never giving actual offense, wrapping his satires in a coating of never-never nonsense that removed them still further from reality. This facet of Gilbert's also carried over to the lighter musicals of the twentieth century, with one major exception. Bertolt Brecht, when he went back to *The Beggar's Opera* for subject matter, took both the shell and the social protest that was at the core of that work. His celebrated line from *Die Dreigroschenoper* (1928; m., Weill), "*Erst kommt das Fressen, dann kommt die Moral*" ("First feed the gut, then invent the moral excuse"), struck at the root of the lighter comedy as it had developed in France, England, and the United States in the nineteenth and early twentieth centuries.

---

(3) This last sung to a parody of England's greatest composer, Handel. G. K. Chesterton considered this song a "mordant criticism" on patriotism (see William Darlington: *The World of Gilbert and Sullivan,* pp. 73–4), but time has definitely softened any such impact.

Chapter Nineteen

The French Libretto
of the Late Nineteenth and
Early Twentieth Centuries

THE IMPORTANCE of the works of Hector Berlioz (1803–69)
to the libretto is manifold, in terms of the history of French
opera in general, of librettistic ideas of the twentieth century, and
of the works themselves as counterweights to the operas of Richard
Wagner. As has been stated before, Berlioz's greatest opera, *Les
Troyens* (composed 1856–8 to his own libretto, a free adaptation
of Vergil's *Aeneid*), was the culmination of the French *tragédie
lyrique*—a sort of winter rose—and more especially the culmination of that strain of the *tragédie lyrique*, never particularly well
remembered in either word or music, to which graftings of Metastasian *opera seria* had been added. Berlioz's theme of the obsessive
concept of duty, seen primarily in Énée's progress toward Italy,
but secondarily in Cassandre's love for Troie and Didon's for
Carthage, is Metastasian (or, if you will, Metastasian by way of
Corneille), whereas the omnipresence of the gods as reminders
of that duty—and the positive use of *le merveilleux* at the end of
the opera—derive directly from Lully and Quinault through countless other examples. A measure of Berlioz's masterly handling of
the story in its reduction to operatic terms is the way in which
he kept the heroic (in *tragédie lyrique* and not Wagnerian terms)
element always in the forefront while working in the love story
of Énée and Didon. The love story has overshadowed the epic
simply because the truncation and dismemberment of the work
for concert performances—and the dearth of complete perform-

ances of the entire opera—have led to a highlighting of the portions featuring the love story: the Royal Hunt and Storm Scene and the love duet. These two excerpts, of course, are excellent examples of Berlioz's abilities. The Royal Hunt and Storm is a classic French *tableau vivant*, combining pantomime and *merveilleux* elements and making use of the corps de ballet in a thoroughly integrated manner. At the end of the scene, the wood sprites mockingly intone the *paroles scéniques* of the opera, thus ironically reminding Énée of his duty while he makes love to Didon: *"Italie! Ha! Italie!"* The love duet shows Berlioz as adept at making constructive use of Shakespeare as Boito would be later; he lifts the *"In such a night . . ."* scene from the end of *The Merchant of Venice*, transposes the references, and puts it to use in a Vergilian epic setting. It not only fits in perfectly, but serves as contrast and complement to the previous, fevered love scene (i.e., the Royal Hunt and Storm).[1] Yet even here Berlioz does not lose the focus: this time the god Mercure appears, to pronounce *"Italie!"*[2] Berlioz may have been a Romantic, but he had enough of a classical education to know when to sacrifice overt romanticism to the demands of a non-Romantic libretto.

Berlioz used librettists for his first opera, *Benvenuto Cellini* (1838; l., Léon de Wailly and Auguste Barbier), which was a failure when first given, and he toyed with the idea of having Scribe write him a *Faust* libretto; but increasingly he realized that, given his own talents as a writer, he and only he could supply the words, as he did for *Les Troyens*. His only other opera, *Béatrice et Bénédict*, again saw him as adapter of the text, this time Shakespeare's *Much Ado About Nothing*.

The chief assets of Berlioz's librettistic work are his verse and his imagination. The latter is only partially in evidence in the two opera librettos that he wrote, because both of them attempt to conform to the conventional idea of what an opera is. *Les*

---

(1) Strangely enough, these two scenes reflect two of the great love scenes of nineteenth-century opera. The first can be compared with *Tristan*, which also has a hunt, if no storm, while the second foreshadows the Act I close of *Otello*. It is evident that Boito modeled the Otello-Desdemona scene, particularly the slow withdrawal upstage into the night, on the Berlioz one.
(2) Note the differing use of dramatic irony from Wagner's: Berlioz's use is more in keeping with the *deus ex machina* tradition of the god removed and above, while in Wagner the god is very much a part of the action and affected by it.

Troyens is a synthesis of prior French classic opera, and as such is an important libretto, but it represents more of a conscious effort of will on Berlioz's part to control the adaptation and to channel it into a *tragédie lyrique* mold. Berlioz was never the master of dramaturgy that Wagner was, but his strong musical sense of drama did much to offset whatever shortcomings he had in stage-craft, and often he supplied touches both appropriate and moving. The beginning of the fifth act of *Les Troyens* is an example. It opens on a scene at night showing the Trojan fleet at anchor. Hylas, a sailor, sings a song of homesickness for his homeland from his post in the crow's nest of the ship, and falls asleep. So far, so Wagner. But then Berlioz focuses on two sentries guarding the tents. "He dreams of his homeland," says one. "Which he will never see again," says the other. The Trojan chiefs come on stage to prepare for the departure, and hear the shades calling *"Italie!"* The focus shifts back to the sentries, who have heard nothing. They do not want to leave Carthage, life being easy for them in the city, and they grumble. They are silenced by the appearance of Énée, who then delivers his great *scène*, *"Inutiles regrets"* ("Useless regrets"), in which he reluctantly capitulates to his duty. The appearance of the sentries is a masterstroke (which Berlioz had used before, in 1854, in *L'Enfance du Christ*), because it gives the scene—and the opera—an added dimension of distance. The sentries have not heard the voices, know nothing of these epic yearnings which drive the great and powerful, and only wish to live as calmly as possible. This use of the common people in *Les Troyens* can only recall its use in Busenello, where the effect was similar.

Berlioz's verse is some of the best French operatic verse of the nineteenth century. It has the merits of a basic musicality, a suppleness—and that directness typical of French writing and in direct contradistinction to Wagner's verse. The tone of the love duet from *Les Troyens* may be Shakespeare's, but Berlioz has managed to capture much of it in his words—no mean achievement, as the English is some of the most beautiful stage poetry in the language.

> *Par une telle nuit, le front ceint de cytise,*
> *votre mère Vénus suivit le bel Anchise*
> *aux bosquets de l'Ida.*

. . . .
Par une telle nuit, la pudique Diane
laissa tomber enfin son voile diaphane
aux yeux d'Endymion.[3]

(IV, last)

Didon's apostrophe to her city and her people, as she prepares for death following Énée's departure is, quite simply, superb:

Adieu, fière cité, qu'un généreux effort
si promptement éleva florissante!
Ma tendre soeur qui me suivis, errante;
adieu, mon peuple, adieu, rivage vénéré,
toi qui jadis m'accueillis suppliante;
adieu, beau ciel d'Afrique, astres que j'admirais
aux nuits d'ivresse et d'extase infinie;
je ne vous verrai plus, ma carrière est finie![4]

(V, i)

Yet the final importance of Berlioz as a librettist rests less on the quality of his verse than on the extent and daring of his imagination—that "romantic" quality which was so extreme as to be his triumph and despair during the nineteenth century. What has become increasingly evident, particularly since 1960 or so, is the extent to which Berlioz as a writer for the stage unconsciously anticipated certain librettistic approaches of the mid-twentieth century. These anticipations cannot be seen in the two works he wrote for the conventional operatic stage, but in the works he called by names other than "opera," but which involve words and scenes—which involve, in short, a libretto. *Roméo et Juliette* (1839), *La Damnation de Faust* (1846, in collaboration with Almire Gandonnière), and *L'Enfance du Christ* (1854) are three of them.

---

(3) "In such a night, her forehead wreathed in cytisus, your mother Venus followed the handsome Anchises into the thickets of Mount Ida . . . In such a night the chaste Diana let fall at last her diaphanous veil before Endymion's eyes."
  The placement of the word *"enfin"* in the line is highly evocative.
(4) "Farewell, proud city, which a concerted effort made to flourish so quickly. Tender sister, who followed my wanderings; farewell, my people, farewell, sacred shore, you who welcomed me when I came as a suppliant; farewell, fair African sky, stars that I admired on nights of rapture and infinite ecstasy. I shall see you no more, my life is over."

Berlioz broke free from the traditional operatic libretto of the Scribe type because his imagination, playing over the glories of Shakespeare and Goethe, could not conceive of those master-pieces being cut up and dried in the accepted manner. Berlioz felt that he had to re-create the essence of the work in music, and thus worked from an emotional rather than from an intellectual point of view (unlike his experience with *Les Troyens*). The French, in turn, considered these works as outside the realm of opera—and, indeed, outcasts from every category—although both Berlioz's *Roméo* and his *Faust* greatly influenced the traditional approach of Gounod's operas musically and librettistically.

Precisely this structural freedom is what commends these Berlioz works to the mid-twentieth century. If the staging problems of a work like *La Damnation de Faust* were such that the "dramatic legend" could only be approximated with the resources available in the nineteenth century—and thus the work could be considered a fevered hybrid performed more for the individual pieces than for the totality—the technical advances of the twentieth century, particularly in terms of lighting, have simplified and clarified a good deal of what remained inchoate even to Berlioz. Further, the twentieth-century celebration of disjunctiveness, which is today a virtue, whereas in the nineteenth century it was a fault, has worked to upgrade these Berlioz works and to allow them to be seen as structural precursors of such librettos as *Sette Canzoni* (1920; m. and l., Gian Francesco Malipiero), *Four Saints in Three Acts*, and *Intolleranza* (1961; m., Luigi Nono; l., Nono, from an idea by Angelo Maria Ripellino).

Having given himself freedom by, in effect, removing his works from a dependence on the formulas of the *opéra* (whatever branch), Berlioz could create works responsive primarily to his own ideas. These works would not necessarily "reproduce" their originals, as even Barbier and Carré's libretto reproduced *Romeo and Juliet*, but they would nonetheless come far closer to the essence of the original. Similarly, this freedom of approach could spill over into other areas, such as the poetry of the work. The hissing and churning chorus of demons and damned in *La Damnation de Faust* is both original and highly effective. Nonsense verse had often been used in a libretto, but almost always in a humorous context. Here Berlioz envisioned it as a verbal counterpart to a musical depiction of Hell. The words themselves are not, therefore, nonsense, but verbalizations in an unknown tongue of horrors too vast and supernatural to be translated:

> *Tradioun marexil firtrudinxé burrudixé*
> *fory my dinkorlitz. O méri kariu! O mevixé!* etc.

Yet these Berlioz works, for all their librettistic daring and appositeness today, are hardly altogether novel. A work like the "dramatic legend" of Faust, taken from the Goethe epic, can be seen as the nineteenth-century French and Italian "number" formula carried to an extreme in which the numbers stand almost by themselves, and in which the "numbers" can include pure music as well as sung texts. Pure music had long been a part of French opera in the form of preludes, intermezzos, and even stretches of ballet music: Berlioz took the idea further in terms of the amount of pure music and its importance in relation to the story. Thus, in *Roméo*, the love scene—the core of the work—is left to the orchestra alone, which bypasses neatly the problems that Gounod's librettists had to face. The structure of these non-operatic works, moreover, in its very loose way does conform to the over-all structure of French opera from Lully to Meyerbeer: *La Damnation de Faust* climaxes before the end, on the tam-tam stroke of the descent to pandemonium and the frenzy of the Hell Scene, then ascends to the skies in pure French *lieto fine cum merveilleux* style with the *Apothéose de Marguerite*.

The one Berlioz work in which this "number" formula is carried to an absolute extreme is, of course, *Lélio*, the sequel to the *Symphonie fantastique*. This piece was held to be, even by the Romantic nineteenth century, too much the heterogeneous product of a fevered mind, easily ridiculed as a farrago of nonsense. The mid-twentieth sees it in a different light. This collection of songs and choruses is bound together by the imaginings and musings of the narrator, Lélio, and as such is less a series of rambling musings than the inner life and thought of an artist, and what to the nineteenth century was a concatenation of disparate elements is, to the world of James Joyce's *Ulysses*, if not logical, at least understandable. Lélio's language is certainly that of the Romantic nineteenth century; his Romantic fulminations and poses (such as finishing an excoriation of those who desecrate Shakespeare, then deciding to become a bandit, and arming himself with pistols, a rifle, and a saber that happen to be lying on a nearby table) are fully tied to the world of Hugo and Lamartine, but in a curious way *Lélio* does more than reflect its age. It foreshadows in a much more comprehensive way than, say, Marie Pappenheim's mono-drama for Arnold Schönberg, *Erwartung* (1909), that inner world of the mind which would have such importance in the twentieth-century novel and would come to be reflected in the movies and, lastly, in opera with works such as *Intolleranza* and Michel Butor's *Votre Faust* (1969; m., Henri Pousseur).

What can quickly be perceived is that Berlioz as librettist is the real antithesis to the Wagnerian esthetic: Berlioz, rather than Meilhac and Halévy or Boito. If *Erwartung* follows *Tristan* in its explorations of the mind, it remains as hermetically sealed as the former work. Berlioz's personal musings, extravagant as they were, open out both in language and in form, and, although they finally are responsive to French theatrical structural ideas, they embrace them in a far looser context. Berlioz was never the *dramaturge* that Wagner was; he never had the knowledge of the stage, and only occasionally (as in *Les Troyens*) showed the continuous control of it that Wagner had. If his characters have no great subtlety, they have a nobility of stature and a personalization through melody and orchestration[5] which are different in intent and result from Wagner's. Berlioz as a librettist is far greater than the sum of his works, and his importance can be judged properly only a century after he died.

Berlioz had little influence on the French libretto of his time. *Les Troyens*, his greatest operatic work, was seen only in shortened form in Paris in 1863, and not again until the twentieth century. Yet the history of the French libretto after the Franco-Prussian War of 1870 is hardly barren. If the *tragédie lyrique* had faded out, and if the enlarged *opéra comique* continued in adaptations of the formulas Scribe had provided, a new injection of purpose was provided by the operas of Wagner.

Wagner's oft-expounded ideals had been largely ignored in France, particularly after the *Tannhäuser* fiasco at the Opéra

---

(5) Whereas Wagner relied on short motives to limn characterization (as with Gutrune), Berlioz used the longer, more Gluck-derived musical lines. Thus Marguerite's great aria, "*L'amour, l'ardente flamme*," becomes in its whole a personalization of her character, and the whole canvas of the flickering darts of orchestration paint both Mercutio (the Mab Scherzo) and Méphisto.

in 1861, but a combination of bourgeois and reactionary critical opposition to them, plus Wagner's insistent claims to artistic purity (typified by his withdrawal to an artistic Valhalla, Bayreuth)—a purity that was a talisman to the nineteenth-century artist—began to have an effect. The existence of the *Revue wagnérienne* (1885–7) drew together the lovers of Wagner and prosyletized for the Master's ideas throughout the French intellectual community, influencing not only the music of the period but the Symbolist poetic movement as well.

It was obvious that this growing popularity of Wagner would debouch upon the French libretto. The insistence on myth, and preferably myth of a semi-savage civilization, the larger-than-life characterizations, the emphasis on virile verse, particularly in its alliterative and allusive guises—all found their way into the French libretto of the eighties and nineties and into the twentieth century.

A curious phenomenon of French musical history is that almost every French composer at one time or another writes an opera; as if the form is a requisite for even those of non-dramatic accomplishments. Henri Duparc, who wrote barely twenty pieces of music during his lifetime, began (and destroyed) an opera, and it is a safe conjecture that the example of Wagner tempted other composers into the field, either in admiration or in opposition.

Ernest Reyer's *Sigurd*, although closely linked thematically to Wagner, is probably the least affected by the German of the later French *Grands Opéras*, being both musically and librettistically more responsive to the *tragédie lyrique* and to Berlioz's *Les Troyens* than to the *Ring* cycle. But, beginning with Emmanuel Chabrier's *Gwendoline* (1886; l., Catulle Mendès)—note, three years after Wagner's death—the Wagnerian strain entered French music and the French libretto and pushed aside the paler replicas of earlier French styles, such as Saint-Saëns' *Henry VIII* (1883; l., Léonice Detroyat and Paul Silvestre) and Massenet's *Le Cid* (1886; l., Adolphe d'Ennery, Louis Gallet, and Édouard Blau). The Wagnerian influence on the libretto in France can be noted at its most pronounced in *Gwendoline* and in Édouard Lalo's *Le Roi d'Ys* (1888; l., Édouard Blau), Vincent d'Indy's *Fervaal* (1897; l., d'Indy) and *L'Étranger* (1903; l., d'Indy), and Ernest Chausson's *Le Roi Arthus* (1903; l., Chausson). The Wagnerian esthetic in assimilated form is seen most clearly in Debussy's *Pelléas et Mélisande* (1902; l., Debussy, from Maurice Maeterlinck's play).

When one examines features of the more obvious Wagnerian-French librettos, two points immediately stand out. The first is that in all cases except that of *Le Roi d'Ys*, the mythologizing has led the subject away from any connection with France or French past history or legend. Whereas one of the major themes of the *Ring* cycle was precisely this retelling of a part of the myth that lay in the background of German history, the French librettists chose to follow Wagner's example in *Tristan* and divorce the myth from any national mythic root. *Gwendoline* is a story of Danes and Saxons, *Le Roi Arthus* is about King Arthur, *Fervaal* is a mysticalization of a Druid tale (replete with Druid names such as Grympuig, Arfagard, and Gwellkingubar). The second point is that, despite all the pseudo-Wagnerian trappings,[6] these French operas retain a large amount of the French Grand Operatic structure. The librettos are still considered in terms of the number of tableaus, and the numbers themselves, although more loosely treated, are still clearly separated. Finally, on no account was the *éclatant merveilleux* ending to be abandoned. Thus *Le Roi d'Ys* ends on a general flood, and *Fervaal*, which in its lengthy monologues and mystical yearnings looks to *Parsifal*, closes on an example of classic French operatic theater:

> A great flash of lightning encompasses the sky, and thunder rumbles under the feet of Fervaal, who . . . has fallen to one knee.
> Sudden calm. Wind and storm have ceased. A roseate glow tints the highest clouds, and the Mystic Chorus begins anew, this time more distinct. Fervaal listens.
>
> . . . .
> Fervaal disappears into the clouds, now ever more tinted with color. . . .

It is almost as if the French, far from understanding the meaning of the Wagnerian concept of the *Gesamtkunstwerk*, took back

---

(6) One Wagnerian feature, the attempt to get away from calling an opera an opera, is reflected in the avoidance of the terms *opéra* and *tragédie lyrique* in categorizing these works. Thus *L'Étranger* and *Fervaal* are called "*actions musicales*," *Ariane et Barbe-Bleue* is a "*conte musical*," and *Louise* a "*roman musical*."

those elements that Wagner had himself taken from the French and pretended they were Wagnerisms, whereas in fact they were nothing but French, though slightly more puffed out with philosophical pretension.

Catulle Mendès's poetic libretto for *Gwendoline* has its moments of unintentional amusement, but is on the whole a stronger poetic effort than most French operas of the time. Mendès was an ardent Wagnerian, a contributor to the *Revue wagnérienne*, and he took over Wagner's verbal virility and his use of assonance. Yet, in the final analysis, Mendès's verse is less indebted to Wagner than to the musical qualities of Victor Hugo, who by the route of Mendès's lesser gifts at last enters the operatic lists *verbally*.

A few excerpts from the love duet in *Gwendoline* will demonstrate this influence. Lines such as *"Laisse-moi respirer le miel de tes cheveux"*[7] and *"Soir nuptial, délice/profond/où notre âme se pâme et glisse/et fond!/Dans le ciel infini de l'amour pur et beau,/nos deux coeurs sont les deux ailes d'un même oiseau!"*[8] owe far less to Wagner than to French poetic sources, and are markedly superior to Scribe's doggerel, and even to the bland poesy of Barbier and Carré.

The story of *Gwendoline* is timeworn: fierce Harald, the cruel leader of the Danes, has come with his warriors to ravage the peaceful Saxon countryside. He sees Gwendoline, and they fall in love, much to the displeasure of Gwendoline's Saxon father. The two are married, but Gwendoline's father uses the marriage to allow the Saxons to attack the unarmed Danes. Harald is struck down by the father ("See, Woden, I die laughing!"), after which Gwendoline commits suicide. But before both of them ascend to Valhalla there is plenty of time for a final duet, for a Saxon-instigated forest fire, and for the final tableau of Harald and Gwendoline, etched against the flames, dying "in arrogant splendor, without falling, their backs against the tree, in a red-lit apotheosis."

Mendès's use of word-sound to duplicate the meaning is well shown in Harald's speech to his beloved:

---

(7) "Let me breathe the honey of your hair."
(8) "Wedding night, profound delight, in which our soul swoons, dissolves, melts away to nothing. In the infinite sky of pure and beautiful love, our two hearts are the two wings of the same bird."

Gwendoline! Ce nom est doux comme le bruit
de l'écume qui court sur la grève la nuit.
Le mien est rudement sonore
comme le choc
de la vague qui bat le roc!
Harald! Harald![9]

(I, iv)

The final duet and chorus, however, though clearly intended as homage to Wagner, only demonstrate the gulf of taste and of talent which separates Wagner from his imitators:

HARALD: *C'est ce soir que Toujours commence!*
GWENDOLINE: *Montons vers les splendeurs du gouffre aérien!*

. . . .

HARALD: *Woden! Woden! l'heure est venue*
de prendre vers le beau Walhalla notre essor.
GWENDOLINE: *Sur un fier cheval blanc je serai dans la nue*
la Walkyrie au casque d'or!

. . . .

CHOEUR: *(dans une épouvantable extatique)*
Le palais du Dieu magnanime
s'ouvre devant les pas du couple glorieux;
ils prennent place enfin dans la salle sublime
à la table auguste des Dieux![1]

(III, last)

If these operas aped certain aspects of Wagner within a still largely French framework, an opera such as *Pelléas et Mélisande*, which is in so many ways the quintessence of French sensibility, nuance, and delicate symbolism, may be said to be musically and

---

(9) "Gwendoline! That name is soft as the sound of the foam that runs across the beach at night. Mine is brutally sonorous, like the shock of the wave that hits the rock! Harald! Harald!"

(1) "Tonight Eternity begins." "Let us climb toward the splendors of the empyrean vast." "Woden! Woden! the time has come to make our way toward the beautiful Valhalla." "On a proud white horse I shall be in the clouds [does Mendès actually intend a pun at this point, so that Gwendoline is transformed into a Folies Bergère tableau?], the Valkyrie in a golden helmet!" (In a tremendous ecstatic transport) "The palace of the all-forgiving God opens at the footsteps of the glorious couple; they take their place at last in the sublime hall at the august table of the gods!"

The regular meter of this chorus argues against the ecstatic instructions, and the "*Dieu magnanime*" seems leagues removed from the barbarous gods of Norseland.

librettistically an assimilation of Wagner's precepts. The manner
of the construction of the libretto, however, apart from the fact
that superficially it was done by the composer, differs markedly
from Wagner's habits and brings into the libretto a new element:
the transference almost intact of a stage play to the operatic
stage. Da Ponte's *Le Nozze di Figaro*—to select an example—
stayed reasonably close to the Beaumarchais original, and works
such as Boito's adaptations of Shakespeare for Verdi captured the
spirit of the original, but in all cases there were changes in emphasis,
in tone, and, most important, in language, not only by translation
but also by adaptation. Debussy's *Pelléas*, however, is Maeterlinck's
Pelléas with minor excisions: its language is Maeterlinck's language,
and Debussy's apprehension of the ethos of Maeterlinck's play
is uncanny.

Debussy perceived the core of Wagner's esthetic, which was
the primacy of the story and its meanings and the use of the music
to heighten, define, and expand the words. The abstract qualities
that Wagner introduced into *Tristan* (and elaborated on at Wagnerian length) are here crystallized but made even more abstract.
Mélisande's "*Je ne suis pas heuresuse*" ("I am not happy") has more
definiteness than the mouthings of Isolde, but is also far more
elusive: does it refer to her human condition, her marriage with
Golaud, her love for Pelléas, her wanting or not wanting a child
—or is she merely shamming?[2] The whole is liquid, shimmering,
unseizable, in contradistinction to Verdi's highly definite use of
the *parola scenica*, and it depends on a fluid and interdependent
correspondence between word and music.

The notion of the *Gesamtkunstwerk* is, of course, integral to
Pelléas, and is reflected there much more pervasively than in
Wagner. It is almost impossible to conceive of the text without
the music—which is paradoxical because the text was, of course,
created without thought of its being used as the basis for an opera
—and, moreover, no part of the whole can be easily separated from
the rest. Maeterlinck's play is lapidary in the sense that what a
character says in one scene adds to what he says five scenes later;

---

(2) This last possibility has been put forward by Edward Green-
field among others, with the suggestion that Mélisande was not the
fragile sweet *ondine* she has always been assumed to be, but rather
a minx, using other people for her own private purposes. The ambiguities of Maeterlinck's play are such that this interpretation can
be justified.

that any single speech or sentence has only limited value (in contrast to *"la maledizione"* from *Rigoletto* or *"E avvanti a lui tremava tutta Roma"* from *Tosca*) but, taken in context of the scene and of all the scenes, contributes to a powerful vision of the whole.

Debussy's libretto, which is Maeterlinck's play, apparently strikes at the root of the librettist's art, for its success both as an enhanced play and as an opera seems to obviate the necessity of a separate form. Of course this is not, and has not been, the case, except in unusual instances, for many reasons. *Pelléas* and the other cardinal example of the play-as-libretto, *Wozzeck*, are both understated works, in which the unspoken overtones are immense. As such, they conform to the dehydrating process that any librettist must to some extent accomplish in his work. Yet this very "play" quality, as well as its symbolist provenance, frees Debussy's libretto from that dependence on either the *opéra comique* "number" formula or any other relics of the French musical stage. *Pelléas et Mélisande* stands alone, and though strands of theatrical influence can be detected in Maeterlinck's work, his "libretto" is by far the freshest example of the genre of its time. Indeed, it is hard to think of another French example that is so free of ancestors—structural, poetic, characterizational—and whose entire tone is so self-contained. Just as the kingdom of Allemonde symbolically embraces the world (*"alle-monde"*) but exists in a world of its own, so *Pelléas* synthesizes Wagner and French opera but remains stubbornly independent and unique. Neither of the other notable uses of Maeterlinck's plays in operatic form—*Ariane et Barbe-Bleue* (1907; m., Paul Dukas; l., adapted from Maeterlinck) and *Monna Vanna* (1909; m., Henri Février; l., Maeterlinck)—approaches *Pelléas* in this quality.

Wagner and his ideas, however, did not command sole attention in the fin-de-siècle French libretto. Besides the works that followed the paths blazed by Scribe, there were other, notable, developments. A curious one, which is of definite relevance in the history of the libretto, is Louis Gallet's idea of *poésie mélique*.

We have seen that, during the nineteenth century and even earlier, the trend of the libretto was steadily toward prose. By the 1890's, even librettists had begun to be aware of the movement, and in 1894, in the preface to his libretto of *Thaïs* for Massenet, Gallet set out his reasoning for *poésie mélique*. In Gallet's eyes the time had come for the (admittedly staggering, in French terms) step of the introduction of prose into the libretto,[3] and Gallet had prepared the ground not only by examining other works for evidences of prose but also by justifying its introduction in the accepted French "logical" manner. He said that because most composers knew little or nothing about literature or poetry (Gallet is tactful enough to excuse Gounod, Saint-Saëns, and Massenet of such faults) and because most composers are egoists, they have "deformed poetry, without regard to its rules, in order to juxtapose it exactly to the contours of their music," and this had resulted in bad verse and monstrous adaptations from the original. Any reading of the previous pages will make clear how inane Gallet's charges are, at least in relation to verse: although there have been isolated examples of composers forcing the use of awkward constructions for music's sake, the use of the alexandrine and the Scribean penchant for choral vapidity owed nothing to any composer and everything to both tradition and librettistic mediocrity.

Gallet claimed that he had found a viable substitute to poetry, one that did not take the libretto into the forbidden realms of prose but still divorced it from dependence on rhyme. This was a system developed by Monsieur Gevaërt, the director of the Brussels Conservatory, who had set out from the logical premise that, melody being so free, why should poetry keep its rhythms? Gevaërt, with an almost hypnotic rectitude, related *poésie mélique* to the ancient Greeks (could he have done otherwise?), and made out a series of rules which included sonority and harmony of words, lack of rhyme and hiatuses, and freer metrical limitations.

What this meant in terms of specifics was revealed in the *Thaïs* libretto: short lines (which could involve rhyme) run together with dashes—in fact, not greatly different from the standard poetry of the later-nineteenth-century French libretto:

> THAÏS: *Ô mon miroir fidèle, — rassure-moi; dis-moi*
> *que je suis toujours belle, — que je serai belle*
> *éternellement; — que rien ne flétrira les roses*
> *de mes lèvres, — que rien ne ternira l'or pur de*

---

(3) Gallet, and all other commentators on prosody in French opera, blandly ignore the fact that the spoken-prose dialogues of *opéra comique* had thoroughly undercut the charmed nature of poetry in French opera.

*mes cheveux; — dis-moi que je suis belle et que
je serai belle — éternellement; éternellement!*[4]
(II, i)

If Gallet's *poésie mélique* did not provide an original approach, it did provide the way station on the road to the prose libretto, which was reached very quickly afterwards. And by coincidence Gallet himself was involved. Charles Gounod, in his preface to the incidental music he wrote for Molière's dark comedy *Georges Dandin* (c. 1873), had called for the creation of the prose libretto, but no one had stepped forward to provide it. But during the 1890's the composer Alfred Bruneau began setting works of Émile Zola as operas. Bruneau adored Zola's works, and tried to get the older man to write him an original libretto. Zola, already a world figure for his novels, was interested but hung back. Louis Gallet thereupon worked up a Zola novel, *Le Rêve* (1891), into a libretto that Bruneau set to music. Zola became interested in the creation of the opera, and involved himself in details of the production. Gallet thereupon provided Bruneau with a second adaptation of Zola, *L'Attaque du moulin* (1893), which recounted an incident from the Franco-Prussian War (although in the opera the war was left obscure) in a manner corresponding to that of the Italian veristic school, and was the direct precursor of Massenet's veristic opera *La Navarraise* (1894; l., Jules Clarétie and Henri Cain). Zola had involved himself even more with the creation of *L'Attaque du moulin,* and when the opera was a success, he decided to take over the writing of Bruneau's librettos. These he wrote in prose.

Zola is the most underrated of the French libretto writers. He came to the libretto at the very end of his artistic life, when he had retreated from the style of naturalism which had made him famous. Although in libretto terms his works in the form are more representative of his talents than are the librettos of other literary figures, such as Hugo and Goethe—and are also far more important

---

(4) "O my faithful mirror, reassure me, tell me I shall always be beautiful, that I shall be beautiful forever, that nothing will fade the rose of my lips, that nothing will tarnish the pure gold of my hair, tell me that I am beautiful and that I shall be beautiful—eternally! Eternally!"

historically—they nevertheless are only a pendant to his novels. Although he wrote six librettos, he died after only two of them were performed, and although the six demonstrate a variety of approach and of ideas about the libretto, they cannot be said to be an oeuvre as can Wagner's or Hofmannsthal's librettos. Finally, they were tied to Bruneau's music, which, while accomplished, was never as strong as the librettos,[5] was accused of being mere declamatory music to highlight Zola's text, and has since lapsed into oblivion. Yet it was Zola, in a curious way an outsider to the libretto—an amateur—who summed up the developments of the French libretto of the nineteenth century in a purely French way: testament to his literary merits and to his deep interest in the art form.

Zola as a librettist invokes continual comparison with his twentieth-century confrère Hugo von Hofmannsthal. Both men came to the libretto from a successful outside career, and both were held in awe by their composer-partners. Further, both of them—like Stravinsky and the neo-classicists in music—were in revolt against the (in this case, librettistic) esthetic of Richard Wagner, and were trying to provide a counterweight of equal importance within their own cultures. In both cases this involved the use of genre elements and of symbolism (and, consequently, at least a partial adoption of Wagnerian traits). Most important, Zola and Hofmannsthal, like Wagner, created their works from the resources of their own minds, and although the finished works, particularly in Hofmannsthal's case, invoked a multitude of sources, they could be termed original. Lastly, both men brought to the fore a humanity and a focus on the meanings of love deeper than the normal libretto idea of love, which together give their work a special appeal and aura.

Zola's six librettos include a one-act retelling of the tale of Lazarus, *Lazare* (set by Bruneau but never performed), and a fairy tale, *Violaine la chevelue* (not set), which, although they demonstrate the range of Zola's work, are not as important as his completed operas. Likewise *Silvanire* (not set), which is subtitled *Paris in Love* and revolves around a sculptor, suffers from direct comparison with such genre works as *La Bohème* and Charpentier's

---

(5) Zola's librettos are a classic example of the libretto overshadowing the music—another example are the operas of Ferruccio Busoni.

Louise, not to mention Zola's own libretto *L'Enfant roi*, which was set after his death by Bruneau. The first of Zola's librettos, *Messidor* (1897; m., Bruneau) will be considered at greater length later. His next work, *L'Ouragan* (1901; m., Bruneau), the last that he was to see completed as an opera, is the story of love and hatred on a distant isle, in which the title (as is Zola's habit) symbolically highlights the theme. The hurricane that sweeps everything to its conclusion is an augmentation of the hurricane existing within the characters, and its focus on various aspects of love—the passionate love of Jeanine, the domineering love of Marianne, and the pure love of Lulu—is contrasted to hatred, which is, as is usual in all Zola librettos, expressed directly and without pretension: "Now, Richard, my brother, I am going to kill you like a dog." Each act is a self-contained entity, and each leads to the next. There is much to admire in the libretto, but a certain staginess and an unresolved quality keep it from being as distinguished as *Messidor* or *L'Enfant roi*, which was set in 1905 by Bruneau.

L'Enfant roi (The Child King) foreshadows Hofmannsthal's *Die Frau ohne Schatten* in its celebration of the begetting of children, but Zola's concern with enlightenment through understanding in love, while part of *Die Frau ohne Schatten*, is far closer to that of Hofmannsthal's posthumous libretto for Richard Strauss, *Arabella*. *L'Enfant roi* revolves around a Parisian baker and his wife: François and Madeleine. That they are deeply in love but childless is a canker in their relationship, but not so dangerous as Madeleine's secret. Before marrying François she had mothered a child, which she has hidden away with its grandmother. François discovers her secret, and the rest of the libretto dwells on his struggle to accept the child as his own and to forgive his wife for her youthful mistake. Needless anger and hurt being resolved in greater understanding is, of course, central to Hofmannsthal in the characters of Barak and his wife and Arabella and Mandryka; in *L'Enfant roi* the preoccupation is the same. Zola underlines the theme by a muted (in keeping with the genre orientation) use of symbolism, not only in the title but also in François' occupation: he provides Paris with the staff of life but cannot provide his wife with children. The two are intertwined in Zola's mind, as is shown in Madeleine's curtain lines: "*Mon François, mon Georget* [*her son*], *la maison est joyeuse et prospère! Paris s'éveille, il faut que*

Paris ait du pain pour la besogne géante de son enfantement!"[6]

As one would expect from a writer of stature, Zola's people are always alive, and his portrait of François in particular is very well drawn. The progress of the man toward understanding is set forward with great skill. At first François believes that his wife has a lover. She confesses her sin in a heartfelt speech, so typical of Zola's librettos and so foreign to most other librettos in its directness: "Forgive me, forgive me, François, forgive me for having lied to you for so long, forgive me for not having had the strength to cry out the truth before our marriage, forgive me for having afterward taken your love under false pretenses, since my love for you turned me into a coward, forgive me for not having confessed my secret womanly wretchedness and for not being able to be more than a wife who loves you!" François says she must choose between the child and himself. She chooses the child, and the two separate, a separation that only makes their torment worse.

Zola uses the character of the young scamp Auguste to set against the couple. It was he who, in a practical joking mood, had poisoned their happiness, and he cannot truly see what evil he has committed, for, in his estimation, children are encumbrances, impediments to a free life ("pleasure without pain"). When the couple splits, François becomes torpid and Auguste takes over the running of the bakery. Yet, because Madeleine and François are genuinely in love, Auguste's reign is doomed. Slowly the couple is forced together, as François begins to be able to understand his unhappiness:

> *Jaloux d'un enfant, je suis jaloux d'un*
> *enfant! Est-ce possible d'être tombé à cette*
> *misère? Moi qui en souhaitais un de tout mon*
> *désir éperdu, moi qui l'aurais adoré de tout*
> *mon coeur attendri! L'enfant, c'est la joie*
> *et la bonheur nécessaire, c'est l'âme sans*
> *laquelle la maison ne peut vivre!*
> *   Mais l'enfant d'un autre, non, non!*
> *cela me déchire. Si je suis jaloux, c'est*
> *que l'autre est toujours là, c'est que cet enfant*
> *d'un autre m'a volé mon enfant à moi, l'enfant*

---

(6) "My François, my Georget, the house is full of joy and prosperity. Paris awakes, and Paris must have bread for the immense task of her childbirth."

*que j'attendais de ma femme tant aimée. Et ma
maison est à jamais vide, jamais je n'y verrai
l'enfant naître et grandir!*[7]

(IV, iii)

Madeleine comes in, and confesses her longing for him in a scene which for human warmth and perception of what is meant by "love" will not be equaled in the libretto until *Arabella*: "I return to you because I love you and I can no longer do without you . . . you are my husband, you have taken everything from my being, my flesh and my heart . . . I was no longer living, I existed in a vacuum. My arms searched for you at night. I needed the household you made for me, my surroundings, my daily tasks. I am your wife, and I shall die if I lose you."

The happy ending is not tacked on, but grows inevitably out of this enlightenment, exactly as it will in *Arabella*.

As can be seen, Zola's librettos depend on symbolism (as the title of *L'Enfant roi* proclaims) but balance it with the immediacy of the genre setting. In this sense, Zola's librettos and that of Charpentier's *Louise* reawaken the spirit of Diderot and apply it to the bourgeois concerns of the fin-de-siècle world, in which the aspirations of Diderot's bourgeois class were transferred to those of the lower class.

Zola's librettos, and particularly that for *Messidor*, involve themselves with people from these lower classes but, unlike his great novels of the Rougon-Macquart series, do not focus on the immediate details or on muckraking treatment of their life. The language and the spirit of rage against injustice are tempered, but in the realm of the libretto even this tempered writing is immensely more direct and forceful than the form had been accustomed to. Indeed, works such as *Messidor* were considered *livrets à thèse*, or message librettos, and are thus in the pure Diderot-Beaumarchais line—although perhaps for that very reason they never achieved

---

(7) "Jealous of a child, I am jealous of a child! Is it possible that I have fallen to this depth? I who wished for one with all my distraught desires, I who would have adored it with all my overflowing heart! A child is a necessary joy and happiness, it is the soul without which no house can live! But the child of another—no! no!—that tears me apart. If I am jealous, it is because the other is there always, it is that this child of another has stolen my own child, the child that I waited for from my beloved wife. And my house is forever empty, never will I see a child born and grow in it!"

success on the essentially middle-class surroundings of the operatic stage. Zola's *Messidor* updates Beaumarchais' *Tarare* and foreshadows Charpentier's *Louise;* but its progeny, in terms of the attack on the injustices of the ruling class, is not French but the Marxist-oriented work of Bertolt Brecht.

Zola of course employed symbolism in his novels, but used it as secondary counterpoint to the overwhelming power of the story itself. By the end of his life (and also perhaps because he was writing for the more genteel arena of opera), this symbolism would assume equal importance with the story, and in fact become intertwined with it, as is shown in *Messidor, L'Ouragan,* and *L'Enfant roi.* Similarly, his prose, which always possessed virility and power that gave impetus to the details of the stories he wrote, had become refined into a language that bordered on free verse. Certainly this is evident in his librettos, and the range of expression that Zola managed to infuse into his *"poèmes lyriques"* and the absolute unpretentiousness of the writing make the lines—as poetry, prose, or free verse—the finest written for the French libretto after Berlioz.

We have seen examples of Zola's dramatic and characterizational writing; here are two of his lyric descriptions, which are at all times not only descriptive but also related directly to the "message" of the work:

> Goël! Goël! île farouche et solitaire, île de
> vierge encore sauvage après des mille années, gardée
> pure de tous côtés, au loin, par sa ceinture de brisants,
> où les navires en voyage au moindre vent s'écrasent![8]
> (L'Ouragan; I, i)

> Midi, la terre brûle, sous l'implacable été; et,
> depuis tant de jours, pas un souffle de vent, pas une
> goutte d'eau! Dans ce creux de montagnes, où la
> chaleur s'amasse, le village perdu flambe comme un
> brasier.[9]
> (Messidor; I, i)

---

(8) "Goël! Goël! Wild and lonely island, virgin island still primitive after thousands of years, kept pure on all sides by a belt of breakers, on which the traveling ships smash themselves at the slightest breeze."
(9) "Noon, the earth burns under the implacable summer heat; and for endless days, not a breath of wind, not a drop of water! In the pit at the foot of the mountains, where the heat gathers, the lost village sizzles like a brazier."

Messidor, Zola's first libretto, merits detailed discussion because it represents his work at its most characteristic and shows how a writer, come to the art form of the libretto as a neophyte, nonetheless managed to create a work making use, in an organic way, of the ever-repeated and distinctive traits of the French libretto, the scenic emphasis, and the necessity for ballet, as well as incorporating the prescriptions of Diderot as to message, genre setting, and noninflated language.

Much of the impetus for the creation of *Messidor* came from Zola's desire to write a libretto that would be a French answer to those of Wagner. In a letter to Bruneau,[1] he confessed his hatred for Wagner's mysticism "because I am in favor of love which brings forth children; I am for the mother and not for the Virgin . . . because all my Latin blood is in revolt against these perverse fogs from the North and only wants human heroes of light and truth." Zola may have considered his wants to be Latin-oriented, but they correspond almost exactly with those of Hofmannsthal. Yet, as with Hofmannsthal, Zola realized the value of Wagner's organically structured librettos, and thus *Messidor* follows Wagner much more than it follows Scribe or *Tarare* in setting forth Zola's "Latin" ideas. There are no "numbers" as such, there are no extraneous characters or situations, and the ballet is fully integrated into the story—and the symbolic meaning—of the libretto.

The symbolism of the title is indicative of the wealth of allusion that Zola has bound up into the work. *Messidor* is, first of all, the French Revolutionary Calendar month signifying harvest,[2] and the word can be broken down into its components, "Mass" (in the religious sense) and "gold" (in a double sense: the color of ripening wheat and the money that comes from it). Zola intends all of these meanings and more, for the gold of the title refers not only to the wheat but also to the waters that must irrigate the land to produce the wheat. In the libretto, these waters flow from the mountains and contain actual gold, which, legend has it, comes from a vast cathedral of gold in their depths. The infant Jesus, seated on his mother's knee, creates the gold by picking up sand and turning it into gold (giving yet another meaning to

---

(1) Lawson Carter: *Zola and the Theater*, p. 192.
(2) Zola used the name of another Revolutionary month, *Germinal* (Seed), as the title of one of his greatest novels.

the title, as *messie* means messiah). Zola's use of symbolism therefore encompasses both the literal and the mystic, and in its richness of allusion compares with that of Hofmannsthal, who took an object as simple as a glass of water and put it to use, in *Arabella,* as the literal and symbolic summation of the story. Further, there is no doubt that Zola, in using the symbolism of gold in all its aspects, good and bad, was developing the same theme that Wagner had employed in the *Ring* cycle.

If Zola did not employ the structure as evidenced in Scribe's *Grands Opéras,* he nonetheless used the well-made play aspect of it (particularly as it was developed by Dumas *fils a*nd Sardou) on which to build his plot. He keeps his characters to a minimum, and has each of them more or less stand for a point of view. He was criticized for this by those who saw in his characters representations of ideas rather than human beings, but Zola's talents as a writer were great enough to ensure his figures a degree of humanity, which talent was denied to lesser librettists.

The story is simple: before the events of the opera, there lived in an abundant valley a group of peasants who tilled the soil and produced their crops. Three of these were Véronique and her husband and Gaspard. Véronique and Gaspard each had one child, a boy and a girl (Guillaume for Véronique; Hélène for Gaspard), who grew up together and were destined for marriage. One day Véronique's husband was found dead in a gully, grasping a piece of gold, and Gaspard is suspected by Véronique of having killed him. Véronique's necklace has also been stolen. At about this time Gaspard, avid for money, had gone up into the mountains and built a gold refinery that used all the water from the stream that irrigated the valley. He became rich at the expense of the peasants, whose crops dried up and who were reduced to poverty. The opera opens during a summer in which a severe drought had added to their woes and brought them to the edge of revolt. No one can scratch a living any more. No water is to be had: it is worth its weight in gold.

Zola brings out the drama by contrasting the characters. Véronique, although she hates Gaspard, is far too superstitious to ascribe everything to his influence. She believes implicitly in the legend of the cathedral of gold—she had a golden necklace to "prove" it—and believes that, if she can find the cathedral, it will then disappear (along with the river) and Gaspard will be ruined. Mathias, her nephew, is scornful of these superstitions. He believes that the peasants should take matters into their own hands and destroy Gaspard's factory. Guillaume, caught in the middle, is in love with his childhood friend Hélène, but is pushed toward action against her father by his and his people's desperate plight. At the end of the first act, Véronique tells Guillaume about her suspicions as to who killed her husband and forbids her son to marry the child of his father's murderer.

In the second act, set in autumn,[3] Mathias has roused the peasants to action against Gaspard. Véronique pleads for patience, saying that destiny alone controls events, that she is setting out to find the secret spot and dry up the supply of the metal. Mathias derides her: "We, my friends, we shall act. Always being patient, always begging, that would be cowardly . . . We shall render justice!" Guillaume, torn, can only stay behind to sow his winter wheat to a parched earth.

Act III opens on the ballet of the Legend of the Gold, which takes place in the cathedral of gold. This ballet was criticized by those who saw in it a continuation of the dreary precepts of the Opéra, but in fact Zola has bent these precepts to his own use. He realized that a naturalistic libretto need not be bound by naturalism (a facet not lost on the librettists of *Louise*); that this legend was so vivid to Véronique that, in her mind at least, it achieved reality. Thus the ballet, which Zola details minutely, can exist as a manifestation of French libretto habits and at the same time as a vision of Véronique's, in the same spirit as the dream ballets of the seventeenth century. Precisely this rationale was used by Wagner in adapting his *Tannhäuser* for the Opéra in 1861.

Zola employed the ballet as a personal ecstatic vision and as a furthering of the story: as soon as Véronique sees the cathedral, it disappears in a thunderclap and night descends. The scene changes to the refinery under a lowering winter sky heavy with snow. Gaspard has installed a new machine and is rejoicing over its promise of new wealth. The crowd of peasants arrives from the town below, now led by Guillaume, who has put himself at their head. He asks that Gaspard render them the water; Gaspard counters by inviting everyone to a banquet celebrating the new machine.

---

(3) "Autumn has come: the last leaves fly in the wet gusts of wind and here is November, with its fogs, which brings back the season of large-scale sowings."

Now Hélène intercedes, but to side with her father—which puts Guillaume in despair. Mathias arrives with several desperadoes and determines to take matters into his own hands. The crowd—now a mob—is won over to his side as snow begins to fall, ever more thickly. Suddenly, the sound of an avalanche is heard, and Véronique appears, to announce the judgment of God. Gaspard, however, knows that what he has always feared has happened: the rock overlooking the stream has collapsed, damming it forever and allowing the water to seep naturally down to the fields. The act ends on the spectacle.

Thus, the legend can be explained in two ways: as a vision corresponding to the eventual natural collapse of the rock under the weight of the snows or as a miracle brought to pass by Véronique's having seen the mysterious cathedral of gold. In either way, the refinery and the wealth of Gaspard have been destroyed, and the literal gold of the river has been turned into the fruitful gold of the wheat-filled plains.

The last act, set in spring, makes this clear: "A triumphal sun bathes the sparkling sheet of grains of wheat, and the entire horizon is resplendent and sings in a thrill of happy fecundity." Mathias is discovered to be the villain who has killed Véronique's husband (and stolen her golden necklace). He has done so, Iago-like, because of his nihilistic evil spirit, and when caught throws himself off a cliff to his destruction. Gaspard and his daughter, now reduced to poverty, are taken in by Véronique, and all ends happily, to the strains of a choral benison of the wheat. Thus the *lieto fine*, with its included *licenza* (here to the god of abundance), becomes an integral part of the libretto and invokes once again the title of the work.

Messidor is more than a little artfully naïve, and its message, in social terms, though partly valuable—it preaches the evils of industrial exploitation—hovers on the edge of agrarian populism: that is, a belief that all evils will be cured if factories are destroyed and everyone returns to the fields. The character of Gaspard is not successful, since Zola must keep a certain sympathy for him if the ending is to succeed, and it is hard to keep sympathy for someone who willfully grinds down others for his own financial gain. Finally, the sudden poverty of Gaspard is unbelievable. Yet *Messidor* contains much of the French libretto in its bones and reflects more of its aspects than any of Zola's other librettos.

Certainly the scenic pictures, which traverse an entire year's cycle (Act I: summer; Act II: fall; Act III: winter; Act IV: spring), keep the focus on the importance of the setting, which was always a part of the French libretto.

The merits of Zola's works for the operatic stage far outstrip their demerits, and establish their author as one of the great practitioners of the art in France. In the artistic life of Zola they assume a smaller role, for his novels and his defense of Dreyfus will always outrank his achievements for Bruneau. Yet in any history of the libretto his position as creator, as continuer, and as summation will always be secure, for more than any other single French librettist he demonstrates the richness and diversity still possible within the format of the French libretto, and his resolute use of *prose mélique* once and for all eliminated the barrier of verse which had held back the libretto (at least in principle) for so long. Verse would continue to be used in the form—and indeed some of the best verse for the libretto was yet to come—but the dike had been broken.

Charpentier's *Louise* deserves mention at the end of this chapter because, although it continues several traits also found in the Zola librettos, it adapts them in different ways, and adds to what Zola contributed. The libretto for *Louise* is an ambitious work, constructed on various levels. At its most immediate, it is a portrait of working life among the poor in Paris; then it is a love story growing out of the frustrations of that working life and accentuated by the temptations of the pleasures that surround any family then living in Paris. Charpentier and his librettists have managed to combine these elements, to which they have added the allegorical figure of Le Noctambule, representing the pleasures of the city, and a host of the artist-dwellers of Montmartre, who are the Bacchants of the opera (as well as providing the excuse for the "ballet," which in this case is the crowning of Louise as the Muse de Montmartre). The directness and honesty of the portraits of Louise's father and mother—the father's near-slavish existence to bring home enough money and the mother's undisguised envy of the luxuries of Paris—were daring novelties at the Opéra-Comique of the time, and the celebration of Louise's reaction against their constricted and unhappy life—that is, flight into "free love"—was novel in that it was stressed and not allowed to slip by on a tide of sentiment, as with both Puccini's *La Bohème* and Leoncavallo's.

Louise rebels for the same reason that the young of all ages rebel—which gives the opera a timeless contemporaneity within its genre setting—and Julien, her painter-lover, is therefore less a figure in his own right than the means to her freedom and the will to force her to act. This is emphasized by Charpentier and his librettists by placing the city of Paris—the City of Love itself—on stage, and by having the father curse Paris and not Julien for Louise's defection.[4] The exact spirit of Henrik Ibsen's landmark play, *A Doll's House* (1879), is represented in Louise's leaving her home at the end of the opera, except that in Ibsen, Nora rebels against the shut-in middle-class world, whereas Louise flees from the suffocating straitjacket of eternal poverty. The popularity of the opera was owing not only to the appeal of its Puccini-like lovers but also to the celebration of the world of Montmartre and Paris—a blend of sentiment, nostalgia, and tourist blarney—but the light sugarcoating should not obscure the sociological truths that Charpentier and his librettists were careful to build into the libretto. No one in the opera is either right or wrong: the father is right in wanting to uphold the sanctity of the family and the moral base of love, Louise is right in wanting to be free of the domination of her parents so that she can live her own life. Louise's flight, though it represents immediate happiness, holds no promise of eternal dawns of sunlight, and she realizes this: she is in agreement with the aged sweeper, who says, "*Moi, j'ai eu ch'vaux et voitures . . . Y a vingt ans j'étais la reine de Paris! Quell' dégringolade, hein? Mais, je ne regrette rien . . . Je me suis tant amusée . . . Ah! la belle vie!*[5]

The language of the libretto is both direct in its passion and colloquial. Although Charpentier and his librettists used both rhymed and free verse, they were always aware that the speech patterns of the people of Montmartre differed from the cadences of the spoken and operatic stage. In this use of localisms they added an element not found in the librettos of Zola, and reinforced the scenic genre touches of the life on the Montmartre streets, in

---

(4) In a Tristanesque passage in the love scene, which is usually cut in performance, Julien states that they are not Julien and Louise but symbols of love faithful only to themselves, beings who want to live without masters, souls in which the holy flame of desire burns.
(5) "As for me, I had horses and carriages . . . twenty years ago I was the queen of Paris; What a comedown, eh? But I don't regret a thing . . . I had such a good time . . . Ah! the good life!" (II, ii.)

the workhouse of the seamstresses, and over the rooftops of Paris with the actual flavor of the language spoken there. Combined with the forcefulness of the characters and the symbolic universalizing of the love story as the story of Paris, the libretto rises above its sentimentality and achieves a distinction to which genre works like the *Bohème* of Illica, Giacosa, and Puccini, for all its merits, cannot lay claim.

The fate of the libretto for *Louise*—that it is hitched to good but not great music—reflects the fate of several other later-nineteenth- and early-twentieth-century French librettos. The lack of strong-enough or individual-enough music dictated that the works themselves, which are better than the music in terms of ideas and execution, would languish in semi-obscurity.[6] Certainly these librettos display a wider scope and a more thoroughgoing approach to subject matter than those of any earlier time in the French libretto, and if they have faults, which they do, those faults are outweighed by the merits they possess.

---

(6) This obscurity is darkened by the French habit, in contradistinction to that of Italy or Germany, of rarely reviving its operas once they have sunk from repertory.

Chapter Twenty

Boito

ARRIGO BOITO is, with Lorenzo Da Ponte, the best-known librettist and he is also the most highly regarded practitioner of the form. Those commentators who see the libretto as essentially a process of adaptation from another medium to the demands of the operatic stage—and thus place the highest priority on adaptive ability—turn to Boito for justification, for his two greatest adaptations of Shakespeare are first-rate achievements. The superiority of *Falstaff* over *The Merry Wives of Windsor* is evident (as even Shakespeare would have admitted), but there exist those who would even credit Boito's *Otello*, when combined with Verdi's music, with being superior to the Shakespeare tragedy. Yet, masterful as those two works are both in terms of adaptation to the operatic medium and faithfulness to the spirit and a good deal of the letter of the original sources, they serve to symbolize the limitations as well as the strengths of the neutral librettist. And this is the paradox of Boito, for Boito as a librettist was an adapter rather than a creator, and yet Boito as an artistic mind should have been the reverse, given the richness and scope of his intellect and interests.

The adaptive rather than creative ethos is of course integral to the Italian libretto, which always proceeded on the assumption that an opera was derived from some other primary source, which had to be made into a libretto (a genre different from any other). Boito, like all other Italian poets-turned-stage artists, grew up and lived with those preconceptions, and he evidenced them in the majority of the librettos he wrote, beginning with his first, which was logically enough an adaptation of Shakespeare's *Hamlet* (for Franco Faccio, 1865). Yet Boito's cultivation, his range of knowl-

edge, and his innate taste led him to choose only the best—
Shakespeare and Goethe, as had Berlioz. When he adapted Victor
Hugo, he hid behind a pseudonym—in part because he liked to
use pseudonyms, which were for him sort of an intellectual game,
but also in part because he did not want to be closely associated
with the work of a man he had come to consider artistically
inferior to Shakespeare and Goethe.[1] Thus *La Gioconda* (1876; m.,
Amilcare Ponchielli) is the work of "Tobia Gorrio."

What must be done in any study of Boito as librettist is to
concentrate on his known strengths, which are adaptive in the
fullest sense, yet do the man the credit of examining just how
much of him there is in the works: just how much Boito the
creator slipped through Shakespeare or Goethe and stood on stage
himself.

Arrigo Boito was born in Padua in 1842, to an artistic family;
after his father had decamped, his mother encouraged his musical
career, sending him to the Milan Conservatory. From his earliest
years, Boito was always much more than a composer, and in
addition to his musical studies read voluminously about the allied
arts. Once he had been graduated, he and his friend Franco Faccio
went to Paris, and Boito returned to Italy a thorough cosmopolite.
He applied himself to a combination of journalism, writing music,
poetry, and librettos, and in his erudition and breadth of interest
became a leading artistic figure in Italy, although he was looked
on by some Italians with suspicion as an eclectic and as only partly
Italian (his mother was Polish). Not only the artistic themes of
his own operas, but also the artistic works themselves— *Mefistofele*
and *Nerone*—were developed in Boito's mind from his youth,
and it can be said that the rest of his life was spent in achieving
their fruition, while he was being distracted not only by the Verdi
collaboration but also by the gnawing doubts of his own critical
soul.

In this sense Boito is very like another half-Italian composer-
librettist, Ferruccio Busoni, and at the opposite pole from such
a craftsman as Felice Romani. Boito's critical snobbism led him
to only the greatest works and forced on him the highest of aims,
yet this same critical spirit stood apart from the result and was able

---

(1) The idea that Boito was trying to disguise his contribution behind
a pseudonym is only partly true: he used an easily decipherable
anagram and made no secret of his authorship.

to pick it apart as not being the equal of the work of Shakespeare
or Goethe or Wagner or Verdi. Boito knew in himself that any
opera on the vast subject of Goethe's epic would have to encompass a great deal not only in terms of length and complexity but
also in terms of the inclusion of Goethe's far-ranging ideas and
ideals. He knew that, though Barbier and Carré had taken the
easier path by setting only the story of merely the first part of
the epic, he had to set both parts and, moreover, to include in
them not only the plot details but also those elements which made
Faust, in his words, not merely the Goethe creation but the
symbol for all earlier Fausts: Adam, Job, Solomon, Don Giovanni,
etc.[2] Thus, though Boito wistfully hoped to have his audience
home by midnight,[3] the first version of *Mefistofele* run over
six hours, at the end of which the audience was in open revolt;
the fiasco (at La Scala in 1868) in turn struck a blow at his pride
and his critical judgment. Boito revised and shortened the opera
for its next incarnation (1875 et seq.), and it was then a success,
but his development in the next years into a librettist for Ponchielli
and Verdi must be regarded, in part, as a critical reaction against
that artistic defeat. Boito had neither the artistic certainty of a
Verdi or a Wagner nor the capacity to absorb just criticism: being
a critic himself, he all too clearly realized his faults and, as a high-
strung, neurotic person was tortured by his vision of the ideal and
his realization of his own inadequacies. A good deal of the duality
that is everywhere evident in his work—the duality of the ideal
and the real, the good and the bad, belief and negation—and which
is expressed in his early poetry, has as its basis neither that Socratic
spirit of inquiry nor, on the other hand, a fevered emotional
vacillation *à la Tannhäuser* but the expression of the essential conflict within himself of what he knew he had to say and the fact
that he knew he would never be able to say it. *Otello* and *Falstaff*—
even *La Gioconda*—provided a respite from these worries, because
in Verdi and Shakespeare Boito was dealing with known great
figures[4] and in Hugo was paying homage to one of the idols

---

(2) Contained in a prose *prologo in teatro* that Boito wrote for the
first version of *Mefistofele* and which paralleled Goethe's. See Stefano
Vittadini, *Il Primo Libretto del Mefistofele.*
(3) At the end of the *prologo in teatro*, the author says: "I hope that
by midnight you can be at home."
(4) A passage from one of Boito's articles reflects on this: "And indeed
the Sublime is simpler than the Beautiful. The Beautiful can be

of his youth, and was using the talents he knew he possessed to a superior degree: that is, his adaptive abilities and his stage poetic sense. With the death of Verdi, his hopes for a *King Lear* libretto vanished and he was thrown back onto the mill wheel of his *Nerone,* which had germinated in the 1860's and which now occupied him for the rest of his life. In 1902, La Scala announced its production, but Boito, fearful of its artistic inadequacies, withdrew it for further revision; when he died in 1918, the opera was not yet finished. It was presented at last at La Scala in 1924 without its final act, and even at that the work sprawled almost as profligately as the first *Mefistofele.* Yet *Nerone* is the receptacle for all that is most creative in Boito, and any appreciation of him as a librettist must include this strange and difficult work, so tremendously flawed when compared with the marble finish of the libretto for *Otello,* but so much more thoroughly Boito's own.

The dichotomy between Boito's adaptive librettos for others and the two—one adaptive—written for his own music cuts deeply into his artistic self. *Otello* and *Falstaff*—and *Amleto*—conform to the Italian librettistic ideals of the reworking of an original source for the operatic stage, and in so doing stress the humanity of the characters while accenting the drama and responding to the demands of *brevità.* *La Gioconda* is an exercise in French *Grand Opéra,* with a show-stopping aria for every vocal category and plenty of variant opportunities for confrontations and tableaus. *Mefistofele* and *Nerone* inhabit another world entirely. The epic nature of their librettos is expressed not only in their scope but also in the grotesqueries of the Brocken Scene in the former and of the fifth act of the latter, and in the figures of Mefistofele and Nerone. Barnabà and Iago hint at the force of evil, which Boito's "Credo" in *Otello* makes evident, but in his operas the characters have shed the bonds of humanity and aspire to ideal characterizations. Boito's Faust, like Boito, lives not for his youth and amours, but for that moment when, like Goethe's Faust, he can believe in something enough to cry out, "*Arrestati sei Bello!*"—"*Verweile*

---

made incarnate with all varieties of form, the most bizarre, the most variegated, the most disparate. The only thing suitable to the Sublime is the immense form—the divine, universal, eternal form: the spheric form." Boito: *Critiche e cronache musicali,* p. 165. In his estimation, this spheric form was represented by Shakespeare. Lurking behind these sentences is the conviction that, for Boito, his own work achieved the Beautiful but not the Sublime.

doch, du bist so schön": Margaret and Helena exist only as man-ifestations of his search. Similarly, Nerone is less a cruel Emperor than a depraved figure being torn apart by the furies and existing in a world bound on one side by the fraudulent and fanatic wizard Simon Mago and on the other by the semi-divine Christian, Fanuèl.

The roots of Boito's operas lie in his early poetry, and especially in the long poem *Re Orso,* which was published in 1865. In an earlier poem, *"Dualismo,"* he set forward his famous duality: *"Questa è la vita!/. . . Un agitarsi alterno/fra paradiso e inferno/ che non s'accheta più,*[5] but in *Re Orso* he found his metaphor: The Eternal Worm. Boito had taken the general idea of the worm as a symbol of evil (i.e., destruction, negation) from Victor Hugo's *L'Épopée du Ver,*[6] but in *Re Orso* he personalized it as his own. Its constant refrain is:

> *Re Orso,*
> *ti schermi*
> *dal morso*
> *de' vermi.*[7]

"The worm never dies; the lion dies, man dies, the eagle dies, but the worm lives forever . . . night and morning the worm goes on . . . over mountain and beach the worm travels." Boito's image is powerful because it embraces not only the immediate— the worm eating the coffined body—but also the general destruc-tive principle: the prevalence of evil and its continual nihilistic scourge.

This pessimistic outlook, which has been noted before in the Italian libretto, is reflected in Boito's work, sporadically in the figures of Barnabà and Iago, melodramatically in that of Mefisto-fele. *Nerone,* of course, brings this pessimism out strongly in the glaring light of Rome on fire and paganism and imperialism sunk into decadence, but even here Boito cannot face the abyss, and contrasts this hell-on-earth with the salvation in Christ of Fanuèl

---

(5) "Such is life . . . a flux between paradise and Hell, which never diminishes."
(6) The worm as such a symbol antedates Hugo and can be found, for instance, in the Gravediggers Scene in *Hamlet.*
(7) "King Bear, beware of the bite of the worms."

and Rubria. This streak of pessimism in the Italian libretto will continue from Boito to the work of another man only half-Italian, Ferruccio Busoni.

Boito was aided in the expressivity of his poems and in the characterizational sureness of his librettos by the quality of his verse. In the period after Romani, Boito was the greatest poet of the Italian operatic stage; unlike Romani, he brought to the libretto a greatly widened concept of poetics, derived in one part from his admiration for the verbal fireworks of Hugo, but certainly derived also from his own extremely sensitive musical ear for shadings of sound. His intellectual curiosity led him to experiment with a variety of verse forms, rhyming combinations and, pre-eminently, verbal sounds. What stands out in his librettos, however, is his use of short lines (*à la Hugo*) and his concentration on sibilants.

Italian operatic verse had always been posited on the mellifluousness of its sounds, as symbolized in the poetry of Metastasio, which were either pastoral or grandiloquent but always fell easily on the ear. If harsher sounds were used, they were almost invariably used within a comic context. Boito, however, had early moved away from the long, songful line and had begun using short, nervous lines that drove wedges between the longer lines of "recitative" which Boito set in nine-syllable lines.[8] Examples of Boito's use of the short line with either harsh sibilants or the relatively softer but still-piquant "i" sounds abound in his works, and indeed their very dominating quality enables them, as verbal sound, to penetrate the thicker orchestral texture of the nineteenth century. The Chorus of the Cherubini in the Prologue to *Mefistofele* is a good example of the lighter use of the "i" sound, which, combined with the shortness of the lines and the repetition, reinforces the over-all idea of eternal celestial spirals:

> *Siam nimbi*
> *volanti*
> *dai limbi,*
> *nei santi*
> *splendori*
> *vaganti,*

---

(8) Boito considered the nine-syllable lines to be the Italian equivalent of the French alexandrine.

siam cori
di bimbi
d'amori.[9] etc.

The more direct use of sibilants is found in the final Gulling Scene of *Falstaff:*

Pizzica, pizzica,
pizzica, stuzzica,
spizzica, spizzica,
pungi, spilluzzica,
finch' egli abbai![1]
(III, ii)

Such departures in the poetics of the libretto were sufficiently novel in Italy so that other librettists and critics, while admiring Boito as a poet, as an intellect, and as a master of a wide vocabulary, nevertheless objected to Boito's tendency toward sibilants, the crudeness of his accentuations, and the asperity of his vocabulary. They also objected to his ostentatious and excessive use of archaic words and obsolete modes of expression—very much a part of Boito's librettos, particularly *Nerone*, which is stuffed with Latinisms forgotten for centuries.

It is too simple, however, to write off these usages as mere intellectual gamesmanship. Boito perceived what Victor Hugo had accomplished with the French language in order to revivify it, and he perceived what Wagner had tried to do with the German in his use of alliteration and word-assonance. What Boito was attempting to do in his works was not to entomb the language in the refuse of its past but to use the past to widen the language and the syntax of the present: to break open once and for all the closed-in world of the Italian libretto with its ingrained and ever-repeated formulas. The words themselves—as with, to a lesser extent, Wagner—were important not in themselves but as differing sound patterns and as building blocks for novel, rather than obsolete, modes of expression. Added to this, the quicksilver nature

---

(9) The translation here is less important than the onomatopoeia of the words, which give their own meaning. Roughly: "We are clouds flying in the celestial ether, wandering amidst holy splendors; we are choirs of babes, of loves."
(1) "Pick at him, peck at him, sting him and buzz at him until he howls."

of Boito's mind could not be content with the monotonous susurrus of the average Italian libretto. The proof of the vitality of Boito's verse, even with its archaisms, its created words, and its often maddeningly hermetic constructions, is a comparison of his works with any of, say, Ghislanzoni's.

What is evident in all of Boito's verse—and reinforces it as a prime aspect of his artistic make-up—is its pithy quality and its characterizational power. This pithy quality is seen in his knack of being able to sum up a scene or a character in an easily apprehended phrase, of which the aforementioned *"Ecco il Leone!"* is the classic example. The pithy is directly related, in addition, to the characterizational, here meant in the widest sense. In one aspect it involves the repetition of words. Such repetition has both a musical and a dramatic function, and ultimately goes back to the fivefold *"Never"* of the last act of Shakespeare's *King Lear*. Two such examples in Boito's librettos are found in *Mefistofele*. Mefistofele's aria, *"Su, cammina, cammina, cammina"* ("Go, onward, onward, onward") (II, ii), brings back an image from *Re Orso* in its specifics and in the leaden quality of the repeated words, which are immediately placed in contrast by Faust's reply, *"Folletto, folletto,/veloce, leggier"* ("Light, quick will-o'-the-wisp"), as light and darting as the will-o'-the-wisp of which it talks. But beyond this the music of the words symbolizes the characters: the immortal ongoing worm that is Satan and the hedonistic, all-searching-yet-never-finding intellect of Faust. Likewise, the final duet of Margherita and Faust, *"Lontano, lontano, lontano/sui flutti d'un ampio oceàno"* ("Far away, far away, on the billows of a vast ocean") (III, i), captures the eternal nature of that love as well as the sadness of it (in the repeated "o" sounds and in the use of a variant word for ocean).

The contrast of vocal sounds and the lightning change of vocal color in the verse are extremely characteristic of Boito. A passage such as the one of the Cherubini quoted above serves to characterize their airiness and their innocence, and is set against the heavier, repeated *"Sanctus!"* of the *Falangi Celesti* and the interjections of Mefistofele. The ironic suavity of the Devil is well set forward in his words, which involve long, unctuous sounds, such as: *"e bello udir l'Eterno/col diavolo parlar si umanamente"* ("it is amusing to hear Old Eternity speaking with such unaffected humanity to the poor old Devil"). The language, in its variety

339

and its ability to mutate, thus complements the music in a way that no other poet—Italian, French, or German—of the nineteenth century was able to achieve, or even sought to achieve.

If Wagner represents the dramatist who labored at his verses and whose music came to dominate both his verse and his dramatic ability, Boito represents the musical mind in its verbal aspect, and it is not going too far to state that the music to which the text should be set can be inferred from the chameleon-like musicality of the words themselves.

There is very little sense of development in Boito's work. *Mefistofele* and *Nerone* were both in his mind from his earliest maturity, and although both underwent changes in emphasis and tone, the ideas behind them germinated in Boito's youth. As a versifier he obviously became slightly more adept as he worked, but the verbal distance between *Amleto*, his first libretto, and *Falstaff*, his last work for Verdi, is small. Likewise, he doubtless learned something about stagecraft during his career, but *Amleto* again shows that, at the age of twenty-three, he knew almost all that he was to know, for his *Hamlet* libretto for Faccio is a fine adaptation of the play, slightly more obviously dependent upon the "number" formulas of the earlier opera than his later Shakespearean adaptations—particularly *Falstaff*—but a masterful job in terms of characterization and incorporation of a great number of Shakespeare's scenes. Also evident in the libretto is Boito's intact transference of "big moments" from the original or from elsewhere, such as the *"To be or not to be"* soliloquy, which would become a hallmark of his adaptive style, and which he culled from Berlioz. He also early showed his ability to transfer with no loss, and often with a gain in dramatic power, as in his setting of Claudio's attempting to say the Lord's Prayer and failing,[2] in the scene after the play within the play. The libretto finally fails not because of being a youthful work but because its ambition was a shade callow: in *Hamlet* there are too many important characters, and the interconnecting strands of the drama are too complex to be finally encompassed in a libretto that does not drastically alter the Shakespearean intent. In his later Shakespearean adaptations Boito avoided this complexity, for *Otello* can be safely reduced to two

---

(2) Contrast with Boito's far more prosaic use of the Lord's Prayer in *Nerone*.

people and a *spirito che nega*, and *Falstaff* to one superman and a host of comic subordinates.

Aside from the works already mentioned, Boito wrote several other librettos, only one of which was produced in his lifetime. This was *Ero e Leandro* (which was originally written for himself, but was set by Giovanni Bottesini in 1879 and by Luigi Mancinelli in 1897), and from which he took the *"Lontano"* duet for the revised *Mefistofele*. *Basi e bote*, a Boito comedy in Venetian dialect, was made into a comic opera in 1927 by Riccardo Pick-Mangiagalli. His other librettos were *Iràm* (never set, though intended for Cesare Dominiceti), a comic opera taken from *The Arabian Nights* which abounds in verbal word-play and pyrotechnics and definitely foreshadows *Falstaff; Pier Luigi Farnese* (c. 1877; set by Constantino Palumbo but never given), another grand opera in the *Gioconda* vein; and a setting of the Semiramide story, *Semir* (or *Semira*), written in about 1876 for Luigi San Germano but never produced. This last exhibits once again the Boitan "duality," and in its settings of the Babylonian Empire foreshadows *Nerone:* its evil high priest, Zoroastro, becomes Simon Mago in the later incarnation.[3] Boito also revised *Simon Boccanegra* for Verdi, translated *Rienzi* and *Tristan* into Italian, translated *Antony and Cleopatra* and *Romeo and Juliet* into Italian for his mistress, Eleonora Duse, and collaborated with Camille du Locle on the French translation of *Otello*. He wrote extensive criticism and was as close to a cosmopolitan man of letters as Italy had seen.

If Boito's verse was one of his major contributions to the Italian libretto, his adaptive abilities have always been the foundation of his fame. The Italian libretto had been the province par excellence of the adaptive spirit, which was broadly interpreted. Yet the nineteenth century saw a growing vogue for the artistic inviolability of the original source, a concept developed partly from the growing concern with the music and literature of earlier ages and partly from Wagner's—and other Romantic writers'—strictures on the artistic purity of the work of art. Boito, as an intellectual and a critic, was conscious of these developments, and he realized that the old-style "adaptations" of, say, a Romani—not to speak of a Metastasio—would no longer suffice. What was

---

(3) Piero Nardi, in his biography of Boito, sees Zoroastro as a precursor of Nerone himself, which to an extent he is, but the parallel is more exact to Simon Mago.

needed was not only a reproduction of the original framework within the terms of the operatic convention, but more importantly the transference of the spirit of the original, and the fidelity to the characterizations and the ideas of the original, in the final creation. Boito thus looked to Da Ponte for his inspiration in his great adaptive works, although it should not be forgotten that the "worm" aspect of Boito's art and the whole of the libretto of *Nerone* invoke Da Ponte's rival Casti rather than the author of *Le Nozze di Figaro*.

Boito's adaptive knack amounted to genius, and raised the art of the "neutral librettist" to a level beyond which there is only the setting of the original, as in *Pelléas*. Yet Boito's adaptations *as adaptations* are greater than transference-intact works because the latter will always be exceptional cases of theater works that in themselves are next door to librettos. Boito demonstrated how a faithful adaptation could be done, and in so doing he injected something of himself into the final work besides his adaptive ability,[4] not being afraid to lay hands on the original in order to make it viable for the operatic stage. The evidences of this in his Shakespearean adaptations for Verdi are today commonplaces of genius: the suppression of the first act of *Othello*, the opening on the storm scene, the ending of the first act on the love duet; and, most impressive of all, the pouring of the character of Falstaff as taken from the two Henry IV plays into the mold of the slight *Merry Wives of Windsor*, a process that improves the original source almost past recognition in artistic, if not in plot, terms. Boito the stage technician is at his finest in the Verdi collaborations, as is shown in the handling of the duologues in *Otello*, in the gradual increase of tension through the four-act form, and in the fluidity and expertness with which he handles the interplay of characters in *Falstaff*.

The loss, which is almost inevitable in an adaptation that is "faithful to the original" but is not an intact transference, is that the adapter must choose the salient facts presented by the original and channel his adaptation to them. Thus any ambiguities or variant readings possible in any of the very great works of art—which were Boito's concern—must necessarily be omitted or toned down,

---

(4) One place is in the final scene of *Falstaff*, where Boito lets the mask hiding his *"prevalence of evil"* side slip and has his fat knight be subjected to one gulling too many by the little people who are less children than fugitives from the Brocken, or dogs hounding a wounded stag. The scene can be read as an apotheosis—and grand fun—but it has never had that effect upon me in the theater.

to the detriment not only of the original but also of the adaptation itself. To take an example: *Othello* the play is not the near-perfect work that *Otello* the opera is, but because of its more sprawling nature and its relative ambiguousness (relatively less than that of *Hamlet* or *King Lear*, relatively more than that of *Macbeth*) it can support variant readings about the characters which the opera has greater difficulty in accommodating. Suppose that Desdemona is guilty as charged by Iago, and that the play is presented from that point of view:[5] extreme as the idea is, we are more likely to find evidence for its support in Shakespeare's play than in Boito and Verdi's opera, which was written from the steadfast assumption of her innocence. Similarly, Boito's addition of the "Credo" to the libretto transforms Iago from Othello's aide-de-camp with, possibly, grandiose visions of his diabolism into an extension of the Eternal Worm himself. Thus, the interpretation that explains Iago's vicious hatred of Othello by unrequited love for him—a highly plausible thesis—would lose the force of its very pettiness, that is, that Othello was brought down not because he was up against the gods but because he was involved in a squalid love triangle, if it were to be transferred to the opera. Verdi and Boito are hardly to blame: the nineteenth century saw *Othello* as they adapted it and so, to a lesser degree, does the twentieth. Yet size has been sacrificed to focus, the focus of a particular age. The very success of Boito's adaptations, therefore, lays bare the gulf that separates adaptation from creation in a work of art.

The quality of Boito's adaptations can be instanced in more immediate terms not in the more famous examples but in Boito's work in revising the libretto of his fellow-librettist, Piave. As is well known, Verdi turned to Boito to help him resurrect *Simon Boccanegra*, which had been a failure in 1857. Boito reworked the libretto, adding the celebrated Council Chamber Scene, which not only was a highly dramatic moment (so dramatic that all the rest is made to look anticlimactic) but also brought to the fore the dynamic and leaderly qualities of Boccanegra, who in Piave's version was seen primarily in his fatherly guise. But Boito's adaptations went well beyond the Council Chamber Scene, and involved the entire libretto.

---

(5) This well-documented thesis is held by the critic Calvin Hoffman, one of the chief advocates of the proposition that Christopher Marlowe wrote Shakespeare's plays.

The changes that Boito made at the beginning of the third act can stand as an example of his masterful adaptive powers, in terms of clarity, language, force, and interrelation of character. Act II had ended with the Doge, Simon, going off to put down the revolt against him led by Paolo (who has already managed to poison Simon with a slow-acting drug). Piave's opening of the third act shows his dramatic fumbling[6] when compared to Boito's reworking. Piave's scene opens on a victory celebration involving the Doge's retinue: Senators and Soldiers, the Doge, Gabriele (the tenor lover about to be married), and the conspirators Paolo and Pietro. The Senators hail Simon in the usual florid style ("Sun of Victory"), while outside the populace sings praise in similar Metastasian terms.[7] The Doge replies, while Paolo mutters about *"la vendetta,"* which is about to occur. Everyone exits to the second choral verse, and Paolo has Fiesco, the aged mortal enemy of Simon, brought in. He tells him that he has poisoned the Doge and counsels Fiesco to flee with him; Fiesco refuses, horror-stricken at the vile nature of the vendetta. Simon now enters once more, and for the first time exhibits the effects of the poison; and the reconciliation scene between the two men follows.

Boito's reworking highlights the power of *brevità*. He empties the stage of its unnecessary forces and reduces the verbiage of the off-stage chorus to the minimum. He keeps Simon off stage at curtain rise, and has Fiesco on stage alone with a Captain of the Guard. The entire scene goes:

> CHORUS: *(off)* Long live the Doge! Victory!
> CAPTAIN: You are free. Here is your sword. *(He gives it to him.)*
> FIESCO: And the Guelphs?
> CAPTAIN: Routed.
> FIESCO: O unhappy freedom! *(Paolo enters, a prisoner between guards.)* What? Paolo? Where are you being taken?
> PAOLO: To the scaffold. My evil demon drove me to the rebels and I was caught there; now Simon has condemned me; but before that I condemned Boccanegra to death!

---

(6) N.B.: Even Verdi was not able to help Piave—because Verdi was not, finally, a librettist.
(7) "Midst the storm clouds of such cruel offenses, Doge, for you there kindles the most serene of stars."

> FIESCO: What do you mean?
> PAOLO: A poison—I no longer fear anything—eats away at his life.
> FIESCO: Wretch!
> PAOLO: Maybe he will precede me to the tomb.
> CHORUS: *(off)* [sings a wedding hymn for Gabriele and Amelia]
> PAOLO: Oh, horror! That wedding hymn, which haunts me, do you hear it? In that church Gabriele Adorno will marry the person I abducted . . .
> FIESCO: *(drawing his sword)* Amelia? *You* were the abductor? Villain!
> PAOLO: Kill me.
> FIESCO: Never: you are reserved for the ax.

What Boito has done, besides focusing the scene on the important characters and leaving aside the others, is to heighten the drama inherent in Piave. Paolo, in Boito's hands, not illogically is drawn into the orbit of the Eternal Worm, but having him captured and condemned makes his confession to Fiesco more plausible—he has, as he says, nothing to lose. Fiesco's patrician reaction is carried over from Piave, but Boito turns the screw by introducing a wedding song (which was, in fact, part of the Piave off-stage chorus, but was so similar to the first chorus as to be indistinguishable from it), and by having Paolo, in a paroxysm of diabolism, confess to having abducted Amelia (who is Fiesco's granddaughter). This development is not a mere piling of horror upon horror, for it brings enlightenment to Fiesco, who had thought that Simon had abducted her. When Paolo leaves Fiesco, then, he (Paolo) is fully debased in the old man's eyes—who will not even soil his blade with Paolo's blood—and, in the ruin of his fortunes, Fiesco can anticipate the reconciliation that will occur, for he knows that his granddaughter is marrying with the Doge's blessing and he knows of the impending death of Simon. Thus, when Boito has Simon enter for the first time in the act suffering the effects of the poison, the moment is heightened: Fiesco, as the upright nobleman he is, *can* only respond with understanding. The passage well illustrates the great adaptive abilities of Boito: his secret of getting to the core of the story and the characters and being able to express both in a dramatic and concise way.

Yet, as has been said, this is only one side of Boito's librettistic work. The other, the creative side, is best expressed in the libretto that haunted his life, and which he never completely set to music: *Nerone*. *Nerone* the libretto is a gigantic sketch, realized to a greater extent than is at first evident, but whose faults are, because of the ambition and the scope, proportionally greater.

In *Nerone* the Eternal Worm is ascendant, in a fuller sense than in *Mefistofele* not only because the libretto ends in destruction but also because the background of the whole is the collapse of a civilization. *"Tutta crolla"* ("All crumbles") could be the motto of the piece, and though Boito provides a positive counterbalance in the rise of Christianity and the martyred deaths of the Christians in the circus, these are clearly considered secondary.[8] The Roman Empire may be finished and the martyrs ready to be vindicated by history, but it is the Eternal Worm who dominates the stage.

The antecedents for the libretto are several, but those uppermost in Boito's mind were clearly the two great epics of the century, Wagner's *Ring* cycle and Berlioz's *Les Troyens*. He took the idea of world apocalypse from the *Ring* cycle, but, as has been suggested, without redemption at the close. In this sense *Nerone* is closer to the twentieth century's idea of finality. In the scale of the project, which transcends all of the figures including Nerone himself, it is responsive to the Berlioz vision and to the historical epics of Mussorgsky, but in the history of the libretto it updates the great epics of Busenello. Boito's tone is closer to Berlioz than to Wagner, and he borrows from the Frenchman his sense of epic time, which differs radically from Wagner's timelessness-in-time. Nerone, as an epic figure, contains all previous "Nerones" within him, and in terms of the opera is most conscious of his precursor Oreste, who has similarly killed his mother and was similarly hounded for it by the Furies. This identification with Oreste becomes complete in the harrowingly grotesque scene of the fifth act. The burning of Rome (which in fact did not signal the end of the Empire), is likewise the collapse of Nerone and his world as well as the continuing evidence of the ultimate nihilism of evil from Babylon and Sodom onward. Thus, although Boito surrounds his tale with the "accurate" trappings and arcane language of ancient Rome, *Nerone* is even further removed from history than Scribe's *Grands Opéras*,

---

(8) The fact that Boito never set the fifth act to music is psychologically interesting, for the opera as it stands ends on the duet of the Christians, a sentimental nineteenth-century close that "works" when the opera is given, but has little relation to *Nerone*.

and the setting exists primarily as a scaffolding for Boito's imagination.

As can be imagined, the characters involved in this epic are overshadowed by the events, and moreover tend to become types or receptacles for ideals and tags of previous historical figures rather than creatures in their own right. Certainly Boito showed in *Nerone* that he needed a primary source to create memorable portraits of the like of Desdemona and Falstaff. Yet in his defense it should be said that in *Nerone* he was not trying to create that type of person, and if he moved away from the nineteenth-century concept of the "rounded" character, his overt intellectualism did not transform his personages into chimeras of his brain. In fact, the weakest characters in the opera are the ever-saintly Fanuèl—a stock figure from the nineteenth century—and Asteria, the complex combination of good and evil who is all too obviously modeled on Kundry.

The titular role, that of the Emperor Nerone (Nero), has always been judged as Boito's greatest incarnation of the Eternal Worm figure. Yet the character, by virtue simply of his identification with Oreste, if for no other reason, is not the inheritor of the Barnabà-Mefistofele-Zoroastro-Iago mantle, which is worn rather by Simon Mago, the bogus wizard-priest. This development is of great import, for it involves a fundamental change in Boito's thinking about evil. In *Nerone* evil has risen above the specific to the general—that is, to the decadence and death of the world—and it is this generalized evil which is plaguing Nerone and forces him to commit his crimes. Simon Mago, on the other hand, is shrunk from the other Worm-figures because he is a charlatan and knows he is a charlatan. His charlatanism also leads directly to his death—a fate that Boito conspicuously holds back from his other satanic totems. If Asteria (who adores Nerone to the point of idolatry) and Nerone are seen as dual-*Doppelgängers* of good and evil, Nerone's stature is greater because of his position and the immensity of his sufferings: he succeeds where she fails. The achievement of *Nerone* is that Boito, like Mussorgsky in *Boris Godunov*, managed to create a single vibrant central character and yet keep the focus on the epic nature of the surroundings.

The story, in terms of "plot," is simple, although the events are often complex because of the overlay of ambiguity with which Boito indulges himself. Nerone is seen at the height of his career, after he has committed the crimes that made him infamous: specifi-

347

cally, just after he has killed his mother, Agrippina. He has also, for purposes of the opera, raped a Vestal Virgin, Rubria, within the sacred precincts. The first act,[9] "The Appian Way," opens on a cloudy night outside Rome, near a sepulcher. Nerone is bringing an urn with the ashes of his mother to be buried, and Simon Mago has agreed to dig the grave so that no one will know. Simon Mago is the leader of a religious mystery cult that depends more on incense, pomp, and cheap miracles than on devotion, and he is hoping to use his growing friendship with Nerone to gain power over him. Nerone, for his part, is clearly under the spell of the Furies. The murder of his mother has unleashed the demons in him, and he has become frightened for his life, afraid of his people, and haunted by his feeling of kinship with Oreste. A mysterious voice (straight from *Les Troyens*) repeats: "*Nerone-Oreste,*" which frightens him further. While Nerone's friend Tigellino keeps watch, they bury the urn as the moon flits in and out of the clouds and voices of Soldiers are heard in the distance. Simon Mago, as part of the ceremony, insists that Nerone pour a cup of blood on the grave; when a veiled creature appears, Nerone, convinced that it is one of the Furies, flees with Tigellino.

The figure is that of Asteria, but Boito wants her to be seen not only as herself, but in her guise of one of the Furies as well. Her first line, "Whoever loves death may touch me," her priestly garb, and her unearthly tone are meant to suggest that she is neither one nor the other but a combination of the real and the supernatural. Simon Mago is not frightened, and discerns her attraction toward Nerone ("The horrible draws me like a lover"). She tells him that this sepulcher is an underground rendezvous of the Christians. Simon Mago takes a torch and goes inside to investigate.

Rubria, in a white robe, now appears to pray at the site, and begins to repeat the Lord's Prayer. Asteria, unseen by her, is moved by the sincerity of the prayer, but tears herself away, saying that she seeks another god. Fanuèl now enters, dressed in sailor's garb. He hardly believes Rubria when she tells him that she has a sin to confess—her seduction—but before she can tell him, he hears Simon Mago. She flees, and he is left with his enemy.

Simon comes out of the sepulcher, sees Fanuèl, takes him up

---

(9) In this synopsis, the version of *Nerone* that Boito published in 1901 as a book is used. There are several changes, mostly cuts, between it and the opera; the most important will be mentioned.

onto it, and shows him the world. The scene is an obvious parallel in Boito's mind with that of Satan tempting Christ, but the moment is not identical because of the change Boito wrought in his portrait of Simon. Simon realizes that he is a fraud, but he is unsure about Fanuèl. He suspects that the man may be a true magician—his mind cannot encompass the Christian charity that motivates Fanuèl's soul—and he wishes to persuade him to join forces with him, so that together they can control the world. Simon's splendid set-piece is, therefore, a far more accomplished tour de force of evil than the "Credo" from *Otello*, and excerpts from it will demonstrate both Boito's verbal power and the majesty of his vision:

> *S'avanza una gran nube*
> *di turbe. Echeggian trïonfali tube.*
> *E il matricida, ei vien col suo corteo*
> *d'istrïoni e d'Eumenidi all'assalto*
> *del mondo reo.*
> *Per te, per te fulgida un'ora ascende!*
> *Dammi la fè che spiri e quella Grazia*
> *che sol l'impronta di tue palme accende*
> *e afferriamo quest'ora!*
> *. . . . .*
> *Guarda quaggiù: pel sangue che l'inonda*
> *l'arca d'oro di Cesare sprofonda,*
> *furibonda ruìna e precipizio;*
> *plebe nefande confuse nel vizio*
> *plaudono a Roma che canta e che crolla.*
> *Tremano tutti: Cesare, la folla,*
> *le coorti. Fischiò negli angiporti*
> *già il greculo rubel. Cadono i morti*
> *nel Circo e cadon nel triclinio i vivi*
> *e i Numi in ciel! Con me su quei captivi*
> *del fango e della porpora distendi*
> *le tue mani, la tua Magìa mi vendi;*
> *due Sovraumani vedrà il mondo allor!*
> *Vendi i prodigi tuoi, t'offro dell'or.*[1]

---

(1) "A great crowd is advancing, in a cloud. Triumphal trumpets echo. It is the matricide; he's coming with his following of actors and Furies to attack the guilty world. For you a resplendent hour is rising! Give me the faith you breathe and that Grace which only the signs of your zeal can inspire. [*Palme* here is a word-play with the Christian symbol of the palm.] Then let us seize this hour! . . . Look there, the golden orb of Caesar is split open by the blood

Fanuèl rejects the bargain with a curse, and Simon replies by vowing eternal hatred. Fanuèl exits, and Nerone and Tigellino return, Nerone now splendidly dressed. He is still anxious about the appearance of the Fury and wants to flee, he knows not where. He is afraid of the reaction of his subjects, and in the distance the sounds of approaching people are heard. He hides in his cloak.

What evolves now is a cross between the Triumphal Scene of *Aida* and something out of Cecil B. DeMille, but before dismissing this spectacle as excessive, we should understand its purpose. Boito gives careful directions as to the *défilade* of the legions of the Empire before Nerone, but to do him justice he does not mean it solely or even primarily as a colossal "tornado" curtain. Again, the naturalistic is mixed with the epic and the supernatural: what transpires is more a vision than an actuality—the vision of Rome in its majesty. Just as Wagner harnessed the spectacle elements of *Grand Opéra* for his purposes Boito used them for his, and the parade of Praetorians, Centurions, Roman Mobs, Young Girls, Subjugated Tribes, Dionysiacs etc., etc., are meant to be built up into a gigantic hymn of praise for Nerone. At its climax the sun breaks forth and reveals Nerone, clothed in gold, as its extension, and the curtain falls on what must be the logical end of the grandiose. What is significant, however, is that this end closes not the opera but merely the first act: in Boito's mind, the rest moves downward to destruction.

Act II, "The Temple of Simon Mago," is set in the cloistered and mysterious precincts, heavy with incense and chanting, that are sacred to the charlatan.[2] He and his followers are seen mocking the rites being performed. Simon has persuaded Nerone to come to the temple to participate, and Nerone has agreed, in his desire to be rid of the Furies. Simon intends to use Asteria as bait. He is under no illusions: "Oh, how fatuous is the faith of man . . . Pray, fools, pray. Meanwhile, dictating worthless fortunes to the oracle,

---

that floods over it—furious ruin and headlong fall—an evil populace confused in vice applauds Rome, which sings and crumbles. Everyone trembles: Caesar, the mob, the cohorts. The Greek rebels have already hissed among the alleys [another word-play, since *angiporti* also means "brothels"]. The dead fall in the Circus, the living in the Triclinium, and the gods in Heaven. With me you extend your hands over those captives of mud and the Purple. Sell me your magic: the world will then see two Supermen! Sell me your miracles; I offer you gold."
(2) Note the Scribean open-closed scene alternation.

the priest laughs behind the altar." He warns Asteria to obey him, and conducts Nerone to the altar. Asteria is seen reflected in a mirror.

Nerone begins his incantations, calling on her as the goddess of death. He works himself into a frenzy, calling her Rubria; she, on the other hand, becomes more and more aroused by his ardor. The Berliozian oracle intones the chant *"Nerone-Oreste"* in the background. Finally, she allows Nerone to kiss her, and he is revolted to find that she is human and not a goddess. He comes to his senses; calls the Praetorian Guard, smashes the idol, and reveals the fraud. Asteria is condemned to be thrown alive into a snake pit[3] and Simon Mago, who has long boasted about his ability to fly, is told that he will get his chance in the Circus. Nerone, now in high good humor, ends the act by striking a pose as Apollo Musagetes and beginning to sing.

If the act ending is, as a stage picture, embarrassing next to Boito's best (Act III of *Otello*), the central portion of the act involves itself with that conflict of the real and the mystic which is so much part of the libretto. The libretto, particularly as it develops in the fifth act, is therefore a remarkable anticipation of Pirandello's dramatic ideas of intellectual dislocation.

The third act, "The Orchard," shifts the focus to the band of Christians led by Fanuèl. He is recounting the Beatitudes to them. Asteria appears, having escaped somehow from the snake pit, and Rubria offers her water;[4] she is greatly moved by their godliness. She warns them that Simon Mago is on his way, and—seized by a sudden convulsion—leaves. Simon arrives, pretending blindness, and tries once more to get Fanuèl to tell him his magic secrets so that he may fly. Fanuèl contemptuously refuses. Simon then denounces all of them, and calls the guards who have been following him to arrest the Christians. Fanuèl counsels non-resistance, and they all leave except for Rubria, who listens to their chanting until it disappears in the distance.

Again, in this act the diabolism of Simon Mago is made clear: not only does he betray the Christians (in an orchard, note), but also he is about to betray Nerone himself. He has arranged for his followers to set fire to Rome before he has to give his imitation

---

(3) In the final libretto, Boito added some lines to Asteria's part so that she reaffirmed her adoration for Nerone despite his sentence.
(4) The parallel to Kundry is here most evident.

of Icarus, and he thus hopes to escape punishment. That the city and its people will be his victims does not trouble him.

Act IV (the last completed) is in two scenes, and is entitled "The Circus Maximus." The first scene is set in the Oppidum, or self-contained portion, at one end of the Circus and which housed the stables. The various gladiatorial troupes pass by. Simon Mago is told that Asteria will set the fire, for, although she hates Simon, she wishes to save the Christians. Nerone arrives, and is warned that a conspiracy against him has been uncovered. But he refuses to listen: he is too absorbed in the progress of the games. Tigellino cannot therefore give the signal to have the conspirators arrested, and Nerone, through his willful obstinacy, becomes accessory to the destruction of Rome. At the moment when the Christians are to be sacrificed, Rubria appears in her Vestal robes and demands their release. Simon strips off her veil and reveals her as a Christian, and she too is led off to die. With the growing clamor Nerone becomes more and more crazed, finally erupting in his famous line: "The Monstrous is the Beautiful." Simon is taken to the highest point of the Circus and pushed off, and the flames begin to invade it.

The second scene takes place in the Spolarium, or place where the bodies of the dead are thrown. Asteria and Fanuèl, who have somehow escaped alive, are searching for Rubria. They find the body of Simon, then discover Rubria, who is still alive. The rest of the scene is a reconciliation between Rubria and Fanuèl, with Fanuèl telling her tales of Christ. The poetry is simple and touching in its use of soft sounds.[5] Rubria dies in Fanuèl's arms. Asteria, after a momentary spasm, like Amneris prays for her peace.

The fifth act, "The Theater of Nerone," is seen surrounded by the smoke and flames of the burning city. Everyone left alive has fallen into a sinkhole of license. Suddenly, from the stage, a Chorus of Furies appears dressed in horrific costumes, searching for Oreste. Oreste appears, in the traditional Greek theatrical garb (including the high shoes): he is Nerone. They begin to play a scene from Aeschylus' *Oresteia.*

---

(5) "*Laggiù,/fra i giunchi di Genèsareth, oscilla/ancor la barca ove prego Gesù./Quella cadenza placida di cuna/invita a stormi i bimbi sulla prora . . .*") ("There, among the rushes in Genesareth, still floats the boat on which Jesus prayed. The gentle rocking, like a cradle, lulls the children in the prow . . .")

This is the most bizarre borrowing from another source which Boito ever used, and it is one of the most bizarre scenes in the history of the libretto. Little wonder that he could not complete his vision with music. Ford's question, *"E sogno, o realtà"* ("Is it a dream or reality?"), has no answer, for the scene is ambiguous: it could be either, or both. The stage picture of a group of people acting out a play while a city burns around them is strange enough, but this only begins the questions. Is Nerone, now playing Oreste on stage, really Oreste, who has been playing Nerone in the opera? Is this excerpt from Aeschylus the only "real" play, while everything else, including the apocalyptic conflagration, has been merely imagination? These Pirandellan elements remain unresolved, for the Furies are both Furies and actors (they are shown being coached by one of Nerone's companions), and Nerone, although he insists on his identity as the Emperor, is both. The end of the world has tipped everything askew, so that nothing is what it seems.

At this moment, Asteria appears holding in her hand a bunch of live snakes, and everyone flees except Nerone. Smoke covers the scene ever more thoroughly, and in the background all that can be seen is the gilded inscription N E R O C A E S A R. She wants him to kill her; she tells him they are united in the fire and the horror of the scene. His mind begins to wander, he sees visions of the innocent dead—he sees Rubria. Asteria must have all of his love, and says that she must die destroyed by his love: kissing him, she kills herself. Now Nerone is left alone amid the ruin of his empire, and the voices call down destruction upon him. Like Don Giovanni, he seeks escape but cannot find it, as the walls crumble around him. He strikes the shield of Pallas, which makes a hollow sound, and the specters reply: "Accursed!"

The last act leaves Nerone alive, as with all of Boito's earlier Worm-figures, but the remorse and the anguish by which he is tortured set him apart from them, and give him a tragic stature. This is perhaps why Nerone is Boito's greatest creation, for Boito's pessimistic mind had an affinity for the Devil-figures which, in his earlier librettos, were painted all too blackly or, as with Mefistofele, with a grandiloquent stage irony that obscured rather than illumined his depths.

Nerone the libretto, despite its central portrait and its astounding picture of a crumbling civilization, must stand as a monumental *oeuvre manquée.* Even in this work, the most personal of all of

Boito's librettos, there are too many tags of other works which have been only partially assimilated into the whole. Whereas Wagner was able to steal from everyone and make the result his own, Boito's adaptive excellence inhibited his creative mind. Yet even given the faults of the work, its merits burn into the mind. To the classical opera that had culminated with *Les Troyens* Boito has added grotesquerie and a pessimistic vision which is world-embracing. The quirky madness of Nerone and of the opening scene of the fifth act will not be effaced, and the vision of the death of man, far more complete than Wagner's at the end of the *Ring* cycle, ushers in the twentieth century with an apocalyptic vengeance. *Nerone*, Boito's work, is Boito's epitaph.

What is evident is that the celebrated duality that haunted Boito's life was less the duality of good vs. evil than the duality of the creative vs. the critical and adaptive mind. Because opera is the combination of libretto and music, and because the question of creativity is secondary to the value of the whole, Boito will live for his Verdi adaptations. Perhaps, then, it is fitting to close on an excerpt from a fragment: the surviving beginning to Boito's *Re Lear*, which he, hopefully, began for Verdi after *Falstaff*. That both men were temperamentally suited for the work is beyond question; that Lear would have become Boito's living Nerone is likewise certain. Symbolically, then, this fragment stands for the man's endeavor, which accomplished so much but left so much undone:

LEAR: *Io voglio affigger qui l'atto supremo*
del regno mio.
La mappa a me.
Sappiate
che abbiam diviso in tre parti il reame,
risoluti a sottrar nostra vecchiaia
alle cure di stato e ad avviarci
senza ingombri al sepolcro.[6]

---

(6) "Meantime we shall express our darker purpose./Give me the map there. Know that we have divided/In three our kingdom: and 'tis our fast intent/To shake all cares and business from our age;/Conferring them on younger strengths, while we/Unburdened crawl toward death." (I, i.)

Chapter Twenty-one

The German and Italian Librettos of the Fin de Siècle and Early Twentieth Century

THE PRE-WORLD WAR I LIBRETTO in Germany and Italy did not have the literary distinction of that in France, with the exception of the Italian operas adapted from the writings of the playwright Sem Benelli and the poet Gabriele d'Annunzio. The German libretto lay under the heavy hand of Wagner, whose posthumous influence extended less to the creation of myth-operas than to the structural idea of the single *dramaturge*. The composer was meant not to adapt but to create, and these creations can be witnessed in not only the imitative Homeric cycle of operas that August Bungert wrote for his intended Bayreuth on the Rhine, but in such other works as Richard Strauss's first, very Wagnerian, opera, *Guntram* (1894), and, latterly, Hans Pfitzner's best work, *Palestrina* (1917), as well as the operas of Franz Schreker, notably *Der ferne Klang* (1912) and *Der Schatzgräber* (1920). Schreker's work, in its tortured neo-Romantic eroticism, reflects the prewar era rather than Wagner, and in its use of supernatural elements goes back to the operas of Marschner. The German libretto, however, emerged from the grasp of Wagner only in the twentieth century, with the work of Hugo von Hofmannsthal, an Austrian poet and playwright, and Bertolt Brecht, whose contributions began in the late twenties and were halted by the advent of Hitler.

The Italian libretto, on the other hand, displayed a greater

amount of originality. Its most original contribution cannot be
ascribed to a single librettist, but became for a time an operatic
genre, and led in turn to one of the cardinal features of the
twentieth-century libretto. This was the development of the
verismo opera. The veristic strain rode to prominence on the fame
of Pietro Mascagni's first opera, *Cavalleria rusticana* (1890; l.,
Guido Menasci and Giovanni Targioni-Tozzetti, from the play of
Giovanni Verga), which was combined with Ruggiero Leoncavallo's *I Pagliacci* (1892; l., Leoncavallo). This duo stood for the
blood-and-hate world of *verismo*. *Verismo*, which spread beyond Italy to Germany (*Tiefland*, 1903; m., Eugene d'Albert;
l., Rudolf Lothar) and France (*La Navarraise*, 1894; m., Massenet;
l., Jules Clarétie and Henri Cain), was in fact a continuation of
the immediate emotional appeal of the middle Verdi operas, but
on a more genre-oriented and melodramatically compressed level.
The vogue for *verismo* died soon after it flowered, but it left several residual evidences. The first was the heightened emotionalism-
for-its-own-sake of the whole, which was metamorphosed into the
decadent—very much a part of fin-de-siècle thought—and which
appeared in the librettos of *Elektra* and, primarily, *Salome*. The
febrile, depraved world of Salome—brought over intact from
Oscar Wilde's *Salomé*—is leagues removed from the treatment
Paul Milliet and Georges Hartmann made in the accepted French
manner for Massenet as *Hérodiade* in 1881, yet its excesses were to
be duplicated—without the compression—in such an opera as
Camille Erlanger's *Aphrodite* (1906; l., Louis de Gramont, from
the novel by Pierre Louÿs), in which (among other events) an
innocent girl is crucified on stage. It was this breeding ground of
the world gone mad which was to produce Berg's two great operas,
the first of which, *Wozzeck*, would depict the individual attempting to exist in such a world and failing, and the second of which,
Lulu, would depict the debased nature of the whole, so that characters are shrunk to animal stature and the farcical grotesque co-
exists with the middle-class genre setting.[1]

The other aspect of *verismo* which survived was the single-
act form. It is curious that, in this case, circumstances dictated the
form, for originally Mascagni had intended to play *Cavalleria* in

---

(1) There is a strong relationship between the Wedekind plays on
which *Lulu* was based and the "boulevard" farces of the time, represented in France by Feydeau and in Austria by Johann Nestroy.

two acts linked by an intermezzo, but the ongoing nature of the piece made it much preferable to perform in a single sitting. The dramatic punch this gave to the story was obvious, and the form, which had once been reserved for light intermezzos between the acts of heavier fare, now became powerful in its own right; it established itself fully with such operas as *Salome* and *Elektra*. The twentieth century would see the broadening of the concept of the one-act form, in part because of its success in veristic opera, but also as a rebellion against the ponderous five-act operas and lengthy myth-dramas of the nineteenth century. Certainly Stravinsky's stage works proceed from this second premise (with the rejection as much motivated by Rimsky-Korsakov's operas as by those of Wagner).

Besides the veristic operas—actually, few in number—the dominant type of late-nineteenth–early-twentieth-century Italian libretto derived, ultimately, from the Scribe well-made play through the modifications made by Scribe's leading French disciple, Victorien Sardou. These were the genre tales of sentimental suspense which are tied in the operagoer's mind to the works of Puccini. The stories take as their basis less the *Grand Opéra* Scribe than the *opéra comique* Scribe, but with added touches of verisimilitude of setting and *mores*. The leading librettist of this genre type was Luigi Illica, who collaborated on the Puccini librettos of *La Bohème*, *Tosca*, and *Madama Butterfly*, but whose other librettistic work was almost invariably done alone. Illica was in no sense a great librettist, and his lack of poetic talent led Puccini to employ Giuseppe Giacosa—himself a playwright—to versify the librettos, but Illica well reflects the type. What is notable in the Illica librettos—he wrote about thirty, a small number compared with the output of earlier librettists but a great many for the end of the nineteenth century—is the extent to which the French influence had penetrated Italy. Love itself plays a more dominating role in the stories, and although hate is also present, most notably in *Tosca*, it is of far less import than in the middle Verdi *melodrammi*. Indeed, in *La Bohème* and *Madama Butterfly* it is absent, and in *Andrea Chénier* (1896; m., Umberto Giordano), an early Illica libretto and one of his most characteristic, it is strongly tempered; for although Gérard the revolutionary dislikes Chénier and loves Maddalena, he is too goodhearted to remain obdurate, repents after he signs Chénier's death warrant, and tries vainly to save him.

Chénier well demonstrates the French influences on the form. It is a genre opera, in the sense that it gives a series of tableau-portraits of France before and after the Revolution, replete with historical characters (Robespierre, Fouquier-Tinville). Illica also includes a measure of social consciousness, for Gérard is portrayed as genuinely inspired by the ideals of the Revolution, and if the focus of the libretto remains on the love story and sentimental touches, such as a woman giving her last son to the Nation as a soldier,[2] the stage picture is far closer to being historically accurate than the *Grands Opéras* of Scribe. The first act is a good representation of the *ancien régime* in its decadence, and the second and third are vivid scenes of Paris during the Terror—the spies, the mobs, the sense of insecurity and panic which underlay each day's activity. Illica also took over the French practice—theretofore rare in the Italian libretto—of providing copious, detailed stage directions and historical justifications in the libretto itself—extending to the genre elements he wanted in the setting. As with Scribe, in the best of Illica's work these elements mitigate or outweigh the standard love plot, or, as in *Bohème*, combine with it to make such an ineradicable whole that the opera has become symbolic of "artist life," even to those artists who know that it is photographed through rose-tinted lenses and gauze scrims but who like to think that this must be the way they live.

In Illica this emphasis on novelty of setting became a repeated trait, so that history and geography were served with librettos on Columbus (*Cristoforo Colombo,* 1892; m., Franchetti); on the awakening of the spirit of freedom in Germany (*Germania*); on Russia and the snow-swept prison camps of Siberia (*Siberia,* 1903; m., Giordano); on the Lady Godiva legend (*Isabeau,* 1911; m., Mascagni); and on Japan (not only *Butterfly* but also the earlier *Iris,* 1898; m., Mascagni). In all of these works there is an entirely Italian quality of naïveté present, which sets the librettos apart from their French progenitors and from the veristic counterparts in Italy.

This quality also sets them apart from the work of two Italian

---

(2) Illica unfortunately was not one to forget a show-stopping moment, and in his libretto for *Germania* (1902; m., Alberto Franchetti) uses it again: the quarrel between two factions fighting for German freedom is ended when a mother donates her son to the cause. But here—added twist—it is not just any woman: it is Louisa, Queen of Prussia, who is the donor!

poet-playwrights whose contributions to the form were incidental to their other work, but who, with such men as Giacosa, exemplified the extent to which the French habit of being first a playwright and then a writer for the musical theater had extended to Italy. These were Gabriele d'Annunzio and Sem Benelli. D'Annunzio, of course, was one of the major figures of fin-de-siècle Italian literature, both as a writer and as a personage modeling himself after the Romantic Victor Hugo and leading a flamboyant life that was to culminate, after the First World War, with a Garibaldi-like raid on the city of Fiume—he held it as a personal fiefdom for over a year. His poetry and his plays combined eroticism with extravagant use of language, heightened by melodrama and *verismo* horror and often enwrapped in inflated symbolism. Although the verbiage remains heavy and, finally, static in its Hugoesque imitations, d'Annunzio's plays are nevertheless very much a product of the fin-de-siècle modes of thought, combining philosophical effluvia from Wagner and the concept of the Superman from Nietzsche and forcing this into an Italian mold. His play *La Nave*, with its invocation of Venetian history, its symbolism of the conquering ship (named "All the World"), and the ecstatic, quasi-religious tone of its closing pages, carried the spirit of nationalism far past the bounds of the early Verdi choruses and brought it to the threshold of national despotism. Not surprisingly, d'Annunzio was one of the strong supporters of Mussolini.

Several of d'Annunzio's plays were made into librettos (e.g., *La Nave* for Montemezzi [1918] and *Francesca da Rimini* for Riccardo Zandonai [1914]—both done by Tito Ricordi), but d'Annunzio himself provided the texts for *Parisina* (1913; m., Mascagni) and *Fedra* (m., Ildebrando Pizzetti). *Parisina* is a sort of amalgam of the Pelléas story with middle Verdi melodrama, symbolism, and effulgence of language. Perhaps the most interesting of d'Annunzio's works for the stage was *Le Martyre de Saint-Sébastien*, which he wrote for Debussy. As a hybrid, part oratorio, part dance, and part drama, it served to break down the barriers between opera and its allied forms, and although the language is considerably faded today, the structure can be viewed as a way station between Berlioz and the twentieth century.

Sem Benelli, on the other hand, moved in a far more restricted —and ultimately more long-lasting—circle. His two most famous play adaptations for the libretto were taken from his two most famous plays, *L'Amore dei tre re* (1913; m., Montemezzi) and *La Cena delle beffe* (1924; m., Giordano). *L'Amore dei tre re*, with its evocation of the Italian legendary past, its strong characterizations and muted symbolism, recalls the plays of Maeterlinck; *La Cena delle beffe* combines the *commedia* spirit with a veristic black humor in which the underdog "comic" has his revenge on his tormentor by cuckolding him and arranging for him to kill his own brother—all of which drives the tormentor mad. Thus, the harmless sexual gavottes of the *commedia* plays have taken a sinister turn, resulting not only in Benelli's work but also in the *Arlecchino* of Ferruccio Busoni.

What is more important than an extended discussion of the Italian librettos of the end-nineteenth and early-twentieth centuries is the realization of the extent to which the Italian librettistic esthetic had changed. Illica still provided what could be termed "an Italian libretto," but it too had been greatly influenced by the French stage. Yet the spirit of adherence to the original, which had been brought home to the Italians by Boito, coupled with the growing power of the Italians as stage artists rather than as librettists, meant that the librettos produced were, in the sense of *Pelléas*, extremely close to the original in language and in spirit. There was no "adaptation" in the sense that Romani had adapted his sources —Ricordi's reductions of d'Annunzio's plays were essentially reductions and not adaptations.

Further, the modern Italian libretto, which has today been confined on stage to the works of Puccini, was remarkable not only for its quality but also for its scope. As had been the case in France, the libretto was not restricted to the *melodramma* formula but could embrace a variety of approaches equally well. The contrasts in tone and spirit within the Italian libretto are well encapsulated in Puccini's *Il Trittico* (1918—*Il Tabarro:* l., Giuseppe Adami; *Suor Angelica* and *Gianni Schicchi:* l., Giovacchino Forzano), in which the first opera is a *verismo* work, the second an exercise in sentiment in the French vein, and the third a brilliant modern *commedia* play. Yet any study of the differing texts set by Mascagni, Montemezzi, Franchetti, Puccini, and Leoncavallo will demonstrate the strength of the Italian libretto of its time, and if many of the conceits of the period have ceased to appeal with the power they once had, the vitality of the period is evident.

Chapter Twenty-two

Hofmannsthal

T HE TWENTIETH CENTURY has seen both a decline in the absolute numbers of operas written and a decline in the artistic
influence of the form itself, but it has also seen a corresponding
widening of the conceptions of what opera and what the libretto
are and should be. This breaking down of structural, organizational, and esthetic-dogmatic barriers was a common occurrence
extending to all the arts; what was equally true was that, unlike
the experience of previous centuries, no one discipline gained even
a pre-eminence in its own country (as, say, *melodramma* did in
nineteenth-century Italy), but a host of differing approaches co-
existed at the same time. Some of these, naturally, were holdovers
from the previous century, either in organizational or esthetic
terms. Thus, the Scribe-Sardou "line" came down through the
librettos set by composers from Puccini and Ermanno Wolf-Fer-
rari to Gian Carlo Menotti; while the Wagnerian esthetic that
called for the composer to create his own world—which would
be a reflection of his inner self—resulted in two incomplete works,
one an oratorio and one an opera, by Arnold Schönberg, *Die
Jakobsleiter* and *Moses und Aron*. Similarly, the refinement of the
"composer as librettist" strain, in which the composer takes over
another work almost intact, extended from *Pelléas* to the *Wozzeck*
and *Lulu* of Alban Berg, while the more traditional adaptations
of another source by librettist and composer for the operatic stage
can be evidenced by the librettos for Benjamin Britten—and numerous other composers.

The twentieth century, likewise, has produced a number of
librettists whose contributions, either as adaptations or as creative
works, have matched those of their predecessors, the major dif-

ference being that the number of librettos written by any one librettist has shrunk drastically, not only from the eighty or so produced by Romani, but even from the more limited number produced by Illica. The most famous inheritor of the title of professional librettist, in terms of quality and number of works produced, is Gian Carlo Menotti, who has written serious and comic librettos, one-act and full-length, and works tailored to television and production in church and amateur groups as well as in the professional operatic theater.

Yet in any study of the libretto of the twentieth century one figure rises above the other librettists: that of Hugo von Hofmannsthal. Hofmannsthal is important not because he necessarily produced greater single examples of librettos than any of the others or because he brought new approaches to the form, but because, in the space of only six opera librettos which he wrote for Richard Strauss,[1] he revealed himself as a creative mind of exceptional penetration and sensibility.

Hofmannsthal was born in Vienna in 1874, and in his earliest youth achieved fame as a poet, under the pen name "Loris." After school, he studied law and took a Ph.D., all the while writing verse. He turned to writing plays as well during the 1890's, and began his collaboration with Strauss with *Elektra* (1909), an adaptation of one of his play adaptations of Sophocles. His work on the libretto paralleled his work for the spoken theater, and in the years in which he created for Strauss he also wrote *Jedermann* (1911), *Die Schwierige* (1918), and *Der Turm* (1925, revised 1927), among other plays. His great friendship with the director Max Reinhardt led the two of them to found what has now become the Salzburg Festival. Hofmannsthal died in 1929, just after sending Strauss the revised first act of their last collaborative effort, *Arabella*.

Hofmannsthal, more than any other librettist, has been used as the touchstone of the proposition that two minds do not have to flow in a single channel in order to create opera, for he and

---

(1) Seven, if the two versions of *Ariadne auf Naxos* are counted. He also adapted Euripides for Egon Wellesz in his one-act *Alkestis* (1924). After Hofmannsthal's death one of his plays, *Das Bergwerk zu Falun*, was made into an opera by Rudolf Wagner-Régeny and given at the Salzburg Festival in 1961.

362

Richard Strauss were profoundly different characters who, it is safe to say, never completely understood one another but worked together for a space of twenty years because of an underlying affinity and because each respected the other's accomplishment.[2] They rarely met, and carried on their collaboration through the mails, a fact that has left posterity with a valuable record of their misunderstandings and concords, their hopes and their vanities, their work habits and their social lives. The men revealed in this correspondence will doubtless always be subject to debate,[3] for the letters answer few questions finally; but the correspondence itself is a detailed ledger sheet of what happens when a composer and a librettist get together to create a work of art, and as such it is of immense value to any student of the art form.

Hofmannsthal, like Boito before him, was a highly educated and sensitive mind, attuned to nuance of word and character and extremely widely read. Unlike Boito, he had no real love of music or great appreciation for it, revering the masters more because they were masters than because of a love for the music they wrote. His poetry, almost all of which was written before the collaboration began, combines beauty of language with this subtlety of nuance and, although tied to the late-nineteenth-century penchant for symbolism, continues to be powerful because of its lyricism and relative directness of appeal.

It is dangerous to simplify Hofmannsthal, for man and artist were always a complex web of interrelated and often conflicting strands of sensibilities. Yet his motivation for entering into a collaboration with Strauss at a time when he was famous throughout Austria and Germany as a poet and becoming equally famous as a playwright can be judged in part as vanity—a wish to join forces with a world-famous composer; in part as ambition—a wish to see his work combined with music to achieve something more than a

---

(2) There is a story that Hofmannsthal once disparaged Strauss's talents vis-à-vis those of Beethoven, but its importance has been exaggerated. Hofmannsthal would never have collaborated with a man whom he artistically despised, nor did he have any need to despise Strauss.

(3) The letters can be interpreted from the point of view of either man to the detriment of the other. They should always be read with the knowledge that each man was in addition writing for posthumous publication.

play; and in part egoistic—a wish to bend Strauss to his own uses. William Mann, in his book on the Strauss operas,[4] has carried this last to the conclusion of viewing Hofmannsthal as a Mephisto figure who prevented the composer from developing into a Schön-berg-like influence on modern music. Although any study of Strauss's personality and music will effectively negate that extreme assumption, the force of Hofmannsthal's will is felt in the col-laboration, and there is no doubt that the choice of subject rested entirely in his hands. Thus, although Strauss would have liked to write prop-and-plot melodramas of the Sardou type and, after *Der Rosenkavalier* (1911), yearned for its repetition, Hofmannsthal led him away to a consideration of the duality of the comic and the tragic (*Ariadne auf Naxos*, first version, 1912; second version, 1916—in the first version it is combined with a straight play), then to a vast symbolically oriented world of fairy tale (*Die Frau ohne Schatten*, 1919), and finally to an exercise in Greek myth (*Die Ägyptische Helena*, 1928) before returning to comedy of man-ners with *Arabella* (1933). This list leaves aside the *Josephslegende*, a ballet built around the Biblical legend of Joseph and his brothers. Little wonder that, in the course of this journey, Strauss abandoned Hofmannsthal long enough to write an autobiographical genre opera, *Intermezzo* (1924).

Yet Strauss's complaisance has great import for the history of the libretto, for his willingness to set to music the fruits of Hof-mannsthal's thoughts re-established, at least in part, that ideal of librettistic pre-eminence which had been disappearing since Meta-stasio's time with the rise in importance of the musical side of the collaboration. The result is that although every one of Hofmanns-thal's librettos after *Elektra* possesses flaws, and in the case of *Helena* the flaws are serious, they represent a librettistic personality and, more, a development over a span of works which had become almost unknown in major librettists—unless, like Wagner, the librettist set his own music. Hofmannsthal's example, then, not only is fascinating from a librettistic viewpoint but also has served to revive and restore the concept of the librettist as a creative artist on a par with the composer. His achievement is reflected in the librettistic work of Bertolt Brecht and has influenced the work of

(4) William Mann: *Richard Strauss, A Critical Study of the Operas*, p. 167. A more reasoned approach is made by Norman Del Mar in the second volume of his life and works of Strauss.

W. H. Auden and Chester Kallman, who dedicated their libretto for *The Elegy for Young Lovers* (1961; m., Hans Werner Henze) to Hofmannsthal.

An examination of the artistic misunderstandings between Strauss and Hofmannsthal is outside the scope of this book, except to note the fact, already stated, that such cross-purpose collaboration does not necessarily work to the detriment of the final result. Strauss's mind did not move with the subtlety or the quick intelligence of Hofmannsthal's, but on the other hand Strauss had a much surer grip on what was theatrically possible. Thus, the compromises effected were often to the betterment of the work—for instance, the second-act finale of *Der Rosenkavalier,* which was essentially Strauss's idea—and if, as in *Die Frau ohne Schatten,* Strauss glossed over a great deal of Hofmannsthal's characterizational and philosophic points, he nonetheless provided the surging power that drives the opera forward. A study of Hofmannsthal's draft first act for *Arabella* and the revision he provided after Strauss's perceptive and just criticism will serve to show the extent of positive collaboration between the two men, and the vast improvement in the revised first act demonstrates how understanding the supposedly arrogant Hofmannsthal could be, as well as the fact that Hofmannsthal, though by no means a master of stagecraft, was better than he is often given credit for being.

What has all too often been overlooked in the examination of the Strauss-Hofmannsthal relationship is the broad area of underlying sympathy between two artistic minds which kept the collaboration from foundering on the rocks of non-understanding and petty vanities. One major cause of this sympathy can be rather easily traced, for it lies in the women that Hofmannsthal created for Strauss—not Elektra, but those women who combine intense femininity with grace and intelligence. Strauss's weakness for this side of the *Ewigweibliche* was brought out fully by Hofmannsthal, and although Strauss translated Hofmannsthal's elegant and charming portraits into something with more sentiment, he nonetheless preserved the essence of Hofmannsthal's characters. Yet, in a larger sense, it is less the characters themselves than the aura that they radiate which attracted Strauss. For Hofmannsthal was the greatest librettist of love: love as understood in its widest sense as a blend of compassion, friendship, and understanding through love—which is expressed at its most perfect in the marriage union between mature individuals and in the consequent creation of a family. Such a focus in an artist can easily become sentimental and mawkish if not tempered with delicacy and understanding. Hofmannsthal luckily possessed both. All of Hofmannsthal's librettos for Strauss contain aspects of this type of love, which is at the opposite pole from what Hofmannsthal called "the intolerable erotic screamings" of Tristan and Isolde. This did not mean, of course, that the sexual element was sacrificed—quite the contrary, as all the librettos attest—but that the neurotic elements of the Wagner opera were replaced by an examination of love in its human and humane terms.

Hofmannsthal viewed this appreciation of earthly love in the form of a progress, not unlike Bunyan's *Pilgrim's Progress* but with its roots more directly in the ethic of *Die Zauberflöte*. This "progress" is most clearly visible in *Die Frau ohne Schatten*, but all of his creative librettos[5] contain the element in a subtilized form, and its elaboration is far more important than the exigencies of the plot line.

Hofmannsthal's librettos themselves mark their own progress, which took the form of a gradual development and efflorescence of the theme of love with each work. Such development within the oeuvre of a librettist is very unusual, and it gives Hofmannsthal's librettos a tighter unity than his stage works, thus allowing them to be judged more cogently as a continuing body of work. Almost certainly the presence of Strauss aided this ordering process, for Hofmannsthal knew that Strauss liked composing to the themes of love, and reserved for his librettos those ideas he had which embroidered on that theme.

Hofmannsthal's dramatic mind worked essentially in two contrasting areas, both of which were reinforced by his poetic gifts and the principles operative in the verse he wrote in his early years. One of these areas was the symbolic myth, or myth-tale, which is reflected in *Die Ägyptische Helena* and, most comprehensively, in *Die Frau ohne Schatten*; the other is the period comedy of manners, seen in *Der Rosenkavalier* and *Arabella*. Both areas have their dramatic counterparts: the first in *Jedermann* and *Der Turm*, the second in *Der Schwierige*. *Ariadne* stands apart, for it is essen-

---

(5) That is, the librettos written after *Elektra*, which was, although free, an adaptation of Sophocles.

tially an exercise, growing out of two experiments that Hofmannsthal was pursuing and which constitute his most daring (and only partly successful) structural novelty. This was the combination of straight play and opera (in the original version), and the combination of the *tragédie lyrique* and the *commedia* art forms, which had been a feature of seventeenth- —and much eighteenth- —century opera in the sense of an opera with light intermezzos between the acts, but which had been forgotten with the arrival of *Grand Opéra* and Wagner.[6] Hofmannsthal, however, took the final step and conflated tragedy and comedy into a single entity, thus preserving the identities of the rival methods but forcing them to coexist, to the ironic benefit of each.

Hofmannsthal's ability may be gauged by the success with which he worked in the two areas, although the comedies of manners show him at his more relaxed and generally more adept. But what saves *Die Frau ohne Schatten* and, lesserly, *Helena* from symbolic and hieratic petrifaction is precisely the qualities more fully developed in the comedies: the superb nuancing of the characters in their humanity, the use of language, and the general excellence of the poetic verse. Hofmannsthal consciously sacrificed suppleness in his two myth-tales in order to achieve monumentality, but he was careful to temper the loss.

What is notable in the myth-tales, and even in the comedies, is the extent to which Hofmannsthal's mind was allusive in the sense that it constantly implied outward from the facts of the libretto. This can be seen on various levels. Because Hofmannsthal was an omniverous intellect, he picked up threads and details from every source, and the list of sources for *Die Frau ohne Schatten* is huge. The same is true of the sources for *Der Rosenkavalier*, with respect to the story, the plot details, and the genre elements. In *Die Frau,* Hofmannsthal's work in constructing the myth-world in which the story takes place was so comprehensive that he felt it necessary to write a very long "Arabian Nights" prose tale on the subject, which amplifies the already comprehensive libretto but which, in itself, is incomplete.

In story terms, this allusiveness pushes the librettos past the

---

(6) It should not be forgotten that, well into the nineteenth century, performances of opera were often interspersed with ballets during the intermissions, thus providing a definite break in continuity, as the ballets had their own "stories."

curtains or the bounds of the stage. Whereas in *Grand Opéra,* the *melodramma,* or Wagner, the libretto was largely self-contained, in Hofmannsthal, particularly in the comedies, the impression is of an unfinished whole of which the scenes are but sketches. One of Hofmannsthal's axioms goes: "Each true work of art is the blueprint for the only temple on earth," and the two key words are "true" and "blueprint." The construction of the temple was left to the mind of the beholder.[7] In this sense Hofmannsthal's comedies are very like those of Beaumarchais, who, after *Le Barbier de Séville,* went on to write a second and a third play about its characters.

More immediately, this allusiveness can be seen as an off-stage dimension that gives depth to the actions on stage. Hofmannsthal constantly invokes beyond the playing area, and the unseen character of Uncle Greifenklau in *Der Rosenkavalier* is only the most famous and touching example of this habit. The Marschallin, in parting from Octavian, tells him: "*Quinquin, Er soll jetzt gehn. Er soll mich lassen./Ich werd' jetzt in die Kirchen gehn,/und spater fahr' ich zum Onkel Greifenklau,/der alt und gelahmt ist,/ und ess' mit ihm; das freut den alten Mann.*"[8] We never see Greifenklau, but the Marschallin's explanation of her sacrifice to him makes her character even more endearing while fleshing out the picture of the world in which she exists. Similarly, the vividness of the portraits of country life painted by Ochs and, contrastingly, by Mandryka in *Arabella* enhance their own characters.

Of course, this last example of Hofmannsthal's allusiveness is bound up with his portrayal of character on stage, and therefore involves his use of language and verse.

Hofmannsthal had an excellent apprenticeship in poetry in his youth, when he was widely celebrated as a poetic prodigy, and he developed that use of verse in his works for the stage. He is one of the greatest librettistic poets, and no librettist since Metastasio has equaled his handling of verse over such a span of works. His poetry is characterized by its thorough professionality: the ease

(7) This "blueprint" nature is evidenced in Hofmannstahl's works, for he continually used earlier works as fodder for later ones.
(8) "Quinquin, you must go now. You must leave me. I am going to church, and later I'll drive to see Uncle Greifenklau, who is old and lame, and dine with him. It will please the old man."

of its clarity and lyric mellifluousness. Unlike Metastasio's, however, this poetic facility never falls into empty sound for its own sake. What is more important is that, at every line, this verse is dramatic, amplifying character and adding to the moment on stage.

Many examples of the beauty of Hofmannsthal's verse exist, and they are paradoxical examples in that the musical quality of the verse is so perfectly expressed that additional music is either superfluous or intrusive; and yet almost any music of the time in which the librettos were written—even given a reduced orchestra —would dominate. Strauss, however, recognized these moments when they appeared and handled them with a gentleness and a humanity that testify to his depth of appreciation for his collaborator. Arabella's dream of the "Right Man" is one:

> *Aber der Richtige—wenn's einen gibt für mich*
> *auf dieser Welt—*
> *der wird einmal dastehn, da vor mir,*
> *und wird mir anschaun und ich ihn,*
> *und keine Zweifel werden sein und keine Fragen,*
> *und selig, selig werd' ich sein und gehorsam wie ein kind.*[9]

Or the love duet in the second act of that opera, which is a distillate of love and some of the most beautiful lines ever penned for a libretto:

> *Und du wirst mein Gebieter sein, und ich dir untertan.*
> *Dein Haus wird mein Haus sein, in deinem Grab*
> *will ich mit dir begraben sein—*
> *so gebe ich mich dir auf Zeit und Ewigkeit.*[1]

Or the song of the Night Watchmen which closes the first act of *Die Frau ohne Schatten*, and which is powerful dramatically in that its call for fruitfulness contrasts with the barrenness of the two couples in the story, and contrasts with the immediately

---

(9) "But the right man, if there is one for me in all this world, will stand before me and will look at me and I at him, and there will be no doubts in me nor any questions, and I shall be happy— happy—and obedient like a child."
(1) "And you will be my master, and I obedient to you. Your house will be my house, and in your grave will I lie with you. So I give myself to you now and forever."

preceding scene, in which Barak's wife has banished him from the
marriage bed:

> *Ihr Gatten in den Häusern dieser Stadt,*
> *liebet einander mehr als euer Leben,*
> *und wisset: nicht um eures Lebens willen*
> *ist euch die Saat des Lebens anvertraut,*
> *sondern allein um eurer Liebe willen!*
> . . . .
> *Ihr Gatten, die ihr liebend euch in Armen liegt,*
> *ihr seid die Brücke, uberm Abgrund ausgespannt,*
> *auf der die Toten wiederum ins Leben gehn!*
> *Geheiligt sei eurer Liebe Werk!*[2]

Or the Marschallin's apprehension of the passage of time:

> *Die Zeit im Grund, Quinquin, die Zeit,*
> *die ändert doch nichts an den Sachen*
> *Die Zeit, die ist ein sonderbares Ding.*
> *Wenn man so hinlebt, is sie rein gar nichts.*
> *Aber dann auf einmal.*
> *Da spürt man nichts als sie.*
> *Sie ist um uns herum, sie ist auch in uns drinnen.*
> *In den Gesichtern rieselt sie, im Spiegel da rieselt sie,*
> *in meinem Schläfen fliesst sie.*
> *Und zwischen mir und dir da fliesst sie wieder.*
> *Lautlos, wie ein Sanduhr.*
> *Oh, Quinquin!*
> *Manchmal hör' ich sie fliessen unaufhaltsam.*
> *Manchmal steh' ich auf mitten in der Nacht*
> *und lass die Uhren alle, alle stehn.*[3]

---

(2) "You married couples in the houses of this town, love one
another more than your life itself, and know this: not for your own
life's sake is the seed of life entrusted to you, but only for the sake
of your love . . . You married couples, who lie in loving embrace,
you are the bridge spanning the gulf over which the dead may return
to life. Hallowed be your work of love."

(3) "Time, *au fond*, Quinquin, time changes nothing. Time is a strange
thing. When one lives for the moment, it is nothing. But then, all of
a sudden, one is aware of nothing else. It's all around us, it is even
inside of us. It trickles in our faces, it trickles in the mirror, it flows
in my temples. And between me and you it ever flows, silently, like
an hourglass. Oh, Quinquin! Often I hear it flowing—ceaselessly.
Often I get up in the middle of the night and stop all—all—the clocks."

To appreciate fully the verse qualities, as opposed to the characterizational qualities, of the Marschallin excerpt, it should be contrasted with some of Ochs's comic verse which occurs earlier in the act. *Der Rosenkavalier*, of course, is a paradise of the nuance in terms both of differing accents employed by the characters (there are at least five) and changing modes of expression (some apparently the inventions of Hofmannsthal himself), which were used to build up layers of patina for the portrait of the Vienna of Maria Theresa.[4] This approach to the genre libretto is thus far more thorough in its structural and formal preparation than the essentially outwardly applied genre touches of a librettist like Illica, for here the verbal sound—archaic or inflected—has joined the visual as reinforcement.

Hofmannsthal's verse, in its fluidity, approaches a melismatic prose, and although he could constrain it to stricter meter and rhyme, he preferred to let it flow freely, accenting the verse qualities by repetition, assonance, and light word-play. But, as with Busenello and every other great librettist, the verse was always subservient to its characterizational aspect, and here Hofmannsthal excelled. The Marschallin is perhaps the greatest of his creations, with Ochs, Octavian, Arabella, and Mandryka only slightly less memorable; but even his more rigidly circumscribed characters, such as Zerbinetta and Ariadne, Barak and his wife, the Empress and the Nurse,[5] and Menelaus and Helena, have a life and vibrancy that is, in the best sense, theatrical, and his thumbnail portraits—Faninal and Waldner especially[6]—are greatly rewarding to actors who know how to play them properly. Hofmannsthal's stagecraft has been often deprecated,[7] and to an extent justifiably, but no one who was not a dramatist could have created a portrait such as that of the Composer in the revised first act of

---

(4) Hofmannsthal used the same techniques in *Arabella*, but in a far less profligate way.

(5) The Nurse is the most interesting of the post-Kundry women torn between various unknown desires and hatreds, and although she is basically more evil than Kundry, she nonetheless represents a development of the Wagnerian premise, whereas Asteria was a re-creation.

(6) And, to a lesser extent, the marvelous hauteur of his Major Domos in *Der Rosenkavalier* and *Ariadne*, the latter of whom disdains even to sing his role.

(7) Even by his close friend Count Harry Kessler: "Hofmannsthal had no dramatic talent but sometimes, with the ravishing power of his lyricism . . . he achieves overpowering dramatic effects." Kessler's *Diary*, as excerpted in *Encounter* (September 1967), p. 24.

Ariadne—an exquisite quintessence of the Cherubino-figure *cum* sketch-of-the-arrogance-of-youthful-genius, all brought to life in the space of one short act. Hofmannsthal was incapable of not creating human beings on stage, a fact that Strauss fully appreciated. Yet the putting of these characters on stage effectively was always the most difficult task for Hofmannsthal, and one at which he worked the hardest: his failures arise from structural faults. *Die Ägyptische Helena,* as a libretto, is not inferior because Hofmannsthal was trying to rework a variant of the Helen story or because he used historical myth-figures, but because he allowed too much else, in the form of needless characters, unfortunate symbols (the all-knowing Mussel Shell, which on stage looks like an ancient phonograph or radio), and drawn-out elaboration to mitigate the essential force of the story.

Symbolism plays a vital role in the librettos of Hofmannsthal, a role intertwined with the characterizational and verbal aspects of the work, and like his allusiveness, it can be seen in various guises. The one-for-one correspondence is the easiest to grasp, and such symbols are used extensively in *Die Frau ohne Schatten,* but this approach to symbolism was only incidental in his subtle mind. Hofmannsthal, as a poet of nuance and half-light, saw symbolism as a reinforcement, not as an end in itself, and he used it—brilliantly, in stage terms—as a reflection and fulfillment of character rather than of meaning. The concept grew out of its use in his poetry. To take an example: the poem, *Die Beiden* (The Two, 1904), tells of a girl who brings a goblet of wine to a young man on a horse. She brings it to him without spilling it, but when she reaches up to him her hand and his tremble; their hands cannot touch and the wine spills. Thus the symbolic experience is total, encompassing the material objects (the glass and wine), the act itself (the handing up), the secondary objects (the hands), the secondary acts (the suddenly activated emotions of the two—even the movement of the horse), and, finally, the result (the spilling). Hofmannsthal is concerned with the whole of the experience, not simply the object itself, and therefore the symbolic moment becomes an instant codification of the preceding actions and intentions, heightened and illumined as a moment but neecssarily and integrally linked to the total work of art.

Hofmannsthal liked to call his use of this all-embracing approach to symbolism *gesture,* or the entire gesture becoming

372

the symbol. As such it is stage-conscious and radiates beyond the concrete manifestation. It is also, in its stylization, linked to the concept of gesture in Metastasio, with whom the exit aria served as the symbol for the preceding events.

This symbolism in gesture can be evidenced throughout Hofmannsthal's librettos, either by itself, without a conscious symbolic reference—as in the Marschallin's movement across the stage to Sophie in Act III of *Der Rosenkavalier*—or linked with a specific symbol such as Octavian, dressed in white, carrying the silver rose (from someone else, but, unbeknownst to himself, actually from him) to Sophie.

The silver rose was one of many concrete symbols that Hofmannsthal used, but the single one that pervades his work is that of water. Water, or liquidity, had a powerful allusive significance to Hofmannsthal, and he returned to its image throughout his life. Its power as a symbol was allied to its nature: pure, transparent, ubiquitous, indispensable, even chameleon in its forms. He used it to represent[8] the human generative process in its widest sense. That is, not simply the procreative aspect—to which it is linked in *Die Frau ohne Schatten* as "the waters of life"—but, beyond that, to the idea of human love which led to the procreation of the species.

Hofmannsthal was an idealist tempered by humanism and irony that took the form of the comic, and as such he is akin to comic writers like Molière, whose works he adored. This humanistic idealism, one of his most endearing traits as a writer, led him to see all of his characters in their best light as human beings, so that none of them, with the possible exception of the Nurse, is a villain in the Boito "worm" sense. His approach to the subject of human love between man and woman was similarly tinged with this idealism. To Hofmannsthal, human love was much more than lust; it was also much more than an end in itself. It represented the necessary beginning along the road to an enlightenment that encompassed both an appreciation of the loved one as the person he or she was and the growth of a friendship out of that love, which would lead to the begetting of children and the creation of a family that would be the ideal expression of the original love. In this sense

---

(8) Hofmannsthal, of course, was too subtle an artist to limit his use of symbolism to any one specific aspect, and the aptness of his choice of water thus symbolizes his symbolic approach.

Hofmannsthal's concept, like his water symbol and like his approach to writing in general, moved outward from the immediate facts toward a nirvana totally different from Wagner's.

It was this very concept, central to Hofmannsthal's being, that he developed during the course of his collaboration with Strauss and which gives the body of his work such vitality and importance in the history of the libretto. Its apparent genesis can be noted in *Der Rosenkavalier*, of course, but it goes back to *Elektra*, and to the character Hofmannsthal himself developed: Chrysothemis. Chrysothemis, Elektra's sister, has been severely criticized as a sentimental and unnecessary addition, but her importance to Hofmannsthal was twofold and she is, in the hands of both Hofmannsthal and Strauss, a character of more importance than she has been credited with. Structurally and emotionally, she was used as a human counterweight to the monomania of Elektra and the burnt-out decadence of Klytemnestra, thus attracting to her person some of the function of the Greek chorus. But Hofmannsthal saw in her more than that, and, in her first scene with Elektra, he had her set forth those human yearnings which would carry forward into his other librettos. Chrysothemis wants to marry and have children, and Hofmannsthal has her use the water image in expressing this wish: ". . . and women whom I have known slender are heavy with the blessing of children, drag themselves to the well, can scarcely lift the buckets, and all at once they are delivered of their burden, return to the well, and from themselves now flows sweet drink, and a new life hangs on to them, sucking, and children grow tall . . ." Already the mutability of the symbol has manifested itself in the use of the German word for well, *Brunnen*, which is also the word for spring or fountain and will be used in that connotation in *Die Frau ohne Schatten*, and in the fact that Hofmannsthal continues the image of life-giving water to life-giving (literally) milk. He furthermore refuses to leave the image static (that is, a one-for-one water-as-good relationship), for in *Die Frau* the fountain itself is no such thing: if the Empress drinks from it, she saves herself but dooms Barak and his wife. It is only when she realizes that her happiness at the expense of others is worth nothing that she is able to drink fully from the waters of life.

In *Elektra*, obviously, this theme had only minor importance, but its presence was signaled, and in his next libretto, *Der Rosenkavalier*, he took up another strand of the web of human love: that of self-realization. Hofmannsthal approached the writing of his comedy as a genre piece, and originally intended to have it revolve around the character of Ochs. Yet the growing preoccupation with the theme of love diverted the course of the libretto, and although *Der Rosenkavalier* as it stands only broaches the subject, it does treat the theme of love in several of its forms, and is thus related to Busenello's *L'Incoronazione di Poppea*. Ideal married love is not seen, but we are given several of its obverse facets: the immediacy of young love, which is a possible prerequisite, and the sadness of a love outside marriage because of an incompatible *mariage de convenance*. Hofmannsthal does not say that the Marschallin will never find love; what he does say is that the chances are that she will not, given the ephemeral nature of her liaisons and the implication that her preference is for younger men. Yet the Marschallin herself is fully aware of her plight, and accepts it, albeit with regret: it is this very awareness which makes her mature. Although her plight is touching and, in stage terms, extremely powerful, it is nonetheless negative, and Hofmannsthal, as he began to work toward his concept, worked away from this cul-de-sac to something positive.

Ariadne auf Naxos introduces the first of Hofmannsthal's female characters who will be the major repositories of this search for love.[1] In keeping with the split nature of the libretto, the character is split between the worldly wise Zerbinetta, the eternal *damigella*, and the gullible Ariadne, who in her feminine way seeks death after abandonment but finds instead (as Zerbinetta predicts) another man. Ariadne is a step backward from the Marschallin in that she is not at all self-aware (partly this situation was owing to the fact that Hofmannsthal was attempting to create an *opera seria* heroine, of more limited subtleties); but unlike the Marschallin she is a positive character, searching for fulfillment in love (or fulfillment in death, as she thinks). The gesture here is redolent of Wagner's *Tristan und Isolde*, but Hofmannsthal's ironic view, evidenced in the comic-with-tragic structure (and particularly stressed in the first version of *Ariadne*, which ends on the comic),

---

(9) Literally, in most cases. Strauss wanted a young woman to play the part, but very few can project the maturity of awareness that an older woman can.

(1) The only men in Hofmannsthal's librettos who approach the women in this respect are Menelaus and Mandryka.

moves the libretto away from *Tristan*. Ariadne's words resound with poetic hyperbole that Ariadne wants to believe rather than believes, and this in turn is reinforced in the second version by a picture of the diva Prima Donna who is singing the role. Finally, her "fate" is to end up with Bacchus, alive and satisfied.

It was with *Die Frau ohne Schatten*, however, that Hofmannsthal began an in-depth study of love which would go beyond the sexual love of *Ariadne* and would occupy him for his last three librettos for Strauss. *Die Frau* repeats cultural history through the working out of a concept in mythic terms before transferring it to a more immediate setting, and Hofmannsthal ensured this overview by creating a world of his own. What is more, he complemented it by enlarging the focus of his study of love.

The whole of *Die Frau ohne Schatten* revolves about a progress, similar to that contained in *Die Zauberflöte*, but here centered about human love. But, for Hofmannsthal, both ecstatic sexual union as represented by the Emperor and the Empress and animal affinity as represented by Barak and his wife are insufficient bases for salvation. What is necessary is not merely self-awareness, which is gained by the Empress and by Barak's wife during the course of the libretto, but something more: self-denial for the sake of others. It is this last quality, already inherent in the behavior of the Marschallin, which is developed in *Die Frau* to a position of importance. The Empress can gain her shadow,[2] but at the price of others' happiness: it is when she realizes this and refuses to jeopardize them that she attains salvation (which is envisioned by Hofmannsthal as a beautiful landscape, through which there flows—of course—a golden waterfall). This emphasis on self, along with the complexities of human behavior, sets *Die Frau* apart from the librettistic naïveté of *Die Zauberflöte*; its superiority lies in the very fact that the Empress, and not Keikobad, must make the decision which affects her life and those of her beloved and Barak and his wife. Thus the characters, however removed from the everyday world, are not puppets on strings manipulated by an unseen god.

---

(2) Again, it should be said that, for Hofmannsthal, the gaining of the shadow does not mean simply the ability to have children. Hofmannsthal incorporated into his symbol a wealth of meanings, and to separate out the most prominent as the only one is to willfully misconstrue his intent and his talents.

Hofmannsthal's next libretto for Strauss, written after a lengthy hiatus, again returned to myth to elaborate on his theme. This time he selected the most famous infidelity in myth, that of Helen of Troy, and combined it with the variant of the myth which told that the Helen who went to Troy was not unfaithful to her husband Menelaus, being but a phantom Helen, the real one being stashed away, pure, in Egypt until Menelaus came and collected her. Hofmannsthal dispensed with the idea of two Helens, since it did not accord either with his humanistic orientation or with his wish to explore self-awareness in love, and manipulated the two as one by means of a magic potion. Thus, Menelaus is about to kill Helena on board his ship, but Helena is rescued to the shores of Egypt by the sorceress Aithra. Menelaus is bewitched into thinking he has slain her and is convinced by Aithra of the story of the two Helens. He goes off for a second honeymoon with what he believes to be the "pure" Helena.

At this point Hofmannsthal intervenes, along the lines he had been developing in the previous librettos. Helena herself could possibly keep Menelaus happy by continued doses of forgetfulness potions, but she refuses to live in that sort of shadow marriage. Menelaus must accept her *as she is*, with full knowledge of her past, must either forgive her for it or kill her. She thus substitutes the potion of remembrance for that of forgetfulness.

Here again was an added element, for in *Die Frau* the story had revolved around couples already married, each member having a measure of knowledge of, though not a complete appreciation of, his partner. Hofmannsthal was insistent that, besides self-awareness and compassion for others, the true marriage must be based on an ability to perceive and forgive the faults of the other spouse. Only then will the two be, in Menelaus' words, *vollvermählt* (fully married). In *Helena*, the courage of Helena leads to the salvation of the marriage, for the restored Menelaus cannot kill his wife, and forgives her.[3]

In his final libretto, Hofmannsthal brought this preoccupation back to the sphere of the comedy of manners, and although he liked

---

(3) Somewhat ironically, this development parallels a similar one in Wagner's works, for the later Wagner librettos arrived at a message of "enlightenment through compassion," specifically applied to Parsifal but also applicable to Brünnhilde. The difference from Hofmannsthal is that, in Wagner, the whole was bound up in some sort of otherworldly consideration, be it Valhallan or Christian.

to say that, for him, myth was "the truest of all forms," his accomplishment in *Arabella* belies his words. As in *Der Rosenkavalier* and his great comedy *Der Schwierige*, he demonstrated that his chief assets, characterizational power and feeling for shades and half-tones of human behavior, were seen at their finest in a restrictive setting. Certainly *Arabella*, despite its very real structural faults, is one of the finest librettos of love ever written.

> Arabella is the story of growing-up; of the growing into womanhood of two sisters, of the growing into understanding first of Arabella and Mandryka and second—and to a lesser extent—of all the major characters. It is the story of the moment when the impetuosity and exuberance of youth becomes the forgiving wisdom of maturity; of the moment of true love and of that moment made permanent. It is the story in which heart and head become one in wisdom and emotion: a story in whose ending there is but a beginning—the future. In that sense Arabella is a fairy tale.[4]

In *Arabella*, Hofmannsthal contrasts two couples—and, in essence, two women—the all-woman Zdenka, who paradoxically must masquerade in men's clothing, and Arabella, who, although she dreams of her "Right Man," approaches love in a more reasoned and cooler way. Further contrast is offered not only by the parents of Arabella but also in the character of Mandryka, a rich landowner of rough, country manners (without the lechery of Ochs and also without the veneer of haphazard breeding that Ochs affects), who has fallen in love with a portrait of Arabella. All three of the principal characters, however, are immature in their love. Zdenka blindly loves Matteo, but, because he is blindly in love with Arabella, has resorted to writing him letters as if from her. Here Hofmannsthal explores the obverse of that compassion for others which was so important an element in *Die Frau ohne Schatten*: if this self-denial is linked with deceit, it (though admirable in itself) cannot lead to good. Mandryka, who cherishes the memory of a "perfect" first wife who died young, wants another such "perfect" experience, and wants it as soon as possible. Arabella, although less emotional than her sister, has been so bowled over by

---

(4) From my unpublished manuscript on *Arabella*, which examines the libretto in some detail. An altered excerpt from it appeared in *Opera News*, December 18, 1965.

the presence of this "Dream Prince" she has always envisioned that she has allowed herself as well to become blinded, however justifiably. Thus she accepts his proposal of marriage and, after gently dismissing each of her three suitors in turn—in an exquisite scene that is a test of a great singing actress—she wanders out into the Vienna night to return home to her family's apartment in a hotel. What she finds at the hotel will jar her out of her reverie and set up the climax of the opera.

The third act of *Arabella* is one of the supreme acts Hofmannsthal wrote, but it suffers both because he died before he could modify certain features of it and because Strauss, lacking Hofmannsthal's guiding words, glossed over the heart of the act—and the story—in order to highlight the final duet. The act nevertheless stands as a testament to Hofmannsthal's long involvement in the question of love and marriage, and it brings the trials and tests of *Die Frau ohne Schatten* down to the level of everyday life. What Arabella and Mandryka must face is the annealing flame of maturity and awareness.

In the weakest part of the libretto, Zdenka, allowing the emotions of her love for Matteo to flood over her (and also knowing that their relationship is almost certainly at an end), has given herself to him—he thinking that he is having a tryst with Arabella. Mandryka has overheard the plans for this assignation and, believing it is with Arabella, has immediately become cynical, feeling that he has been played for a fool by the sophisticated girl. When Arabella, completely ignorant of this turn of affairs, arrives back at the hotel in her semi-daze of joy, she cannot understand the behavior of Matteo—who likewise cannot understand hers. His inexplicable familiarity is followed closely by the arrival of Mandryka with Arabella's parents, and she is confronted with something far more serious: an ugly situation of which she knows neither the cause nor the facts. She maintains her self-possession amid recriminations from Mandryka, the bewilderment of her parents, and the loaded silence of Matteo. Her inner strength is the distinction that Arabella has over her softly feminine sister; it is typified by her comment, "What good is anything in this world if this man is so weak that he hasn't the strength to believe me?" She realizes that Mandryka is not the "Dream Prince" but a mortal, with mortal faults, and it is at this point that the heart of the libretto is reached.

Mandryka, having worked himself up in an orgy of self-pity, has just arranged a duel with Arabella's father, Waldner (who has been persuaded to defend the honor of the family), when Zdenka, who has been listening to everything, can no longer stand the deception. She runs down the staircase of the hotel, now dressed in a négligée, as a girl, and kneels before her father. Her overriding emotions have thus swept away the bric-a-brac of convention.

It is of course Arabella who immediately senses the truth and who immediately acts. "*Ich bin bei dir,*" she says to Zdenka— "I stand by you." Her forthright decision to support her sister in front of witnesses, and not to divorce herself, however subtly, from a very compromising situation, again demonstrates the strength of her character. It is now Mandryka's turn to gain maturity, and to learn humility. What is taking place in him is what has been taking place in Arabella: the realization that selfishness has strict limits. He apologizes abjectly to her, and Arabella, not looking at Mandryka, speaks to Zdenka. This is the key speech of the whole libretto.[5] Romantically sentimental, it is now the romanticism of awareness:

> *Zdenkerl, du bist die Bess're von uns zweien.*
> *Du hast das liebevollere Herz, und nichts ist da für dich,*
> *nichts in der Welt, als was dein Herz dich tuen lässt.*
> *Ich dank dir schön, du gibst mir eine grosse Lehre,*
> *dass wir nichts wollen dürfen, nichts verlangen,*
> *abwägen nicht und markten nicht und giezen nicht,*
> *nur geben und liebhaben immerfort!*[6]

The roles of the two principals have been reversed; it is now Arabella who is the stronger and who leads her beloved. Mandryka now realizes that he must make an act of apology above words, and goes to Waldner on behalf of Matteo to ask for Zdenka's hand. What he is doing, of course, is to ask for Arabella's forgiveness.

The final scene between Arabella and Mandryka, therefore, is

---

(5) The extent to which Strauss did not grasp what Hofmannsthal was doing in this act is shown by the nondescript quality of the music he gives Arabella at this point—so nondescript, in fact, that the passage is usually cut in performance, a cut that disfigures the opera.
(6) "Zdenkerl, you are the better of us two. You have a heart more filled with love, and nothing exists for you, nothing in the world, except what your heart lets you do. Thank you, you have taught me a great lesson: that we shouldn't desire anything, or demand anything; we shouldn't weigh or bargain or keep back—only keep giving and loving always."

not the climax of the opera, but its fulfillment. Arabella and Mandryka have been made aware of each other in a deeply personal way, and both have made acts of sacrifice. It is at this point that Hofmannsthal introduces his final homage to the symbolism of water: the glass of pure water from a well which, in Mandryka's home town, every fiancée brings to her beloved as token of her betrothal. Its introduction *after* each character has gone through this process of awareness—and not at the moment they fell in love "at first sight"—is perfectly gauged, for Hofmannsthal has no intention of using the symbol in any simplistic sense.

It may be useful here to quote from a letter from Hofmannsthal to Strauss to show the inclusiveness which Hofmannsthal demanded in his symbolic use. Strauss had objected to the glass of water on the basis that it was simply another trick of "somewhat childish symbolism" akin to poetic raspberry syrup. Hofmannsthal replied:

> Nor do I think that I shall be able to find anything better and at the same time equally simple . . . if on the other hand one takes something more complicated, it may easily look forced, intentional and almost theatrical if staged by Arabella at midnight. Instead of any ceremony at this point, one could of course have the still outstanding engagement kiss. Yet this simple ceremony of carrying the filled glass down the stairs has immense mimic advantages. A kiss she cannot *carry toward him*, she would simply have to walk up to him and give him the kiss; the other implies the most bridal gesture in its chastest form, and it can be followed by the kiss which thus gains solemnity, something that raises it out of the ordinary . . .[7]

And so Mandryka sends up a glass of water to Arabella's room, not knowing what to expect, and she, the focus of the libretto, makes the final gesture of forgiveness and love. She comes down to him and says: ". . . *dass ich mich nicht erfrischen muss an einem Trunk:/nein, mich erfrischt schon das Gefühl von meinem Glück,/und diesen unkredenzten Trunk kredenz' ich meinem Freund/den Abend, wo die Mädchenzeit zu Ende ist für mich.*"[8]

---

(7) Letter of August 5, 1928: *Strauss–Hofmannsthal Correspondence*, pp. 501–2.

(8) "I don't need to refresh myself with a drink: no, I am refreshed already by the consciousness of my happiness. And this untouched drink I offer to my friend, on this evening when my maidenhood is at an end."

She uses that beautiful word of true human love, *Freund*, when passion and liking become fused in one: a unity which, unlike the passion of *Tristan*, presages commencement.

Mandryka drinks, smashes the glass, and asks her: "And you will stay just as you are?" She replies: "*Ich kann nicht anders werden, nimm mich, wie ich bin*" ("I cannot be another—take me as I am"). They kiss, and the opera is at an end. The simplicity of Arabella's last sentence, which contains within it the whole of the preceding libretto, is the simplicity and purity of the last scene, symbolized in the glass of pure water. The moment, the poetry, and the gesture are one, and the one is perfect in its understanding humanity.

Arabella is the logical culmination of Hofmannsthal's librettistic development, and, although he did not realize it, rounds out his librettistic work with logical finality. Although this discussion of the development of the idea of love has left aside a number of other considerations operative in the Hofmannsthal librettos, it has served to highlight the one area in which Hofmannsthal made a strong contribution to the history of the form. Another element in his librettos that should be mentioned in passing is his handling of the duologue, which was such an important facet of the Wagner librettos. With Hofmannsthal, the duologue becomes far less a contrast and more a subtle interaction of personality. The duologues between Kari and Helena in *Der Schwierige* are carried over into the librettos, particularly the comic librettos, and an example such as the Mandryka-Waldner scene in Act I of *Arabella*—certainly one of the masterful duologues in the history of the libretto—can stand as representative of Hofmannsthal's handling of juxtaposed character.

Hugo von Hofmannsthal was, like Romani, something of an anachronism as a librettist: his work breathes the air of the nineteenth rather than the twentieth century. Yet, unlike Romani,[9] Hofmannsthal's work transcends the prison of time, and can be viewed as a self-contained entity. Given the support and acquiescence of a composer whose spirit of denial must stand as one of his strongest traits, Hofmannsthal was able to re-establish the librettist as a creator in his own right, as a man whose work was sufficiently important to be treated as a work-in-progress and not

_____

(9) Except for *Norma*.

butchered or altered for the sake of the specific opera. Thus Strauss ceded to Hofmannsthal the right to create his own world, with characters whose personalities did not have to depend on the music to be brought to life. As a result, he contributed to a series of operas, none of which is as faultless as *Otello* or *Pelléas et Mélisande* but the importance of which as a body of work is only beginning to be realized.

Finally, however, it is the *caritas* with which all of Hofmannsthal's creative librettos are saturated that serves to negate their deficiencies. Like Arabella, Hofmannsthal tells us to take him as he is, and as with Schubert, that is enough.

Chapter Twenty-three

Aspects of the
Later Twentieth-century Libretto

Although the developments in the libretto in the broad period from the First World War to the present are in many ways too close to us to be viewed with any perspective or final understanding, nonetheless certain features and trends are observable and deserve comment as features particularly of this century. Although the twentieth century—already over two-thirds completed —has produced a smaller number of operas than the comparable period in any earlier century in its history, it has produced a greater number than may at first be evident, the strongly nineteenth-century orientation of opera performance having allowed many twentieth-century works to lapse in semi-obscurity.

The majority of this librettistic output has been along traditional lines familiar to readers of the foregoing pages and not differing to any radical extent from earlier practices. Plays and novels continue to be turned into librettos, with a greater attention paid to fidelity to the original source—often extending to the setting of the actual words. The reign of Scribe and his successors continued, replete with the "tornado" curtain and the immediate, heightened emotional response.

The librettos to the operas of Benjamin Britten and Gian Carlo Menotti can be instanced as demonstrating the continuing power of nineteenth-century ideas on the shaping and content of the libretto. Menotti himself, as a librettist, must stand as an important, if anachronistic, figure, for all of his work looks backward to the achievements of the preceding century in its melodramatic, sentimental, and comic phases. Indeed, as with so many earlier buffo librettists, Menotti reserves an element of the comic for parody of current modes and vogues in music and the arts (e.g., *The Last Savage*, 1963; *Help! Help! the Globolinks!*, 1968).

Yet the twentieth century has seen the development in the libretto (and in other arts) of a new approach to the traditional which is not a continuation but a revival. Conscious archaism has been one of the prime ingredients of the twentieth-century libretto: a return or exploration of an art form unknown or fallen into disuse which can also be updated by additional, contemporary, elements.

Stravinsky's *Oedipus Rex* (1927; l., Jean Cocteau), one of the better examples, did not, in its statuesque, hieratic, and verbally obscure terms, revive Greek tragedy but reflected what Cocteau would have us believe Greek tragedy was like. Carl Orff's experiments with a purer type of Greek re-creation (e.g., *Antigone*, 1949; l., Friedrich Hölderlin's translation of Sophocles) and Britten's experiments with the adaptation of the Japanese Nō play techniques (e.g., *Curlew River*, 1964; l., William Plomer) are current examples of this trait.

W. H. Auden and Chester Kallman in their librettos have also worked with this archaism. Auden in particular has been fascinated with opera, and, as a major poet, has with Kallman done numerous translations of Mozart and other operas and has written widely on the form. Their libretto for Stravinsky, *The Rake's Progress* (1951 —symbolically first given in Venice), is a conscious attempt to re-create the shell and the feeling of Mozartean opera without forgetting to add crowd-pleasing nineteenth-century devices, such as the final "reminiscence" duet *à la Gounod. Elegy for Young Lovers* is their homage to the spirit of Hofmannsthal, although the symbolism and the story are far removed from his work and are closely akin to Auden's play *The Ascent of F6*, with additional philosophical speculations on the nature of artistic creation. Finally, *The Bassarids* (1966; m., Henze) combines archaism in the form of an opera with a contrasting lighter intermezzo and a wrenching updating of Euripides' *The Bacchae*, in which the depravity portrayed by the Greek playwright is given a thoroughly modern application.

The Auden-Kallman librettos achieve less than their intentions, partly because their verse is inferior to Auden's other poetry but largely because the works show too clearly their philosophical and structural seams without the mitigation of strength of character or of scene. *The Rake's Progress* is the most successful, but with the later works the indulgences of the librettists result in a tonal fluctuation among ponderosity, pretentiousness, banality, and genuine emotion. As with Hofmannsthal, the librettos, particularly for Henze, reveal the minds of the librettists, but unlike Hofmannsthal's they do not exist as works in their own rights, but more as patchworks of half-assimilated ideas.

The first main feature of the twentieth-century libretto is the development and use of the one-act form. We have seen how the form passed from the comic works of the preceding centuries to the *verismo* operas of the late nineteenth; from there it went to *Salome* and *Elektra* and became an integral part of opera. From the "minute operas" of Darius Milhaud and the short works written for radio or television—or school performance—to longer and more complex works, the one-act opera is a constant part of the century.

The main impetus for shorter operas was an attempt to get away from the overblown forms of the nineteenth century, particularly the works of Wagner, but as in so many cases the Bayreuth magician had a hand in the result. He had been one of the first to call for the single-idea libretto, as opposed to the tableau librettos of *Grand Opéra*, and *Der fliegende Holländer*, whatever its other relations with Meyerbeer, was written as an exemplification of this concept (and is ideally meant to be played without pause). Secondly, the internalization of the libretto, as shown in *Tristan*, had led directly to the psychological monodrama, of which Schönberg's *Erwartung* is one example; Bartók's *Bluebeard's Castle* (*A Kékszakállú Herceg Vára*, 1918; l., Bela Balácz) is another, as well as a brilliant librettistic achievement.

The anti-Wagnerian strain can be noticed in the simplification of the story and the characters and in the emphasis on what could be called "snapshot scenes": a variety of short, variegated stills of life. This can be seen as a diminution of the standard *Grand Opéra* technique of scenic variety, and, like *Grand Opéra* but more compactly, emphasized the disjunct rather than the continuous. Accompanying this scenic emphasis was a conscious attempt to depersonalize the characters on stage. This led to the so-called "puppet operas," in which the characters were intended to be played, not by humans, but by puppets. Manuel de Falla's *El Retablo de*

Maese Pedro (1923; l., adapted by de Falla from Cervantes) is an example of a one-act opera specifically designed for puppets, but all of Busoni's operas, according to him, were meant to be played *against* their humanity as if by puppets (if not by actual puppets), and certain early Stravinsky works—not only *Oedipus Rex* but also *Histoire du Soldat* (1918; l., C. F. Ramuz)—moved away from the "rounded" characters that had been so important to the later nineteenth century.

Closely related to "puppet opera," and in fact an integral part of the work of Stravinsky, was the fairy tale opera, which was aided by this revolt against the "reality" of the later nineteenth century. Stravinsky took the idea for fairy tale opera from the importance of the fairy tale in Russia and from the examples given in the operas of his teacher, Rimsky-Korsakov, but the rationale behind the form lay in its qualities of artificiality and fantasy. As had been stated before, with the twentieth century the ghost of Carlo Gozzi was vindicated, by direct use, as in *The Love for Three Oranges* (1921; m. & l., Prokofiev), or by indirect homage, as in *Le Rossignol* (1914; m., Stravinsky; l., Stravinsky and Stepan Mitusov, from an Andersen tale).

Other developments were taking place in opera which struck at the form itself. These had to do with the question of what was opera, and what the libretto was meant to be. The French had always closely defined the categories, and had excluded what did not pertain; but, in a looser way, so had other countries. With the twentieth century, composers and librettists began to transcend the disciplines of opera, comic opera, operetta, play with incidental music, ballet, monodrama, masque, pantomime, and oratorio and to write works without category, which were frequently performed in an opera house and broadly considered operas. *Histoire du Soldat* is a good example in that it bridges many forms, being partly balletic, partly chamber-instrumental (the few orchestral performers are placed on stage), partly narrational, and not at all sung—all the words are spoken. Yet in a curious way it is an opera, or at least something between an opera and a ballet,[1] and as such can fit under the enlarged umbrella of the form. Many other hybrid works have followed Stravinsky's lead—*Die sieben Tode-*

---

(1) Alfred Loewenberg includes it in his *Annals of Opera*.

sünden der Kleinbürger (1933; m., Weill; l., Brecht) can be considered another—and, as the years passed, the rules lessened in importance. The movement away from classical ballet, begun in earnest by the Diaghilev company, and the spirit of Dada revolt against not only the attitudes of the nineteenth century but also the forms themselves hastened this process, and the development of new methods of communication which could be used for artistic purposes, such as moving pictures, radio, recordings, and, later, television, granted composers and librettists new forums for their experiments.

Hovering over all of these departures from the traditional, however, was the radical change in outlook which distinguishes the librettos written in this century from those of the preceding ones. Opera has too often, and too loosely, been categorized as "an exotic art" only peripherally involved with problems of the times; this book has already demonstrated the amount of falsity with which that comfortable view is burdened. The general optimism and faith in man, science, or the state that had prevailed in the nineteenth century gave way, in the holocausts of the twentieth, to a much more severe, cynical, and pessimistic outlook, which Boito expressed in nineteenth-century terms in *Nerone*, but which Georg Büchner, even earlier, had expressed in *Wozzeck*, in terms completely in accord with the twentieth century. Dramatists such as Luigi Pirandello[2] and Frank Wedekind had highlighted this dislocation of order by juxtaposing the fantastic and the real, the farcical and the tragic, the grotesque and the prosaic, which increasingly came to mirror the activities of society. George Steiner's diamond image of the Auschwitz guard who, in his off hours, works on a thesis on Goethe's humanity pinpoints this dislocation at its most extreme. Alban Berg's instinctive realization of the *ur*-themes of the times in his choice of operatic subject matter is one of his chief traits as a composer.

This pessimism is well reflected in the librettistic work of the composer, writer, and theorist Ferruccio Busoni (1866–1924). Busoni wrote his own librettos, and as a librettist is, within the limits of his two greatest operas—*Arlecchino* (1917) and *Doktor*

---

(2) Who himself wrote an interesting original libretto for Gian Francesco Malipiero, *La Favola del figlio cambiato* (1934).

Faust (1925; music unfinished and completed by Philipp Jarnach) —an artist of superior gifts. For his *Doktor Faust* he went back beyond Goethe to the medieval legend, and saw it in terms of the play of opposing intellects rather than as a "story." He unfolds the tale as a succession of scenes, emphasizing the fantastic aspects (magic) and the grotesque (Faust is dressed for his wedding in outlandish clothes, with a train carried by monkeys), and he banishes entirely the aspects of salvation, except as ironically employed and outworn relics (when Faust agrees to the bargain, an off-stage chorus is singing Alleluias and Hosannas). The ending is likewise barren. Faust dies in an empty, snow-filled street at night, still clutching his dream of immortality, and Mephistopheles, as a Night Watchman, pronounces his epitaph: *"Sollte dieser Mann verunglückt sein?"* ("This man must have met with some misfortune").[3] In its viciously understated blandness the moment undercuts the transcendental closes both of Goethe and of the nineteenth-century adaptations (or imitations) and brings it within the sphere of Wozzeck's end, but the moment is further reinforced by the fact that Mephistopheles *speaks* the words. Music has been shed with the shedding of the uplift ethos of the nineteenth century —and is one of the distinguishing marks of twentieth-century opera.[4] Busoni carried this idea through in his one-act "theatrical capriccio," *Arlecchino*, the titular role of which is entirely spoken, as if Arlecchino refuses to sing out of contempt for the convention.

Arlecchino has been consistently misjudged as a libretto because it has consistently been taken as a lighthearted exercise in the *commedia dell'arte* style. In fact, Busoni has taken the conventions of the *commedia* to point up the obverse of the comic muse: that is, the streak of nihilism that lies within every clown, brought out in pathetic terms in Shakespeare's fools, here in sardonic terms. Arlecchino, the hero, creates the world in which he exists, and he exploits it ruthlessly—in this sense, he is the character Da Ponte's Don Giovanni should have been. He cares nothing for any of the

---

(3) Busoni, half Italian and half Austrian, wrote his librettos in German.
(4) The development of *Sprechstimme* is closely allied to this usage, as both an attempt to get away from the confinement of singing and to make greater expressive use of the voice.

others, except for his own amusement, and his cynical approach to life is total. He breathes contempt:

Was ist ein Soldat? Etwas, das sich selbst aufgibt.
Eine kenntliche Kleidung. Ein Hunderttausendstel.
Der künstliche Mensch . . . Was ist das Recht? Was man
anderen entreissen will . . . Was ist das Vaterland?
Der Zank im eigenen Hause.[5]

Similarly, the world in which he exists is a darkening place. All is rootless, suspended in a void: Matteo the tailor is shuffled off stage as a conscript to fight the illusory but somehow immanent barbarians so that Arlecchino can cuckold him; he returns, his nose still buried in his Dante, none the wiser. The Doctor and the Abbate are both pious frauds whose response to the presence of danger (the approach of the barbarians) is to head for the nearest tavern.

Busoni makes brutal fun of the Verdi and Wagner heroics (and the scene between Arlecchino and his abandoned wife, Colombina, is a twisting of the first Giovanni-Elvira scene), which has in part led to the opera's being considered mere parody. But Busoni intends something far more thoroughgoing. He has Arlecchino dispose of the Lohengrin-Trovatore tenor with ease, and then escape. Darkness falls on the scene; the Doctor and the Abbate emerge drunk from the tavern and are shown the body by Colombina. They dither in pedantic drunkenness—strongly recalling the behavior of the Doctor and the Captain in scene iv of Act III of *Wozzeck*—while around them in the town the people come to their windows and then go away again, not wanting to help. This closing off, this alienation of man, is entirely characteristic as an attitude of the twentieth century. Finally, a passing carter with his donkey arrives to take away the body (which turns out to be still alive), while the Abbate intones a prayer to the *"asinus providentialis."* Arlecchino sets the seal on the scene by appearing on the roof of Matteo's house, gesturing widely to the heavens and saying, with great contempt, *"Die Welt is offen! Die Erde is jung! Die Liebe ist frei! Ihr Harlekins!!"* ("The world is open! The earth

---

(5) "What is a soldier? Something that gives itself away. A handsome uniform. A hundred-thousandth part. A false man . . . What is Right? What someone will grab from another . . . What is the fatherland? A squabble in one's house."

is young! Love is free! You Harlequins!!"), which grinds in the irony of the lost souls who inhabit it.

Arlecchino is as finely wrought a libretto as the form has produced, and it distills the rejection of the nineteenth-century esthetic in parodic and sardonic terms. It demonstrates the continuing power of the *commedia* form to be put to use to reflect not a dying art but the living spirit, and in its pessimistic tone invokes Gozzi rather than Goldoni.

This pessimism is carried to a far more comprehensive condemnation of capitalistic society in the librettos of Bertolt Brecht. Brecht (1898–1956) spent his life as a writing animal, working mainly in the theater, but also writing poetry and prose; and because of his strong opinions was forced to lead a nomadic life that stretched from Germany to the United States (by way of Asia) and back again to Germany, where he died. All of his writing talent he placed at the service of his world-view, which in essence was a loathing of the rapacity and greed of man and a loathing of that form of government which he felt embodied that greed: capitalism. Since his death Brecht has continued to grow in stature as a playwright and poet, and his ideas and his unwavering didacticism have been of major importance in the history of the theater.

Brecht was a convinced Marxist, and he applied the Marxist tenets not only to his works but also to the form that they took. What he wanted was communication: the transference of the message from the playwright to the audience without the use of emotionalism or sentimentality, in such a way that the audience itself would be "converted"—but through reason rather than pity. As a Marxist, he wrote constantly for the working classes, and even invited them to participate in production: to discuss the points made and to make alternate suggestions. He was, in fact, so completely dedicated to the Marxist ideology that he was willing to submit to "higher authority" for correction (as his play *Galileo* details), for although Brecht saw as well as anyone the faults of Marxism as applied to the governing of a specific society, he was willing to choose such government—inevitably communist—rather than any of its alternatives (either watered Marxism or capitalistically oriented), which he considered immeasurably inferior.

Brecht liked to use music as an integral part of his plays because he appreciated the immediacy of its appeal to the audience.

Most of his works, however, are plays with music (i.e., songs) in the *comédie mêlée d'ariettes* manner rather than through-composed librettos, and even his "operas," such as *Die Dreigroschenoper* (1928; m., Weill) and *Aufstieg und Fall der Stadt Mahagonny* (1930; m., Weill), include spoken portions. Other than with Weill, whose music brought Brecht his fame, he worked chiefly with the composers Hanns Eisler and Paul Dessau.[6]

As can be imagined, given Brecht's strength of will, his ideas as a librettist were not subject to the whims of composer control in the manner of the nineteenth century. The last thing Brecht wanted was to water down or prettify his works for public consumption: what he wanted was to make the audience think, to force it to face unpleasant truths and to take sides. Ironically, he is remembered in the operatic sphere for the stagily evil words for the *Morität* ("Mack the Knife") aria in *Dreigroschenoper*, but any reading of this libretto or that of *Mahagonny* will reveal the vigor of his attack on society.

What must never be overlooked in the work of Brecht is the depth of his humanity and his allegiance to the "little people" who are inevitably crushed in any clash of opposing powers. It is this quality that keeps Brecht from becoming a didactic propaganda machine or a series of revealed truths. Brecht would have seen the *Ring* cycle from the point of view of the least of the Nibelungs. His celebrated lines from *Galileo* ("Pity the country that has no heroes." "Pity the country that needs heroes.") demonstrate his concern, as well as set him apart from the esthetic of the nineteenth century. It was around this allegiance that Brecht built all of his tenets, from his hatred of the tyrant to his hatred of the oppressive society to his hatred of war. The peasant girl Grusche in his play *The Caucasian Chalk Circle* is perhaps his finest creation of this simple figure, who, despite tribulation, exile, and the burden of a child not hers, not merely endures but prevails. The way in which Brecht takes this essentially sentiment-oriented tale, strips it of sentiment, and puts it to didactic use is symbolic of his work as a writer for the stage.

Die Dreigroschenoper, however, and *Mahagonny* are involved with the obverse side: that is, the evils of society. Brecht took the

(6) *Das Verhör des Lukullus* (The Trial of Lucullus), a radio play, was set as an opera by Dessau in 1951; a second version, more overtly in line with Communist dogma, was set by Dessau in the same year.

shell and the content of *The Beggar's Opera* and updated them so
that the social picture remained the same and the milieu remained
the same but the reference was to Germany in the 1920's. The
tawdry underworld was put into the limelight, with its petty
thieves, its pimps and its whores, who are fleeced by Peachum and
are ground under by a society that uses them and then lets them
rot. If Peachum is Brecht's picture of the capitalist, who bends
the society's *mores* to his own standard, Mackie, the romantic
highwayman, is what he sees as the hero of a diseased society: a
man of no morals whatsoever—an Arlecchino in sharkskin—who
preys on everyone, but who is excused because he gets away with
it. Peachum's creed is set forth, appropriately, to a chorale tune:

> *Wach auf, du verrotterer Christ!*
> *Mach dich an dein sündiges Leben!*
> *Zeig, was für ein Schurke du bist*
> *derr Herr wird es dir dann schon geben.*
> *Verkauf deinen bruder, du Schuft!*
> *Verschacher dein Ehweib, du Wicht!*
> *Der Herrgott, für dich ist er Luft?*
> *Er zeigt dir's beim Jüngsten Gericht!*[7]

What is notable about Brecht's verse, besides its force, is its
directness. He fully exploits the harshness of the German language
to achieve his purpose of hitting the audience directly, without
euphemism and without sentiment. His poetic approach, then,
stands opposed to that of Hofmannsthal, who brought out the
softer, more lyric side of the language. Brecht could also write lyric
verse, as his duet of the flying cranes in *Mahagonny* demonstrates,
but even here the order and form of the lines separates them from
the liquidity of Hofmannsthal.[8] Brecht and Hofmannsthal, be-

---

(7) "Awake, you rotting Christian! Get on with your sinful life!
Show us what a rascal you are: the Lord will soon repay you for it.
Sell your brother, you blackguard! Barter away your wife, your poor
wight! The Lord, does he mean nothing to you? He'll show you on
Judgment Day!"
    Note the use of "*Wach auf,*" with its strong Bach-chorale as-
sociations.
(8) "*Sieh jene Kraniche in grossem Bogen!/Die Wolken, welche
ihnen beigegeben zogen/mit ihnen schon, als sie entflogen/aus einem
Leben in ein andres Leben./In gleicher Höhe und mit gleicher Eile/
scheinen sie alle beide nur daneben./Dass so der Kranich mit der
Wolke teile/den schönen Himmel, den sie kurz befliegen.*" ("See each

tween them, brought the range of poetic possibility of its language to the German libretto, which had not had first-class poetry, and both accomplished the task in a century in which the poetic libretto had given way to its prosaic counterpart.

Brecht's characterizational abilities are shown in the ballads that he fashions for his characters. Jenny's famous "Ballad of the Sea-pirate Jenny" is cast in the mold of a fantasy of what Jenny's hopes are: what they are is not marriage and home but a gang of ruffians who will arrive and put to death all her tormentors. Brecht constantly drives at his main point of the double standard of morality, one for the rich and one for the poor, and he makes his cruelest fun by mocking at the *deus ex machina* ending. Just as Mackie is about to die on the gallows for his many crimes, the Royal pardon arrives—not only a pardon, but also a title and a life pension. By exaggerating the ludicrousness of the "happy ending" Brecht (like Gay before him) grinds in the reality of the situation, which is put into wistful words by Mrs. Peachum: "So everything has a happy ending. How nice and peaceful our lives would be, if the King's messengers on horseback always arrived."

Brecht's libretto for Weill's *Mahagonny* is a bleaker, more pervasive look at society. In the libretto Brecht created his own vision of Hell, which he set in a mythical United States but which is in fact a portrait of the dissolution of the Weimar Republic. Mahagonny, the city of nets, is a "free city" that a gang of thieves have founded in order to get rich quick. Instead of breaking their backs in the gold fields of the "West," they create a libertine environment and wait for the gold to come to them in the form of the prospectors looking for fun. They are of course successful, and they catch in their net Paul Ackermann,[9] a lumberjack, who is all too willing to subscribe to their anarchistic tenet that "Everything is permitted," but who finds that even anarchy has its limits—determined by those in charge.

The inhabitants of this city are under no illusions. When a hurricane approaches, Begbick says:

---

crane sweep through the sky! The clouds, which have joined them, accompany them as they fly up from one life to another. At the same height and speed they appear next to each other. So that the crane will share the beautiful heavens with the cloud across which they both fly so briefly.") (Act II, number 14.)

(9) Called Jimmy Mahoney in the score.

Schlimm ist der Hurrican
schlimmer ist der Taifun
doch am schlimmsten ist der Mensch.[1]

The credo of this bread-and-circuses city, so akin to the Rome seen by Boito in *Nerone*, is set forth:

Erstens, vergesst nicht, kommt das Fressen
zweitens kommt der Liebesakt.
Drittens das Boxen nicht vergessen
viertens Saufen; laut Kontrakt.
Vor allem aber achtet scharf
Dass man hier alles durfen darf.[2]

Paul joins in the license, but finds out its limits when he has lost all his money: everything is permitted except not being able to pay. He is arrested and brought before the totally corrupt court, which he cannot bribe (having no money). No sentiment will suffice: neither friend nor sweetheart will let him have money and because, as he is told, lack of money is the greatest crime possible, he is condemned to death. No king's messenger arrives, and Paul dies in the electric chair, after which the city of nets collapses into its final flaming anarchy.

Mahagonny carries Brecht's pessimistic didacticism to an extreme, and its unrelieved catalog of man's inhumanity in a materialistic society is wearying in its obsessional compulsion, but what dominates is Brecht's cry of outrage at the collapse of his world at the hands of the barbarians. For *Mahagonny* appeared at a time when the Weimar Republic was in serious trouble, and when the Nazis were growing in power. At the Berlin staging in 1931, gangs of them disrupted the performance. If *Mahagonny*, in its agony, sounded the death knell of humanism in Germany, the power of its truths is such that they remain applicable today. In the history of the libretto there is no more searing indictment of a society and a way of life.

This German pessimistic streak did not die out with the flight of Brecht from Germany nor with the rise to power of the

---

(1) "Hurricanes are bad, typhoons are worse, but worst of all is Man" (Act II, number 11).
(2) "First, don't forget, is gluttony, next comes lust. Third, don't forget, is boxing, fourth is swilling to the full. Above all note well that here you can do anything you want." (Act III, number 13.)

Nazis. It can be found in an elaboration of a Grimm fairy tale which Carl Orff wrote in Germany during World War II, *Die Kluge* (1943; m. & l., Orff). Courageously, he uses the characters of three beggars to set forward a litany of the anarchy of the times, the trio *"Als die Treue"* (scene vii), the refrain of which he sets to a pseudo-beer hall tune (i.e., to just the kind of tune that the Nazis liked to use for propaganda purposes).[3] The beggars, in their despair, do exactly as Busoni's Doctor and Abbate did: they get stinking drunk, for in this world they know there will be no release through Siegfried.

If the librettos of Busoni and Brecht well represent the prevalence of decay and unreason which has been so much a part of the twentieth century, other librettos have brought to the fore different aspects of the century. The holocaust of the First World War resulted in a general shattering of values, and the most immediate reaction was seen in the Dada movement of the early 1920's, which made fun of what had previously been held sacred. Yet the Dada spirit went well beyond the nose-tweaking japes of painting a mustache on the Mona Lisa or enshrining a urinal as a work of art, and in literature led to experiments in shattering the structure of language itself. Edith Sitwell's abstract poems, some of which were collected and set to musical accompaniment by William Walton in *Façade* (1922)—the poems were spoken, not sung—caused the expected furor, but demonstrated a truth that had been evident to many even earlier: that linear coherence was not necessarily the only coherence possible, and that assonance and word-patterns and repetitions could establish their own meaning. Likewise, Cocteau's deliberate choice of a dead language, Latin, which could be understood by only a few in the audience, for his setting of *Oedipus Rex* for Stravinsky, and then his adding a Narrator who explained the story, were only partly a trick. What Cocteau was attempting to do was to achieve a hieratic monumentality by the use of words which, though imposing in their sonority, actually meant little to the audience and had to be interpreted. Thus, the very unintelligibility of the words—so long a distinctive

---

(3) *"Fides* is struck dead. *Justitia* lives in dire need. *Pietas* lies on straw. *Humilitas* cries murder. *Superbia* is chosen. *Patientia* has lost the battle. *Veritas* has flown to Heaven. Truth and honor have fled across the sea. Piety goes begging. *Tyrannis* holds sway. *Invidia* is loose. *Caritas* is naked and bare. Virtue has been driven out of the land. Dishonor and evil have stayed behind."

feature of the libretto, even when sung in the language of the country—was considered an asset, not a liability, to the final result, much as the gibberish of Berlioz's devils, while meaningless, held great meaning.

The step from these developments to the appearance of the "abstract libretto" was short, and it was taken by Gertrude Stein (1874–1946). The famous American expatriate writer wrote two such works for Virgil Thomson, both of which have an assured place in the history of the libretto.[4] In fact, *Four Saints in Three Acts* (1934) and *The Mother of Us All* (1947) differ as works, but they both represent the final and complete liberation of the word from its prison as a meaning-symbol, so that it becomes, primarily, a sound or collection of sounds. In that sense, Stein's use of words frees them from their associative context and forces them into conjunction with words of similar sounds. Likewise, sentences, such as they are, do not follow each other with any logic. Stein's prose is free-form verse, and its fluidity is extreme. Because of repetition and absolute disregard for syntax—except as Stein's own syntax—each of her sentences seems to flow on with no end.

Four Saints, the more abstract of the two librettos, is one of the landmark works in the form. Logic cannot be applied to its subject matter because there is no subject matter other than a vague celebration of saints (many more than four, and many who are saints only in Stein's calendar), with special emphasis on Saint Theresa of Ávila.[5] There is no story; there are a prelude and four, not three, acts; Act II has one scene, after which Act I resumes, and the second Act I plays scenes iii and iv together, then a separate scene iv and eight scene v's, one of which contains nothing. Scene x precedes and follows scene xi, and the two are different. There are, moreover, no singers directed to sing any one speech or set of speeches, and indeed there is no cast of characters. For the production as given, Maurice Grosser contrived a scenario that gives some order to the libretto, but other, quite different, scenarios could be devised to the same text and music.

---

(4) Other works of Stein which have been set to music are *The Wedding Bouquet* (1937; m. Lord Berners), *In a Garden* (1949; m., Meyer Kupferman), and *In Circles* (1967; m., Al Carmines).
(5) In the opera, called Saint Terese. All references have been taken from the published libretto (Random House, 1934).

It is all too easy to limit the scope of Stein's libretto to Dada japeries, but to do so underrates the extent of her accomplishment. There are superficial resemblances to French sources in the ballets and in Stein's debts to Satie,[6] but *Four Saints* is a far more interesting libretto than a Dada example such as *Les Mamelles de Tirésias* (1945; m., Francis Poulenc; l., Guillaume Apollinaire), amusing as that one is. The difference, of course, is in the approach to language itself. Stein perceived the essential divorce between the words and what they were intended to mean which had always been a part of the libretto. *La vendetta* had a signpost quality that was meaning enough, but great stretches of love poetry had become emasculated through repetition and were, in fact, lifeless words of no real meaning. Thus they could be eliminated and other words substituted.

In one of the passages that Stein did suggest a meaning for, according to Grosser, she intended a Vision of the Holy Ghost to come to Theresa. What Barbier and Carré would have concocted for Gounod can be imagined; what Stein saw as an ecstatic vision, however, cannot be imagined, and that is why it is a vision:

> *Pigeons on the grass alas.*
> *Pigeons on the grass alas.*
> *Short longer grass short longer longer shorter yellow grass*
> *Pigeons large pigeons on the shorter longer yellow grass alas*
> *pigeons on the grass.*
> *If they were not pigeons what were they.*
> *If they were not pigeons on the grass alas what were they.*
> *He had heard of a third and he asked about it it was a magpie in the sky. If a magpie in the sky on the sky can not cry if the pigeon on the grass alas can alas and to pass the pigeon on the grass alas and the magpie in the sky on the sky and to try and to try alas on the grass alas the pigeon on the grass the pigeon on the grass and alas.*

In an era of hallucinatory drugs and psychedelic experimentation, the foregoing does not have the bizarre quality it had when it was written, but even then it was not nonsense. The image of a bird is, of course, central to the appearance of the Holy Ghost, and a pigeon is a secularized Paraclete. The magpie was introduced

---

(6) Wilfred Mellers: *Caliban Reborn*, p. 86.

because Stein had a vivid image of the bird hanging in the air around Avila, the home of Saint Theresa. Finally, the repetitiousness of the passage, in its obsessional aspect, recalls the endless Church litanies.

Stein's approach to language was in great part textural, a closely woven carpet of interlocking sounds, and as such her writing does not depend on the *parole sceniche* as much as the pattern of key words, which are threaded in and out of the texture. In the following sentence the last word, so different in sound, sticks out: *"Saint Therese in a storm in Avila there can be rain and warm snow and warm that is the water is warm the river is not warm the sun is not warm and if to stay to cry."* Or a simple playing around with words: *"They might in at most not leave out an egg. An egg and add some. Some and sum. Add sum. Add some."* Or the juxtaposition of words in a sentence:

> *To be interested in Saint Therese fortunately.*
> *Saint Ignatius to be interested fortunately.*
> *Fortunately to be interested in Saint Therese.*
> *To be interested fortunately in Saint Therese.*

Which leads to a new idea: *"Interested fortunately in Saint Therese Saint Ignatius and Saints who have been changed from the evening to the morning."*

The comparison of Stein's libretto to an abstract painting is apt, because both work with the primary techniques, color and sound, and manipulate them directly without regard to an outside ordering process, such as characterization or a story line. The sounds thus built up and juxtaposed can be used to create a feeling or an approach from which a scene may be constructed for the stage, a scene that may differ in different conceptions but will ultimately refer back to the words of the text. It is interesting to note that by abstracting the sounds and the words from the context of the story and the character and thus highlighting them Stein was only anticipating a development that has since taken place in the staging of opera: the use of the work itself, be it *Aida* or *Pelléas*, as a basis for widely differing conceptions as to the meaning of the work in production. The fact that *Four Saints* may be staged in any one of a variety of ways is obvious; what has become increasingly obvious is that more traditional works are subject to the same variety of approach.

The Mother of Us All differs in that it is a pageant-libretto on a more specifically designated topic: Susan B. Anthony and the winning in the United States of political rights for women. Parenthetically, it should be noted that both librettos are not plucked out of the void, but involve figures—Theresa and Susan Anthony —who were very important to Stein. Stein characteristically destroys the concept of time in her pageant, so that many American historical figures of different periods coexist, moving in and out of the frame of the stage, and so that Ulysses S. Grant can say: *"He knew that his name was not Eisenhower. Yes he knew it. He did know it."* The structure here is an elaborate mosaic of parts, which include Stein and Thomson as well as the characters, and the scenes are more clearly evidenced by the text than in *Four Saints*.

This closer approach to a conventional libretto means that the characters are built up over a span of scenes, with Miss Anthony emerging at the end out of a welter of American historical figures into the position of pre-eminence which Stein wishes to carve for her. In so doing, Stein shows an instinctive knowledge of the powers of the stage. One of the scenes (I, ii) is a debate between Daniel Webster and Susan Anthony—that is, the classic duologue. Stein emphasizes the historicity of the characters by conducting the debate entirely in a pastiche of snippets from speeches made by Webster and rejoinders by Anthony. Yet the total non sequitur of the snippets underlines the total non-understanding of the two (or, at least, Webster's non-understanding of Anthony), and his constant reference to his opponent as *"he,"* although called "parliamentary punctilio" by Maurice Grosser in his preface, is more likely haughty disdain or sheer ignorance.

ANTHONY: *I understand that you undertake to overthrow my under-taking.*[7]

WEBSTER: *I can tell the honorable member once for all that he is greatly mistaken, and that he is dealing with one of whose temper and character he has yet much to learn.*

ANTHONY: *I have declared that patience is nevermore than patient. I too have declared that I who am not patient am patient.*

---

(7) This sentence is a rebus.

WEBSTER: *What interest asks he has South Carolina in a canal in Ohio.*
ANTHONY: *What interest have they in me, what interest have I in them, who the head of whom, who can bite their lips to avoid a swoon?*
WEBSTER: *The harvest of neutrality had been great, but we had gathered it all.*

The picture of American political life that Stein puts forward in *The Mother of Us All* is rich in its diversity within complexity, and there is no doubt that her timeless approach has heightened the mythic and pageantic qualities of the libretto. Gertrude Stein must be considered as the librettist who created a positive approach to a redefining of language and play structure out of an essentially negative, or at best only immediately pleasing, tradition, which was Dada. In this sense she stands in relation to Erik Satie in music.

This increasingly expressed lack of coordinates or lack of guideposts within the work itself is reflective of the growing hold that the disjunctive has had on the later twentieth century. Where the smoothly logical, as seen most clearly in the librettos of Metastasio, or contrastingly in the Gluck reform operas, had powered the libretto down past Wagner into the twentieth century, the disjunct, growing from the tableau opera of Scribe, and romanticized to expressionistic excess by Berlioz, had come to be considered representative of the age. To this has been added the element of chance or the glorification of the irrelevant within the framework of the libretto and of the music.

The final libretto to be considered here uses some of these techniques, and returns to the theme of Faust: it is Michel Butor's *Votre Faust* (1969; m., Henri Pousseur). The subjects and the title are significant, for Faust in the Gounod version has had a great hold on the French artistic mind—one that it is loath to admit. The title is a play on Paul Valéry's discussion-play, *Mon Faust*, which was modeled on the Don Juan in Hell Scene from Shaw's *Man and Superman* and uses the Gounod shell as Shaw had used the Mozart one.

Butor calls his libretto "*Fantaisie variable genre opéra*" ("a changeable fantasy in the operatic genre"), and it was the result of a suggestion by a theater director who wanted an opera with one condition: that it be about Faust. Thus, Butor has written a libretto about a young composer (Faust) who is asked by a theater director (Méphisto) to write an opera, with one condition, etc. At the end of the libretto, he has not yet written a note, but is about to start.

Butor, in the course of the libretto—a series of short, disjunctive scenes—throws in references to earlier operas, such as Monteverdi's *Orfeo,* Gluck's *Orphée, Don Giovanni,* and *Tristan,* and such plays as Marlowe's *Doctor Faustus* and Goethe's epic, all in their own languages, and insists that even this, the created libretto, is a work in progress that can and should be changed. At the end of it he suggests that the work be played backward.

The *Votre Faust* aspect is emphasized through the involvement of the audience in the creation: at one point a question is put to the audience as to whether Henri (i.e., Faust) should attend a marionette show with Maggy (Marguerite) or with another girl. The audience votes, and the libretto proceeds with the appropriate text.

Votre Faust is more an experiment than a finished work, but it demonstrates the lengths to which the development of the libretto has gone in the course of the twentieth century. Although the text contains within it echoes of previous works in direct quotation, it is something on its own, in a genre which is not of any century but the twentieth. As such it can stand as a culmination and continuing beginning of its own genre, the art form of the libretto, which the foregoing pages hopefully have given something of the due that "The Tenth Muse" has for so long lacked.

APPENDIX

My dear Monsieur Hasse has never been absent from my heart since I quitted Vienna; but, hitherto, I have not been able to devote myself to your service, because in this most idle bustle I am hardly my own master [except] when I sleep. So fully am I engaged in walking, shooting, music, cards, and conversation, that not a moment remains for private meditation, without defrauding society. Yet, in spite of all these impediments, I am penetrated with such remorse for having so long neglected you, that I am now determined to obey your commands. But what can I possibly suggest to you, which has not already occurred to your own mind? After so many illustrious proofs of knowledge, judgment, grace, expression, invention, and ingenuity, with which you only have been able to dispute the palm of harmonic primacy with our nation: after having breathed with your seducing notes into so many poetical compositions that life and soul which the authors themselves were unable to furnish or imagine, what light, advertisement, or instruction, can you expect me to furnish? If I were only to mention things with which you are *not* acquainted, my letter would already be finished; but if you wish me to converse with you, God knows when I should have done.

And now, as *Attilio Regolo* is to be the subject of my letter, I shall begin by developing the characters, which, perhaps, are not expressed in so lively a manner in the piece, as I had conceived them in my mind.

In *Regolo*, it has been my intention to delineate the character of a Roman hero of consummate virtue, according to the pagan idea, not only in principle, but practice; whose fortitude has been

403

long tried, and is proof against every caprice of fortune. A rigid and scrupulous observer, as well of justice and probity, as of the laws and customs which time and the great authority of his ancestors have rendered sacred to his country. Sensible to all the gentler passions of humanity, but superior to each. A great commander, good citizen, and an affectionate father; but never considering these characters as distinct from his country, or otherwise among the blessings or evils of life, than as they eventually contribute to the welfare or injury to that whole of which he considered himself as a part. A great friend to glory, but regarding it merely as a reward to which individuals should aspire, by sacrificing their own interest and happiness to public utility.

With these internal qualities, I attribute to my prototype a magnetic exterior, without pomp; reflecting, but serene; authoritative, but humane; equal, considerate, and composed. I should not like that his voice or gestures should be violent, except in two or three situations of the opera, in which a sensible deviation from the constant tenor of his subsequent conduct, would exalt his ruling passions, which are patriotism and glory. You must not be alarmed, my dear Sir, I shall be much shorter in the description of the other characters.

In the personage of the Consul, *Manlio*, I have tried to represent one of those great men, who, in the midst of every civil and military virtue, suffer themselves to be carried away by the rage of emulation, beyond all warrantable bounds. I wish this rivalry to be strongly marked, as well as his hostile disposition of mind towards Regolo. These will appear in the first scene with Attilia, as well as in the beginning of the next, in which the Senate hears Regolo, and the Carthaginian Ambassadors. His subsequent change of sentiment into respect and tenderness for Regolo, will render his character more admirable, and more pleasing; it will exalt the virtue of Regolo, by demonstrating its efficacy in producing such stupendous effects, and will add to the second scene of the second act, which is that for which I feel the greatest partiality. The characteristic of Manlio is a natural propensity to emulation, which when he discovers, he corrects, but does not relinquish.

Publio is the young lion that promises all the force of the sire, but is not yet furnished with tusks and claws; and it may easily be conjectured through his impetuosity, passion, and the inexperience of youth, what he will be, when arrived at maturity.

Licinio is a pleasing young man, valiant and resolute, but extremely impassioned. Hence it is very difficult to convince him of the necessity of sacrificing the genius of his wife, and even the life of his benefactor to glory, and the service of his country.

Amilcare is an African, not accustomed to the maxims of probity and justice, which the Romans, at this time, professed, and much less [accustomed] to their practice: hence, from the beginning, he remains in astonishment, being unable to comprehend a way of thinking so diametrically opposite to that of his country. He is, however, ambitious of imitating what he sees; but, for want of moderation, goes awkwardly to work. However, during his short residence at Rome, if he did not acquire the Roman virtue, he at least learned to envy those who possessed it.

The ruling passion of *Attilia* is tenderness and veneration for her father, whom she not only prefers to Rome itself, but to her lover. Convinced by authority and example, she, at length, adopts her father's sentiments, but in the trial of that fortitude, which she wished to imitate, she manifestly sinks under the weakness of her sex. In *Barce*, I figured to myself a pleasing, beautiful and lively African. Her temperament, like that of her nation, is amorous, and her tenderness for Amilcare extreme. In him, all her hopes, her fears, thoughts and cares, are centered. She is even more attached to her lover than the manners of her country; and is not only more indifferent than him about the Roman passion for glory, but thanks the Gods for having preserved her from its contagion.

These are the general outlines of the portraits I meant to draw; but you know that the pencil is not always faithful to the traces of the mind. It therefore depends upon you, who are not only an excellent artist, but a perfect friend to clothe my personages in so masterly a manner, that if their features should not strike, they may be recognized, at least, by their dress and ornaments.

And now, to come to particulars, according to your desire, I shall speak of the recitatives, some of which I should wish to be animated by instruments; but in pointing them out I do not pretend to limit your ideas: where mine meet with your wishes, adopt them; but where we disagree, I beg of you not to change your opinion, in mere complacency.

In the first act, I find two situations in which instruments may assist me. The first is the whole harangue of Attilio to Manlio, in the second scene, beginning: *"A che vengo! Ah! sino a quando"*.

405

After the words *A che vengo*, the instruments should begin to be heard; and, afterwards, sometimes silent, sometimes accompanying the voice, and sometimes by reinforcing, to give energy and fire to an oration in itself violent; and I should like this accompaniment to continue to the end of the verse: *"La barbara or qual è? Cartago o Roma?"*

But I believe that it will be necessary, particularly in this scene, to avoid the inconvenience of making the singer wait for the chord; otherwise all the heat and energy of the speech would be chilled, and the instruments, instead of animating, would enervate the recitative, and render the picture disjointed, obscure, and suffocated in the frame. So that it seems here, as if all *ritornelli*, or interstitial symphonies, should be avoided.

The other situation is in the seventh scene of the same act; and is precisely one of those little places in which I should wish Regolo to quit his moderation, and think more of himself than usual. There are only twelve verses that I should wish to have accompanied; which begin at: *"Io venissi a tradirvi—"* and end with: *"Come al nome di Roma Africa tremi"*.

If you should think accompaniment necessary here, I recommend the same economy of time as before; that the actor may not be embarrassed or obliged to wait, by which that fire would be diminished, which I wish to have increased.

And now we are speaking of the seventh scene of the first act, if you have no objection, I should wish to have a very short symphony after this verse of Manlio: *"T'acheta: ei viene"*, to give time for the Consul and the Senators to take their places, and to allow Regolo leisure for advancing slowly, and in a pensive manner. The character of the symphony should be majestic, slow, and sometimes interrupted; expressing as it were the state of Regolo's mind, in reflecting upon his now entering that place as a slave, in which he formerly presided as consul. I should like, that during one of these breaks in the symphony, Amilcare should come in to speak; when, during the silence of the instruments, he should pronounce these verses: *"Regolo, a che t'arresti? è forse nuovo/per te questo soggiorno?"* And the symphony should not be concluded, till after Regolo's answer: *"Penso qual ne partii, qual vi ritorno"*. But after these words, I should not wish the instruments to perform any thing more than a mere close.

In the second act, there seems to me no other recitative which requires accompaniment, than the soliloquy of Regolo, which begins thus: "*Tu palpiti, o mio cor!*" This ought to be recited sitting, till after the following words: ". . . *Ah! no. De' vili/questo è il linguaggio . . .* " The rest to be performed standing; for as the exit of Regolo happens at the change of scene, it would be difficult if he were sitting. But in order that he may have time and space to move about slowly, stopping from time to time, and manifesting himself to be immersed in thought, it is necessary that the instruments should introduce, assist, and second, his reflections. While the actor is sitting, as his reflections consist of doubts and suspensions, they will afford an opportunity for extraneous modulation, and short *ritornelli* for the instruments; but the instant he rises, the rest of the scene requires resolution and energy: so that I recur to my former wish, for economy of time.

And now we are speaking of this scene, I must beg of you to correct the original, which I transmitted in the following manner. There is a meaning implied, which upon reflection seems to want clearness in the expression. ". . . *Ah! no. De' vili/questo è il linguaggio. Inutilmente nacque/chi sol vive a se stesso; è sol da questo/nobile affetto ad obliar s'impara/se per altrui. Quando ha di ben la terra/alla gloria si dee . . .* "

Though there are places in the third act, as well as in the other two, which I may have neglected to mention, where violins may be opportunely employed; yet I must observe, that this ornament should not be rendered too familiar; and I should be glad, if in this third act, particularly, no accompanied recitative occurred, till the *last scene*. This is prevented by the noise and tumult of the people, who cry out, "*Regolo resti.*" The noise of these cries ought to be great, to imitate reality, and to manifest what a respectful silence the mere presence of Regolo could obtain, from a whole tumultuous people. The instruments should be silent when the other personages speak; and, if you approve of it, may be employed whenever the protagonist speaks in the last scene; varying, however, the movement and modulation, not merely to express and enforce the words or sentiments, as is thought a great merit by other composers, but to paint also the situation of mind of him who pronounces these words and sentiments, at which such masters as you always aspire. For you know, as well as I, that the same words and sentiments may be uttered, according to the diversity of situation, in such a manner as to express either joy, sorrow, anger or pity. I should hope from such hands as yours, that a recitative always accompanied by instruments, would not be such a tiresome thing as it usually is, from others. In the first place, because you will preserve that economy of time which I have so much recommended; particularly, as you likewise so well know how to perfect the art, by the judicious and alternate use of *pianos* and *fortes,* by *rinforzandos,* by *staccatos,* slurs, accelerating and retarding the measure, *arpeggios,* shakes, *sostenutos,* and above all, by new modulation, of which you alone seem to know the whole arcana. But if, in spite of so many subsidiaries, you should be of a different opinion, I shall readily give way to your experience, and be perfectly contented, if the following verses are accompanied by violins; that is, the first ten, from: *"Regolo resti! ed io l'ascolto! ed io . . ."* to the verse: *"Meritai l'odio vostro?"* Then from the verse: *"No, possibil non è: de' miei Romani . . ."* to *"Esorto cittadin, padre comando,"* and lastly from *"Romani, addio: siano i congedi estremi . . ."* to the end.

You imagine now, I suppose, that this tiresome discussion is over. No, Sir, we have still a short addendum to tack to it. I should wish that the last chorus were one of that kind, with which you have excited in the audience a desire of hearing it, unknown before; and that there should be such a stamp set on the *addio,* with which the Romans take a final leave of Regolo, as shall demonstrate, that this chorus is not like most others, a superfluity, but a most essential part of the catastrophe.

I here quit the subject, not indeed, for want of materials, or will to converse with you longer; but because I am really tired myself, and fearful of tiring you.

Signor Annibali,[1] is desirous that I should write something to him, concerning his part. But I must entreat you to read to him such passages of this letter, as you may think likely to afford him any satisfaction. I have not time to peruse what I have written; think then, whether it is possible for me to transcribe any part of it.

Present a thousand affectionate compliments in my name, to the incomparable Signora Faustina,[2] and believe me, upon all occasions, yours most truly.

---

(1) Domenico Annibali, the contralto *castrato,* sang the role of Attilio Regolo.
(2) Faustina Bordoni, one of the greatest mezzo-sopranos in operatic history, was the wife of Hasse.

Metastasio's Letter to Johann Adolf Hasse

. . .

The translation, with minor changes, is that of Charles Burney (*Life of Metastasio*, vol. I, pp. 315 *ff*.), to which Burney adds a footnote: "Regarding these memoirs as a kind of supplement to my *General History of Music*, I have inserted a translation of this letter, at full length, however long and technical it may appear to some of my readers; as I cannot help regarding the instructions of such a Poet, to such a Musician, as precious relics, not only worthy of preservation, but of being contemplated with reverence, by young opera composers, ambitious not only to embellish, but enforce the imagery and sentiments of the Poetry which they have to clothe with melody and harmony."

SELECTIVE BIBLIOGRAPHY

I HAVE purposely made this a selective bibliography, both because better general bibliographies exist of works on opera (an excellent one, for instance, is contained in Donald Jay Grout's *A Short History of Opera*) and because, by and large, the librettos themselves have furnished me with more useful information than many of the writings which have been done on them. In general, all books specifically referred to in the preceding pages are listed here, and in addition I have included books that have been particularly useful or deal with librettists.

I would like, however, to include in this bibliography a few words on the sources of the librettos themselves, for any detailed study of the libretto must proceed from them. Libretto collections of sorts exist in most large libraries and in music libraries, but most collections possess severe restrictions, either because of gaps within them or because of insufficient cataloguing. This last is the most pervasive fault, for very few libretto collections are triply cross-referenced (by title, librettist, and composer), and unless that is done, any collection is to an extent restricted in usefulness. Even this amount of cross-referencing is often not enough, for, particularly in the earlier examples, the researcher should also know the date and the city from which the libretto derives—as I have shown, a libretto was subject to change from city to city and from production to production. Because up to now very little librettological work has been done, it is not surprising that many references in library catalogues contain errors.

Because, as has been stated before, the libretto has been for much of its history the neglected stepchild of music and of literature, libraries have never sought to obtain or build integral collections. The difficulty in so doing has been compounded by the transitory nature of the "little book," which was printed not for posterity but for immediate use. Not only have most copies, therefore, disappeared, but those which have survived have survived in far less than perfect condition, and the effects of time upon the inferior paper used in their production has led to further deterioriation. Finally, libraries have all too often allowed such examples as they have to molder unattended because other facets of their collections demand prior attention and expenditure of funds. Thus, the librettos, badly catalogued, are hardly ever consulted, and the source for the libretto becomes the text as printed in the vocal or orchestral score.

Most great collections of librettos have been the result of the efforts of single specific collectors who made the field of the libretto their hobby and then transferred their collections intact to a library by either gift or sale.

The most famous such collection was made in the late nineteenth century by a German, Albert Schatz, and it was purchased for the Library of Congress by Oscar T. Sonneck. In any history of the libretto, Schatz and Sonneck are owed a debt of gratitude, for Schatz's librettological work in connection with his collection was the first such systematic endeavor in the field, and Sonneck's further research on it was codified by the publication of the *Catalogue of the Librettos Written Before 1800 in the Schatz Collection of the Library of Congress* (Washington, 1914). The volume did not include the complete collection, but the librettos written before 1800 were, by much, the most important in terms of virgin librettistic territory and formed the majority of those in the collection. As it was triply cross-referenced and packed with Schatz's research findings and Sonneck's notes, the catalogue was then, as it remains today, the single most valuable work on the libretto. The catalogue, which it is not hyperbolic to call monumental, has long been out of print, but recently the New York printing firm of Burt Franklin has reprinted it. The Schatz collection itself, numbering *in toto* over twelve thousand volumes, is of course one of the major sources of. pre-1800 librettos, and is rivaled in scope as a collection chiefly by the Rolandi collection in Venice (very roughly, the Schatz has more examples of German librettos or Italian works given in Germany whereas the Rolandi remains better focused on Italy).

Ulderico Rolandi, an Italian doctor, devoted his life to the hobby of libretto collecting and, at the end of it, wrote a book, *Il Libretto per musica attraverso i tempi,* which until the present book was the only general study of the libretto. In certain areas, notably those of the specifics of the librettos themselves—the changes in appearance and format, the variants, the parodies, the effects of censorship, etc.—the book deals with aspects of the libretto only briefly considered, if at all, in the present work, and as such it is still useful to those wishing information about the art form. Its over-all view, however, remains bound by the specifics of the Rolandi collection itself and by the fact that it is ever Italian-oriented. It does not pretend to do more than remain on the surface of its subject—no small achievement, given the general lack of books on the libretto—but in so doing it misses any chance to achieve a synthesis or an appreciation for the interrelationship of themes and approaches in the various national schools of the libretto which I have tried to suggest.

At Rolandi's death, his collection, comprising over thirty-two thousand librettos, including many for oratorios, was left to the Fondazione Cini on the Isola San Giorgio in Venice, and it has since been superbly catalogued. It is hoped in the future to be able to publish a catalogue of this collection.

The collection itself is, of course, excellent, particularly in the field of Italian opera, and includes a full range of nineteenth- to mid-twentieth-century librettos that the Schatz collection lacks. With the Schatz collection, which is housed in the Music Division of the Library of Congress, it has the great advantage of being contained in a small-sized library, and thus is easier to use than, for instance, the fine British Museum libretto collection, which is catalogued as part of the Main Reading Room books. Indeed, the Rolandi librettos are stacked in the working room, and can be used directly by the researcher. Anyone doing extensive work in a subject will appreciate what an incalculable boon this arrangement is.

Other useful collections include that of Manoel de Carvalhães (about twenty-one thousand librettos), which was bought by the Italian government and is now in the library of the Accademia Santa Cecilia in Rome (the cataloguing, however, is haphazard and not triply cross-referenced), and collections in the Munich Staatsbibliotek and in Paris, Brussels, Bologna, Florence, Naples, and the Marciana Library in Venice.

What is now needed, of course, is a thoroughgoing attention to the librettological side of the libretto. The intensive spadework that has been going on in the last twenty years on the musicological

aspects of sixteenth-, seventeenth-, and eighteenth-century works
has perforce led to ancillary work being done on the libretto, but
a great deal more needs to be accomplished. Particularly important,
as this book has attempted to show, is the exploration of the
dramatic and poetic roots and interrelationships of the libretto and
its sister arts.

ADORNO, THEODOR: *Versuch über Wagner*. Frankfurt, 1952.

APOLLONIO, MARIO: *L'Opera di Carlo Goldini*. Milan, 1932.

ARNOLDSON, LOUISE PARKINSON: *Sedaine et les musiciens de son temps*.
Paris, 1934.

ARRUGA, FRANCO LORENZO: *Incontri fra poeta e musicisti nell'opera
romantica italiana*. Milan, 1968.

ARVIN, NEIL COLE: *Eugène Scribe and the French Theater*. Cambridge,
Mass., 1924.

BAUR-HEINHOLD, MARGARETE: *The Baroque Theater*, London, 1967.

BENTLEY, ERIC: *The Dramatic Event*. New York, 1954.

BRANCA, EMILIA: *Romani*. Turin, n.d., but 1892.

BRICQUEVILLE, EUGÈNE DE: *Le Livret d'opéra français de Lully à Gluck*.
Paris, 1888.

BRUNEAU, ALFRED: *À l'Ombre d'un grand coeur*. Paris, 1932.

BUKOFZER, MANFRED: *Music in the Baroque Era*. New York, 1947.

BURNEY, CHARLES: *Memoirs of the Life and Writings of the Abate* [sic]
Metastasio. 3 vols. London, 1796.

BURT, NATHANIEL: "Opera in Arcadia," *The Musical Quarterly*, (October, 1955).

CAMETTI, ALBERTO: *Jacopo Ferretti*. Milan, n.d., but 1898.

CARLSON, MARVIN: *The Theatre of the French Revolution*. Ithaca,
1966.

CARTER, LAWSON A.: *Zola and the Theater*. New Haven, 1963.

CELLA, FRANCA: *Indagini sulle fonte francesi dei libretti di Gaetano
Donizetti*. Milan, n.d.

———: *Indagini sulle fonte francesi dei libretti di Vincenzo Bellini*.
Milan, 1968.

———: *Prospettive della librettistica italiana nell'età romantica*. Milan,
1968.

COOPER, MARTIN: *French Music from the Death of Berlioz to the Death
of Fauré*. London, 1951.

———: *Opéra-comique*. New York, 1949.

CROSTEN, WILLIAM L.: *French Grand Opera*. New York, 1948.

CUCUEL, GEORGES: *Les Créateurs de l'opéra-comique français*. Paris,
1914.

CURTISS, MINA: *Bizet and his World*. New York, 1958.

DARLINGTON, WILLIAM: *The World of Gilbert and Sullivan.* New York, 1950.

DE RENSIS, RAFFAELLO, ed.: *Critiche e cronache musicale di Arrigo Boito (1862–1870).* Milan, 1931.

DEAN, WINTON: *Bizet.* London, 1948.

————: "Shakespeare and Opera," in Hartnoll, Phyllis, ed.: *Shakespeare and Music.* London, 1964.

DELLA CORTE, ANDREA, ed.: *Drammi per musica.* 2 vols. Turin, 1958.

DEL MAR, NORMAN: *Richard Strauss.* 2 vols. New York, 1964–9.

DEMUTH, NORMAN: *French Opera: Its Development to the Revolution.* Sussex, 1963.

DENT, EDWARD J.: *Busoni's Doktor Faust,* in *Music and Letters,* VII (1926).

————: *Mozart's Operas.* New York, 1947.

DOISY, MARCEL: *Musique et Drame.* Paris, 1949.

DONADONI, ALESSANDRO: *Dalla Didone all' Attilio Regolo.* Rome, 1897.

DONINGTON, ROBERT: *Wagner's Ring and Its Symbols.* London, 1963.

EINSTEIN, ALFRED. *Gluck.* London, 1936.

ESSLIN, MARTIN: *Brecht.* New York, 1961.

EWEN, FREDERIC: *Bertolt Brecht.* New York, 1967.

FITZLYON, APRIL: *The Libertine Librettist.* London, 1955.

FONT, AUGUSTE: *Favart.* Paris, 1894.

FORBES, ELIZABETH: "Scribe," *Opera* (June 1968).

FREEMAN, ROBERT: "Apostolo Zeno's Reform of the Libretto," *Journal of the American Musicological Society,* Vol. XXI, No. 3, 1968.

GALLET, LOUIS: *Notes d'un librettiste.* Paris, 1891.

GARCIN, LAURENT: *Traité du Mélo-drame.* Paris, 1772.

GASSNER, JOHN: *Masters of the Drama.* New York, 1940.

GAY, PETER: *Weimar Culture.* New York, 1969.

GILBERT, WILLIAM S.: *New and Original Extravaganzas.* Boston, 1931.

GINISTY, PAUL: *Le Mélodrame.* Paris, n.d.

Goethe-Eckermann Conversations. London, 1906.

GOLDONI, CARLO: *Mémoires.* Mercure de France edn. Paris, 1965.

GROS, ÉTIENNE: *Philippe Quinault.* Paris, 1926.

GROUT, DONALD JAY: *A Short History of Opera,* 2nd edn. New York, 1965.

GUIET, RENÉ: *L'Évolution d'un genre: le livret d'opéra en France de Gluck à la révolution (1774–1793).* Paris, 1936.

GUTMAN, ROBERT: *Richard Wagner.* New York, 1967.

HARTOG, WILLIE G.: *Guilbert de Pixérécourt.* Paris, 1913.

HOGARTH, GEORGE: *Memoirs of the Opera.* 2 vols. London, 1851.

HOLST, IMOGEN: *Tune.* New York, 1968.

HOOVER, KATHLEEN O'DONNELL: *Makers of Opera.* New York, 1948.

HUGHES, SPIKE: *Famous Verdi Operas*. New York, 1968.

IACUZZI, ALFRED: *The European Vogue of Favart*. New York, 1932.

ISTEL, EDGAR: *The Art of Writing Opera Librettos*. New York, 1922.

LANDORMY, PAUL: *La Musique française de La Marseillaise à la mort de Berlioz*. Paris, 1944.

LANG, PAUL HENRY: *Handel*. New York, 1968.

————: *Music in Western Civilization*. New York, 1941.

LEE, VERNON: *Studies of the Eighteenth Century in Italy*. London, 1887.

LESSING, G. E.: *Hamburg Dramaturgy*. Dover edn. New York, 1962.

LIVINGSTON, ARTHUR: *La Vita veneziana nelle opere di Gian Francesco Busenello*. Venice, 1913.

LOESCHER, ERMANNO: *Romani, critico artistico-scientifica*. Rome, 1884.

LOEWENBERG, ALFRED: *Annals of Opera*, 2nd edn. 2 vols. Geneva, 1955.

————: "Lorenzo da Ponte in London," *Music Review*, IV (1943).

LONGYEAR, REY M.: "La Pièce bien faite: The Opéra-comique Librettos of Scribe," *Southern Quarterly*, I (1963).

LORENZ, ALFRED: *Das Geheimnis der Form bei Richard Wagner*. 4 vols. Berlin, 1924–33.

MACDONALD, DWIGHT, ed.: *Parodies*. New York, 1965.

MAGEE, BRYAN: *Aspects of Wagner*. New York, 1969.

MANN, WILLIAM: *Richard Strauss: A Critical Study of the Operas*. London, 1964.

MARTIN, GEORGE: *Verdi*. New York, 1963.

McGOWAN, MARGARET M.: *L'Art du ballet de cour en France (1581–1643)*. Paris, 1963.

MELLERS, WILFRED: *Caliban Reborn*. New York, 1967.

MIRAGOLI, LIVIA: *Il Melodramma italiano nell'ottocento*. Rome, 1924.

MOBERLY, R. B.: *Three Mozart Operas*. New York, 1968.

NARDI, PIETRO: *Vita di Arrigo Boito*. Rome, 1942.

NEWMAN, ERNEST: *Opera Nights*. London, 1943.

————: *Wagner*. 4 vols. New York, 1933–46.

————: *The Wagner Operas*. New York, 1949.

NICOLL, ALLARDYCE: *The World of Harlequin*. Cambridge, Eng., 1963.

NIVELLINI, VITTORIO: "Goldoni, librettista," *La Scala*, No. 69 (November, 1957).

NOSKE, FRITS: *La Mélodie Française de Berlioz à Duparc*. Paris, 1954.

OLIVER, ALFRED R.: *The Encyclopedists as Critics of Music*. New York, 1947.

PIRROTTA, NINO: "Commedia dell'arte and Opera," *The Musical Quarterly* (July 1955).

POUGIN, ARTHUR: *Monsigny et son temps*. Paris, 1908.

POWERS, HAROLD: "Il Serse trasformato," *The Musical Quarterly* (October 1961 & January 1962).

PRUNIÈRES, HENRI: *L'Opéra italien en France avant Lulli.* Paris, 1913.

RINALDI, MARIO: *Felice Romani.* Rome, 1965.

ROBINSON, MICHAEL F.: *Opera Before Mozart.* London, 1966.

ROLANDI, ULDERICO: *Amilcare Ponchielli . . . librettista.* Como, 1935.

————: *Il Libretto per musica attraverso i tempi.* Rome, 1951.

ROLLAND, ROMAIN: *Essays on Music.* New York, 1915.

————: *Histoire de l'opéra en Europe avant Lully et Scarlatti.* Paris, 1895.

SALERNO, HENRY F., ed.: *Scenarios of the Comedia dell'arte* (Flaminio Scala's *Il Teatro delle favole rappresentative*). New York, 1967.

SCHRADE, LEO: Monteverdi. London, 1964.

————: *Tragedy in the Art of Music.* Cambridge, Mass., 1964.

SMITH, PATRICK J.: "Hofmannsthal's 'Arabella.'" Unpublished manuscript.

SOLERTI, ANGELO, ed.: *Gli Albori del melodramma.* 3 vols. Milan, n.d., but 1904.

————, ed.: *Le origini del melodramma.* Turin, 1903.

STEINER, GEORGE: *The Death of Tragedy.* New York, 1961.

STRAUSS, RICHARD, and HUGO VON HOFMANNSTHAL. *Correspondence.* London, 1961.

STRUNK, OLIVER, ed.: *Source Readings in Music History.* New York, 1950.

TIERSOT, JULIEN, ed.: *Lettres des musiciens écrites en français du XVᵉ au XXᵉ siècle.* 2 vols. Turin, 1924.

TINTORE, GIAMPIERO: *L'Opera napoletana.* Milan, 1958.

TORREFRANCA, FAUSTO: *L'Opera come spettacolo.* Rome, 1916.

VAN DEN BERGH, HERMAN: *Giambattista Casti, l'homme et l'oeuvre.* Amsterdam, 1951.

VANLOO, ALBERT: *Sur le Plateau: souvenirs d'un librettiste.* Paris, 1914.

VERDI, GIUSEPPE: *I Copialettere.* Milan, 1913.

WAGNER, RICHARD: *On Music and Drama.* New York, 1964.

————: *Opera and Drama.* London, n.d.

WALKER, FRANK: *The Man Verdi.* New York, 1962.

WALKER, J. C.: *Historical Memoir on Italian Tragedy.* London, 1799.

WEISSTEIN, ULRICH, ed.: *The Essence of Opera.* New York, 1964.

WELLESZ, EGON: *Essays on Opera.* London, 1950.

WILKINS, ERNEST H.: *A History of Italian Literature.* Cambridge, Mass., 1954.

WORSTHORNE, SIMON TOWNELEY: *Venetian Opera in the Seventeenth Century.* Oxford, 1954.

YORKE-LONG, ALAN: *Music at Court.* London, 1954.

ZUCKERMAN, ELLIOT: *The First Hundred Years of Wagner's Tristan.* New York, 1964.

Index

INDEX

i

Index

v

Index

A NOTE ABOUT THE AUTHOR

TRIPLY IMMERSED *in the world of music, Patrick J. Smith is at once critic (his reviews and critical essays have appeared in* The Musical Quarterly, Opera, Opera News, *and* High Fidelity), *book editor of* Musical America, *and Editor-Publisher of* The Musical Newsletter. *He was born in 1932, was graduated from Princeton University, and lives, with his wife and son, in his native New York.*

A NOTE ON THE TYPE

THIS BOOK *was set on the linotype in Janson, a recutting made direct from type cast from matrices long thought to have been made by the Dutchman Anton Janson, who was a practicing type founder in Leipzig during the years 1668–87. However, it has been conclusively demonstrated that these types are actually the work of Nicholas Kis (1650–1702), a Hungarian, who most probably learned his trade from the master Dutch type founder Kirk Voskens. The type is an excellent example of the influential and sturdy Dutch types that prevailed in England up to the time William Caslon developed his own incomparable designs from them.*

The book was composed, printed, and bound by The Haddon Craftsmen, Inc., Scranton, Pa. Typography and binding design by

W A R R E N ⚏ C H A P P E L L